A

DICTIONARY

OF

SUPERSTITIONS

AND MYTHOLOGY

BY

BIREN BONNERJEA, D.Litt. (Paris)

[Virendra Vandyopādhyāya]

FOLK PRESS LIMITED

RANELAGH ROAD, LONDON, S.W.1

Detroit: Reissued by Singing Tree Press, Book Tower, 1969

This book was originally published in 1927

Library of Congress Catalog Card Number 69–17755

JIT ROY
NEPOTIS AMANTISSIMI MEI
IN MEMORIAM
D.D.

PREFACE

OWING to the great volume of existing literature on the subject, it may seem an unnecessary waste of time and energy to offer the following work to the public ; a few words of explanation, therefore, may not be out of place here.

A number of years ago, when I was making a comparative study of mythology and folklore I began to collect notes, which gradually grew to such an extent that I felt myself justified in curtailing the mass of material and rearranging the whole in the form of a short dictionary. It would have been an easy task to enlarge this book to at least four times its present size, but I purposely restricted myself to what, in my opinion, was absolutely essential and at the same time most trustworthy.

As the book is primarily intended as a reliable guide for serious students of mythology and folklore, I have given under every heading the country or countries where the superstition is prevalent and the authorities with the pages of the works where it is to be found ; wherever no localities are given, it is to be understood as pertaining to Great Britain, unless the book referred to deals with one particular country or province. I have deviated from the course mentioned above when either the subject is too well known, or when the superstitions were collected by myself and no printed work on the subject was available. To further facilitate references, I have given at the end of the lexico-graphical part, a complete bibliography of the works chiefly made use of in the compilation of this book. I have included only those British, French, German, Bohemian and Indian superstitions which I could actually verify on the spot ; owing however to my ignorance of the Czech language, I was forced to avail myself of the kind services of a friend who helped me in my task.

A complete understanding of the gradual development of the human mind can be arrived at only by means of a study of the superstitions of the various nations. It is a well-known fact, that the more advanced a nation is, the less superstitious are the people. The moment anything can be logically answered, superstition comes to an end ; but as long as we cannot understand the causes and effects, we are groping in the dark, and

5

our imagination is given full play. It is also a well-known fact
that advancement influences our imagination to a very great
extent. There are several very important factors in the making
of superstitions, the foremost of which is our environment.
We can dream our day-dreams amidst green fields with the
birds singing above us, or beside the rippling stream under
the clear moonlit sky, but it would be difficult, if not impossible,
to indulge ourselves in those same dreams amidst the noise
and bustle of a busy city life, or while rushing through the
Continent of Europe in the *wagon-lit* of the Nord Express.
Every man is born primitive, but the conditions of his living
tend to form his ideas. A villager living his primitive semi-
savage life is naturally more prone to be imaginative than his
town-bred cousin ; hence imagination is to be found more
in villages than in towns, more amongst savages than among
civilized races—and in Imagination is the seed of Superstition. Imagination combined with Ignorance is Superstition full-born.

Superstition may be defined subjectively as the disposition
or tendency to ascribe phenomena which admit of natural
explanation to occult or supernatural causes ; or objectively,
it is any system of religious belief or practice which manifests
such a tendency. Superstition is excessive belief or credulity ;
it arises from the encroachment of faith on the rights of
reason and knowledge, and is applied in popular usage to various
forms of polytheism. It is an unreasonable belief in things or
phenomena which, although owing their origin to perfectly
natural and logical causes, are attributed to some supernatural
force or power, or again, the natural results of these are dis-
torted by popular imagination into something fantastic. Thus
for example, in the Middle Ages, when science was in its infancy,
the violent wind was supposed to have been caused by Wodan
and his spectral followers, riders and hounds in full chase,
rushing through the woods, or athwart the sky, in quest of
some poor human soul ; the French have their prototype
in the Grand Veneur riding in the forests of Fontainebleau,
and we in our legend of Herne the Hunter haunting the ancient
oak tree in Windsor Forest. " Superstition would seem to be
simply cowardice in regard to the supernatural. The superstitious man is one who will wash his hands at a fountain,
sprinkle himself at a temple font, put a bit of laurel-leaf into
his mouth, and so go about for the day. If a weasel run across
his path, he will not pursue his walk until someone else has
traversed the road, or until he has thrown three stones across it.
When he sees a serpent in his house, if it be the red snake, he
will invoke Sabazius ; if the sacred snake, he will straightaway

place a shrine on the spot. He will pour oil from his flask on the smooth stones at the cross-roads as he goes by, and will fall on his knees and worship them before he departs. If a mouse gnaws through a meal-bag, he will go to the expounder of the sacred law and ask what is to be done. . . . He will not tread upon a tombstone, or come near a dead body or a woman defiled by childbirth, saying that it is expedient for him not to be polluted. Also on the fourth and seventh days of each month he will order his servants to mull wine, and will go out and buy myrtle wreaths, frankincense, convolvuluses."*

Every natural thing our forefathers could not understand was attributed, as it is attributed to-day by the savage races, to some good or evil spirits ; diseases were caused by malicious demons, ill-disposed fairies or malignant witches ; shipwrecks were the direct acts of Nixes or Water-demons ; anæmia was caused by those horrible monsters, vampires, sucking the patient's blood ; the eclipse of the sun and the moon was the result of their being devoured by some bloodthirsty and revengeful demons, such, as Râhu or Ketu ; Werewolves, or men who by means of black arts transformed themselves into beasts of prey, devastated the land. An eminent author relates how, during an eclipse, he heard a French peasant exclaim with deep anguish: "*Mon Dieu! Qu'elle est souffrante!*" and as an explanation pointed to the almost totally obscured moon. The Rev. Mr. S. Baring Gould found it impossible to find anyone to guide him through a certain wood in France, for fear of the "Loup-garou."

As an example of what superstitions lead to we need only mention the awful days of the Hexenverfolgungen and Hexenprozessen when hundreds, nay even thousands, of innocent human beings were burnt at the stake on the mere supposition of being witches : as witness whereof the trial and condemnation of the famous Lancashire Witches. With the advancement of culture and civilization, these superstitions have happily vanished ; but it would be safe to assert that no matter how advanced the people are, there is not one nation in the world which is entirely free from superstitions of every kind. We, living in civilized Europe, cannot understand the mentality of the Zulus in employing "witch-doctors" to "smell out" culprits, or of the Hindus in prostrating themselves before a hideous idol and praying for riches or the recovery of stolen goods, yet very few of us would willingly walk under a ladder, or make up a party of thirteen at the dinner table. The origin of most of

*THEOPHRASTUS: *The Characters*, translated by R. C. Jebb (1870) xxvii.

our modern superstitions is lost in antiquity. Dr. Adolf Lehmann in his admirable book, *Aberglaube und Zauberei* has discussed this question of the evolution of superstitions at great length ; it is therefore, unnecessary for me to go into the matter any further, or to give any explanation as to their origin. I have contented myself with a simple list of these superstitions with their different variations in different countries as they exist at the present day.

With regard to Oriental words and names, I have not restricted myself to any definite system of transcription, and have been guided only by the pronunciation. The various superstitions connected with folk-medicine have been sparingly dealt with, as my own *Ethnologie du Bengale,* BLACK, *Folk Medicine* and HOVORKÁ AND KRONFELD, *Vergleichende Volksmedizin* give sufficient information.

It remains for me now to acknowledge my indebtedness particularly to the following works, from which I have freely borrowed : Sir James G. Frazer, *The Golden Bough* ; E. Tylor, *Primitive Culture* ; Dr. Brewer, *Reader's Handbook* ; J. Dowson, *Hindu Classical Dictionary* ; Dr. A. Wuttke, *Der deutsche Volksaberglaube der Gegenwart* ; L. Strackerjan, *Aberglauben und Sagen aus dem Herzogtum Oldenburg* ; Dr. A. Lehmann, *Aberglaube und Zauberei* ; Fanny D. Bergen, *Current Superstitions*, Berenger-Féraud, *Superstitions et survivances etudiées au point de vue de leur origine et de leur transformations* ; and Brand, *Observations on the Popular Antiquities of Great Britain.* Since completing my MS. it has been my good fortune to come across *Lean's Collectanea* by Mr. V. S. Lean ; unfortunately, therefore, I could not make as much use of this vast treasurehouse of research and information relating to folklore as I would have liked. I must also not forget to tender my thanks to the various friends at home and abroad who have helped me with valuable contributions and advice.

Last, but not least, my best thanks are due to my wife for her untiring help in the arduous task of collecting, selecting and arranging the material.

Should this book be of some little service to serious students whose criticism alone I value, I shall be amply rewarded for the amount of time and labour I have spent thereon. It has been a labour of love for me; and incomplete though it may be, I send it forth to the world to earn as much appreciation for itself as it is worth.

BIREN BONNERJEA.

Paris,
   March, 1927.

PRONUNCIATION

a in Indian words as *a* in " fall."

ā in foreign words as *a* in " father."

c in Slav words as *ts*.

č in Slav words as *ch* in " church."

ch in French words as *sh*.

ch in German words before e, i as *sh*; before other vowels or consonants as *ch* in Scotch : " loch."

ch in Greek words as *k*.

e in foreign words as *e* in " met " or *a* in " mate."

gh in Arabic words as the Modern Greek γ or the North German *g*.

g in German words as *g* in " garden."

ḥ in Semitic words as a strongly aspirated *h*.

ï in foreign words as *ee* in " meet."

j in foreign words as *j* in " judge."

j̈ in Teutonic words as *y*.

kh in Semitic words as *ch* in Scotch " loch "

l in Slav words between two consonants is pronounced as *li.*

q in Semitic words as a guttural *k*.

r in foreign words is always distinctly pronounced.

r in Slav words between two consonants is pronounced as *ri*.

s in foreign words as *ss* in " hiss."

s in German words at the beginning of a syllable as *z*.

s in French words between two vowels as *z*.

š in Slav words as *sh* in " shy."

sch in Teutonic words as *sh*.

st in German words as *sht*.

t in foreign words has usually a soft sound as in French or Italian.

u in foreign words as *oo* in " fool " or *u* in " full."

v in Teutonic words as *f*.

w in Teutonic words as *v*.

z in Teutonic words as *ts*.

ž in Slav words as the French *j* or as *s* in " pleasure."

ai in Indian words as *a-i*.

au in Indian words as *a-u*.

au in German words as *ou* in " house."

äu in German words as *oy* in " boy."

ei in German words as *y* in " my."

9   B

eu   in German words as *oy* in " boy."
ö in German words as *eu* in French.
φ in Danish words as the German *ö*.
u in French is pronounced by rounding the lips and saying *ee*.
ü in German is the same as the French *u*.
ou in French words as *oo* in " fool."

All consonants with diacritical marks : ḍ, ṇ, ṣ, s̤, ṭ, t̤, ẓ, z̤
are pronounced as their corresponding Latin equivalents.

A

Aalu : This was the name by which the Egyptian Elysium was designated.

Aasgaardsreia : "Aasgard's Chase"; a frequent appellation of the Wild Hunt (q.v.) of Northern mythology.

Abaris : Gr. Myth. It was Abaris to whom Apollo (q.v.) gave a golden arrow on which to ride through the air.

Abhac : It is the Irish cognate of an Afanc (q.v.).

Abhaswaras : Hindu Myth. A class of deities, sixty-four in number, of whose nature little is known. (DOWSON, *H.C.D.*)

Abraxas : A stone with the word Abraxas engraved on it is said to be a famous talisman. The word symbolizes the 365 intelligences between deity and man.

Acacia : Acacia-wood was held in ancient times to be the "Wood of Life." According to Kercher, it was sacred to the sun god of Egypt.

Academus : Gr. Myth. A hero of Attica. He told Castor and Pollux where Theseus had hidden Helen.
He is sometimes identified with Cadmus (q.v.).

Acca Laruntia : According to a legend, she was the wife of Faustulius. She saved Remus and Romulus exposed on a hill and brought them up. These children afterwards founded the city of Rome.

Accidental upsetting of a cup : In Japan if a cup of medicine destined for a sick person be accidentally upset, it is a sure sign of his speedy recovery. (GRIFFIS, *M.E.*, p. 467.)

Acco : Gr. Myth. A class of beings belonging to the same species as Lamia (q.v.).

Acephali : A fabulous race of people, reported by ancient writers to have had no heads. cf. *Blemmyæ, A-Siras.*

Achæus : Gr. Myth. Brother of Ion, nephew of Helen, ancestor of the Achæans.

Achelous : Gr. Myth. God of the river bearing this name, and father of the Sirens (q.v.).

Acheri : Indian Folklore. They are the ghosts of little girls, who live on the tops of mountains, but descend at night to hold their revels in more convenient places (CROOKE, *P.R.I.*, Vol. I, p. 263; TRAILL, *Asiatic Researches*, XVI, pp. 137 *seq.* ; N.I.N.Q., Vol. II, p. 27; *Ethnologie du Bengale,* p. 99).

Acheron : The " River of Grief " ; one of the four rivers of Hell. Hell itself is sometimes designated by this name. The name is taken from the Greek ἄχος ῥέω meaning " I flow with grief."
 " Et l'avare Achéron ne lache point sa proie."
                                                  Racine.

Achilles : Gr. Myth. Son of Thetis and Peleus, the most famous Grecian hero of the Iliad. In the siege of Troy he killed Hector, and was himself mortally wounded by a poisoned arrow shot by Paris. In his infancy he was dipped in the river Styx by his mother, so that he became invulnerable ; his only vulnerable part was his heel. He was brought up by the centaur Chiron. Achilles disguised as a woman lived with the daughters of Lycomede but was discovered by Ulysses. The lance of Achilles cured all wounds that were caused by it.

Achilles' Horses : The two horses belonging to Achilles possessed the power of human speech. cf. *Arion, Al-Borak, Balaam's Ass*

Acis : Sicilian Myth. A Sicilian shepherd loved by the Galatea (q.v.). The monster Polypheme, a Cyclops, was his rival and crushed him with a huge rock. The blood of Acis was changed into a river which bears the same name and flows at the foot of Mt. Etna (DR. BREWER, *R.H.*, p. 5.)

Acorn : To dream that you are eating an acorn indicates that you will gradually rise to riches and honour. Vide *Sweet-flag.*

Acrisius : A fabulous king of Argos, father of Danaüs. He was accidentally killed by a disc thrown by Perseus his grandson.

Acteon : Gr. Myth. A hunter who surprised Diana in her bath. The goddess was enraged and changed him into a deer ; in this form he was devoured by his own hounds.

Adad : Babyl. Myth. He is an ancient god who personifies winter storms. He is depicted as armed with a thunderbolt and lightning ; he has many other names.

Adamida : A planet on which reside the unborn spirits of saints, martyrs and believers (KLOPSTOCK).

Adder : The bite of an adder can be cured by an ointment made from its liver (LEAN, Vol. II, p. 485).
 It is said in fable that the adder, in order to prevent hearing the voice of a charmer, lays one ear on the ground and sticks its tail into the other.

Address : Vide *Change of Address.*

Aderyn y Corph : In Welsh folk-lore it is a kind of supernatural bird which appears as a foreteller of death. Vide *Death Warnings, etc.*

Adhyatman : Hind. Myth. The supreme spirit ; the soul of the universe (DOWSON, *H.C.D.*, p. 2).

Admete : Gr. Myth. Founder and king of Pheres in Thessaly, and one of the Argonauts. He was husband of Alceste (q.v.) whom he offered as a sacrifice in order to prolong his own life. Apollo guarded his troops.

Adolf : He was bishop of Cologne ; he is popularly believed to have been devoured either by mice or by rats in A.D. 1112. cf. *Hatto, Freiherr von Güttingen, Widerolf, Graaf.*

Adona : A seraph who was the first of the twelve martyrs. Adona was the tutelar spirit of James.

Adon-Ai : He was the spirit of love and beauty.

Adonis : Class. Myth. A beautiful youth beloved by Aphrodite. He was born of a myrrh tree. In the flush of his youth, he was slain by a wild boar. After his death, he was changed into an anemone by Venus.

Adultery : Many of the indigenous tribes of Sarawak are firmly persuaded that were their wives to commit adultery while their husbands are searching for camphor in the jungle, the camphor obtained by the men would evaporate (FRAZER, *G.B.*, Vol. I, p. 29).

Among the inhabitants of the hills near Rajmahal, Bengal, it is believed that adultery undetected and unexpiated will cause epidemics in the villages. (FRAZER, *Psyche's Task*, 2nd Ed., p. 45).

Aëdon : Gr. Myth. A queen of Thebes who killed her own son by mistake. Zeus relieved her grief by turning her into a nightingale.

Ægeon : Gr. Myth. A huge monster with one hundred arms and fifty heads who, with his brothers Cothus and Gyges, conquered the Titans by hurling at them three hundred rocks at once.

Ægeus : Gr. Myth. The father of Theseus, who, in grief at the supposed loss of his son, threw himself into the sea, which was named Ægean Sea after him.

Ægina : Gr. Myth. A daughter of the river-god Asopus. Zeus in the form of an eagle carried her off to an island which bears her name.

Ægir : In old Norse mythology this was the name of a water-demon. Vide *Rán.*

Ægisthus : Gr. Myth. Son of Thyestus and Palopea. He killed Agamemnon, after having seduced his wife Clytemnestra.

Ægle : Gr. Myth. One of the Hesperides.

Ægyptus : Gr. Myth. A son of Balus, twin brother of Danaüs and king of Libya, who conquered and gave his name to Egypt.

Aello : Gr. Myth. One of the Harpies (q.v.).

Æolus : Class. Myth. The happy ruler of the Æolian Isles, who had dominion over the winds.

Æsculapius : Rom. Myth. The god of medicine.

Æsir : Teut. Myth. The chief gods of the Teutonic pantheon. With the Æsir were associated the Asynjur or goddesses, of whom there were eighteen.

Aesma : In Persian mythology this is a clearly defined, outrageous and assaulting demon, whose name has been thought to be reflected as Asmodæus in the Book of Tobit. (*D.R.E.*, Vol. IV, p. 620.)

Æthra : Gr. Myth. Mother of Theseus.

Afanc : In Wales an Afanc is regarded as a kind of crocodile, but it was originally, in the opinion of Sir John Rhŷs, a kind of monster in human form, as is suggested by the Irish cognate Abhac. (*D.R.E.*, Vol. IV, p. 576.)

Afrit : In Arabic demonology Afrit is the chief of the demons. The word in Arabic simply means a " demon."

Afterbirth : If dogs eat of the afterbirth of mares, they will go mad. (STRACKERJAN, Vol. I, p. 49 ; see PLOSS, *Das Weib*, Vol. II. p. 221 *et seq.*).

Agamemnon : Son of Atreus, brother of Menelaus, husband of Clytemnestra by whom he was slain with the help of Ægisthus.

Agate : Agate quenches thirst, if kept in the mouth ; it also has the power of allaying fever. It is supposed to render the wearer invisible ; it turns the swords of foes against themselves.

    The agate is the emblem of health and long life and is dedicated to June.

    In the Zodiac it stands for Scorpio. cf. *Alectoria*.

Agatha, St. : She protects from fire (q.v.).

Agdistis : Gr. Myth. The Great Mother was so called at her reputedly original shrine at Pessinus from the rock Agdus on Mt. Dindimus.

Age : One should never tell his age to others, lest he die. (STRACKERJAN, Vol. I, p. 49.)

To ascertain a girl's age, pull a hair from her head, tie a ring to it and hang this inside a tumbler or a goblet in such a manner that it does not touch the sides of the glass ; the ring will begin to oscillate and will strike the sides as many times as the number of years the girl's exact age is. (*Parts of Gt. Britain*).

Aghasura : Hind. Myth. An Asura (q.v.) who was Kansa's general. He assumed the form of a vast serpent, and Krishna's companions, the cowherds, entered its mouth, mistaking it for a mountain cavern ; Krishna rescued them. (DOWSON, *H.C.D.*, p. 6).

Aglaia : Class. Myth. One of the three Graces (q.v.)

Agni : " Fire." One of the most ancient and sacred objects of Hindu worship. It appears in three phases—in heaven as the sun, in mid-air as lightning and on earth as ordinary fire. (DOWSON, *H.C.D* , p. 6.)

(ii) The most important of the Vedic gods ; originally the god of the altar fire, he yet represents a trinity in which to earthly fire are joined the lightning and the sun. He is the mediator between gods and men. He is represented as red and with two faces.

Ague : The two patron saints for this disease are : St. Pernel and St. Petronella. Vide *Iliad, Spider*. (Various remedies are given in Lean's *Collectanea*, Vol. II, pt. ii, pp. 483 *et seq.*)

Ahasverus : A legendary personage better known by the name of the Wandering Jew (q.v.).

Ahi : Hindu Myth. A serpent. A name of Vritra, the Vedic demon of drought (DOWSON, *H.C.D.*, p. 9).

Ahlmakoh : In the Vancouver Islands this is a kind of demoniac wood-spirit. He plays an important part in the ritual as an amulet-dispenser. His nasal mucus is valued as an amulet for invulnerability.

Ahnfrau : In German superstition she is an ancestress of some noble family, whose spirit appears to give warning of an approaching disaster or death. cf. *White Lady, Mélusine, Bertha, Death Warnings.*

Ahriman : In Zoroastrianism he is the spirit of evil. He stands at the head of the host of evil spirits ; he is the prince of darkness personified and is malevolent in the extreme. He was the Evil Principle or Being of the ancient Persians.

Ahura-Mazdas : Vide *Ormazd.*

Airāvat : Hind. Myth. A fine elephant. An elephant produced at the churning of the ocean and appropriated by the god Indra (q.v.).

Airi : Indian Folklore. The ghost of someone who was killed in hunting. " Those who see Airi face to face are burnt up by the flash of his eye, or are torn to pieces by his dogs, or have their livers extracted and eaten by the fairies who accompany him." (CROOKE, *P.R.I.*, Vol. I., p. 262 ; *Ethnologie du Bengale*, p. 100). cf. *Wild Huntsman.*

Ajagava : Hindu Myth. The primitive bow of Siva (q.v.), which fell from heaven at the birth of Prithu. (DOWSON, *H.C.D.*, p. 10.)

Ajax : Gr. Myth. The names of two heroes of the Trojan war, which has remained synonymous with impetuous warriors.

Akhkhazu : " The Seizer." In Babylonian superstition it was an evil spirit, who had the power of securing his victim under his control. cf. *Labasu.*

Akratos : Gr. Myth. It was the potent spirit of the unmixed wine.

Akupara : Hind. Myth. The tortoise or turtle on which the earth rests. (DOWSON, *H.C.D.*, p. 10.)
Vide *Earthquake.*

Akuti : Hindu Myth. The daughter of Manu, who was given to the patriarch Ruchi. She bore twins, Yajña and Dakshina, who became husband and wife and had twelve sons, the deities called Yamas (DOWSON, *H.C.D.*, p. 10).

Aladin's Wonderful Lamp : 'Alâ-ud-Dîn (Aladin), the son of a poor tailor, obtains a certain lamp. Every time this lamp is rubbed, a *jinn* (q.v.) appears and executes all his commands. Aladin becomes a rich man, but the lamp is afterwards obtained by a trick by a magician. After a series of adventures, Aladin succeeds in killing the magician and recovering his lamp. (BURTON, *Alif laila wa laila.*)

Alasnam's Mirror : This mirror remained unsullied when it reflected a chaste and pure-minded woman, but became dim when the woman reflected on it was faithless, wanton and light. cf. *Florimel's Girdle*, etc.

Al-A'war : A son of Iblis, a jinn (q.v.), who encourages debauchery. (*Jew. Enc.* Vol. IV, p. 521.)

Albatross : In sailors' superstition, this bird is supposed to cause the wind to blow; if this bird be killed, some terrible disaster will happen to the ship. (BASSETT, p. 128.)
" And I had done a hellish thing,
And it would work 'em woe :
For all averred I had killed the bird
That made the breeze to blow.
Ah wretch ! said they, the bird to slay,
That made the breeze to blow."
COLERIDGE : *The Ancient Mariner*, II, 3.
Vide *Petrel*.

Al Borak : This is the name of the animal which conveyed Mahomet to the seventh heaven. He not only spoke good Arabic, but had also a human face. He was brought by Gabriel. His other peculiarities were : he had the cheeks of a horse and the wings of an eagle. cf. *Balaam's Ass, Arion, Achilles' Horses.*

Alceste : Gr. Myth. Daughter of Pellias and wife of Admete (q.v.). After her death Hercules entered the infernal regions to bring her back to earth again.

Alceus : Gr. Myth. Son of Perseus, grandfather of Hercules.

Alcide : Gr. Myth. Grandson of Alceus. Surname of Hercules and his descendants.

Alcmæon : Gr. Myth. A son of Amphiraüs, leader of the Epigoni against Thebes. He was driven mad by the Erinyes for killing his mother Eriphyle (q.v.). He was slain by a son of Phegeus.

Alcmene : Gr. Myth. The wife of Amphitryon and mother of Herakles (Hercules) by Zeus.

Alcyon : A fabulous bird which was supposed to build its nest on the calm waters of the sea. It was regarded as a bird of good omen. (*Petit Larousse illustré*, p. 26.)

Alcyone : Gr. Myth. Daughter of Eolus, wife of the King of Trachis. She and her husband were changed into alcyons.

Alectoria : It is a stone extracted from a capon. It is said to render the wearer invisible, to allay thirst, to antidote enchantment and to ensure love. cf. *Agate*.

Alecto : Gr. Myth. One of the three Erinnys or Furies.

Alectryon : Gr. Myth. A youth sent by Mars to guard against surprise. He fell asleep, and Apollo surprised Mars and Venus in each other's arms. Mars, in anger, changed Alectryon into a cock.

Alexandrite : A species of beryl found in Siberia ; it shows the Russian imperial colours—red and green—and is named from the Emperor Alexander of Russia.

Allatu : In Babylonian mythology this is the name of the wife of Nergal (q.v.). Vide *Aralu*.

Aloka-nanda : One of the four branches of the river Ganges, which flows south of the country of Bharata. This is said by the Vaishnavas to be the terrestrial Gangâ, which Siva received upon his head. (DOWSON, *H.C.D.*, p. 11.)

Alpe : In Germany the Mara (q.v.) is usually designated by this name.

Alphito : In Classical mythology these were beings which belonged to the same class as the Lamia (q.v.).

Al Raqim : In the Qor'an (Sura xviii) this is a name connected with the legend of the Seven Sleepers ; it usually refers to their dog, now in Paradise and in charge of letters and correspondence.

Alraune : It is a kind of Kobold who brings gold through the chimneys. (*East Friesland, Oldenburg,* WUTTKE, p. 230).

Alrinach : In Eastern mythology it is the demon who causes shipwrecks and presides over storms and earthquakes. When visible, it is always in the form and dress of a woman (BASSETT, p. 69). cf. *Nixe, Lorelei, Siren, Jal Pari, Bugarik.*

Al Sirat : An imaginary bridge between the earth and the Mahometan paradise ; it is not so wide as a spider's web. Those laden with sin fall over into the abyss below. cf. *Bifrost.*

Alsvid : Vide *Arvak*.

Altar : To dream that you are kneeling at an altar is a bad omen.

Alte : " Old one " ; it is the name of a Teutonic field-spirit in human form.

Alu : In Babylonian superstition this was a demon. The word signifies " the strong one."

Alukah : The blood-sucker or vampire (q.v.) of Jewish super-stition whose two daughters continually cry : " Give, give." It is none other than the Ghoul (q.v.) of the Arabs. (WELLHAUSEN, Vol. III, pp. 135-7).

Alwantin : In the Deccan it is the spirit of a pregnant woman, one dying on the day of childbirth or within the puerperal pollution. (JACKSON, *F.L.N.*, Vol. II, p. 55.)

Amalthea : Class. Myth. The goat which nourished Jupiter. One of her horns became the horn of abundance.

Amara-Kanṭaka : " Peak of the Immortals " ; it is a place of pilgrimage in the table-land east of the Vindhyas. (DOWSON, *H.C.D.*, p. 11.)

Amarum : Among the Quichas of Equador this is one of the most formidable demons known ; it is of the form of a huge water-boa. It is the father of witchcraft, and the souls of sorcerers are said to take up their abode in these monsters. (KARSTEN, *Indian Tribes of Equador*, p. 70.)

Amatongo : A Zulu generic name for the ghost-folk (CALLAWAY; HAGGARD, *Nada the Lily*, pp. 60, 99, 113, 217, etc.)

Amazons : Gr. Myth. A race of female warriors, generally supposed to have inhabited the coasts of the river Thermedon, in Cappadocia, with whom the Greeks repeatedly warred. They were said to expose their male children and to burn (or cut off) their right breasts. The most famous queens of the Amazons were : ANTIOPE who attacked Theseus and was vanquished by him ; PENTHESILEA who was killed by Achilles ; THOMYRIS who caused the death of Cyrus ; and THALESTRIS who encountered Alexander.

Amber : It is said to be a concretion of birds' tears. The birds which wept amber were the sisters of Meleager, called Meleagrides, who never ceased weeping for their brother's death.
Amber is a cure for sore throats and all glandular swellings.

Ambergris : It is said to be the petrification of some interior part of the whale. (BASSETT, p. 240, quoting O'Reilly.)

Ambondrombe : The Hovas of Madagascar believe that the ghosts of men and beasts live on this great mountain, and occasionally walk among the tombs and execution places (q.v.) of criminals.

Amchi-malghen : It is the guardian-nymph of the Chilians. (MOLINA, *Chili*, Vol. II, p. 86.)

Amenti : Egypt. Myth. The region of the dead ; it is the subterranean realm, whither the sun descends. The soul entering Amenti was conducted by Anubis (q.v.). was judged by the forty-two judges, and was then passed on to Aalu (or Elysium), or tortured according to its due. It corresponded to the Greek Hades or the Hebrew Sheol.

Amethyst : The amethyst is an emblem of humility and sobriety. It is dedicated to January and Venus. In the Zodiac it stands for Sagittarius ; in metallurgy, for copper ; in Christian Art it is given to St. Matthew, and in the Roman Catholic Church it is set in the pastoral rings of the bishops ; whence it is called " Prelate's gem."
Amethyst banishes a desire for drink and promotes chastity. The Greeks thought that it counteracted the effects of wine.

Amon : Egypt. Myth. Originally a local deity, and later one of the chief deities of the Egyptian pantheon ; subsequently, he was called by the name of Amon-Ra (q.v.).

Amon-Ra : Egypt. Myth. He was called " the father of the gods, the fashioner of men, the creator of cattle, the lord of all being, etc." He is represented as a man wearing on his head a disc, surmounted by two tall ostrich plumes. His wife was Mut, and Chunsu was his son. The ruins of Carnac are the remains of his great Theban temple.

Amphiaraus : Gr. Myth. A hero and seer of Argos, who took part, among others, in the Expedition of the Seven against Thebes. He was worshipped as a god at Orpus.

Amphion : Gr. Myth. Son of Zeus and Antiope ; twin of Zethus, and husband of Niobe.

Amphitrite : Class. Myth. One of the Nereids (q.v.); wife of Poseidon (q.v.).

Amphitryon : Class. Myth. Zeus takes the form of Amphitryon and visits Alcmene, his wife, entertains her with a feast and becomes the father of Hercules.

Amset : Egypt. Myth. He was the man-headed genius of Amenti. He was associated with the North.

Amulets : In India all kinds of diseases are superstitiously believed to be cured by wearing different kinds of amulets. (See advertisements in the daily, weekly or monthly papers of Calcutta, Bombay, etc.)

Anadyomene : Gr. Myth. An epithet of Aphrodite, alluding to the legend of her rising out of the sea at birth.

Anæmia : It is believed to be caused by vampires (q.v.) sucking the blood of the living. (FOSTER, *Observations during a Voyage round the World*, p. 543 ; *Enc. Brit.*, Vol. VIII, p. 6 ; SKEAT, *Malay Magic*, pp. 326 *et seq.;* RHYS, *Celtic Folklore*, p. 673 ; ENNEMOSER, *History of Magic*, Vol. II, pp. 185, 480 ; KRAUSS in *Mitteil. d. anthrop. Gesell. zu Wien.* Vol. XVIII. p. 183).

Anafielas : In Lithuanian legend it was a high, steep mountain, up which all souls of the dead had to clamber ; claws of bears and lynxes were therefore burnt with the bodies to help the deceased in this arduous task.

Anaka-dundubhi : " Drums " ; a name of Vasu-deva who was so called, because the drums of heaven resounded at his birth. (DOWSON, *H.C.D.*, p. 14.)

Ananga : " The bodyless " ; it is a name of Kāma, god of love.

Ananta : " The infinite " ; it is a name of the serpent Sesha. (DOWSON, H.C.D.)

Anat : Vide *Antum.*

Anchor : If you dream of an anchor, you will, if a man, be a sailor, or if a woman, marry one.

Andhaka : A demon, son of Kasyapa and Diti, with a thousand arms and heads, two thousand eyes and feet ; he was called Andhaka, because he walked like a blind man, although he could see very well. (DOWSON, *II.C.D!*, p. 15.)

Andromache : Wife of Hector. After the fall of Troy, she became a slave of Pyrrhus, son of Achilles. Her name is symbolic of conjugal love.

Andromeda : Gr. Myth. Daughter of Cepheus and Cassiopeia. By the decree of Zeus, she was chained to a cliff, to be devoured by a monster. Perseus returning after slaying Medusa, killed the monster and married her. When Phineus, her betrothed, interfered, Perseus changed him into a stone by means of the Gorgon's head. Vide *Medusa.*

Angdistis : Vide *Agdistis.*

Angel : Angels in popular belief are the supernatural messengers of God.

Children who like to talk of angels, or are unusually clever, will not live long. (STRACKERJAN, Vol. I, p. 35.)

To dream of seeing an angel is good, to dream of being one yourself is better, but if you dream you are speaking to one or calling on one, it is of evil significance.

Angerboda : Norse Myth. She was a giantess who, by Loki, was the mother of the wolf Fenrir (q.v.), the Midgard Serpent (q.v.) and Hel (q.v.), goddess of the dead.

Angling : To dream of angling presages affliction and trouble.

Angus : Celt. Myth. A Gaelic god of love and amorous dalliance. He was son of Dugda, whom he cheated out of his underground palace. His harp was of so sweet a tone that whoever heard must follow ; his kisses became invisible love-whispering birds.

Anilas : Hindu Myth. A class of deities, forty-nine in number, connected with Anila, the wind. (DOWSON, *H.C.D.*, p. 17).

Animal : No animal dies near the sea, except at the ebbing of the tide. (*Gt. Britain.*)

Animal under Yoke : Vide *Stones*.

Animisha : " One who does not wink " ; a general epithet of all Indian gods. (DOWSON, *H.C.D.*, p. 17)

Animism : (As the subject is too vast to be dealt with in a few lines, the reader is referred to TYLOR : *Primitive Culture.*)

Anito : The Irayas and Catalangans of Luzon worship the souls of their ancestors under the name of Anitos. These are household deities ; some of them reside in pots, and miniature houses standing near the family dwelling are sacred to them. (FRAZER, *G.B.*, Vol. II, p. 463.)

Ankle Bones : The ankle bones of a hare are superstitiously believed by the Arabs to be a powerful weapon against Jinns, Ghouls and even Satan himself. (HASTINGS, *Dic Bib.*, Vol. IV, p. 603.)

Anne, St. : Vide *Riches, Wealth Bestowers*.

Annwn : Celt. Myth. The British Hades, represented as a sea-girdled, revolving fortress. Gwyn was the leader of the dead.

'Anqa : Turkish Folklore. A fabulous bird of enormous size, said to inhabit the Caucasus range (REDHOUSE, *Turkish-English Lexicon*, Constantinople, 1890, p. 1325; KUNOS, *T.F.T.*).

He whose head touches the shadow of a flying *'anqa*, will wear a crown (ZENKER, *Dictionnaire turc-arabe-persan*, Leipzig, 1876, p. 640.).

Ant : When ants are unusually busy, foul weather is at hand (SKEAT, *Malay Magic*, p. 535).

Ants never sleep. (EMERSON, *Nature*, Vol. II, p. 53.)

To have an ants' nest made near your door portends security and riches (LEAN, Vol. II, p. 53).

If you dream of ants, you will live in a great town, and be happy, industrious, well-married, and have many children.

According to Alexander Ross, the cruel battle between the Venetians and the Insubrians, as also the one between the Liégeois and the Burgundians, in which 30,000 men were slain, was presignified by combats between two swarms of ants. Vide *Worm*.

Anteus : Gr. Myth. A giant, son of Neptune and the Earth, who was killed by Hercules. Vide *Bernardo del Carpio*.

Anthony, St. : Cures erysipelas.

Antigone : Gr. Myth. A daughter of Œdipus (q.v.) and Jocasta, typical of faithfulness and heroism in the Greek ideal of womanhood. She was her father's guide after he had torn out his eyes.

Antiope : A Theban princess carried off by Epopeus. She became the mother of Amphion and Zethus. She was maltreated by Dirce, wife of Lycus, and unknowingly took refuge with her sons, who were ordered by Dirce to tie her to the horns of a wild bull. They, on finding out that she was their mother, treated Dirce herself in the aforesaid manner.

Antum : Babyl. Myth. The consort of Anu.

Anu : Egypt. Myth. A mighty king, the first-born of the gods. (SAYCE, p. 483.)
    In Babylonian mythology he is the god of the sky or heavens, and is one of the most ancient deities. His consort was Antum or Anat.

Anubis : Egypt. Myth. A jackal-god of the necropolis ; he is usually regarded as a son of Isis and Osiris (q.v.) ; a god of the dead ; he guards the dead and superintends their embalmment and shares with Thoth (q.v.), the office of the conductor of the dead to the Judgment Hall of Amenti, whither he guides them by the hand and where he weighs their hearts against the Feather of Truth and Right. (WIEDEMANN, *Rel. of Ancient Egyptians*, p. 230.)

Anukit : Egypt. Myth. A goddess of Libyan origin, depicted as wearing a feather crown. She was worshipped in the neighbourhood of Philae.

Annuit : Babyl. Myth. A goddess, who was later identified with Ishtar.

Anunnaki : Babyl. Myth. A group of powerful earth-spirits, genii or demons, who were servants of gods ; on the whole, they were hostile to men. They were closely associated with the Igigi (q.v.).

Apaosa : In Persian means " Drought " ; hence drought personified.

Apepi : Egypt. Myth. The great serpent, who led the onslaught of the demons against the sun, by whom they were duly overcome ; thus symbolizing the struggle of darkness and light.

Aphrodite : Gr. Myth. The goddess of love and beauty, and of life as expressive of the cosmic power of love.

Apis : Egypt. Myth. The sacred bull, which was considered as the highest form of animal life.

Apocatequil : In Peruvian legend he was the first son of the mortal who descended on earth. He recalled his mother to life, and made an aperture in the earth with a golden spade, through which the race of the Peruvians emerged and took possession of the land. (GASKELL, p. 54, quoting *Non-Class. Myth.*, p. 12.)

Apollo : Gr. Myth. One of the most important of the Olympic gods, especially conspicuous as the god of manly youth and beauty, of poetry and music, and of the wisdom of oracles.

Apollyon : One of the various names of the Devil.

Apoplexy : Vide *Fever*.

Apparel : If you dream of losing wearing apparel, your character will be injured by another.

Apparition : An unnatural appearance of a real being ; a spectre : a phantom.

> " The dominant spirit . . . is the apparition of a figure on horseback without a head."—W. IRVING, *Sketch Book*, II.

Apple : If an apple tree blossoms in autumn, it is considered to be a sign of an approaching marriage. (*Lower Saxony*, WUTTKE, p. 35.)

If the first apple of a young tree be plucked and eaten by a woman who has borne many children, the tree will be sure to bear many apples. (*Bohemia*, GROHMANN, p. 143; FRAZER, *G.B.*, Vol. I, p. 39).

Appolina, St. : Vide *Toothache*.

April : Vide *Diamond, Sapphire*.

Apron : In Vogtland a girl does not allow her lover to dry his hands on her apron, for fear this would bring about a quarrel.

If a man wipes himself on a girl's apron, he will fall madly in love with her (PLOSS, *Das Weib*, Vol. I, p. 443.)

Apsaras : The Apsaras are the celebrated nymphs of Indra's heaven. They are the daughters of pleasure and of fascinating charms, who lure heroes and sages from their devotions and penances. They are fairy-like beings, beautiful and voluptuous, and number about thirty-five millions. (DOWSON, *H.C.D.*, p. 20 ; TYLOR, *Primitive Culture*, Vol. II, p. 173; WARD, *Account of the Writings . . . of the Hindoos*, Vol. II, p. 151.) cf. *Siren, Lorelei, Houri, Peri*.

Arachne : A young Lydian maiden who excelled in the art of embroidery. She was changed into a spider, for having defied Minerva in her arts.

Aracho : It is the Mongol name for Râhu (q.v.).

Aralu : Babyl. Myth. The abode of the dead, represented as a vast and gloomy cavern in the midst of the earth, surrounded by seven walls and ruled over by Nergal (q.v.) and his wicked consort, Allatu, and their attendant demons. In this place the dead were supposed to lead an existence with no hope of return to a brighter life.

Arch Enemy :
Arch Fiend : } Other names for the Devil.

Ardat lili : "Maids of the night." These, in Babylonian superstition, were evil spirits who, like the Lilu (q.v.), plied their trade at night.

Ardha-nārî : "Half woman"; a form in which Siva is represented as half male and half female, typifying the male and female energies. (DOWSON, *H.C.D.*, p. 21.)

Ares : Gr. Myth. The god of war and, sometimes, of pestilence ; son of Zeus and Hera, and lover of Aphrodite. The Romans identified him with Mars.

Arethusa : Class. Myth. A wood-nymph of Elis who, when pursued by Alpheus, a river, was changed into a river running under the sea.

Argonauts : Gr. Myth. The heroes who went to win the "Golden Fleece." They were about fifty in number.

Argus : A mythical monster with a hundred eyes; guardian of Io.

Ariadne : Class. Myth. Daughter of Minos. She fell in love with Theseus, who afterwards abandoned her.

Ariane : Gr. Myth. Daughter of Minos. She gave Theseus a skein of cotton to guide him back after killing the Minotaur (q.v.) in the labyrinth. Theseus threw this away and fell into the sea.

Arianrod : Celt. Myth. A Cymric goddess, wife of Gwydion, mother of Dylan and Llen.

Arion : Gr. Myth. The wonderful horse which Hercules gave to Adrastos. It not only spoke good Greek, but both its fore-feet were those of a man. cf. *Al Borak, Balaam's Ass, Achilles' Horses.*

Arishta : Hindu Myth. A Daitya (q.v.), son of Bali, who attacked Krishna in the form of a savage bull and was slain by him. (DOWSON, *H.C.D.*, p. 21.)

Aristæus : Class. Myth. A son of Apollo and the nymph Cyrene. He was deified as the protector of flocks, shepherds, the vine and the olive ; he was also the instructor in bee-keeping.

Arjuna : Hindu Myth. The hero of the great epic Mahâbhârata. He was one of the five Pândava brothers.

Arm : If a person has hairy arms, it is a sign that he will be wealthy. (*North Ohio*, BERGEN, *C.S.*, p. 35.)

Arsaphes : Another spelling for Hershef.

Artemis : Gr. Myth. An Olympian goddess of various attributes. In mythology she is a virgin huntress and goddess of wild nature. She is the same as Diana (q.v.) of the Romans.

Artemisia : Leaves of artemisia, tied in a bundle and placed near beds, drive demons away. (*China*, WILLIAMS, *M.K.*, Vol. II, p. 255.) Vide *Sweet-flag*.

Arthur, King : In current English superstition he is supposed to be still living in fairy-land and will come back to earth when the proper time arrives. He is said to sit at the Round Table. Vide *Morgaine la Faye, Papillon, Charlemagne, Raven*.

Aruru : Babyl. Myth. A goddess to whom is ascribed the creation of Gilgamesh and Eabani.

Arva : " A horse." One of the horses of the moon ; a fabulous animal, half horse, half bird, on which the Daityas are supposed to ride. (DOWSON, *H.C.D.*, p. 25.)

Arvak : Norse Myth. One of the horses of the sun, the other being Alsvid.

Arvan : Another spelling for Arvâ.

Aryskoui : An ancient war-god of the Red Indians of America.

Asakku : In Babylonian superstition the Asakku were the demons who carried and spread plague.

Ascalophos : Son of Acheron. In a Greek tale he was turned into an owl for telling tales and trying to make mischief.

Ascension Day : In Swabia, on this day, wreaths of red and white flowers are hung up over stable doors, as a preventive against lightning. (WUTTKE, p. 21.)

In North Germany it is believed, that melons planted on this day grow well. (ib.)

In Hessen it is believed that herbs plucked or collected on Ascension Day are especially powerful for medicinal purposes. (ib.)

Ascanius : Class. Myth. The son of Æneas and Creusa, who accompanied his father in his wanderings after the fall of Troy ; later, he succeeded his father.

Asclepius : In later Greek religion he is the god of medicine and healing.

Ases : Scand. Myth. Gods of benevolence.

Asgard : Norse Myth. It is the abode or the citadel of the gods. It is situated at the zenith, and can be reached only by the bridge Bifrost, the rainbow.

Ash : If ash is thrown into the room from a burning log, troubles and anxieties must be expected. (*Greece*, LAWSON, p. 328.)
On the tenth night after the death of a person, he who fired the funeral pyre is required to sift some ashes, near which a lamp is placed, and the whole covered with a basket. Next morning the ashes are examined, and the ghost is said to have migrated into the animal whose mark appears on the ashes. (*India*—N.I.N.Q., III, p. 35; CROOKE, *P.R.I.*, Vol. II, p. 74; *Ethnologie du Bengale*, p. 73).

Ashmodai: Jewish lore. A demon, generally regarded as the same as Asmodeus.

Ashtoreth : The Phœnician goddess Astarte, the goddess of fertility and reproduction. She was worshipped from time to time by the Israelites. Vide *Astarte*.

Ashur : Assyr. Myth. The chief deity of the Assyrian pantheon. He was the god of military prowess. His symbol was the winged circle.

Ash Wednesday : Cattle must not be tied up on this day, as they lose their strength by so doing ; neither must they be sold—it brings ill-luck. (WUTTKE, p. 22.)

A-Siras : A race of spirits or beings without heads. (DOWSON, *H.C.D.*, p. 26.) cf. *Acephali, Blemmyæ*.

Askefruer : "Ash-nymphs." These are Danish forest-spirits of present-day superstition. Their bodies are covered with hair, their faces are wrinkled, they have hanging breasts and dishevelled hair and are usually dressed in moss. They are endowed with various occult powers and especially with that of curing diseases. (THIELE, *Danmarks Folkesagn.*)

Asmodeus : In Jewish demonology it is the name of an evil spirit of anger and lust. Later, he was the king of the demons.

Asp : Queen Cleopatra of Egypt is said to have committed suicide by holding an asp to her bosom.

To dream of an asp is good ; it promises wealth and a rich wife.

Asrael : Mahometan Myth. An angel of death. He is immeasurable in height, insomuch that the space between the eyes equals a journey of 70,000 days. Vide *Azrael*.

Ass : The mark running down the back of an ass and the cut at right angles over the shoulders is the cross of Christ, impressed on the animal, because Christ rode an ass during his triumphant entry into Jerusalem.

Three hairs taken from the " cross " of an ass, will cure whooping cough, but the ass from which the hairs are plucked will die.

The blood of a she-ass will cure epilepsy. (STRACKERJAN, Vol. I, p. 84.)

Vide *Beans*.

Aṣ-Ṣayyāhun : These are the " pious travellers " of Mohammedan mythology. They are angels who scour the country with the intention of frequenting only those gatherings where the name of Allah (God) is being repeated.

Assides : A plant in the country of Prester John. It not only protects the wearer from evil spirits, but forces every spirit to tell its business. (BREWER, *R.H.*) cf. *Tulsi, Chikuli, Che*.

Astarte : The Phœnician goddess of fertility and of sexual love. By the Classical nations she was also regarded as a moon goddess. Human sacrifices were often offered to her. (See FRAZER, *Adonis, Attis and Osiris*).

Asthma : Asthma can be cured by foam (q.v.) from a mule's mouth. (FRAZER, *G.B.*, Vol. III, p. 23; *Ethnologie du Bengale*, p. 140).

Asto-vidatu : In Persian superstition it was a spirit who divided the bones at death.

Astræa : Class. Myth. Daughter of Zeus and Themis. She was a goddess of justice, and was the last of the divinities to leave the earth at the end of the Golden Age. She became the constellation Virgo.

Asur : Same as Ashur.

Asura : Hindu Myth. The word " Asura " was originally used as an epithet of the higher gods ; later, it became synonymous with an evil spirit or demon and an enemy of gods or *devas*. The Asuras were created from the downward breathing of a Prajāpati, and had darkness and magic ascribed to them.

In the Rig Veda this was the name given to Varuṇa (q.v.) ; later, it denoted a ghostly and demoniacal being of a lower order. (OTTO, *Das Heilige*, p. 153.)

Asvins : Vedic Myth. Two gods of dawn, twin brothers, young and beautiful, capable of assuming any forms they chose, and said to be sons of a nymph. They are the physicians of heaven and benefactors of mankind. cf. *Dioscuri*.

Asynjur : Norse Myth. They were the goddesses of Asgard (q.v.), associates of the Æsir (q.v.) and distinguished from the Vanir (q.v.) goddesses.

Ataguchu : A Peruvian god who helped Apocatequil (q.v.).

Athanas : Gr. Myth. The mad paramour of Ino (q.v.) who slew Ino's two sons.

Athena : One of the greater Olympian deities, prominent as a civic goddess, wise in the industries of peace and in the arts of war.

Atlantides : The Pleiades or seven stars, fabled to be the daughters of Atlas and Pleione.

Atlantis : A mythical island in the west, said to have been sunk beneath the ocean by an earthquake. The Atlantic Ocean is said to derive its name from this island.

Atlas : In later Greek mythology he was a Titan, son of Iapetus and Clymene. He was forced to support the heavens on his head and hands, as a punishment for warring against Zeus.

Atli : In the Volsunga Saga Atli is a king corresponding to Etzel in the Nibelungenlied ; he marries Gudrun and invites her brothers to court, where they are treacherously slain. Gudrun avenges them by killing her own and Atli's two sons, and later, Atli himself.

Atma, Atman : The soul, the principle of life ; the supreme soul.

Atropos : Gr. Myth. One of the Fates (q.v.), or goddesses of destiny. She is the one who cuts off the thread of life. cf. *Bidhātāpurusha, Fates, Norn, Parca, Hathor, Sudičky*.

A Tsze : A fox (q.v.) in human form is known among the Chinese as *A Tsze*. (MAYER, *Chin. Read. Man.*, p. 65.)

Attis : Class. Myth. A god of vegetation and of young life. According to a legend, violets sprang from his blood. He was beloved by the goddess Cybele.

Audhumla : Norse Myth. The cow formed from frost. She nourished Ymir with four streams of milk, and licked out of the salty frost stones a being, called Buri (q.v.).

August : Vide *Onyx*.

Aurora : Rom. Myth. The goddess of dawn. Vide *Eos*.

Aurora Borealis : It gives warning of an impending war ; the red light in it denotes the blood to be shed in the war. (STRACKERJAN, Vol. II, p. 63.)

Auxo : Gr. Myth. One of the three goddesses known as Heures (q.v.)

Avalon : The place where Morgaine la Faye (q.v.) keeps Holgar the Dane entranced.

Axe : If cows, the first time they are taken out in spring, be made to step over an axe, they will be invulnerable to all kinds of magic and witchcraft. (*East Prussia*, WUTTKE, p. 98.) cf. *Weather Bad*.

Azi : In Persian means " Greed " ; hence greed personified.

Azrael : Another spelling for Asrael, 'Azraîl.

'Azrail : Same as Azrael above. In Mahometan mythology he is the angel of death. He consigns the souls he has seized to the angels of compassion or to the angels of punishment, according as they are believers or unbelievers.

B

Baal: The chief male divinity of the Phœnicians. The Assyrians identified him with Beal (q.v.)

Baba-Yaga : The Baba Yaga of Russian folklore is a hideous old beldam, whose children are the evil spirits. She is said to steal children for the purpose of gratifying her desire for human flesh. She has teeth and breasts of iron, with which she rends her victims ; her home is in a far distant forest. (See RALSTON, *Folktales of the Russians*.)

Baby : In Bohemia if a pregnant woman wishes to have a baby boy, she puts poppy seeds outside on the window sill ; if a baby girl, sugar.

New-born babies must not be carried over cross-roads ; ignoring this precaution is equivalent to the signing of the death sentence of the child. (*Pomerania*, WUTTKE, p. 194.)

Bacchus : Rom. Myth. The god of wine and riotous merriment, son of Jupiter and Semele. He is the prototype of Dionysus of the Greeks. He helped his father in his wars with the giants.

Backache : Backache can be cured by keeping chestnuts in the pocket. (STRACKERJAN, Vol. I, p. 85.)

Bachelor : At the funeral of a bachelor, cast sand before the coffin, to blind the eyes of the unbegotten children of the deceased. (*Kurdistan. Jew. Enc.*, Vol. IX, p. 600.)

Bacon : Bacon, especially if it is stolen, is a powerful medicine for various diseases, such as warts, fever, constipation, etc. (STRACKERJAN, Vol. I, p. 83; Vol. II, p. 85). Vide *Pig, Moon.*

Badhava : Hindu Myth. It is a flame with the head of a horse ; called also Haya-Siras, "horse-head." (DOWSON, *H.C.D.*, p. 39.)

Bagouly : The modern name for Pactolus (q.v.).

Bahman's Knife : When Prince Bahman started on his exploits, he gave his sister Parizādi, a knife which, he told her, would remain bright and clean as long as he was safe and well, but, immediately he was in danger, or dead, would become dull or drop gouts of blood. cf. *Canace's Mirror, Sophia's Picture, Florimel's Girdle, Ring Bertha's Emerald.*

Balaam's Ass : An ass which is said to have spoken Hebrew on one occasion to Balaam cf. *Al Borak, Arion, Achilles' Horses.*

Balder : Teut. Myth. Son of Odin and Frigg, god of light and peace, and of the good, beautiful, eloquent and wise. He was slain by the contrivance of the evil Loki. Vide *Hoder, Mistletoe.*

Bali : Hindu Myth. A good and virtuous Daitya king ; through devotion and penance he defeated Indra, humbled the gods and extended his authority over the three worlds. (DOWSON, *H.C.D.*, p. 42.)

Bali, Balin : A monkey-king of Kishkindhyā, who was slain by Rāma, and whose kingdom was given to his brother Su-griva, a friend of Rāma. He was supposed to be the son of Indra and to have been born from the hair (*bala*) of his mother, whence his name. (DOWSON, *H.C.D.*, p. 42.)

Balin : Balin and Balun of Arthurian legend were two knights who, though brothers, slew each other by mistake.

Balmung : In the Nibelungenlied it is the name of the famous sword of Siegfried. cf. *Excalibur, Tizona.*

Balor : Celt. Myth. A king of the Fomors (q.v.), whose eye blighted all he looked at. It was therefore always kept closed, except in war. In the wars with the gods, he slays Nuada, and is slain by Lugh who blinds his fatal eye with a magic missile.

Balun : Vide *Balin.*

Ban : Babyl. Myth. She is the consort of Nin-girsu and one of the most prominent goddesses of the pantheon.

Bana : A Daitya, eldest son of Bali ; he had a thousand arms. (DOWSON, *H.C.D.*, p. 42.)

Bandicoote : If a woman eats the flesh of bandicootes after she has passed her eleventh or twelfth year, she will be barren (*Western Australia*—PLOSS, *Das Weib*, Vol. I, p. 508).

Bāngmā (masc.), **Bāngmi** (fem.) : A fabulous bird in India, which is not only supposed to have human speech, but is also oracular. (DAY, *Folk-tales of Bengal.*) cf. *Bulbul Hezar.*

Banmānus : In some Indian dialects means a "monkey." (Sanskrit : vana=wood ; manushya=man ; man of the wood.) cf. *Monkey, Orang-utang.*

Bannik : In Russian folklore this is the name of a household spirit, who lives in the bathroom. (*D.R.E.*, Art., *Demonology, Slavic.*)

Banquet : It is good to dream of a banquet ; it denotes prosperity.

Banshee : It is a supernatural being, supposed by the peasantry of Ireland and of the Highlands of Scotland, to wail under the windows of a house, where one of the inmates is about to die. Certain families of rank were reputed to have a special spirit of this kind. (LADY WILDE, pp. 135-7 ; D. R. MACANNALAY, *Irish Wonders*, p. 110 ; KENNEDY, *Fireside Stories*, pp. 143-4 ; T. CROFTON CROKER). cf. *Bodachun Dun, Božaloshtsh, Death Warnings, Gwrach y Rhibyn, Smrtnice, Cyhiraeth.*

Banyan : Indian folklore. The banyan tree is a representation of the god Siva. One who cuts this tree is punished with the extirpation of his family. (JACKSON, *F.L.N.*, Vol. I, p. 136.)

Baptism : If a child cries during baptism, it is the devil going out of it. (*Niagara Falls, Ont.*, BERGEN, *C.S.*, p. 21.)

Baptismal Water : If a baby girl be baptized with the same water with which a boy has been baptized just before, she will, in later life, have a growth of beard. (*East Prussia, Mark, Oberlausnitz.* WUTTKE, p. 198)

Barahoot : A well in the province of Hadramot, in which the souls of unbelievers reside. (LANE, *A.S.M.A.*, p. 264.) Vide *Zemzem*.

Barbara, St. : Vide *Storms, Dying*.

Barbarossa : Frederick Barbarossa, " Redbeard," a German king, is supposed to sit at a marble table in Kyffhäuser. His beard is growing through the table. In another variation of the legend, his beard is growing round the table, and when it grows three times round the table, he will wake up.

> " Er ist niemals gestorben,
> Er lebt darin noch jetzt ;
> Er hat im Schloss verborgen
> Zum Schlaf sich hingesetzt.
>
> Sein Bart ist nicht von Flachse,
> Er ist von Feuerglut,
> Ist durch den Tisch gewachsen,
> Worauf sein Kinn ausruht."
> —FR. RÜCKERT : *Barbarossa im Kyffhäuser.*

cf. *Holgar the Dane, Charlemagne, Alfred King*.

Barley gaffer : The English name of the Gerstenalte.

Barn : To dream of barns stored with corn denotes that you will marry well, overthrow your adversaries at law and grow rich.

Barnacle : A barnacle broken off a ship turns into a Solan goose. (BASSETT, p. 265.)
" There are in the north parts of Scotland certaine trees, whereon do grow shell fishes, etc., etc., which falling into the water, do become fowls, whom we call *barnacles*." (GERARD, *Herbal*, 1597, p. 1391 ; BRAND, *Observations*, Vol. III, p. 362.)
" Like your Scotch barnacles, now a block,
Instantly a worm, and presently a great goose."
MARSTON, *The Malcontent* (1604).

Barrenness : Barrenness can be cured by drinking water in which moss growing on the Temple walls has been boiled. (*Jews of Palestine.* SCHIFFER, *Urquell*, V, p. 235.) Menstrual blood cures barrenness (STRACK, p. 16.)

In Bosnia and Herzegovina, it is believed that barrenness is caused by the woman cohabiting with the devil (PLOSS, *Das Weib*, Vol. I, p. 507, quoting GLÜCK, *Die Tatowierung der Haut, etc.*) ; among the Chippeway Indians, because she is untrue to her husband.

According to the Magyars, a woman may be made barren if the genitals of a corpse be rubbed with her menses (PLOSS, *op. cit.*, Vol. I, p. 508, quoting V. WLISLOCKI). Vide *Bandicoote, Pig, Swallow, Mandrake.*

Basilisk : An animal which comes out of the egg of a black cock. It is so extremely poisonous that it can kill at a distance by its glance. It is a monster with a human face ; no human being can look at it and live. cf. *Dragon, Gin-sai, Bazaliček.*

Basin : To dream of a basin signifies a good maid.

Basket : If children carry baskets on their heads, they will not grow tall. (GRIFFIS, *M.E.*, p. 470.) cf. *Gun.*

Bastard : A woman by giving birth to seven bastard children regains her virginity (!) (STRACKERJAN, Vol. II, p. 127).

Bat : Bats flying about in a house foretell a death. (*India*; see also STRACKERJAN, Vol. I, p. 24.)

Of all animals the luckiest is the bat, and happy is he who keeps a bat's bone about his person. (*Macedonia*—ABBOTT, p. 110).

The right eye of a bat, carried in the waistcoat pocket, makes a man invisible. (*Bohemia*—GROHMANN, p. 58.)

Bathing : If you dream of bathing in clear water you will prosper ; but if in muddy water shame and sorrow will be your portion.

Bat horin : It is a demon of Jewish folklore, which brings diseases of the eye to one who fails to wash his hands after meals. (BRÜHL, *Jahrbuch*, Vol. I., p. 157.)

Bath-tub : Among the Jews of Galicia it is said that a child's bath-tub must not be used for any other purpose, or the child will not prosper. (SCHIFFER, *Urquell*. Vol. V, p. 141.)

Battle : On the day a battle is expected to take place, the wives of the Tschi-speaking men, who are away with the army, paint themselves white and run about armed with guns, or sticks made to look like guns, and taking some melon-like fruits hack them with knives, as if they were chopping off the heads of the enemies. (ELLIS, *The Tschi-speaking Peoples of the Gold Coast*, p. 226.)

Baudoin : Balaam's Ass (q.v.) was called by this name.

Bay tree : The withering of a bay tree prognosticates death.

The Romans called the bay " the plant of the good angel," because neither sickness nor evil will infest nor have anything to do in a place where a bay tree is.

Bazalíček : In Bohemian superstition it is a kind of a spirit which is born out of the egg of a black cock. Its look is so poisonous that no one can look at it and live. (GROHMANN, p. 18.) cf. *Basilisk, Dragon, Gin-sai.*

Beads : Among the Hindus, a necklace of beads, used in the same manner as a rosary (q.v.), is a powerful charm against malevolent spirits. As an antidote to the Evil Eye blue beads are especially valued, and are hung round the necks and pasterns of horses and other valuable animals. (CROOKE, *P.R.I.*, Vol. II, p. 19; ABBOTT, p. 144.) cf. *Crucifix.*

Beans : If you eat no beans on Christmas Eve, you will become an ass (RAGNER).

If you dream of beans, you will have a rich and cruel enemy.

On the last night of the year, the head of a Japanese household scatters beans about the house with ceremonial rites, in order to exorcise evil spirits (A. HUMBERT, *Le Japon illustré*, Paris, 1870, Vol. II, p. 326 ; BERTHOLET, p. 43. cf. *Ethnologie du Bengale*, p. 118.)

Bear : Bears scare diseases away ; hence children are taken for a ride on the back of a bear, or one of his hairs is worn round the neck as an amulet (*India*, CROOKE, *P.R.I.*, Vol. II, p. 242.)

According to a legend, the young of a bear is born a shapeless mass; the dam licks her cub into its proper shape and life.

When a bear is slain by the North American Indians, they will beg pardon of the animal and sometimes even go through a form of smoking a " pipe of peace " with him, lest his spirit return to do them harm. (SCHOOLCRAFT ; FRAZER, *G.B.*, Vol. II, p. 398; BERTHOLET, p. 12.) Vide *Heart.*

Beard : In Macedonia a beardless man is regarded as particularly ill-omened. (ABBOTT, p. 105). In India the same superstition is prevalent.

If a baby girl be baptized with water with which a boy has been baptized, she will have a growth of beard later. (WUTTKE, p. 198.)

Beast : In China it is generally believed to the present day, that demon witches can assume the form of foxes and other beasts. (DE GROOT, *Religious Systems of China*, Vol. IV, pp. 156, etc.)

The Stiens of Cambodia ask pardon of the beasts they have killed (MEUHOT).

Beautiful : In Arabic demonology, Jinns (q.v.) sometimes appear in the form of human beings ; if they are good spirits, they appear beautiful; if evil, horribly hideous. (LANE, *A.S.M.A.*, p. 35).

Beauty : Beauty can be acquired by bathing in May dew. (WUTTKE, p. 176), or by drinking cold coffee, or by bathing in human blood. (STRACK, p. 10, quoting GRIMM, 181.)

Beaver : When a beaver is hunted, it bites off the part which the hunters seek and then, standing upright, shows the hunter that it is useless to continue the pursuit.

Becket, St. : This saint has the power of curing blindness.

Bed : Girls sit on the bridal bed for luck (MEAKIN, *The Moors*, p. 441).

To dream of beds indicates approaching marriage. Vide *Hydrophobia*.

Bedclothes : Picking the bedclothes is a sign of an impending death (LEAN, Vol. II, p. 573).

Bedstead : The foot of a bed should not point towards the door ; those who lie on such a bed will be taken out of the room as corpses. (*Hessen, Lauenberg*, WUTTKE, p. 132.)

Bedsteads should not be carried into a room with the foot-end first ; those lying on such beds will die. (*Silesia*, ib.)

Bee : The buzzing of a bee in a room indicates that a stranger is about to pay the house a visit. (*Ethnologie*, p. 117.)

If a member of the family dies and the bees are not " put into mourning," they will forsake their hive (FRAZER, *Death and Burial Customs, Scotland, F.L.J.*, 3, 281 ; ELWORTHY, p. 95).

Bees building their hive in a house foretell that the house will catch fire (*Malay Peninsula*, SKEAT, *Malay Magic*, p. 535).

It is unlucky for a stray swarm of bees to flight on your premises (ELWORTHY, *E.E.*, p. 95.).

If bees swarm on a rotten tree, a death will occur in the family within the next twelve months.

Bees will never thrive if you quarrel with them or about them.

A swarm of bees suddenly forsaking their hive foretells a death (LADY WILDE, p. 181). Vide *Virginity, Beehive.*

Beehive : If bees build their hives on a house, the house is sure to catch fire. (*Silesia, Tyrol*, WUTTKE, p. 32 ; cf. above.)

When going along the street with a beehive, you must never look round ; if this precaution be taken the bees will never forsake their hives. (*Wetterau, Westphalia*, WUTTKE, p. 183). Vide *Bee.*

Beelzebub : One of the Devil's numerous names.

> " One next himself in pow'r and next in crime
> Long after known in Palestine and named
> Beelzebub . . ."
>
> MILTON : *Paradise Lost*, Bk. I, 79-81.

Beetle : Beetles in popular superstition are both deaf and blind.

To kill a beetle brings rain, thunder and lightning (LEAN, Vol. II, p. 136).

Beggar : The curse of a beggar is considered by the Jews of Byelostok and Kiev to be effective. (*Jew. Enc.*)

If you dream of beggars coming in the house and taking things away, you will have great adversity.

Bel : Babyl. Myth. A deity belonging to the supreme Triad, which comprised Anu (q.v.), god of the heavens, Bel, god of the earth and Ea (q.v.), god of the waters. (*Enc. Brit.*, Vol. III, p. 114.) Vide *En-lil.*

Belial : It is the Hebrew name for the spirit of evil personified. The word was used from early times as a name for the Devil or one of his fiends, and by Milton in his *Paradise Lost*, as the name of one of the fallen angels.

Belit : Assyr. Myth. A goddess, wife of Ashur.

Bell : You will be sure of toothache if you eat while a funeral bell is tolling. Be warned in time by this American superstition, or take the consequences. Vide *Death Omens.*

Bells in the ear : A buzzing sound—generally called "bells in the ear "—in the right ear of a person denotes that something good is spoken about him, or that he is praised ; in the left ear, something bad, or that someone is back-biting him. (*Gt. Britain, Germany, France, Greece, Bohemia, India* ; cf. STRACKERJAN, Vol. I, p. 31 ; LAWSON, p. 328).

It is an indication that someone is thinking of you,

" Left your mother,
Right your lover."—*Popular Rhyme.*

Bellerophon : Gr. Myth. A Corinthian hero, son of Glaucus, grandson of Sisyphus, who killed the Chimera (q.v.) with the help of the winged steed, Pegasus.

Belphegor : The name of a certain arch-demon. According to a story, he was chosen by Lot to live on earth for ten years, in order to test the truth of the statement that wives brought their husbands to hell. Belphegor tried, but was dismayed and fled from the terrors of the married state.

Belt : Magicians and witches are supposed to possess the power of transforming themselves into animals, mostly of a ferocious nature (see *Werewolves, Bereserker*), by means of putting on certain belts. (See ENNEMOSER, *Geschichte der Magie* ; TYLOR, *Primitive Culture* ; GRIMM, *Deutsche Mythologie* ; O'DONNELL, *Werewolves.*)

Bendis : Class. Relig. A Thracian goddess. She was generally identified with Artemis by the Greeks.

Ben nefilim : In Jewish folk-lore the demon of epilepsy is usually called by this name.

Benten : In Japanese superstition she is the goddess of luck. She is also goddess of knowledge and eloquence. (CHAMBERLAIN). See *God of Luck*.

Berenice's Hair : Berenice, Queen of Ptolemy III, hung up her hair in obedience to a vow, in the temple of Nuwar. The hair disappeared and is fabled to have been carried to Heaven, where it was changed into a constellation.

Bereserker : In Norse folk-lore it is the name of one of a class of wild warriors, who are supposed to be capable of assuming animal shapes, especially those of the bear and the wolf. When in these forms, a rage or frenzy comes upon them, they howl like wolves or growl like bears, foam at the mouth, have enormous strength and are believed to be invulnerable to fire and iron. cf. *Werewolves.*

Bërlic : A certain Swiss spirit of mischievous nature. (JALLA, *Leg. Vaud.*, p. 27).

Bernardo del Carpio : He lifted Orlando in his arms and squeezed him to death, because his body was proof against any instrument of war. Anteus (q.v.) is also reputed to have been squeezed to death by Hercules.

Bertha : Vide *Perchta, White Lady*.

Bes : Egypt. Myth. A god of varied attributes, but chiefly a deity averting the evils of omen and witchcraft, and god of pleasure. In some myths he plays an important rôle in creation, separating Heaven and Earth from their primordial union.

Bhaga : Hindu Myth. A deity who is supposed to bestow wealth ; he presides over marriage. (DOWSON, *H.C.D.*, p. 43.)

Bhairava : Hindu Myth. A guardian spirit.

Bhairava (m.) ; Bhairavi (f.) : " The terrible " ; names of Siva and his consort, Devi (q.v.). The Bhairavas are eight inferior manifestations of Siva, all of which are of a terrible character. They are : (i) Asitānga, black-limbed ; (ii) Sanhāra, destruction ; (iii) Ruru, a dog ; (iv) Kāla, black ; (v) Krodha, anger ; (vi) Tāmra-chudā, copper-crested ; (vii) Chandra-chudā, moon-crested; (viii) Mahā, great (DOWSON, *H.C.D.*, p. 45.)

Bhūta : A ghost, imp, goblin. These are malignant spirits which haunt cemeteries, lurk in trees, animate dead bodies and delude and devour human beings. They are fierce and are eaters of flesh ; they were created by the Creator, when He was incensed. (DOWSON, *H.C.D.*, p. 55.)

Bhūta, like our English word " ghost," is a general term for demons in India. They emanate from those who die an unnatural death by violence, accident, suicide, etc., or those who have been robbers, evil-doers, etc. The Bhūts eat filth and drink any water, however impure. As a rule, they are powerless by day and become active only at night. (See CROOKE, *P.R.*, Vol. I, pp. 234 *et seq.* ; *Ethnologie du Bengale*, p. 94.) Vide *Goblin, Filth, Desert, Treasure*.

Biasd na Srogaig : Celt. Folklore. A mythical animal peculiar to the Isle of Skye. It had but one horn on its forehead and dwelt in lochs. It is the Celtic equivalent of the Bogey (q.v.), Bubák (q.v.), Bumann (q.v.). (CAMPBELL, *Sup. of Scot. Highl.*, p. 218.) cf. *Unicorn*.

Bible : An open bible keeps away evil spirits. (*Christian Countries.*)

The bible is subject to a host of superstitions. cf. *Qorān, Prayer Book.*

Bidhātā Purusha : Hindu Myth. He is equivalent to the Classical Fates and the Scandinavian Norns. He is a god of fate ; he writes the child's future life on its forehead, on the sixth day of its birth. (DAY, *Folk Tales of Bengal,* p. 9.) cf. *Parca, Fates, Norn, Sudičky, Hathor.*

Biersel : In German superstition it is a kind of Kobold, who lives in the cellar, cleans the jugs and bottles, but must have his jug of beer for his pains. (*Torgau District,* WUTTKE, p. 230.)

Bifrost : Norse Myth. The bridge leading to Agard (q.v.). cf. *Al Sirat.*

Bilocation : The power of being present in two different places at one and the same time. St. Alfonso di Liguori was said to have had this power.

Bilwis : Teut. Myth. It was a supernatural being of maleficent powers, whose season of activity was Walpurgis Night. This was a soul-like character, which flitted through the fields and wrought havoc to the crops.

Bîr : In Indian superstition it is a very malignant village demon (CROOKE, *P.R.I.,* Vol. I, p. 254).

Bird : When birds are shot or are dying, they fly to the nearest water.

Fish are sometimes transformed into birds (*China—* MAYER, *Chin. Read. Man.,* p. 301.)

The single, or twice repeated, cry of a bird is a good omen ; but if the cry be repeated three times, the meaning is reversed (*Greece—*LAWSON, p. 313).

If birds enter the house and fly round in a room, it is a sign of death (LE BRAZ, Vol. I, p. 7, quoting TIERNEY, *Hermine,* Vol. XXXIII, p. 235).

Birth : Children cannot be born till the tide comes in.

If you are born at sermon-time on Christmas morning, you can see spirits. (RAGNER.)

" First a daughter, then a son,
The world is well begun.
First a son, then a daughter,
Trouble follows after."

Maine and Massachusetts (BERGEN, *C.S.,* p. 24).

Vide *Night, Distaff, Star, Crow, Friday, Kitten, Stork, Sugar, Tomb, Underclothing.*

Birthday : To die on one's own birthday is considered by the Jews to be a good omen. (*Jew. Enc.*, Vol. IV, p. 486.)

Bishamon : Jap. Myth. A god of luck (q.v.), represented as being in complete armour and carrying a spear.

Bittern : The cry of a bittern foretells some misfortune, probably death. (STRACKERJAN, Vol. I, p. 26.)

Biu : In Egypt they have usually hawks' or jackals' heads ; but some *biu* are entirely birds.

Blaakula : Like Blocksberg of the Germans, it was the favourite resort of the Swedish witches. (LEHMANN, *A.Z.*, p. 112 ; ENNEMOSER, *Hist. Mag.*, Vol. II, p. 195.)

Black : Black denotes death and guilt ; therefore the Devil is always black. (STRACKERJAN, Vol. II, p. 68.)

Blackbird: To see two blackbirds in one place is an omen of good luck in the East. (ST. CLAIR TISDALL, *Mod. Pers. Conv. Gram.*, 2 Ed., p. 45, Exercise II.)
  If you dream of a blackbird and a thrush sitting on the same tree, you will have two wives, or two husbands as the case may be.

Blain : St. Cosmos is the one who can cure them.

Blaise, St. : Vide *Quinsy, Sore Throat, Disease.*

Blarney Stone : An inscribed stone in the wall of an old castle at Blarney, near Cork, Ireland ; whoever kisses it will have a cajoling tongue (*Ireland*).

Blast : It is a large round tumour which is thought to rise suddenly on the part affected by the baneful breath cast on it by fairies at the time of their vindictive malice. (ELWORTHY, *E.E.*, p. 534.)

Blemmyæ : A race of people described by Pliny, and said to be headless ; they have their eyes and mouths in their breasts. cf. *Acephali, A-Siras.*

Blindness : The human saliva is a cure for blindness (ELWORTHY, *E.E.*, pp. 420, 663 *note*).
  St. Thomas à Becket has the power of curing this disease.
  If the copper coin from the eyes of a corpse be washed in wine or water, and the liquid given to husbands to drink, the husbands will be blind to their wives' peccadilloes (KRAUSS, *Volksglaube und religiöser Brauch der Südslaven*, p. 140.)
  To dream of blindness indicates want of money. Vide *Shabriri, Saliva.*

Blindness, Moon : It is commonly believed to be produced by sleeping exposed to the full light of the moon. " There is a great difference of opinion as to facts, some quoting experience as incontrovertible, others regarding the thing merely as a vulgar prejudice, without substantial foundation " (YULE and BURNELL, *Hobson Jobson,* 2 ed., p. 580).

Blindness, Night : This can be cured by eating a fire-fly, enclosed in a piece of banana or some other soft fruit. (*Bengal, Ethnologie du Bengale,* pp. 118, 141.)

Blocksberg : It is believed to have been the favourite place of rendezvous of the German and the Danish witches. The Devil himself is said to have attended the gatherings there. (GRIMM, *Deut. Myth* ; LEHMANN, *A.Z.,* p. 112 ; ENNEMOSER, *Hist. Mag.,* Vol. II, p. 195.) cf. *Blaakula, Brocken, Hekkenfeldt, Hekla, Lyderhorn.*

Blood : To see blood is a sign of good fortune, probably money. (*Gt. Britain.*)

Witches sign their names on a great book with their own blood and swear allegiance to the Devil. (LEHMANN, *A.Z.,* p. 114. cf. GOETHE, *Faust* ; STRACK, *Das Blut.*)

The burning of blood from the body of a dead animal is a very common method of appeasing the spirits of disease (*Cornwall*—HUNT, *Pop. Rom.,* p. 213).

It is an Esthonian belief that men who see women's blood will suffer from an eruption of the skin (F. J. WIEDEMANN, *Aus dem inneren und äusseren Leben der Ehsten,* p. 475).

The blood of a virgin mixed with different molten metals helps to mix them thoroughly. (*China,* PITMAN, *A Chinese Wonder Book,* p. 34.) The same belief is prevalent among many other nations. (FRAZER, *G.B.,* Vol. I, p. 361.)

If a young man cuts the little finger of his left hand, and secretly gives the blood flowing from this wound to his sweetheart to drink, she will be madly in love with him. (PLOSS, *Das Weib,*Vol. I, p. 444, quoting v. SCHULENBURG, *Windisches Volksthum.*)

Draw blood of a witch, and she cannot harm you (*Lancashire*). Vide *Hydrophobia, Nose, Menstruation, Beauty, Epilepsy.*

Blood-stone : A kind of stone which is believed to have the power of stopping a flow of blood. (TYLOR : *Early History of Mankind.*)

Blood-sucker : In East Prussia the Vampire (q.v.) is usually designated by this name.

Bloody Hand : The family of the Kincardines in Scotland have the Spectre of the Bloody Hand.

Blud : The Wend name for a Will-o'-the-wisp (q.v.) ; it is the soul of an unbaptized child.

Blue : The Devil appears in the form of a blue flame (STRACKER-JAN, Vol. II, p. 69), especially in fires (*Gt. Britain*). Vide *Bride*.

Blue Goblin : It is a particularly malevolent type of demon in Carnarvonshire.

Blue Men : " The fallen angels were driven out of Paradise in three divisions, one became the Fairies of the land, one the Blue Men in the sea and one the Nimble Men . . . or Merry Dancers of the sky."—CAMPBELL : *Sup. of Scot. Highl.*, p. 199.

Boar : In Morocco most wealthy Moors keep a wild boar in their stables, in order that the jinn or evil spirits may be diverted from the horses and enter into the boar. (A. LEARED, *Morocco and the Moors*, Lond., 1876, p. 301 ; FRAZER, *G.B.*, Vol. III, p. 15.)

Boat : It is unlucky to mention a horse or a mouse on a fishing boat (*Celtic*, RHYS, *C.F.*, p. 345 ; FRAZER, *G.B.*, Vol. I, p. 453).
   A boat would not proceed if there is a man on board who has failed to keep his word (*Turkey*, KUNOS, *T.F.T.*, p. 185).
   If a girl dreams of falling off a boat and being rescued by a man, she will marry her rescuer.

Boback Gartin : Is the name of the one-time spirit of Gartinbeg House.

Bodachun Dun : " The ghost of the Hill ; " it is said to appear to the family of Rothmurchas in Scotland when a person belonging to the family is about to die.   cf. *Banshee, Death Warnings, Božaloshtsh, Smrtnice*.

Bogey : In English children's superstition it is a spirit of a vague and indefinite nature, whose only aim in life seems to be that of frightening children.   cf. *Bubák, Bumann, Biasd na Srogaig*.

Boggart : In Lancashire this is a peculiarly mischievous spirit and is closely allied to the Brownies.

Boil : Boils can be cured by keeping muscatels in one's pocket. (STRACKERJAN, Vol. I, p. 85.)
   St. Rooke can also cure boils.

Bolt : Vide *Lock*.

Bone : It is lucky to find bones (WUTTKE, p. 96). Vide *Lucky Finds*.

Bonnet : To dream of losing a bonnet prognosticates a speedy marriage.

Bonze : If a Japanese fisherman, while going to fish, meets a *bonze* (priest), he is sure to have bad luck in fishing ; the strict bonze does not eat fish. (GRIFFIS, *M.E.*, p. 470 ; BASSETT, p. 108.) cf. *Priest*.

Boobrie : The Boobrie of Celtic superstition was a Water-bird, which inhabited the fresh water and the sea wells of Argyllshire. (CAMPBELL, *Tales of the Highlands ;* Bassett, p. 272.)

Book : To drop your books on the way to school signifies that you will make mistakes in your lessons. (*Chestertown, Md.*)

Boreas : It is the name of the North Wind personified.

Bornholm : In Danish superstition, the king of the elves is said to reside in the island of Bornholm. (THIELE.)

Boxing : If you spit on your hands your blows will be more telling.

Bozaloshtsh : " God's plaint " ; among the Wends she is a messenger of death. She is a little woman with long hair, who cries like a child, beneath the window of a house where someone is about to die. cf. *Banshee, Smrtnice, Death Warnings*.

Bracelet : Vide *Nurjehan's Bracelet*.

Bragi : Norse Myth. One of the Æsir, god of poetry and husband of Ithunn (q.v.).

Brahmā : Hindu Myth. The first member of the *Trimurti*. He is the Creator himself. In the Rigveda he signified power. He is represented as red with four heads, the fifth one being destroyed by Siva. His consort is Saraswati, the goddess of eloquence.

Brahmadaitya : In India it is the spirit of a murdered Brahman. In Bengal such spirits are especially powerful and malicious. Sometimes they are headless trunks, with eyes looking from their breasts ; at others, they are harmless and even well-disposed towards human beings. (See *Ethnologie du Bengale*, p. 96.)

According to Rev. L. B. Day, Brahmadaityas are the ghosts of Brahmans who die unmarried. (*Folktales of Bengal*, p. 201.)

Brawn's Head : A boy brought to King Arthur's court a brawn's head, over which he drew his wand thrice and said. " There's never a traitor or a cuckold, who can carve that head of brawn." Sir Kay was the only knight in King Arthur's court who succeeded in doing so. cf. *Drinking Horn, Mantle.*

Bread : Bread baked on Christmas Eve will not turn mouldy. (THIERS, *Traité des Superstitions*, Vol. I, p. 317).

To burn or throw bread away brings ill-luck ; do so and you will need bread yourself one day. (*Gt. Britain.*)

He who cuts a slice of bread more than the number of persons eating has a hungry relative somewhere. (*Silesia, Tyrol,* WUTTKE, p. 37 ; *Bohemia.*)

To drop a slice of bread with the buttered side up is a sign of a visitor. (*Memoirs of the Amer. Folk Lore Soc.,* Vol. IV, pp. 89 *seq.*)

The Mohammedans never cut bread with a knife, but " break " it, saying it is impious to wound bread with steel. (ABBOTT, p. 103.)

In Scotland (GREGOR, p. 21), and in Brittany (LE BRAZ, Vol. I, p. 267), on the night following a burial, bread and water are kept in the room where the body lay before the burial. Failure to comply with this precaution causes the deceased to lose his repose in the other world. In Ireland, potatoes and baked cakes are substituted for bread, and serve the same purpose. (LADY WILDE, p. 118.)

> " In your pocket for a trust
> Carrie nothing but a crust.
> For that holy piece of bread
> Charms the danger and the dread."

HERRICK : *Hesperides,* ed. HAZLITT, 1869, p. 346.

If a piece of bread which has been carried in the pocket of a mourner, be afterwards eaten, the teeth will fall out. (*Hunsbruck,* WUTTKE, p. 213.)

It is good to dream of bread ; it indicates prosperity. Vide *Fruits, Change of Address, Disease.*

Breadcrumb: Maras (q.v.) can be killed by shooting them with a gun filled with breadcrumbs ; ordinary shots have no effect on them. (STRACKERJAN, Vol. I, p. 385.)

Breakage: If you break something, you will break two other things. (*Memoirs of the Amer. Folk Lore Soc.,* Vol. IV, pp. 130, 134; *Great Britain.*)

Bream: In Hungary the bream is said to attack men voraciously. (GUBERNATIS, *Z.M.*, Vol. II, p. 344 ; BASSETT, p. 261.)

Breath: In Chinese superstition it is said that the breath of a living person or the snuffing by a cat or a dog partly revives a corpse. (*Chin. Volksmärchen*, p. 202.)

Breeze: A sudden breeze which neither disturbs nor disarranges anything is a death signal for certain Irish families. It is said to be caused by the passage of the soul. (LADY WILDE, p. 139.)

Scratch a foremast with a nail, you will get a good breeze. (KÜHN UND SCHWARTZ, *N.D.S.*, p. 454 ; BASSETT, p. 143.) Vide *Chapel*.

Breidablik: Norse Myth. The bright abode of Baldar in Asgard.

Bress: Celtic Myth. A Fomor, son of Elathan, known for his great beauty.. In his attempt to recover his kingdom, he roused the Fomors to the war in which they were overthrown by the gods.

Briar: If you dream of being pricked by briar, you desire to do something, and if you are young, it denotes that you are in love.

Bridal Clothes: It is unlucky to wear the bridal clothes before the wedding day ; the marriage will be broken off by so doing. (*Pomerania, Silesia*, WUTTKE, p. 204 ; *France, Great Britain.*)

Bride: It is extremely lucky for a bride to see a rainbow or a black cat. (*Great Britain.*)

A bride on her wedding day should wear
" Something old, something new,
Something borrowed, something blue."
Vide *Green, Stones*. *Popular rhyme.*

Bridesmaid: " Three times a bridesmaid, never a bride." (*Great Britain.*)

It is lucky for bridesmaids to touch the bride during the marriage ceremony, with their clothes ; if they succeed, they will themselves be married soon. (*Munich. Zeitschrift für deutsche Mythologie*, 2, 103.)

Bridge: If you dream of crossing a bridge, it shows that you will leave a good situation to seek a better one.

Brigit: Celtic Myth. The Gaelic goddess of fire and hearth and of poetic inspiration. She was the daughter of Dagda and wife of Bress.

Brisingamen: Norse Myth. A jewel or necklace, belonging to Freya, which was obtained from the dwarfs.

Brocken: In the Harz Mountains (Germany) it is believed to be the favourite haunting place of witches. (ENNEMOSER, *Hist. Mag.*, II, 195.) cf. *Blocksberg, Blaakula, Hekkenfeldt, Hekla, Lyderhorn*.

Broom: Witches fly through the air on broomsticks (*General*).
   Two crossed brooms in front of a house door or cattle-shed, is a sure method of keeping witches and evil spirits at bay.
   Tables should not be dusted with a broom lest one of the household die. (*England ; Jews of Galicia*, SCHIFFER, *Urquell*, Vol. V, p. 46.)
   A Hamburg tradition says that if you have long had a contrary wind, and meet a ship bound in the opposite direction, throw a broom before her, and you will get fair wind. (THORPE, *N.M.*, Vol. III, p. 183.)
   In Indian folklore, if a man sees a broom the first thing after getting up in the morning, he does not pass the day happily ; if a broom be kept erect in the house, a quarrel will follow. (JACKSON, *F.L.N.*, Vol. I, p. 149.) Further, children affected with a cough are sometimes fanned with a broom. (*Ethnologie du Bengale*, p. 140.)

Broomstick: Witches cannot stride over a broomstick. (STRACKERJAN, Vol. I, p. 344.) Vide *Broom* above.

Brother: Three married brothers should not dwell in the same town. (*Jew. Enc.*, Vol. IX, p. 600, quoting SEFER HASIDIM, p. 33 ; cf. Deut. xxv. 5.) This probably accounts for the roving propensities of the Jews.

Brownie: A benevolent spirit or goblin of shaggy appearance, supposed to haunt old houses, especially farm-houses in Scotland, and sometimes to perform useful household work while the family is asleep. (See HAZLITT, p. 79.)
   " The brownie formed a class of beings, distinct in habit and disposition from the freakish and mischievous elves."—SCOTT, *Ministr. Bord.*

Brunhilde: In the Nibelungenlied, a young and stalwart queen, a Valkyrie, whom Siegfried, making himself invisible by means of the Tarnkappe, wins and tames for Gunther. When she learns of this deception from Siegfried's wife, Kriemhild, she induces Hagen to treacherously murder Siegfried by stabbing him at the back between the shoulders, the only part where he was vulnerable.

Brunnehilde: In the "Ring of the Nibelungen," a Valkyrie who aids Siegmund against the will of Wotan (Wodan), and is placed in a fire-guarded stronghold. She sleeps there until awakened by Siegfried, upon whose pyre she eventually immolates herself.

Brushwood: The Khonds place brushwood in the paths leading to places decimated by smallpox and other diseases, in the hope of making the disease-demon retrace his steps. (*Enc. Brit.*, Vol. VIII, p. 6. *Ethnologie du Bengale*, p. 132.)

Brynhild: In the Volsunga Saga, a Valkyrie who for having disobeyed Odin, was condemned to become mortal, and was placed in an enchanted castle. Sigurd wakes her from her sleep and they fall mutually in love. She is, however, married to Gunnar. Brynhild procures the death of Sigurd, slays herself with the same sword, and is burnt on the same pyre.

Bubák: In Bohemian superstition, it is a kind of spirit, whose name is very frequently mentioned to frighten children. cf. *Bogey, Bumann, Biasd na Srogaig.*

Bubble: A group of bubbles on a cup of tea or coffee signifies money. (*Great Britain*; *Memoirs of the American Folk Lore Society*, Vol. IV, p. 87.)

Bucket: It is unlucky to come across an empty bucket on first going out, but lucky to pass a full one. (*General*; *Jew. Enc.*, Vol. IX, p. 600.)

Bug: Bugs never infest a dying person (LEAN, Vol. II, p. 579.) Vide *Flea, Vermin.*

Bugarik: The Gāros of Assam believe this to be a lovely siren, whose head floats on the current. She has the body and arms of a woman, but no legs. She is supposed to kill women and men too, if she can catch them. (A. PLAYFAIR, *The Garos; Ethnologie du Bengale*, p. 99). cf. *Mermaid, Nixie, Siren, Lorelei, Alrinach.*

Building: If during the building of a house someone accidentally dies, it is a sign that many deaths will occur in the house. (STRACKERJAN, Vol. I, p. 35.)

To dream of an unfinished building denotes future prospects for you, though the present may seem black.

If a house be newly built, the owner thereof will shortly die (GOODRICH-FREER, *Folklore*, XIII, 52; LE BRAZ, Vol. I, p. 157.)

Houses in which someone has been burnt to death are not rebuilt. (CURTIN, *Tales of the Fairies*, p. 113.)

(See *Word-Lore*, Vol. I, p. 195.)

Bulbul Hezar: Muham. Myth. A nightingale which not only had human speech, but was oracular also. (BURTON, *Alif laila wa laila*, LANE.) cf. *Bāngmā*.

Bulderbasse: The Danish name for a Poltergeist.

Bull: According to the Moslems, a bull supports the earth on its back.

Bulla: An ornament, worn by Roman children, which contained charms and was originally intended to ward off ghostly anger.

Bullet: "Among the Galelareese, who inhabit a district in the northern part of Halmahera, a large island to the west of New Guinea, it is a maxim that when you are loading your gun to go out shooting, you should always put the bullet in your mouth before you insert it in the gun ; for by so doing you practically eat the game that is to be hit by the bullet, which therefore cannot possibly miss the mark." (FRAZER, *G.B.*, Vol. I, p. 25, quoting M. J. VAN BAARDA, " *Fabelen, verhalen en overleveningen der Galelareezen*" in "Bijdragen tot de Taal, Land . . . en Volkenkunde van nederlandsch Indië, XLV (1895), p. 502.)

Bullkater: "Tom-cat " ; is a German field-spirit.

Bullock: If a woman dreams of a bullock, it warns her of a powerful enemy.

Bumann: In German children's superstition, it is a bogey of an indefinite nature. (STRACKERJAN, Vol. I, p. 422.) cf. *Bogey, Bubák, Biasd na Srogaig*.

Bur: Babyl. Myth. Another name for Adad.

Buri: Norse Myth. The progenitor of the gods, licked out of the stones by Audhumla.

Burial: Male and female slaves were buried alive with the dead headsmen of various African tribes to administer to his wants in the spirit world. (HAGGARD, *Nada the Lily*, p. 166.) This practice is, in the opinion of some authors, still in vogue among the Chavas of the Zambesi district.

In the foundations of houses, towns, cities, etc., people were once buried alive in Teutonic countries. (GRIMM, *Deut. Myth.*, 2 Aufl., pp. 38 etc., 1095 ; TETTAU UND TEMME, *Volkssagen*, p. 109) ; in Siam (*Enc. Rel. Eth.*, Art. "Siam ") ; among the Slavs (cf. the legend of the Kremlin Palace in Moscow) ; in France (BERENGER-FÉRAUD) ; in India (see *Yak, Yaksha*) ; in Wallachia

(St. John, *Legends of the Christian East*, p. 187). See also *Word Lore*, Vol. I, p. 195 ; Frazer, G. B., Vol. I, p. 145 ; Schmidt, *Das Volksleben der Neugriechen*, pp 194 seq.; Elworthy, E. E., p. 82 ; Bertholet, *Transmigration of Souls*, p. 12 ; Pröhle in *Zeitschr. f. deut. Myth.*, Vol. I, p. 202. cf. *Sati, First Buried, Last Buried*.

To dream of being buried signifies a serious fit of illness.

Burning Ghāts: They are the favourite haunts of many evil spirits and are therefore not safe at night. (*India.*)

Buschweiber: The " Wild-maidens " or forest-spirits of German superstition.

Bush-asp: A Parsi demon with long hands, who lulls men to sleep and attacks them. (Venidad, XVIII, 38.)

Busyasta: In Persian mythology it is the typification of inordinate sleep and sloth.

Busiris: A legendary King of Egypt who sacrificed all strangers at the altars of the Egyptian gods. He was slain by Hercules.

Butter: The first butter churned should not be sold or given away, but it should be eaten at home ; if this is not done the cow will not give any more milk. (*Mecklenburg.* Wuttke, p. 135 ; *Bohemia.*)

Stolen butter cures warts (q.v.). (*N. and Q.*, 24-10-1925.)

Butterfly: If you do not kill the first butterfly you see in the year, some bad luck will befall you (*W. England.* Lean, Vol. II, p. 32.)

Butterflies are the souls of ancestors. (*Ireland.* Rhys, *C.F.*, p. 612.)

Butterflies flying by night presage death. (G. Henderson, *Survivals in Belief among the Celts*, p. 79.)

Button : In America, superstitious women usually ascertain the profession of their future husband by counting the buttons on their skirts and repeating the following verse :

" A doctor, a lawyer, a merchant, a chief,

A rich man, a poor man, a beggar-man, a thief."

Vide *Doubt*. —Knortz, p. 98.

Butze: A German household spirit.

Bwgan: The Welsh generic name for ghosts.

C

Cabbage: Vide *Full Moon, Moon Waxing*.

Cacus: Rom. Myth. A thieving, crafty giant, a son of Vulcan. He was killed in his cave in the Aventine by Hercules.

Cadmus: Gr. Myth. A son of Agenor, king of Phœnicia, founder of Thebes. He killed a dragon, from whose teeth a host of armed men sprang up and fought each other, till all but five were killed ; later, these five became the ancestors of the Theban families.

Cæsarian Operation: Babies brought into the world by this means are said to possess extraordinary strength ; also they are endowed with the power of seeing hidden treasures and spirits. (STRACKERJAN, Vol. II, p. 156. cf. SHAKESPEARE, *Macbeth*, v. 7.)

Cage: If a maiden dreams that she has let the bird out of the cage, it is a sign that she will be the mistress of the first man who chooses to ask her.

Cake: If you dream that you are making a cake, you will have joy and profit. Vide *Wedding Cake.*

Calcutta: There is a story : One of the first European settlers in India came to the place now known under this name, and asked a native what the name of the place was. Owing, however, to the bad pronunciation of the European who wished to say *kyā kahtā* ? (What is it called ?), but said instead, *kab kāṭā* (When did you cut ?), the native misunderstood him and thinking that he was referring to a tree that had recently been felled, answered, *kal kāṭā* (felled yesterday) ; hence the name.

Calf: Witches sometimes ride on calves. (STRACKERJAN, Vol. II, p. 84.)

Call: Calling a dead person three times in succession by his name, forces him to appear and to lose his tranquillity in the spirit world (*East Prussia*) ; in Silesia, this holds good only on Christmas Eve. (WUTTKE, p. 216.) Vide *Death Omens.*

Calliope: Gr Myth. The muse of epic poetry and eloquence, mother of Linos and Orpheus. She is represented either with a tablet or with a roll of paper.

Callirhoë: Class. Myth. (i) Wife of Alcmæon, and the cause, through covetousness, of his death. (ii) An ocean nymph, wife of Chrysaor.

Callisto: Gr. Myth. Daughter of Lycaon, king of Arcadia. She was changed by Juno into a bear, in which shape she was killed by Artemis. Jupiter took her to Heaven and she became the constellation Great Bear.

Calydonian Boar-Hunt: Gr. Myth. It was the pursuit by a band of heroes of the boar, sent by Artemis to ravage Calydon. The boar was finally slain by Meleagor.

Calypso: Gr. Myth. A sea-nymph who kept Odysseus (Ulysses) in her island, Ogygia, for seven years.

Camel : Arabs sacrificed camels on the grave of the owner (BERTHOLET, p. 12 ; cf. *ibid.* p. 22 ; MACDONNEL, *Vedic Mythology,* p. 165 ; *Handbook to the Ethnographical Collections of the British Museum,* 1910, p. 33, fig. 30.) cf. *Burial, Horse, Sati.*

Camphor: Vide *Adultery.*

Canace's Mirror: It indicated by its lustre if the person, whom the inspector loved, was true or false. cf. *Bahman's Knife, Sophia's Picture, Florimel's Girdle, Ring Bertha's Emerald.*

Candle: To have three candles burning at the same time in a room is unlucky. (*Great Britain.*)

In Ireland, twelve candles are kept alight around a dead body because otherwise the devil may carry the soul away. Evil spirits cannot cross a circle of fire. (LADY WILDE, p. 118.)

A film of tallow, called a " winding sheet," shot from the top of a lighted candle, gives warning to the house of an approaching death.

A candle burning with two distinct flames is, in parts of Germany, an omen of an approaching death ; in Austria, Silesia, Hesse, Tyrol and Swabia, this is a sign of a letter. (WUTTKE, p. 37.)

If you dream of a candle burning brightly, you will receive a pleasing letter from your sweetheart.

Candle Glowing: Virgins have the power of blowing into flame a candle still glowing. (STRACKERJAN, Vol. I, p. 90 ; GRIMM, *Deutsche Rechtsalterthümer,* 1828, pp. 932-933.) cf. *Light.*

Cane: " Salonica schoolboys hold that a hair stretched across the palm of the hand will make the master's cane split. English schoolboys entertain an identical belief in a hair, but it must be a horse hair. ' If the hair be plucked fresh from the tail of a living horse so much the better.' " (ABBOTT, p. 301, quoting T. PARKER WILSON, " School Superstitions " in *Royal Magazine,* September, 1901.)

Cannon-ball: The Chinese fire cannon-balls at the bore in Canton river, while some shoot arrows. (BASSETT, p. 23, quoting DENNYS.)

Canopic Jars: The four jars containing the principal intestines of a deceased person and buried with the mummy.

Canwyll Cyrph: Welsh name for Corpse Candles.

Cards: During a game of cards, the devil sits under the table, and if any of the party swears, up jumps the devil behind him, tail and hoofs and all. (STRACKERJAN, Vol. I, p. 262.)

Carpo: Gr. Myth. One of the Heures (q.v.).

Carrying: It is unlucky to carry anything out of a house on Christmas morning until something has been brought in. (RAGNER.)

Cassia tree: High medicinal virtues are attributed to the leaves and barks of the cassia tree. (*China.* MAYER, *Chin. Read. Man.*, p. 101.)

Cassiopeia: Gr. Myth. She boasted that her beauty was equal to that of the Nereids. As a punishment, Poseidon afflicted the land with floods and a devouring monster, which was afterwards slain by Perseus. Vide *Andromeda.*

Castor: One of the Dioscuri (q.v.).

Cat: If a domestic cat washes herself, visitors will come. (*Alsace.* LAMBS, p. 31.)
   Cats on the deck of a ship are said to " carry a gale of wind in their tail," or to presage a coming storm.
   When cats are very assiduous in cleaning their heads and ears, it prognosticates rain (HAZLITT, p. 96 ; ABBOTT, p. 110) ; or it indicates the point of the compass from which wind is expected (*Greece.* LAWSON, p. 328).
   The sneezing of a cat indicates good luck for a bride. If a cat sneezes thrice, a cold will run through the family (*Great Britain*).
   If a cat crosses your path, ill luck will follow you (*Germany, Bohemia*) ; a cat cleaning herself denotes guests (*North and Central Germany.* WUTTKE, p. 32).
   Satan's favourite form is that of a black cat, hence it is the familiar of witches. (*General ;* ENNEMOSER, *Hist. Mag.*, Vol. II, p. 148.)
   A cat has nine lives.
   Whoever kills a cat will never have good luck (*Macedonia*, ABBOTT, p. 110 ; *Malay Peninsula*, SKEAT, *Malay Magic*, p. 191).
   In Teutonic countries a cat or a dog was made to run into a new house before others entered it, as a precaution against possible accidents (GRIMM, *Deut. Myth.* pp. 972, 1,095).
   Black cats bring luck.
   A strange tortoiseshell cat coming into the house is unlucky. (*Great Britain*).

Tom-cats of a tortoiseshell colour are highly prized in Japan as a preventive against shipwreck. (CHAMBERLAIN, Ger. tr. p. 297) ; or they bring luck to the owner (*England*).

There is a Hungarian proverb that a cat does not die in water, hence its paws disturb the surface. " The cat in folklore is commonly diabolical, and in the bag of proverbs has probably a diabolical allusion. The popular idea that she has nine lives, expresses its mystic character." (GUBERNATIS, *Z.M.*, Vol. II, pp. 64 seq.)

A cat jumping over a dead body causes vampirism. (*Greece*. LAWSON, p. 410.)

If a man dreams of a cat, and the cat scratches him, his sweetheart is a spiteful termagant ; if a woman dreams the same, she has a rival.

Vide *Dogs, Shingles.*

Caterpillar: These will be plentiful if you go into the garden on a Good Friday. (WUTTKE, p. 18.)

Catherine, St.: She resolves doubts.

Catseye: It is considered by the Cingalese as a charm against witchcraft and to be the abode of some genii.

Cattle: To dream of cattle portends money. (*U.S.A.* KNORTZ, p. 21.)

Excessive lowing of cattle indicates much rain or snowfall. (INWARDS, p. 153 ; ABBOTT, p. 111.)

Caul: Children born with a caul are lucky ; they cannot be drowned (*Great Britain*, BRAND, *Observations*, Vol. III, p. 114; *Times*, 20-2-1813, 27-2-1813, 8-5-1848 ; HAZLITT, p. 99 ; ABBOTT, p. 139), and they are impregnable to the machinations of evil spirits. (STRACKERJAN, Vol. II, p. 127.)

Celæno: One of the Harpies (q.v.).

Celestial Fox : Chinese Folklore. It is of a golden colour and possesses nine tails ; it serves in the halls of the Sun and the Moon, and is versed in all the secrets of nature. (MAYER, *Chin. Read. Man.*, p. 65.)

Cemetery : A handful of earth taken from a cemetery, and thrown at a mill will stop its motion. (GREGOR, p. 216.)

Centaurs : Gr. Myth. A race of savage beings, said to have lived in Thessaly. They were exterminated in a furious battle by the Lapithes. Poets have regarded them as monsters, half human and half horse.

Cerberus : Class. Myth. A dog, described by Hesiod as fifty-headed, and by later writers as three-headed, with a serpent's tail and serpents about his body, guarding the entrance of the infernal regions. cf. *Garm.*

Ceres : Rom. Myth. Daughter of Saturn and Cybele, the Latin goddess of agriculture. She was later identified with the Greek Demeter. Vide *Corn Spirit.*

Chair : If three chairs be accidentally placed in a row, a death will occur either in the house or in the family. (*Ohio.*)

Chakora : A kind of partridge ; a fabulous bird, supposed to live upon the beams of the moon. (DOWSON, *H.C.D.*, p. 65.) cf. *Manucodiata.*

Chameleon : They are believed to live on air only. (HAZLITT, p. 101.)

"Excellent, i' faith, of the chameleon's dish : I eat the air. . . ." SHAKESPEARE : *Hamlet*, Act III, Scene 2.

Chamunda : Hindu Myth. An emanation of the goddess Durgā, sent forth from her forehead to encounter the demons Chanda and Munda. (DOWSON, *H.C.D.*, p. 65.)

Chanda, Chandi : Hindu Myth. The goddess Durgā, especially in the form she assumed for the destruction of the Asura called Mahisha. (DOWSON, *H.C.D.*, p. 66.) Chandi means " the fierce." Vide *Devi, Kāli, Durgā.*

Chandra-kānta : "The moon-stone"; a gem or stone, supposed to be formed from the congelation of the rays of the moon. It is believed to exercise a cooling influence. (DOWSON, *H.C.D.*, p. 68.)

Change of Address : To take a cat with you, when you are changing your lodgings is unlucky ; it denotes a death. (STRACKERJAN, Vol. I, p. 49.)

Before changing your address, you should take some bread, salt and a broom into the new one ; this would be a safeguard against possible starvation. (*Mark.—* WUTTKE, p. 176.)

It is well to let a cat or dog run in before entering a new house. (GRIMM, *D.M.*, pp. 972, 1095.)

Changeling : A child, usually stupid and ugly, supposed to have been left by fairies in exchange for one taken (HARTLAND, *Science of Fairy Tales*) ; sometimes, it is an old fairy (KÜHN UND SCHWARZ, p. 92 ; WOLF, *Beiträge*, Vol. II, p. 304) ; or the bastard children of water-nixies and human beings whom they have dragged under the sea.

Chang Sien : Chin. Myth. A divinity worshipped by women desirous of offspring (MAYER, *Chin. Read. Man.*, p. 10.)

Chapel : Sardinian sailors obtained a good breeze by sweeping a chapel after Mass, and blowing the dust from it after departing ships. (BASSETT, p. 143.)

Charlemagne, Emperor : He is believed to be reposing to this day within a mountain near Salzburg, in Austria. cf. *Holgar the Dane, Arthur King, Barbarossa.*

Charon : Class. Myth. Son of Erebus and Nox, whose duty it is to ferry the souls of the dead over the Styx (q.v.).

Charontas : Another form of Charos.

Charos : In Modern Greek superstition it is the name of Charon. He is represented as a demon of supernatural size and power, is enveloped in a black mantle and is equipped with a golden sword and a quiver full of arrows. He is the personification of death. (GOETHES WERKE, *Bibl. Inst., Leipzig*, p. 293 ; LAWSON, p. 98.)

Chastity : St. Susan protects chastity. Vide *Bees, Salt Cellar, Canace's Mirror, Drinking Horn, Florimel's Girdle, Mantle, Sophia's Picture, Boar's Head, Water of Jealousy, Light Dying, Candle Glowing, Grotto of Ephesus, Alasnam's Mirror, Amethyst.*

Che : A plant of supernatural growth and auspicious omen. (MAYER, *Chin. Read. Man.*, p. 20.) cf. *Assides, Chikuli, Tulsi.*

Chederles : Muham. Myth. A Moslem hero who, like St. George, saved a virgin exposed to the tender mercies of a huge dragon. He also drank of the Water of Immortality and is still living to render aid in war to any who invoke him.

Chemise : If a man dries himself on a chemise which has already been worn, he is sure to propose marriage to the owner of the article. (For a possible explanation vide *Perspiration.*)

Cherry Tree : To dream of the branch of a cherry tree is unlucky. (STRACKERJAN, Vol. II, p. 72 ; *U.S.A.*, KNORTZ, p. 43.)

Cherub : (pl. Cherubim). Muham. Myth. They are angels who are absorbed in the holiness of Allah ; their function is to repeat the *tasbih* (Glory to God !) night and day. They inhabit a secluded part of the sky, removed from the attacks of the devil, Iblis (q.v.).

Chestnut : Chestnuts kept in one's pocket are a good preventative against backaches. (STRACKERJAN, Vol. I, p. 85.)

Chichi Vache : "Sorry cow," a monster that fed on good women only. It was all skin and bone, because its food was so extremely rare. (BREWER, *R.H.*) cf. *Unicorn.*

Chikuli : It is a kind of cactus which grows in Mexico, and is superstitiously believed by the American Indians, to bring luck to anyone who carries it in his belt. The wearer is not only protected from the attacks of bears, but deer and other game allow themselves to be killed by him. (*Prager Tagblatt,* 21st April, 1925.) cf. *Assides, Tulsi, Che.*

Child : St. Germayne is the patron saint for children, but unless the mothers bring a white loaf and a pot of good ale, he will not look at them.

A dying child may be released from death's grasp, if nominally sold by the parents to some friend for a shekel ; a change of name may also serve the same end. (*Jews— Jew. Enc.,* Vol. IV, p. 486.)

Children cannot be born till the tide comes in. Vide *Stepping over a child, First-born Children.*

Childbed : Women in childbed must not spin, lest they spin a halter for the child. (*Franken—*WUTTKE, p. 196.) (For various superstitions see PLOSS, *Das Weib,* Vol. II, pp. 354 *et seq.*)

Chimera : Gr. Myth. A monster, represented as vomiting flames and having the head of a lion, the body of a goat and the tail of a dragon. He was killed by Bellerophon.

Chimney : They are the favourite entrances and exits of witches and all evil spirits. (cf. WUTTKE, p. 171.)

Chimney Sweep : It is lucky to meet a chimney sweep the first thing in the morning. (*Great Britain, France, Germany, Bohemia*).

Chintā-mani : "The wish-gem." A jewel which is supposed to have the power of granting all desires. It is said to have belonged to Brahmā, who himself is called by this name. It is also named "Divya-ratna." (DOWSON, *H.C.D.,* p. 72.) cf. *Aladin's Wonderful Lamp.*

Chira-jivan : "Ever-lived." Gods or deified mortals who live for long periods.

Chiron : Gr. Myth. A Centaur, tutor of Achilles and other heroes.

Chitra-lekhā : Hindu Myth. "A picture." A nymph who was skilled in painting and in the magic arts.

Chlvnik : A Russian household spirit who lives in the cattle-shed.

Choking : Vide *Hiccough.*

Cholera : In cases of epidemics of this disease, Obla Bibi is invoked by the Hindus.

Cholera can be detected by throwing up in the air a piece of raw meat, which will immediately turn black. (*Great Britain.*)

To cure cholera, people sleep in churchyards. (*Australia.*)

Chomoriri : A lake in Tibet. According to a story, it derived its name from a woman (Chomo), who was carried into it by the yak she was riding, and cried out in terror : ri-ri !

Choorail : The Moslems of India designate the ghost of a pregnant woman by this name.

Chopstick : To break the chopsticks while eating is an extremely bad omen ; if children strike anything with their chopsticks while at meal, they are believed to be struck dumb. (*Japan.*—GRIFFIS, *M.E.*, p. 470.)

Christmas : Lights are kept burning all night on this day, in order that the spirits of the dead returning to the world, may warm themselves. (*East Prussia.*—WUTTKE, p. 216.) Vide *Xmas.*

Christopher, St. : Vide *Bad Dreams, Earthquake, Flood, Fire, Night Alarms.*

Chronos : Class. Myth. The name of the oldest god.

Chrysaor : Gr. Myth. Son of Poseidon and Medusa, husband of Callirhoë, by whom he was the father of Geryon and Echidna.

Chunsu : Egypt. Myth. A moon-god and god of healing. The chief seat of his worship was Thebes where he formed one of the Triad, the other two being Mut (q.v.) and Amon-Ra (q.v.). He was son of Amon-Ra.

Church : To dream of a church and the altar and priests in white denotes a speedy marriage.

Church bell : When church bells are ringing for a funeral service, nothing must be eaten, lest the teeth become hollow. (*Mark, Hessen.*—WUTTKE, p. 214.)

Churchyard : All churchyards are haunted. (cf. HAZLITT, p. 129.)

Churel : In the Deccan, it is the spirit of a pregnant woman, one dying on the day of childbirth or within the puerperal pollution. The Churel is particularly malignant to her own family and appears in various forms, but she invariably has her heels in front and toes behind. (CROOKE, *P.R.I.*, Vol. I, p. 270.)

Cinder : A cinder bounding from a fire is either a purse or a coffin ; those which rattle, when held to the ear, are tokens of wealth ; those which are mute and solid, indicate sickness or death.

Cigar : If you step on a cigar end, you will marry the first man you meet. (*Salem, Mass.*—BERGEN, *C.S.*, p. 65.)

Cigarette : If you light three cigarettes with the same match, one of the persons smoking will die before the year is out (*Europe*).

Circasea Lutetiana : It is considered in Silesia, Hessen and Hunsbruck, to have great magical properties and is a safeguard against witchcraft. (WUTTKE, p. 90.)

Circe : Gr. Myth. A famous enchantress who transformed Ulysses' (q.v.) companions into pigs.

Circle : A circle drawn round a person keeps ghosts and evil spirits away, hence it has always borne an important share in occult purposes. (cf. STRACKERJAN, Vol. I, p. 154 ; Vol. II, p. 17 ; GOETHE : *Faust* ; DALYELL, *Dark. Sup.*, p. 120.)

Cirein Crôin : The sea-serpent of Celtic superstition was the largest animal in the world. (CAMPBELL : *Sup. of Scot. Highl.*, p. 220.)

    " Seven herrings are a salmon's fill,
    Seven salmons are a seal's fill,
    Seven seals are a whale's fill,
    Seven whales are the fill of a Cirein Crôin
    And seven Cirein Crôin are the fill of the big devil
        himself."   *—Caithness Rhyme.*

City of Giants : The Arabs call Jericho, in Palestine, by this name. (*Jew. Enc.*, Vol. V, p. 659.)

Claire, St. : She cures bad eyes.

Claw : Tigers' claws are worn by the Chinese to ensure good fortune or to ward off sickness, fire or fright. (WILLIAMS, *Mid. King.*, Vol. II, p. 256.)

Cleverness : Extremely clever children will be short-lived. (STRACKERJAN, Vol. I, p. 35.) Vide *Angel.*

Climbing : If you dream you are climbing and reach the top, you will have success in love.

Clinking : The clinking of spoons on All Hallows' Eve indicates that the spirits of dead relatives are hungry. (*Tyrol.*— WUTTKE, p. 216.)

Clock : Clocks stop the moment the owner dies. (LEAN, Vol. II, p. 590.)

Clio : Gr. Myth. The Muse of history. She is represented either as sitting down or as standing, and either with a roll of papers in her hand or with a case of books beside her.

Clootie : The Scotch name of the Devil.

Clootie's Croft : In Scotland a piece of village land, left untilled and uncropped by the inhabitants of most villages. It is traditional that such pieces were set apart as propitiatory gifts to the Devil. (WEBSTER.)

Clothes : To put on clothes inside out by accident, is sure to bring good luck, if not changed (*Great Britain*, CHAMBERS, *Book of Days*, Vol. II, p. 321 ; *Macedonia*, ABBOTT, p. 144) ; or it indicates that you will be lucky in love (*Bohemia*).

To stitch clothes on your person means a foe for every stitch you make (*Great Britain*, *U.S.A.*—KNORTZ, p. 99), or that you will die (*Great Britain*). Vide *Coffin*.

Clotho : Gr. Myth. The goddess who spins the thread of life. Vide *Fates*.

Cloud : If clouds assume the form of droves of sheep or lambs at the time a baby is born, it prognosticates good luck for the newly-born. (*Swabia*.— WUTTKE, p. 30.)

If you dream of clouds, and they are white, you will have joy and prosperity ; but if they are black, trouble.

Cloven Hoof : In the superstitions of various nations, the cloven hoof is supposed to be a constant attribute of the devil and his followers.

Clover : Vide *Four-leaved Clover*.

Clover Mannikin : It was a Teutonic field-spirit who lived in the clover fields.

Cluricaune : Irish Lore. A fairy being having the appearance of a tiny old man, supposed to have a knowledge of buried treasures, and to haunt wine-cellars (CROKER.)

Clymene : Gr. Myth. Daughter of Oceanus, mother of Atlas and Prometheus.

Clytemnestra : Gr. Myth. Half-sister of Helen and wife of Agamemnon. Owing to her infidelity during Agamemnon's absence she was slain by Orestes.

Clytie : Class. Myth. An ocean nymph, who pined away for love of Apollo and was changed into a heliotrope.

Coach : In Kilcurry, Ireland, a dead coach is a spectral coach drawn by four headless horses and driven by a headless driver. This coach goes about noiselessly, and gives warning of death, but not necessarily of the person seeing it. (JONES and YEATS, *Folklore*, X, pp. 199, 122 ; CROFTON CROKER, *Fairy Legends*, p. 250.)

In Cornwall, the appearance of this coach foretells the death of the person seeing it. It is driven by two headless horses, and its rumbling noise may be heard at midnight. (MISS COURTNEY, *Cornish Folklore*, " Folklore Journal," Vol. V, p. 109.)

Coal : A piece of coal kept in one's pocket brings luck. (*Great Britain.*)

It is unlucky to give a neighbour a live coal to kindle a fire with on Christmas morning. (RAGNER.)

If you dream of burning coal, you will have shame and reproach, but if of dead coal, expedition in business.

Coblyn : A Welsh modification of Goblin ; it is used to denote spirits that are thought to haunt the mines.

Cobra : According to the Hindus, the hood of a cobra bears the imprint of the foot of Krishna. Vide *Kāliyā*.

Cobweb : If a girl finds a cobweb on the door, it is a sign that her beau calls elsewhere. (*North Ohio.*—BERGEN, *C.S.*, p. 62.)

A cobweb in the kitchen is a sign that there is no courting there. (*Boston.* Ib.)

Cock : A black cock brings luck (*Silesia.*—WUTTKE, p. 176.)

The crowing of a cock before midnight is a sign of death ; if heard however, on the way to business, it denotes good luck. (*Great Britain.*)

The Persians are superstitious respecting the crowing of a cock (MONIER, *First Journey through Persia*, 1810, p. 62).

The favourable hours for the crowing of a cock are at nine, both in the morning and in the evening, at noon, and at midnight.

If a cock crows in the afternoon, it is either a sign of great joy or of great sorrow (LE BRAZ, Vol. I, p. 6) ; if it crows three times at night, it is a sign of death (DEENEY, *Peasant Lore from Gaelic Ireland*, pp. 55, 60, 78 ; *N.E. Scotland—Folklore Journal*, Vol. VIII, p. 43 ; *Wales—* OWEN, p. 297.).

The crowing of a cock before midnight is held in Macedonia to be a sign of death (ABBOTT, p. 107 ; THOMAS

HARDY, *Tess of the D'Urbervilles*, Ch. XXXIII) ; in Scotland, it is regarded as an indication of coming news. (CAMPBELL, *Sup. Scot. Highl.*, p. 257) ; amongst various African tribes such cocks are held as prognosticating some dire misfortune, and are accordingly killed. (ELLIS, *Ewe-speaking Peoples*, p. 96 ; TREMEARNE, *Hausa Superstitions and Customs*, p. 141.)

Vide *Alectryon, Basilisk, Bazaliček, Dragon, Lion, Fire.*

Cockatrice : Another name for a Basilisk (SHAKESPEARE, *Rape of Lucrece*, 78.)

Cockchafer : If the first cockchafer seen be stitched in a piece of cloth and worn as an amulet, it will be a safeguard against attacks of fever. (*Köten, Silesia.*—WUTTKE, p. 95.)

Coeyte : Gr. Myth. A river in Hades.

Cœus : Gr. Myth. A Titan.

Coffee : Coffee drunk cold promotes beauty.

Coffin : To lie inside a coffin, though in fun, is to invite certain death.

If the clothes of a living person be enclosed in a coffin, their rightful owner will die as the clothes gradually rot away. It is for this reason, that people are afraid of giving away discarded clothes to the poor. (*Holstein, Saxony, Silesia, Hessen, Mecklenburg.*—WUTTKE, pp. 83, 211.)

The noise of a coffin being deposited at the door is an omen of death. (GREGOR, p. 203.)

Coin : In Tyrol, coins found during a storm of rain are considered to have been dropped from heaven, and are used as amulets for luck. (WUTTKE, p. 96.)

To find a coin with a hole in it, is extremely lucky ; such coins should never be given away. (*Great Britain.*—LEAN, Vol. II, p. 34 ; *India.*)

Colic : St. Erasmus relieves colic.

To cure colic stand on your head for a quarter of an hour (HUNT), or carry a hare's foot on your person (PEPYS' Diary, 31, XII, 1664).

Comb : If a comb which has been used for a dead person, be used again, the person who combs his hair with it will shortly die. (*East Prussia.*—WUTTKE, p. 214.)

If you comb a child before it has teethed, its teeth will be separated from each other like those of the comb. (FRAZER, *G.B.*, Vol. I, p. 44.)

Constipation : This may be cured by means of stolen bacon (q.v.)

Consumption : It may be cured by sleeping over a cow-house or by sucking the blood of a person in health (LEAN, Vol. II, p. 489).

Comet : The Samoan Islanders hold that the appearance of a comet always indicates the death of a chief. (PRICHARD, *Phys. Hist. of Mankind*, II, p. 154.)

The appearance of a comet prognosticates war, pestilence, famine, destruction of the world or some other grievous calamity. (WUTTKE, p. 30 ; STRACKERJAN, Vol. I, p. 23 ; LEHMANN, *Aberglaube und Zauberei.— Great Britain, France, Germany, Italy, Spain, Netherlands, etc.*)

Conch-shell : The conch-shell is sacred to Vishnu. It is the bone of the demon Pañchājana, who, according to the *Vishnu Purāna* (v. 21), "lived in the form of a conch-shell under the ocean. Krishna plunged into the water, killed him, took the shell which constituted his bones, and afterwards used it for a horn. When sounded, it fills the demon hosts with dismay, animates the gods, and annihilates unrighteousness."

Consus : Rom. Relig. An early Italian god of the earth and its harvests.

Coral : Coral is a talisman against enchantments, witchcraft, thunder and other perils and all maladies ; hence the use of a coral necklace. It was consecrated to Jupiter and Phœbus.

Red coral worn about a person is a certain cure for indigestion.

A coral ring is used to keep off the influences of the sun. (CAMPBELL, *Notes on the Spirit Basis of Beliefs and Customs*, Bomb., 1885, p. 69.)

Corn : To cure corns take a pearl button and steep it in the juice of a lemon in which it will become dissolved ; place a piece of lemon soaked in this on the corn, and repeat it daily, or oftener if required, and it will extract the corn. (LEAN, Vol. II, p. 491, quoting N. IV.)

Cornelius, St. : Vide *Epilepsy, Palsy.*

Corn Spirit : Any of the various personifications, interpreted by folklorists, as representing the vegetative energy of growing grain, with which it flourishes and dies, also the type to which these personifications conform. Many harvest customs are traced to the ancient prevalence of this belief, while such deities as Ceres, Demeter and Persephone are believed to have been the result of this form of superstition. (WEBSTER.)

Cornucopia : The horn of plenty. It was a goat's horn filled to overflowing with flowers, fruits and corn, etc., and was the symbol of plenty and peace.

Corpse : If a corpse becomes stiff too quickly after death, call him thrice by his Christian name ; the corpse will become pliable again. (*Silesia.*—WUTTKE, p. 210.)

Do not look at a corpse after it has been thrown overboard ; if you do so, you will soon follow the same path. (STRACKERJAN, Vol. I, p. 46.)

Sailors do not like to have corpses on board the ship they are sailing in (*Great Britain*).

" In a secret murther, if the dead carkasse be at any time thereafter handled by the murtherer, it will gush out of blood, as if the blood were crying to heaven for revenge of the murtherer." (KING JAMES, *Dæmonology*, p. 136.) cf. *Mummy* ; *Dead Body*.

Corpse Candles : A lambent flame seen in a churchyard or over a grave, and superstitiously believed to appear as an omen of death in Celtic countries, or to indicate the route of a coming funeral. (RHYS, *C.F.*, p. 275 ; HAZLITT, p. 88.)

" These fiery apparitions (corpse candles) which do, as it were, mark out the way for corpses to their κοιμητηριον and sometimes before the parties themselves fall sick."—AUBREY : *Miscellanies* (1696).

The *ignis fatuus*, called by the Welsh *canwyll cyrph*, prognosticates death. If small and of a pale blue colour, it denotes the death of an infant ; if large and yellow, the death of a grown-up person.

In Wales the corpse candle appears to warn a family of an impending death. (OWEN, pp. 298-301.)

In Carmarthen scarcely any person dies but someone sees his light or candle.

Captain Leather, Chief Magistrate of Belfast, in 1690, being shipwrecked off the Isle of Man, was told that thirteen of his crew were lost, for thirteen corpse candles had been seen moving towards the churchyard ; it is really a fact that thirteen of the men were drowned in this wreck. (cf. BASSETT, p. 317.)

Cosmos, St. : This saint cures blains.

Cotton : A piece of cotton sticking on a dress, denotes a letter ; the initial of the name of the person from whom the letter is to come may be seen from the form of the cotton.

Cough : In India children affected with a cough are fanned with a broom. (JACKSON, *F.L.N.*, Vol. I, p. 149.)

Coupe enchantée : Vide *Drinking Horn.*

Courage : A man who is of a nervous temperament, can become courageous by carrying the tongue of a fox with him (*Bohemia*—GROHMANN, p. 54), or by eating a piece of a lion's heart (*Arabia*—FRAZER, *G.B.*, Vol. II, p. 355.) Vide *Pillow.*

Cow : The cow is a sacred animal in India.
" Curst cows have curt horns." (" Curst " means " Angry, fierce.") Vide *Death Omens.*

Crab : In Siamese belief there are giant crabs and great scorpions in the sea who drag ships down. ' (BASSETT, p. 218.)

Cracking : Cracking of the finger joints when pulled, denotes that the owner is loved by someone. (STRACKERJAN, Vol. I, p. 91.)

Cradle : The child which sleeps in a cradle procured before its birth, will be short lived. ((STRACKERJAN, Vol. I, p. 44).
To rock an empty cradle brings evil or calamity to the child which sleeps therein later on. (*Great Britain.*)
" Rock a cradle empty,
Babies will be plenty."
Peabody, Mass. (BERGEN, *C.S.*, p. 24).
To dream of a cradle is a certain sign of marriage.

Cramp : Tying the garter round the left leg below the knee cures cramp.
Cramp may be avoided by using mole's paws, or hare's ankle-bone. (LEAN, Vol. II, p. 492.)
Vide *Shibbeta, Eel, Slipper, Sheep.*

Cream : To dream of cream being spilt on you denotes the infusion of some grace from above.

Cremation Grounds : In Hindu superstition these are said to be the favourite haunts of demons and witches. TAWNEY, *Kâtha—sarit—sâgara*, Vol. I, p. 159.)

Creon : Gr. Myth. Brother-in-law of Œdipus, who espoused the cause of Etiocles against Polynices. He condemned Antigone to be buried alive for having performed funeral rites over Polynices.

Cricket : Crickets in a house presage good fortune. (*England*, cf. STRACKERJAN, Vol. II, p. 112), but if they suddenly forsake the house, it is a sign of an approaching death or disaster. (LEAN, Vol. II, p. 19, quoting Sir W. Jardine).
To kill a cricket is extremely unlucky.

E

Criminal : The spirits of executed criminals are said to become vampires, Brahmadaityas and other kinds of malevolent ghosts.

Crocodile : Crocodiles are said to be reincarnations of murdered Brahmans, and are therefore duly respected (cf. ELLIS, *Ewe-speaking Peoples*, p. 71).

Crocodiles are said to weep over a person's head after they have devoured the body, and then eat the head.

They moan and sigh like a person in distress in order to allure passers-by, and then make them their prey.

Humming birds and lapwings will fearlessly enter the crocodiles' mouth, and the creatures will never injure them, because they pick their teeth.

Cronus : Gr. Myth. A Titan who dethroned his father and was in turn dethroned by his son Zeus. He was a god of harvest and was identified by the Romans with Saturn.

Crop : Vide *Moon, Spindle.*

Cross-eye : To meet a cross-eyed person of the opposite sex is lucky.

Cross Roads : Cross roads are the favourite meeting places of witches from all parts of the world.

In Cornwall cross roads are avoided after nightfall. (*Folklore Journal*, v, 218.)

If you go to a cross road between eleven and twelve o'clock on Christmas day and listen, you will hear what most concerns you for the coming year (RAGNER).

" At cross roads, or in the neighbourhood of cemeteries, an animated corpse often lurks watching for some unwary traveller whom it may be able to slay and eat." (RALSTON, *Folk Tales of the Russians*, p. 311.)

Crow : Many crows in the early morning foretell a gale (*Tibet.*—WADDELL, p. 135), if they thereby gape at the sun, the weather will be hot and dry ; but if they stalk at nightfall into water, rain is at hand.

When crows forsake a wood in a flock, it is a sign of a famine.

A crow appearing to one on the left hand side is a good omen (HAZLITT, p. 51), or it indicates some impending evil to the person ; flying over a house and croaking thrice, it foretells evil at hand to someone of the inmates.

If a crow flutters about the window and caws or sits down (*Bohemia*), it forebodes a death.

The croaking of a crow indicates rain (HAZLITT, p. 51.).
" One crow—sorrow,
Two crows—mirth,
Three crows—wedding,
Four crows—birth."
—*Maryland* (KNORTZ, p. 134).
A crow cawing on the chimney gives warning of a death
in the family. (*Macedonia.*—ABBOTT, p. 108.)

Several crows fluttered about the head of Cicero
on the day he was murdered by Popilius Laenas; one
of them even made its way into his chamber, and
pulled away the bedclothes.—MACAULAY : *History of
St. Hilda*, p. 176.

cf. *Blackbird, Raven.*

Crucifix : Evil spirits are afraid of the crucifix ; it is therefore a powerful charm against them. (*Christian Countries.*)

In Serbia if a pregnant woman kisses the crucifix
her child will be epileptic. (PLOSS, *Das Weib*, Vol. I, p. 617.)

cf. *Rosary, Beads, Qor'an, Prayer Book.*

Cruelty : The spirits of those who have been cruel during
their lifetime, can find no peace in death, but must return
to earth as ghosts.

Crumb : The crumbs saved up on three Christmas Eves are
good to give as a physic to one who is disappointed
(RAGNER).

Crust : The first crust from a loaf of bread must not be given
away, but should be eaten at home ; if this is not done,
you will be in need (*Bohemia*).

Crying : If a sick person cries, it is a sign that he will
recover from his illness. (WUTTKE, p. 43 ; WOLF, *Beiträge*,
Vol. II, p. 368.)

One must not cry before at least three hours have
passed since the death of a person, otherwise the hell-
hounds may be attracted by the noise and devour the
soul before it has had time to reach the throne of God.
(LADY WILDE, pp. 118, 214.)

Crystal : Crystal induces visions, promotes sleep and ensures
pleasant dreams. It is dedicated to the moon ; in metallurgy it stands for silver.

Cuckold : Vide *Mantle, Boar's Head, Drinking Horn.*

Cuckoo : The same superstition as with the swallow (q.v.)
is prevalent in Silesia, Bavaria, Mark and Swabia.

If you hear the first cuckoo in spring, you will have
luck all the year round (*Great Britain, Bohemia*).

In Celtic superstition the cuckoo is said to have its winter dwelling underground. (CAMPBELL, *Sup. of Scot. Highl.*, p. 5.)

Cuckoos lay their eggs in other birds' nests. (*Alsace.*— LAMBS, p. 31.)

If you hear a cuckoo in your dream, your sweetheart will prove to be a coquette.

A cuckoo calling on the top of a house or on the chimney presages death. (LADY WILDE, p. 318; CAMPBELL, *op. cit.*, p. 35.)

Cuichi supai : The Indians of Ecuador call the rainbow (q.v.) by this name. It is said to be a demon that makes women pregnant. (KARSTEN, *Ind. Trib. Ecuad.*, p. 70.)
cf. *Incubus, Succubus, Jhoting, Tulúlu Supai.*

Cup : Vide *Accidental upsetting of a cup.*

Cupid : Rom. Myth. The god of love. He is represented as a little naked boy with bow and arrows. He shoots people with his darts and they immediately fall love-sick.

If you dream of Cupid breaking his dart, your love will change ; but if he breaks his bow, you will remain a spinster all your life. cf. *Kāma, Venus.*

Curetes : Gr. Myth. Earth-born demons, attendants upon Rhea, who, when she gave the infant Zeus into their charge, executed a wild dance and thus concealed the child's presence from Cronus (q.v.).

Curing diseases by transferring them to other things : See E. B. TYLOR, *Primitive Culture*, Vol. II, pp. 136 etc. ; DALYELL, *Dark. Sup.*, pp. 105-111 ; FRAZER, *G.B.*, Vol. III, pp. 13 sqq., 26 sqq. ; BLACK, *Folk Medicine*, pp. 34-48.

Curse : The curse of a dying man, of a Brahmin (*Hindus*), or that of a beggar (*Jews of Byelostock and Kiev*) is effective.

Cuttlefish : Cuttlefish with their many legs, swimming on the top of the water and striving to be above the waves presage a storm. (BRAND, *Observations*, Vol. III, p. 291.)

Cwn y Wybr : The Welsh name for " dogs that haunt the air."

Cybele : The great nature goddess of the ancient people of Anatolia. She was the deification of the earth as sustaining and reproducing the wild life of nature. She was thought to haunt mountains and forest fastnesses, accompanied by trains of wild attendants bearing torches and dancing to music.

Cyclops : Class. Myth. One of a race of giants having but one eye in the middle of the forehead, fabled to inhabit Sicily, and in later traditions supposed to assist in the workshops of Hephæstus (Vulcan) under Mt. Etna. According to Homer, they were shepherds.

Cycnus : Gr. Myth. Son of Stenelus, king of Liguria, and friend of Phæton. He was changed into a swan and placed among the stars.

Cyhiraeth : In Wales it is a kind of dreadful and doleful moan in the night proceeding from an invisible source. It is a " spectral female used to be oftener heard than seen ; but her blood-freezing shriek was as a rule to be heard when she came to a cross road or to water, in which she splashed with her hands. . . . These cries meant the approaching death of the hearer's husband, wife, or child as the case might be ; but if the scream was inarticulate it was reckoned probable that the hearer himself was the person foremourned." (RHYS, *C.F.*, p. 453 ; BASSETT, p. 317.) cf. *Death Warnings, Death Omens.*

D

Dædalus : Class. Myth. An Athenian architect, who built the Labyrinth of Crete. He was cast into the Labyrinth, but escaped with his son Icarus, by flying through the air with artificial wings, of which he was the inventor. Dædalus reached Sicily in safety, but his son Icarus flew too near the sun ; the wax on the wings melted, he fell and was drowned in the sea.

Dagan : Babyl. Myth. God of the earth. He was identified with Bel (q.v.) and was worshipped as early as the ninth century B.C.

Dagda : Celtic Myth. A Gaelic god, perhaps of earth, famous as a warrior, harpist and eater of porridge. He was king of the Tuatha de Danann (q.v.) after their defeat by the Milesians.

Dagger : To dream of daggers denotes hot contest with others.

Daikoku : Jap. Myth. A god of luck (q.v.), who stands on a bale of rice and is accompanied by a rat.

Dāini : In Bengal this word signifies a witch. The line of demarcation between a Dāini and a Dākini is extremely fine (see *Ethnologie du Bengale*, p. 95).

Daitya : Hindu Myth. Titans, descendants of Diti by Kāsyapa. A race of demons and giants who warred against the gods and interfered with sacrifices. They were in turn victorious and vanquished. (DOWSON, *H.C.D.*, p. 76.)

In later Indian mythology, they were evil beings and deadly foes of the gods.

Ḍākini : In Indian superstition it is a female spirit of a malicious nature.

Ḍākinis are of two kinds : human and ghostly. Girls born on the second, seventh and twelfth day of a month are human ḍākinis. They cause the death of their husbands, and their evil eye injures all things and individuals that come under its influence. Women who die in childbirth become ḍākinis. A ghostly ḍākini dresses in fine clothes, and decks her person with ornaments ; but she does not cover her back, which is horrible. It is so frightful that anyone happening to see it dies of horror. They trouble only women. They are said to live with men who gradually become emaciated, and ultimately die within about six months. They cause cattle to yield blood instead of milk. They live upon the flesh of corpses, can assume any form, or swell or shrink their body at will ; their feet are reversed. They haunt trees, cemeteries, deserted tanks, cross roads, mines and other desolate places. (JACKSON, *F.L.N.*, Vol. I, p. 152 ; *Ethnologie du Bengale*, p. 95).

Damkina : Assyro-Babyl. Myth. Consort of Ea.

Danaë : Gr. Myth. Daughter of Acrisius, king of Argos, and mother of Perseus by Zeus.

Danaides : Gr. Myth. They were the fifty daughters of Danaüs. All of them except one killed their husbands on the night of their marriage. As a punishment they were condemned to fill a barrel without bottom with water.

Danaüs : Gr. Myth. A mythological personage, king of Egypt and later, of Argos ; father of the Danaides.

Dānava : Indian Myth. An ancient name for demons.

Dancing : Witches are very fond of this sport ; they try to find many other votaries. Goblins and Elves are also addicted to it. (STRACKERJAN, Vol. I, pp. 312, 316, 398.)

To dream of dancing denotes poverty, grief and despair after great enjoyment.

Dando : In Cornwall it is a ghost who rides about accompanied by his hounds. (HUNT, *Pop. Rom.*, p. 223.)

Dāno : A kind of Indian demon who is nowadays hardly to be distinguished from the Bīr. (CROOKE, *P.R.I.*, Vol. I, p. 254.)

Danu : Celt. Myth. The Gaelic mother of the gods, cognate with the Cymric goddess Don. She is represented as the ancestress of the forces of knowledge and light, the Tuatha De Danann, who overcame the powers of darkness, the Fomors.

Darbas : " Tearers " ; Rākshasas and other destructive demons.

Darkness : Spirits can only appear in the dark.
If you dream of losing your way in the dark, you will be blinded by some passion and have much trouble.

Dasim : Muham. Myth. A son of Iblis, a jinn, who causes hatred between husband and wife. (*Jew. Enc.*, Vol. IV, p. 521.)

Davy Jones : In sailors' superstition, it is a malignant spirit having power over the sea ; hence the sea itself is called Davy Jones's Locker.

Dead Body : It is unlucky to pass a dead body lying on the ground. (*Tibet.*—WADDELL, p. 135.) Vide *Corpse.*

Death : Death is caused by the soul leaving the material body which served as a resting place for the soul ; it is merely a transitory stage from one form to another.
Immediately after the death of someone in the house, all those who are sleeping must be awakened, otherwise it would be their sleep of death. (*East Prussia, Silesia.*—WUTTKE, p. 209.)
To dream of death denotes happiness and long life. Vide *Pigeon, Tide, Lock.*

Death Omens : Death is foretold by the ringing of a bell that cannot otherwise be accounted for. (*Southern Ohio.*)
A cow lowing after midnight foretells a death.
If a doctor is called on a Friday, the patient will surely die. (*Cambridge, Mass.*)
If you meet a funeral train, it is a sign of death. (*Prince Edward Islands.*)
Lie down on the table and you will die within a year. (*Mattawamkeag, Me.*)
Ringing in the ears is a sign of death. (*U.S.A.*)
Three chairs placed accidentally in a row means death. (*Ohio.*)
If sparks are accidentally kept overnight, it is a sign of death. (*Cumberland, Me.*)

To hold a lamp over a sleeping person causes death (*Massachusetts.*)

To knock on the door and receive no answer is a sign of death. (*Virginia and Englewood, Ill.*)

A film of tallow shot from the top of a lighted candle gives warning to the house of an approaching death. (*Great Britain.*)

To imagine that you hear someone calling you by your name soon after dusk, is an omen of death. (*India.*)

The dismal moaning of a dog prognosticates a death in the near future.

Dogs give warning of death by scratching on the floor of the house. (*Great Britain.*)

Pictures falling off the wall without anyone touching them is a sign of death (*Great Britain.*)

(For other forms of Death Omens see LEAN'S *Collectanea*, Vol. II, pp. 548-580 ; BERGEN, *Current Superstitions*, pp. 125-130.)

Vide *Coffin, Cock, Change of Address, Hoop, Salt, Comet, Bittern, Broom, Dog, Picture, Rat, Raven, Pleiades, Fir tree, Lamb, Cinder, Candle, Cricket, Louse, Star, Winding Sheet, Yellow Light, Bedclothes, Clothes, Bat, Bay tree, Bedstead, Bee, Building, Crow, Eye, Egg, God-mother, Hand, Knock, Match, Mayflower, Meteor, Mirror, Mouse, Nail, Needle, Owl, Pigeon, Salt, Shoe, Smell, Smile, Sweeping, Will, Turpentine, Umbrella, Wedding ring, Whistle, Worm, Menstruation, Portrait, Panel, Bird, Cuckoo, Goose, Breeze, Knocking, Water, Blood, Reed, Butterfly.*

Death Warnings : In Great Britain : Vide *Banshee, Corpse-Candles, Bodachun Dun, Edgewell Oak, Aderyn y Corph, Doubles, Gwrach y Rhibyn, St. John's Eve, Wag-at-the-Wa', Cyhiraeth.*

In France : Vide *Mélusine.*

In Germany : Several princes of Germany have their special warning-givers of death. In some it is the roaring of a lion, in others it is the howling of a dog ; in some it is the tolling of a bell, or the striking of a clock at an unusual time, in others it is a bustling noise about the castle.

Vide *White Lady, Habergeis, Ahnfrau.*

Among the Wends : Vide *Božaloshtsh.*

In Austria : Vide *Habsburg.*

In Bohemia : Vide *Smrtnice.*

" Spectrum fœmineum vestitu lugubri apparere solet in arce quandam illustris familiæ, antequam una ex conjugibus dominorum illorum è vita decedat."

—DELRIO : *Disquisitiones Magicæ*, p. 592

In Beyrout : Vide *Weeping Chamber.*

(Other forms of death warnings are given under separate headings.)

Death Rattle : A particular kind of noise made in respiring by a person in the extremity of sickness ; it is considered an omen of death. (HAZLITT, p. 171.)

Death-watch : The tapping made by a small beetle, called a death-watch, is said to be a warning of death to someone in the house. (OWEN, p. 325 ; BRAND, *Observations*, Vol. III, p. 225.)

December : " December's frost and January's flood
Never boded the husbandman's good."

(LEAN, Vol. I, p. 367, quoting *Times*, Jan. 1, 1884.)
Vide *Turquoise, Ruby.*

Decuma : Rom. Myth. One of the three goddesses of Fate ; she is identical with Lachesis.

Deer : Cherokee hunters ask pardon of the deer they kill. If they failed to do so, the chief of the deer tribe would track the hunter and put the spirit of rheumatism into him. (FRAZER, *G.B.*, Vol. II, p. 406.)

Defilement : St. Susan preserves from defilement.

Deformity : In Japan the birth of a deformed child is attributed to some great sin of the parents (GRIFFIS, *M.E.*, p. 472) ; or in India to the non-fulfilment of the mothers' wishes (JOLLY, *Medicin, Grundr. d. Indo-Arisch. Phil.,* p. 52, quoted in *Ethnologie du Bengale*, p. 81, n. 1 ; cf. CROOKE, *P.R.I.*, Vol. II, p. 3).

Deianira : Gr. Myth. Wife of Hercules, whose death she unwittingly caused. Vide *Nessus.*

Deino : Gr. Myth. One of the Grææ.

Delhan : Muham. Myth. A demoniacal being of Arab superstition, who inhabits the islands of the seas ; it has the form of a man and rides an ostrich. It eats the flesh of men, whom the sea casts on the shore from wrecks. (LANE, *A.S.M.A.*, p. 44.)

Delphian Oracle : Gr. Relig. The most famous oracle in the world. The oracles were given forth by a priestess, the Pythia, who seated herself upon a golden tripod above a chasm, whence issued mephitic vapours.

F

Demeter : Gr. Myth. She is identified with Ceres of the Romans.

Demi-Gods : The heroes of ancient mythology, sons of mortals and gods or goddesses, who raised themselves to the standard of gods by their acts of bravery, are usually designated by this name ; thus Hercules, Achilles, Castor and Pollux, etc., are all considered as demi-gods.

Demon : In ancient Greek mythology δαίμων or demon was a supernatural being of a nature intermediate between that of gods and men. In popular superstition it means a malignant spirit of a superhuman nature.

"The three special characteristics of mediæval demons were horns, hoofs . . . and tails."
—WRIGHT, *Hist. Caricat.* (1865).

Deo : Hindu Folklore. Originally this term was applied to the thirty-three great divinities. "Now the term represents a vague class of the demon-ogre family. The Deo is a cannibal, and were he not exceedingly stupid could do much harm." (CROOKE, *P.R.I.*, Vol. I, p. 253.) Tempests are often caused by him (*Ethnologie du Bengale*, p. 101.)

Deodand : "Given to God." In Old English law not only every animal which killed a man, but every instrument or tree or cart-wheel, etc. which caused the death of a man was deodand. (cf. R. DOUGLAS, *China*, 4th ed., p. 83).
"Omnia que movent ad mortem sunt Deodanda."
—BRACTON.

Desert : All deserts are a resort of Bhût. (CROOKE, *P.R.I.*, Vol. I, p. 278, quoting Henderson, *Folklore of Northern Countries*, p. 278 etc.)

Desert Goats : Amongst the Malays of the Lower Siamese States it is believed that if a desert goat fall over a cliff, it immediately licks itself whole. Accordingly, the tongue of a desert goat is carried as an amulet against falling, and is a sure cure for wounds caused by falling.

Despoina : Gr. Myth. Persephone was often called by this name.

Deucalion : Gr. Myth. A king of Pythia in Thessaly, son of Prometheus and Pyrrha. He is the Noah of Greek mythology. During the inundation, Deucalion and Pyrrha took refuge in a barge which stopped on Mt. Parnasse. They alone were the sole survivors of the flood. They repopulated the world by throwing stones behind them ; each stone thrown by Deucalion became a man and each thrown by Pyrrha a woman.

Deva : (Nom. Devas—Deus, from the root Div, to shine.) Hindu Myth. God. The gods are spoken of as thirty-three in number ; eleven for each of the three worlds. (Dowson, *H.C.D.*, p. 84 ; Macdonnel, *Vedic Mythology.*)

Devala : Hindu Myth. Music personified as a female.

Devas : Zoroastrianism. The spirits of evil.

Devatā : Hindu Myth. A divine being or god. The name " Devatā " includes the gods in general or, as most frequently used, the whole body of inferior gods. (Dowson, *H.C.D.*, p. 85.)

Devi : Hindu Relig. The consort of Siva and daughter of Himāvat (Himalaya Mountains). She is the Sakti or female energy of Siva, and is considered either as a beneficent or as a malignant deity. In the former she is called Devi " goddess," Gauri " the yellow or brilliant," Umā " light," Pārvati " the mountaineer," etc., in the latter, Durgā, Kāli, Chandi.

Devil : In Jewish and Christian theology it is the popular appellation of the supreme spirit of evil, the tempter and spiritual enemy of mankind, the foe of God and holiness.

To dream of the devil denotes trouble ; if he appears in fire, some immediate misfortune will befall you, if he vanishes in smoke, expect returning calm.

Dhātri : Hindu Myth. " Maker, Creator." A deity of no very defined powers and functions ; he is described as operating in the production of life and preservation of health. He promotes generation, brings about matrimony, presides over domestic life, cures diseases and heals broken bones. He is said to have " formed the sun, moon, sky, earth, air and heaven." (Dowson, *H.C.D.*, p. 90.)

Diamond : The diamond is an emblem of innocence. It is dedicated to April and the sun. In the Zodiac it stands for Virgo ; in Christian art, for invulnerable faith.

Diamond produces somnambulism and promotes spiritual ecstasy.

Diana : Rom. Myth. An ancient Italian goddess whose worship was early widespread throughout the Peninsula. She is represented, like Artemis, as a huntress.

Diancecht : Celt. Myth. A Gaelic god of medicine.

Diarmaid : Celt. Myth. He was noted for his beauty spot which was always kept covered up with his cap, for if any woman chanced to see it, she would instantly fall in love with him.

Diarmait O'Duibhne : According to a Gaelic legend he is said to have eloped with Finn's betrothed.

Dickepoten : In the provinces of Mark and Lower Saxony the Jack-o'-Lantern (q.v.) is designated by this name.

Dictyna : The Cretan goddess Britomartia, probably a local counterpart of Artemis.

Digestion : Topaz promotes digestion.

Dimple : Dimples are the impressions of God's fingers, hence a dimple on the chin is considered lucky (*Great Britain*).
" Dimple in chin
Devil within."
—*Chestertown, Md.* (BERGEN, *C.S.*, p. 32).

Dindymene : Gr. Myth. The Great Mother (q.v.) was so called from Mt. Dindimus. Vide *Agdistis*.

Dionea : Class. Myth. A nymph, daughter of Uranus and the Earth, or of Oceanus and Tethys. She was loved by Zeus, and became the mother of Venus.

Dionysos : Gr. Myth. The god of wine and riotous merriment. The Romans identified him with Bacchus.

Dioscuri : Class. Myth. The twins Castor and Pollux. They were typically represented as horsemen and were patrons of games and equestrian exercise. Castor alone was mortal. Vide *Asvins, Leda, Pollux*.

Dirce : Gr. Myth. The second wife of Lycus. Antiope's sons tied her to a wild bull which dragged her about until she died. After her death she was changed into a fountain by Bacchus. cf. *Pirene*.

Dirge : A music or song of a mournful character to accompany funeral or memorial rites.

Dis : Rom. Myth. Pluto was so called by the Romans.

Disappointment : Vide *Feast, Foot, Pig, Scissors, Sneeze, Song*.

Disease : Diseases are superstitiously believed to be caused by various demons. (For authorities see under separate headings.) cf. *Jew. Enc.*, Vol. IV, p. 517 ; ROTH, *Superstition, Magic and Religion in North Queensland* ; *Ethnolog. Bulletin*, No. 5, Brisbane, 1903, §116; TAPLIN, *The Narrinyeri*, pp. 62 seq. ; HOWITT, *Native Tribes*, pp. 356, 358 ; ELLIS, *Yoruba-speaking Peoples*, pp. 113 seq.)

The Dyaks of Borneo are firm believers in diseases being caused by spirits. (ST. JOHN, *Far East*, Vol. I, p. 217 ; TYLOR, *P.C.*, Vol. II, p. 134.)

Bread consecrated on St. Blaise's day (3rd February) cures all cattle's diseases.

St. Rooke cures diseases, because he had a sore; St. Sebastian, because he was martyred with arrows and St. Blaise cures all children's diseases. Vide *Bear, Blood, Brushwood, Claw.*

Distaff : In Hungaria if a young married woman takes her distaff and her needle case with her to her husband's home, she will give birth to baby girls only. (PLOSS, *Das Weib*, Vol. I, p. 551, quoting V. CZAPLOVICS *Gemälde von Ungarn.*)

Diti : Hindu Myth. A goddess, daughter of Daksha, wife of Kasyapa and mother of the Daityas. (DOWSON, *H.C.D.*, p. 93.)

Div : Turkish Folklore. A giant, a demon, a fiend, of a gigantic size, and ugly. (REDHOUSE, *Turkish-English Lexicon*, p. 940 ; KUNOS, *T.F.T.*)

Divé ženy : "Wild women"; female forest-spirits of Bohemian folklore.

Divining Petrel : A kind of sea-bird, considered by sailors as extremely unlucky to kill. cf. *Albatross, Petrel, Mother Carey's Chickens.*

Divining Rod : A forked hazel rod suspended between the balls of the thumb was, at one time, supposed to indicate the presence of water springs and precious metals by inclining towards the earth, beneath which these are to be found.

Dobhar-Chu : (pronounced *dooar, dour*). The Celtic name for a Water Dog ·(q.v.).

Dobrochot : A Russian pet-name for a demon, especially the domestic spirit.

Doctor : If you call a doctor on a Friday, the patient will die (*Cambridge, Mass.*)

Dog : Dogs are supposed to see spirits, when human beings cannot ; thus in Old Scandinavia, the dogs could see Hela, the death goddess, moving about. (GRIMM, *D.M.*, p. 632.)

The Esquimaux lay a dog's head in a child's grave, in order that the dog may guide the infant to the land of souls. (CRANZ : *Grönland.*)

When dogs wallow in the dust expect foul weather. (BRAND, *Observations*, Vol. III, p. 189.)

The howling of a dog at night near a house forebodes the death of an inmate. (OWEN, p. 304 ; LAWSON, p. 328 ;

LE Braz, Vol. I, p. 7 ; Cambry, *Voyage dans le Finistère*, Vol. I, p. 71 ; Dalyell, p. 503 ; Hazlitt, p. 184 ; *F.L.J.*, 1883, pp. 217, 355), or the presence of spirits in the air (St. John, *Leg. Chr. East*, p. 193.)

Dogs give warning of death by scratching on the floor of the house. (*Great Britain, India.*)

If a black and white spotted dog crosses your path when you are on your way to some business, you are sure to have success (*Great Britain*), or you will have a disappointment (*India*).

A dog running between two friends indicates the end of the friendship (*Alsace*, Lambs, p. 29).

A dog coming and staying in your house, is an omen of wealth (*China*—Doolittle, Vol. II, p. 328).

Sailors on the sea do not mention dogs by their name. (Bassett, pp. 125, 279.)

If a dog howls the night before Christmas, it will go mad within the year. (Ragner.)

Among the Zulus it is a very bad omen for a dog to climb on the roof of a hut. (Haggard, *Nada the Lily*, pp. 36, 38) ; among the Orāons, see Sarat Chandra Roy, *The Oraons of Chota Nagpur*, p. 273 ; Frazer, *Folklore in the Old Testament*, Vol. III, p. 264, quoted in *Ethnologie du Bengale*, p. 125.

" Cane præviso funere disce mori."

R. Keuchen, *Crepundia*, 115.

Capitolinus tells us that the death of Maximinus was presaged by the howling of dogs.

Pausanias says, the dogs broke into a fierce howl just before the overthrow of the Messenians.

Virgil says the same thing occurred just before the battle of Pharsalia.

Vide *Rat, Owl, Fire, Ulcer, Madness, Fisherman*.

Dog's Blood : The Chinese say that the blood of a dog will reveal a person who has rendered himself invisible (!)

Dolphin : Dolphins pursuing one another in fair and calm weather, foreshow wind ; but if they thus play when the seas are rough and troubled, it is a sign of fair and calm weather to ensue. (Brand, *Observations*, Vol. III, p. 241 ; *Ethnologie du Bengale*, p. 114.)

Dolya : Slav. Myth. A personification of the good or the evil fortune of an individual ; the Dolya accompanies the person throughout his life. (*Dic. Rel. Eth.*, Vol. IV, p. 625.)

Domovoy : In Slavic folklore it is a domestic spirit. Every house has its *domovoy*, who lives with his wife and family. Generally speaking, he is of a merry disposition. cf. *Brownie, Nisse, Gardsvor.*

Don : Celt. Myth. A Cymric goddess, ancestress of gods.

Donaufürst : An Austrian water-spirit who asks all who come to the river what they wish most, and then ducks them in the river where is all and everything, (SIMROCK, *D.M.*, p. 150 ; BASSETT, p. 161.)

Door : Maras (q.v.) and other evil spirits never come in through doors.

If doors open themselves without any apparent cause, it is a sign that a ghost has just entered. (*Silesia, Lower Saxony.*—WUTTKE, p. 223 ; *Ethnologie du Bengale*, p. 91.)

In Scotland, doors and windows are opened at the moment anyone is dying in the house. (GREGOR, p. 206 ; FRAZER, " Death and Burial Customs, Scotland," *Folklore Journal*, Vol. III, p. 282.) Vide *Slamming, Window.*

Dotterels :
" When dotterels do first appear,
It shows that frost is very near ;
But when that dotterels do go,
Then you may look out for heavy snow."
—Salisbury Sayings.

Double Fruits : If fruits which are growing double, be divided and eaten by two persons, they are sure to have a fulfilment of their desires. (*Great Britain, India.*)

If a pregnant woman partake of such fruit, she will give birth to twins. (*Mecklenburg.*—WUTTKE, p. 193 ; *India* ; FRAZER, *G.B.*, Vol. I, p. 40 ; cf. KARSTEN, *Indian Tribes of Equador*, p. 74 ; *Ethnologie du Bengale*, p. 81, n. 2.)

Doubles : The apparition of a living person visible either to himself or to some other person and superstitiously believed to foretell a great calamity or death.

" The appearance of a double or ' fetch ' has ever been held . . . to signify approaching death."—PROCTOR, *Light Sc.*

Doubt : If one is in doubt, he should count the number of buttons on his coat ; if they are of an even number, he is right ; if of an odd number, wrong. (*Jews of Bohemia.*)

St. Catherine resolves doubts.

Dove :   In Popayan doves are immune from attacks or slaughter, as they are supposed to be inspired by departed souls (TYLOR, *P.C.*, Vol. II, p. 6) ; sometimes they are said to be animated by the souls of lovers (*India*).

Witches cannot assume the form of doves. (cf. *St. Mark*, i, 10 ; *St. John*, i, 32, 33 ; *St. Matthew*, iii, 16).

According to a legend, doves were the messengers of Venus.

In sailors' superstition, doves are birds of good omen. (BASSETT, p. 276.) cf. *Swallow, Lamb.*

Dragon :   A mythical monster, represented as a large and terrible reptile with strong claws like a beast or bird of prey and a scaly skin. It is generally represented with wings and sometimes as breathing out fire. The dragon was consecrated to Minerva, goddess of sagacity and wisdom, in order to symbolise that wisdom is ever-awake.

In Corea it " is the embodiment of all forces of motion, change and power for offence and defence in animal life, fin, wing, tusk, horn, claws, with the mysterious attributes of the serpent." (GRIFFIS, *Corea*, p. 301.) It can transform itself and fly away.

In China the dragon is not a myth, but a real mysterious animal with all the qualities attributed to it by the imagination of the Coreans. (DE GROOT, *Rel. Sys. Chin.*)

In modern superstition there are four dragon kings, each bearing rule over one of the four seas, which form the border of the habitable earth. A peculiar description of pearl, possessing magic virtues, is said to be carried by the dragon upon its forehead. (MAYER, *Chin. Read. Man.*, p. 153.)

Dragons must be killed by one blow only. (KUNOS, *T.F.T.*, pp. 139, 276, 304, etc.)

A black cock when it is seven years old, lays an egg, from which a dragon comes out. It has the body of a snake, has four feet and devours human beings. (ALPENBURG, *Mythen*, p. 376 ; WUTTKE, p. 235.)

In Teutonic literature the favourite food of the dragon is said to have been a virgin.

Dragon is another name of the Devil, and in Christian legends it is the personification of the spirit of evil. Vide *Sturgeon, Treasure.*

Dream :   According to some people, e.g., the Indians of North America, dreams are caused by the soul leaving the body during sleep and wandering over strange lands. The Karens say that dreams are what the *lâ* (soul) has seen on its journey.

Generally speaking, dreams are interpreted by contraries in Japan (GRIFFIS, *M.E.*, p. 472, and in India) ; thus, it is lucky to dream of being murdered and unlucky to dream of finding money.

If you dream the same dream three times in succession, it is sure to be fulfilled. (*U.S.A.*—KNORTZ, p. 43.)

It is lucky to forget your dreams of the previous night. (*Great Britain, India.*)

If one has a bad dream which it is desired to forget on waking in the morning, the advice is given to spit three times in order that the desired effect may be produced. (*Mittheilungen der Gesellschaft für Jüdische Volkskunde*, X, 114 ; *Jew. Enc.*, Vol. XI, p. 599.)

St. Christopher protects from bad dreams.

Historic Dreams :

Jacob had an historic dream on his way to Haran (*Gen.* xxviii. 12-15). Joseph, son of Jacob, had an historic dream revealing to him his future greatness (*Gen.* xxxvii. 5-10). Daniel had an historic dream about four beasts which indicated four kingdoms (*Dan.* vii.). Pharaoh's butler and baker had warning dreams, one being prevised thereby of his restoration to favour, and the other warned of his execution (*Gen.* xl. 5-23). Nebuchadnezzar had an historic dream which Daniel explained (*Dan.* ii. 1, 31, 45). Abimelech, King of Gerar, was warned by a dream that Sarah was Abraham's wife and not his sister (*Gen.* xx. 3-16.) Joseph, husband of Mary, was warned by a dream to flee from Judea ; and when Herod was dead, he was warned again by a dream to "turn aside into the parts of Galilee" (*Matt.* ii. 13, 19, 22). In the Old Testament Pharaoh had a warning dream of a famine which he was able to provide against (*Gen.* xli. 15-36).

For the interpretation of dreams see under different headings.

Drebkuls : The Lettish equivalent of Poseidon, the Earth-Shaker.

Dress : If a girl breaks the needle (STRACKERJAN, Vol. I, p. 34) or pricks her finger while making a new dress, it is an omen that she will be kissed wearing that particular dress.

If you dream of being dressed in gay dresses, you will be blessed with good health.

It is considered lucky to put on any article of dress, especially stockings, inside out ; but this should not be done on purpose, neither should it be changed (CHAMBERS, *Book of Days*, Vol. II, p. 321 ; ABBOTT, p. 144.)

Drink : Drinks should not be stirred with a knife, as this will cause stomach-aches. (STRACKERJAN, Vol. I, p. 49.)

If you dream you are drinking something cold, it is a good omen ; but if something hot, you will have a severe illness. Vide *Amethyst*.

Drinking Horn : King Arthur had a horn, from which no one could drink who was either unchaste or unfaithful.

The Cuckold's Horn, as this was called, was brought to King Arthur's court by a mysterious boy who also brought the Mantle (q.v.) ; it gave warning of infidelity inasmuch as no one unfaithful in love or " unleal " to his liege lord could drink therefrom without spilling the liquor.

The *Coupe enchantée* of the French possessed a similar property. cf. *Brawn's Head, Mantle*.

Drowning : It is caused by water-nixies who keep the souls of the drowned inside pots. These souls must become water-nixies themselves, unless the pots are turned over by some human being. (WOLF, *Beiträge*, Vol. II, pp. 293, 297.)

The body of a drowned sailor is preserved as long as he would have lived had he not been drowned. (*Mélusine*, Vol. II, Col. 253.)

The body of a drowned person may be located by floating some straw, which will come to rest above the spot where the body lies (HADDON, in *Folklore*, IV, p. 360) ; or by floating a loaf of bread at the spot where the person fell into the water ; the bread will come to rest and begin to turn round where the body lies submerged (GREGOR, p. 208.). Sometimes a luminous light is perceived at the exact spot where the body of a drowned person lies (FRAZER, in *Folklore Journal*, III, p. 281 ; BASSETT, p. 311.).

Idiots cannot be drowned because it is the weight of the brain that drags a person down to the bottom of the water ; it is the same with persons who have a mole mark above their mouth (GOODRICH-FREER in *Folklore*, XIII, p. 61).

When people drown at sea, a. water-sprite appears in the shape of a headless old man. (GRIMM, *Teut. Myth.*, Vol. I, p. 491.)

Where a person has been drowned, a button from his waistcoat, mounted on a piece of wood, will indicate the spot where the body lies, by ceasing to float on its arrival thither. (HAZLITT, p. 193.)

Druj nasu : " Corpse-fiend " ; in the Avesta it is the veritable incarnation of pollution and contagion arising from decomposition of a dead body.

Drunkard : Vide *Song, Splashing.*

Dryad : Certain kinds of nymphs. In Classical Mythology, she was a wood-nymph, or more correctly, a nymph whose life was bound up with that of a tree.

Dullahan : Irish lore : A malicious sullen spirit, or goblin.

Dumb : Children if, while eating, you strike anything with your chopsticks, you will be dumb ! (*Japan.*—GRIFFIS, *M.E.*, p. 470.) Vide *Wolf.*

Dumu-zi : " Child of life." A Babylonian god of the solar type.

Dumu-zi-zuab : Babyl. Myth. A deity of a local character. Nebo (q.v.) appears under this form, which describes him as a son of the " deep."

Dung : Dung is considered offensive to ghosts.
   In India, cow-dung is a panacea for all evils ; it cures various diseases, purifies everything and serves many other purposes. (DAY, *Folktales of Bengal; Ethnologie du Bengale*, p. 133 ; LAROUSSE, *Grande Dic. du* XIXe *Siècle*, Vol. XIV, p. 1255b.)
   Horse-dung placed before a house, or inside the door brings good luck. (*Great Britain.*)

Dun-shagga : Babyl. Myth. A deity of a local character.

Durgā : Hindu Myth. Devī (q.v.) in her malignant form is known as Durgā " the inaccessible." She is represented as a yellow woman riding a tiger.

Dusou : The *Dusou* or *Giavanel* of the Swiss peasants is a big supernatural bird of the owl family which speaks to belated travellers and says : *Doumlou* (donne-le-moi—give it to me). Woe betide the man who answers in the affirmative. (JALLA, *Lég. Vaud.*, p. 28.)

Dutchman, Flying : Vide *Flying Dutchman.*

Dvorvoy : A Russian household spirit who lives in the yard.

Dwarf : Teut. Folklore. Diminutive old men with large heads and long, white beards. They shunned the light of day, for the sun's rays would transform them into stones. They became invisible at will and their principal occupation was smith's work.
   For a man to meet a female dwarf (a person of a short stature) and for a woman to meet a male one, is considered lucky. (*Great Britain, India, Canada.*)

Dyaks : Vide *Head-hunting.*

Dyaus : In Vedic mythology : (i) heaven ; (ii) the father of the gods ; hence also called Dyaus-pitri.

Dying : St. Barbara relieves the dying.

Dylan : Celtic Myth. A Cymric sea-god, son of Arianrod.

E

Ea : Assyro-Babl. Myth. A deity belonging to the supreme triad. He was god of the watery element, giver of arts and sciences, healer of the sick, and according to one version, creator of mankind. His consort was Damkina. Vide *Bel.*

Eabani : Babl. Myth. A wild man created by the goddess Aruru to withstand Gilgamesh, but is lured into the service of the latter by Ukhat.

Eacus : Gr. Myth. Son of Zeus. He was celebrated for his justice, and, after his death, was made one of the three judges of the infernal regions ; the other two being Minos and Rhadamantos (q.v.):

Eagle : The eagle is an emblem of royalty.

Tarquinus Priscus was assured that he would be king of Rome by an eagle which swooped down upon him, took off his cap, rose in the air and let the cap fall again upon his head.

Aristander assured Alexander of his victory over Darius in the battle of Arbela, by the flight of an eagle (LLOYD: *Stratagems of Jerusalem,* 290). Vide *Mountain Climbing.*

Eagle-Owl : The screeching of the eagle-owl is especially considered as a portent of disaster. (*Macedonia,* ABBOTT, p. 108).

Eagle-Stone : " The pebble commonly called the aetites, or eagle-stone was found in the eagle's nest, and . . . the eggs could not be hatched without its assistance." (PENNANT, *Zoology,* 1776, Vol. I., p. 167.)

Ear : Small ears indicate that a person is mean ; large ones show that he is generous.

If the left ear tingles, it indicates that someone is talking evil of you ; if the right ear, someone is praising you. (ABBOTT, p. 111). The evil foreboded by the tingling of the left ear may be averted by biting the little finger of the left hand.

A burning sensation of the ear indicates that someone
is speaking of you ; thus

> " Left your lover,
> Right your mother."
> —*Gt. Britain.*

A burning sensation in the ear denotes that you will
receive some news (CAMPBELL, *Sup. Scot. High.*, p. 258).
cf. *Bells in the ear, Death Omens.*

Earth Mother : Vide *Great Mother.*

Earthquake :   Among the North American Indians earthquake is supposed to be caused by the movement of the
earth-bearing tortoise; in Celebes, by the world-supporting Hog rubbing himself against a tree ;   among the
Caribs, because Mother Earth is dancing.   The Elephant
of the Hindus, the Bull of the Moslems, the Frog of the
Mongol Lamas are creatures who carry the earth on
their backs or heads and shake it when they stretch or
shift. According to the Japanese, earthquakes are
caused by huge whales creeping under the earth.

In European mythology earthquakes owe their origin
to the struggles of Loki (q.v.), Atlas (q.v.), Prometheus
(q.v.), Drebkuls (q.v.), etc.

Cattle give warning of an earthquake by their un-
easiness.

St. Christopher protects from the dangers of earthquakes.

> " These are things
> An earthquake brings :
> At nine of the bell
> They sickness foretell ;
> At five and seven they betoken rain ;
> At four the sky is cleared thereby
> At six and eight comes wind again."
> —LEAN, Vol. II. p. 325.

If you dream of an earthquake, it warns you to be
cautious.

Easter :

> " He who is born on Easter morn
> Shall never know want, or care, or harm."
> —BERGEN : *Cur. Sup.* p. 21.

Eating : In Congo if a king be looked at while eating, he will
shortly die. (ELWORTHY, *E. E.*, p. 426).

It is a bad omen to dream of others eating.

In eating, if you miss your mouth and the victuals fall, it is very unlucky, and denotes approaching sickness. (HAZLITT, p. 205).

In Bengal strangers, especially women, are not allowed when a child is eating, for fear of the evil eye (cf. *Ethnologie du Bengale*, p. 85 and n. 2).

Ebisu : Jap. Myth. A god of luck who is represented as carrying a fish.

Eblis : English spelling for Iblis.

Echidna : Gr. Myth. A monster, half maid and half serpent. She gave birth to other monsters, such as Cerberus, the Hydra, the Chimera, the Sphinx, the Dragons, the Gorgons, etc.

Echinus : An echinus fastening itself on a ship's keel, will arrest its motion like an anchor. (BASSETT, p. 258). cf. *Remora*.

Echo : Class. Myth. A nymph who, having displeased Juno, was changed into a rock and condemned to repeat the last words of anyone speaking to her.

The Anglo Saxons thought that the echo was a spirit. (A. S. : *wudu-mære*=echo; from *wudu*=wood, *mære*=elf, spirit ; hence, wood-spirit.)

Among the primitive races, the echo is believed to be an evil spirit.

In Bengal the echo is a wood-spirit mocking people speaking to it, or in its presence.

Eclipse : The eclipse of the sun and the moon is supposed by many people to be caused by a demon swallowing them (*Ethnologie du Bengale*, pp. 101, 102).

The Irish and the Welsh run about beating kettles and pans during eclipses. (HAZLITT, p. 341).

In Sumatra it is the sun devouring the moon, or vice versa. (MARSDEN, p. 194).

Among the Caribs, it is caused by Maboya, a demon and a hater of all light, attempting to devour the sun or the moon.

Among the Hindus, it is caused by the demons Rāhu or Ketu devouring the sun or the moon.

During an eclipse of the sun, poison falls from heaven ; therefore cattle must be herded, wells kept covered, and other precautions taken. (*Hessen, Westphalia.*— WUTTKE, p. 145. cf. the Jewish and Indian superstitions. CROOKE, *P.R.I.*, Vol. I. p. 21). Vide *Rāhu, Ketu, Maboya, Aracho.*

Edgewell Oak : This oak indicated the coming death of an inmate of Castle Dalhousie by the fall of one of its branches. cf. *Death Warnings.* (DALYELL, *Dark. Sup.*, p. 504 ; HAZLITT, p. 205).

Eel : In Scottish superstition eels grow from horse hairs. (CAMPBELL, *Sup. Scot. High.* p. 221).

An eel skin tied round the leg is a cure for cramp. (*India*, CROOKE, *P.R.I.*, Vol. II, p. 258 ; *Ethnologie du Bengale*, p. 115.)

Eel fat is used as a magic ointment, and gives the power of seeing the fairies. (HARTLAND, *Sc. F.T.*, p. 65.)

The eel is a totem of the Munda Kols of Bengal, and of the Oraons, neither of whom will eat it.

Egeria : Class. Myth. A nymph endowed with prophetic powers. According to a Roman legend, Numa is said to have asked her advice in the forests of Aricia.

Egg : If you eat a raw egg, fasting, on Christmas morning, you can carry heavy weights (RAGNER).

The tenth egg is always the largest. (*Gt. Britain*).

If you steal an egg, you will have seven years of poverty. (*Jews of Pinsk, Byelostok, Jew. Enc.* Vol. IX., p. 600).

To find an extremely small hen's egg in the house, is an omen of an impending death. (STRACKERJAN, Vol. I., p. 25).

Dragons come out of the egg of a black cock. (ALPENBURG, *Mythen*, p. 376 ; WUTTKE, p. 235).

It is unlucky to dream of eggs (*U.S.A.* KNORTZ, p. 43).

It will addle eggs if you bring them over running water. (*N. Lincoln*, LEAN, Vol. II., p. 149).

Bringing eggs into a house after sunset brings ill luck (*ib.*)

Eggshell : After you have eaten eggs, you should crush the shells ; you will never suffer from epilepsy if you take this precaution. (*Gt. Britain* ; *Alsace*, LAMBS, p. 39).

Ladies, take care ! If you step over an egg-shell, you will go mad. (*Japan.* GRIFFIS, *M.E.*, p. 469).

It is lucky to find egg-shells (*Silesia*, WUTTKE, p. 96 ; *Gt. Britain*).

Ehlose : The guardian spirit of the Zulus, which may take many forms, and warn a person of an approaching danger. (HAGGARD, *Nada the Lily*, pp. 11, 22, 94, 99).

Eirek : Scand. Myth. Eirek, journeying toward Paradise, came to a stone bridge guarded by a dragon ; he entered its maw, and found that he had arrived in a world of bliss.

Ekimmu : In Babylonian superstition it was the ghost of a man ; it represented a class of demons that infest the graves. cf. *Ghoul*.

Elathan : Celt. Myth. A king of the Fomors, father of Bress.

Elbow : Itching of the elbow denotes "a strange bed" (*Gt. Britain*), or that you will sleep with a stranger. (*Boston, Mass.*)

If you accidentally knock your elbow, look out for a disappointment ; the evil, however, may be averted by knocking the other one. (*Gt. Britain, India.*)

If someone is speaking deprecatingly of you in your absence, and you have the natural desire of punishing him by getting him drenched, just bite your elbow ! Easier said than done ! (STRACKERJAN, Vol. I., p. 31).

Elder : If you burn elder on Christmas Eve, you will have revealed to you all the witches and sorcerers of the neighbourhood (RAGNER).

Elderberry Tree : The Danish women will never break off a branch of an elderberry tree without first apologizing to the spirit of the tree.

Electra : Gr. Myth. A daughter of Agamemnon. Her rôle is to urge Orestes, her brother, to vengeance ; and, in Euripides' version, actively to assist him.
Vide *Aegisthus*.

Elementals : They are nature spirits, such as those of land, water, fire, etc., and are personifications of natural phenomena, or are associated with particular departments of nature.

"To rise to intercourse with these elemental spirits of nature was the highest aim of the philosopher." —Lecky : *Ration.* (1865).

Elephant : The Hindus believe that earthquakes are caused by the earth-bearing elephant shaking himself.

In popular superstition elephants are supposed to celebrate religious rites.

Elephants have no knees. (HAZLITT, p. 207).

The flesh of an elephant is thought by the Ewe-speaking peoples of West Africa to make the eater strong. (ELLIS, *Ewe-speaking People*, p. 99).

Eleusinian Mysteries : The most famous religious mysteries of the world.

Eleutheria : Gr. Myth. The goddess of liberty was called by this name.

Elf : The name of a class of supernatural beings supposed in early Teutonic belief to possess magical powers. They were of a dwarfish form, produced diseases of various kinds, stole children, caused nightmares, acted as succubi (q.v.) and incubi (q.v.), etc.

Elian, St. : Leads to the discovery of lost goods.

Elixir : In Alchemy, a preparation by the use of which it was sought to change metals into gold. It was a supposed drug or essence with the property of indefinitely prolonging life. (Elixir Vitae).
> " I know too where the Genii hid
> The jewell'd cup of their King Jamshid
> With life's Elixir sparkling high."
> —MOORE, *Lalla Rookh.* (1815).

Ellefolk : The Elves of Danish superstition.

Elle Woman : In Danish superstition it is the spirit of the elder tree.

Elmo's, St., Light : In Brittany it is called a wandering candle, and is a menace. It is sometimes a lost soul for whom prayers are asked. In Greece this light is a bad omen ; it is a demon which breaks masts, destroys ships and crew, and can be expelled only by the diabolical cries of a pig. According to the German sailors, it is a good omen when it mounts up, and the contrary is shown by its descent. It is the spirit of a defunct comrade.— (BASSETT, p. 314).

Elyll : In Welsh superstition it is a hairy, clumsy creature, and is the same as a brownie.

Emerald : Emerald promotes friendship and constancy of mind.
If a serpent fixes its eye on an emerald, it goes blind.
The emerald is an emblem of success in love. In the Zodiac it signifies Cancer ; it is dedicated to Mars and May ; in Metallurgy it means iron, and in Christian art it is given to St. John.

Empusa : Gr. Myth. A demoniac apparition that appeared sometimes at midday, sometimes at night. She had the power of continually changing her shape, but could be detected by the donkey's leg which was her constant attribute.

Emu : Some Victorian tribes regard the fat of the emu as sacred. Anyone who threw away the fat or flesh was held accursed. (FRAZER, *G. B.*, Vol. III., p. 203).

Enceladus : Gr. Myth. One of the most celebrated of the Titans who revolted against Zeus. He fled to Sicily, but was captured on the way, and imprisoned in Mt. Etna. His vain efforts to free himself and his breath of fire made Etna a fire-emitting volcano.

Enchantment : Alectoria (q.v.) is an antidote for enchantment.

Endor, Witches of : Name of the three supernatural beings who appeared to Macbeth. (SHAKESPEARE : *Macbeth.*)

Enemy of God and Man : An epithet of the Devil.

En-lil : Babyl. Myth. In the oldest inscriptions Bel is styled by this name, thus designating him as the chief god (or demon) Nipur. The name merely describes him as a powerful demon, but he manifested himself in storms and other violent disturbances of nature.

Entrance : As a rule, ghosts and spirits must leave a place the same way as they entered it. (cf. THORPE, *Northern Myth.*; GRIMM, *Deut. Myth.* ; WUTTKE, *Volksaberglaube,* etc.) Vide *Exit.*

Enyo : Gr. Myth. One of the Grææ.

En-zu : Babyl. Myth. The moon-god Sin is ordinarily designated ideographically En-zu which describes him as a " lord of wisdom."

Eolus : Class. Myth. Son of Zeus and the nymph Menalippa, a god of the winds ; it was he who let loose the winds.

Eos : Gr. Myth. The goddess of dawn corresponding to the Roman Aurora.

Ephesus : In Arabia a talisman consisting of a piece of paper containing the names of the Seven Sleepers of Ephesus is still used to ward off ghosts and demons.
Vide *Grotto of Ephesus, Seven Sleepers of Ephesus.*

Ephialtes : In Greece the name given by the ignorant to account for the nightmare which results from indigestion.

Epiales : In Greece it is a cold shivering fit which precedes an attack of fever.

Epidemic : During epidemics open the door only when the person outside has knocked three times. (*Jews of Galicia* SCHIFFER, *Urquell,* ii. 202 ; *Jew. Enc.,* Vol. XI. p. 600). Vide *Plague.*

Epigones : Gr. Myth. One of the sons of the seven heroes who were beaten before Thebes.

Epilepsy : Three drops of a sow's milk cure epilepsy (*Irish*). The skull of a dead person used to make broth in, cures of epilepsy (LEAN, Vol. II., p. 493).

Epilepsy can be cured by wearing a heavy silver ring (*East Friesland*, WUTTKE, p. 163) ; or by drinking the blood of a she-ass (STRACKERJAN, Vol. I, p. 84), or of the executed (STRACKERJAN, Vol. I, p. 83), or the hot blood of a weasel (*Tyrol*, ALPENBURG, *Mythen*, p. 390) ; or let the patient carry a golden peacock's feather under his shirt (SCHIFFER, *Urquell*, v. 290) ; or let him drink the blood of a black cat ; or let his shirt be buried at the junction of two roads, after it has been pulled over his head and carried out through the chimney. (*Minsk.—Jew. Enc.*, Vol. V, p. 426).

If all the above remedies fail, the patient will have nothing left but to invoke either St. Cornelius or St. Valentine. Vide *Ben nefilim, Eggshell, Ass, Crucifix.*

Epimethus : Gr. Myth. Brother of Prometheus. In spite of his brother's advice not to receive any present from Zeus, he accepted Pandora as his wife, and thus brought sorrow to the human race.

Epitaph : If you would preserve your memory, be warned against reading epitaphs. (*U.S.A.*)

Erasmus, St. : Cures colic and gripes.

Erato : Gr. Myth. One of the Muses ; she presides over elegiac poetry and is represented with a lyre.

Erebus : Class. Myth. Father of Charon.

Erinys : Gr. Relig. (pl. Erinyes). One of the avenging spirits who bring retribution upon those who have violated the laws of natural piety, hospitality, etc. Originally, they were the revengeful ghosts of the slain ; later, they were conceived as snaky-haired women pursuing the offender, and inflicting madness. They were three in number : Alecto, Megæra and Tisiphone.

Eriphyle : Gr. Myth. Wife of Amphiraüs, who foretold to her husband the disastrous end of the expedition against Thebes. She was slain by her son Alcmæon.

Erl King : In Teutonic and Scandinavian folk-lore, a personification of a spirit or natural power, supposed to work mischief, especially to children.

" Dem Vater grauset's, er reitet geschwind,
Er hält in den Armen das ächzende Kind,
Erreicht den Hof mit Müh' und Not ;
In seinen Armen das Kind war tot."
—GOETHE : *Erlkönig.*

Eros : Gr. Myth. The god of love, corresponding to Cupid of the Romans.

Erymanthean : Gr. Myth. A devastating boar which wandered about in Arcadia. Its capture was one of the labours imposed upon Hercules.

Erysipelas : The tongue of a fox, worn near the heart, is a preventive against this disease. (STRACKERJAN, Vol. I, 85). Vide *Anthony, St.*

Eshshata : Jewish Folk-lore. The name of a spirit of fever. (*Jew. Enc.*, Vol. IV. p. 517).

Esprit Follet : The French equivalent of a Puck, Poltergeist, etc.

Eteocles : Gr. Myth. A king of Thebes, son of Œdipus and Jocasta. His refusal to give up his throne to Polynices led to the expedition of the Seven against Thebes, in which the brothers killed each other.

Eternal Jew : In popular superstition it is the Jew who hurried on Jesus Christ, when He was led to crucifixion. As a punishment, he is compelled to wander about the world, homeless and restless, till the Day of Judgment. (S. BARING GOULD, *Myths of the Middle Ages*; EUGÉNE SUE, *Le Juif errant*, HAZLITT, p. 618). Also known as the " Wandering Jew."

Ethelbert, St. : Leads to the recovery of lost goods.

Ethra : Class. Myth. Mother of Theseus.

Etzel : In the Nibelungenlied, the second husband of Kriemhild, king of the Huns. Vide *Gunther, Siegfried, Hagen, Kriemhild.*

Eucharis : A nymph belonging to the goddess Calypso ; heroine of an episode of Telemachus.

Eumeus : Gr. Myth. A faithful servant and guardian of the troops belonging to Ulysses.

Euminides : Gr. Myth. A name by which the Erinyes or the Furies are often designated.

Eumolpus : Gr. Myth. A son of Neptune and founder of the famous Eleusian mysteries.

Euphrosyne : Gr. Myth. One of the three Graces.

Euronomus : A grizzly Greek demon who ate the flesh of corpses. He was blue-black in colour, like a carrion fly, his teeth were bared, and he is represented as sitting on the skin of a vulture. (Painted by Polygnotus).

Europa : Gr. Myth. A daughter of Agenor, king of Phœnicia. She was carried away to Crete by Zeus disguised as a bull and became the mother of Minos.

European : The finger-nails of Europeans are in popular belief a deadly poison. (*India*—CROOKE, *P.R.I.*, Vol. I, p. 279).

Eurus : Gr. Myth. God of the east wind.

Euryale : Gr. Myth. One of the Gorgons.

Euryclea : Gr. Myth. The old nurse of Odysseus, who, on his return in disguise, recognized him by his scar.

Eurydice : Gr. Myth. A nymph beloved of Orpheus. After her death by snake-bite, Orpheus descended to the nether regions, obtained Pluto's permission to bring her back to earth, but on his way back he turned round, which he was forbidden to do, and she had to return to Hades.

Eurynome : Gr. Myth. A sea-goddess, daughter of Oceanus.

Eurystheus : Gr. Myth. A Mycenæan king to whose service Hercules was bound.

Euterpe : Gr. Myth. The muse of lyric poetry ; she is represented with a flute.

Even : Vide *Odds and Evens*.

Evil Eye : A supposed power of bewitching by spiteful looks, attributed to certain persons as a natural endowment. The belief is widespread both among savage and civilized people. (LEHMANN, *Aberglaube und Zauberei*, p. 32 ; BUDGE, *Egyptian Magic*, p. 97, etc. ; LANE, *Customs and Usages of the Egyptians of To-day* ; ELWORTHY, *The Evil Eye* ; KOHUT, *Jüdische Angelologie u.s.w.*, p. 58 ; DALYELL, *Dark. Sup.*, p. 3 *et seq* ; HAZLITT, p. 216, 379 ; ABBOTT, p. 139 ; *Ethnologie du Bengale*, pp. 81, 84, 85, 131, 137).

A woman who believes herself to be overlooked is to take the shift off over her head, turn it three times withershins (=against the course of the sun), then hold it open, and drop a burning coal through it three times ; then put it on again (ELWORTHY, E.E. p. 429).

The evil eye, or in fact any evil, can be averted by the mother kissing the child thrice, and spitting after each kiss. (*Jew. Enc.*, Vol. IX. p. 598). Vide *Bread, Tulsi, Horseshoe, Palm, Ribbon, Thread, Stag, Horn.*

Evil One : An epithet of the Devil,

Excalibur : King Arthur's brand, which, when flung back into the lake, was caught by an arm clothed in white samite. cf. *Balmung, Tizona.*

Excrement, Human : This substance, thinned with water and given to animals, cures inflammations. (STRACKERJAN, Vol. I, p. 84). Inflammations of human beings can also be cured by external use of the same. (*ib.*)

The Bhûts of India feed on human excretion.

Execution : The bones and the blood (STRACK, p. 20) of the executed are a powerful talisman for procuring wealth. (*Silesia.*—WUTTKE, p. 177. cf. DAVIS, *Chronicles of Newgate.*)

Uncanny things go on at midnight in places where executions usually take place ; therefore, it is not safe for people to go there at this time.

To dream of an execution, or places of execution, denotes that you will suddenly be sought after for relief. Vide *Hand.*

Exeter : Derives its name, according to a belief, from the Romans exclaiming in delight : " Ecce terra ! " when they came in sight of where this ancient city now stands.

Exit : A mara or another evil spirit can make her exit only the way she made her entrance.

Exorcism : The act of driving an evil spirit from the body of one possessed by adjuration, especially by the use of a holy name or by magic rites. Vide *Beans, Peachwood.*

Eye : If the right eye itches, you will be pleased ; if the left, you will have sorrow. (*Gt. Britain, India.*)

If the eye of a corpse remains open, or if he smiles, it is a sign that someone else from the same house will die soon. (STRACKERJAN, Vol. I. p. 30).

St. Claire and St. Ottilie cure bad eyes.

It is a very bad omen to dream of losing an eye ; your friends and relations will die, and you may even lose your liberty.

" Blue-eye beauty, do your mammy's duty,
Black-eye, pick a pie,
Run round and tell a lie ;
Grey-eye, greedy-gut
Eat all the world up."
—*U.S.A.* (BERGEN, *C.S.* p. 33).

Vide *Smile, Evil Eye, Soreness, Gutta Percha, Kite, Rubbing.*

Eye of Balor : Vide *Balor.*

Eyebrows : People with meeting eyebrows are superstitiously believed to be either vampires or werewolves. (O'DONNELL, *Werewolves*; BARING GOULD, *Book of Were Wolves*; RANFT, *Tractat von dem Kauen und Schmatzen der Todten in Gräbern.*)

Eyelid : For a man, the twitching of the right upper lid is considered lucky, and of the left unlucky ; for a woman, vice versa. (*Gt. Britain, India*, SCHIFFER, *Urquell*, ii, 80-82 ; ABBOTT, p. 112).

F

Fafnir : In the Volsunga Saga, a giant who, in the form of a venom-breathing dragon, possesses and guards a great treasure. He was slain by Sigurd.

Fair : To dream that you are going to a fair denotes that your pockets will be picked.

Fairy : One of a class of supernatural beings of diminutive size ; in popular belief they are said to possess magical powers and to have great influence for good or evil over the affairs of men.
  " Heavens defend me from that Welsh fairy, lest he
  Transform me into a piece of cheese ! "
    —SHAKESPEARE: *Merry Wives of Windsor*, v., 5.

Faithfulness : If your beloved is untrue to you, light three candles by the wrong ends and say the Paternoster three times ; then he is sure to come back to you. (*Bohemia*).

False Report : If a man is falsely reported dead, he will live ten years longer. (*Silesia, Hesse.*—WUTTKE, p. 39).

Famine : When crows, robins or rooks forsake a wood in a flock, it forebodes a famine.

Fangen : Forest spirits of German mythology.

Fantine : Swiss Folk-lore. A class of well-disposed fairies.
  " On y voit encore la grotte où vivaient les *fantines* ou *masques*, tout occupées à procurer le bien-être des habitants du vallon. Elles faisaient prospérer l'agriculture, procurant des saisons favorables. Dans leur retraite, elles fabriquaient des clochettes pour que le bétail ne s'égarât pas dans les bois, alors plus touffus qu'aujourd'hui."—Prof. JEAN JALLA: *Lég. Vaud.* p. 20.

Farce : If you dream you see a farce, you will have good success in business.

Fascination : Human saliva is a charm against fascination.

Fate : Class. Myth. The goddess, or one of the goddesses of fate and destiny. In Greek mythology they were three in number : *Clotho, Lachesis,* and *Atropos.* cf. *Norn, Parca, Bidhâtâpurusha, Hathor, Sudičky.*

Father-in-law : It is an evil omen to dream of your father-in-law.

Faun : Rom. Myth. An Italian deity of fields and woods, represented as having human form with pointed ears, small horns and sometimes a goat's tail, or as half goat and half man.

Faunus : Rom. Relig. A rural deity, god of animal life and fruitfulness, patron of husbandry, hunting and herding and guardian of the secret lore of nature.

Faust : Faust was a young German student who, after studying magic, sold himself to the Devil. The legend has been immortalized by Goethe.
> " Faust : O Faustus,
> Now thou hast but one bare hour to live,
> And then you must be damn'd perpetually."
> MARLOW : *Dr. Faustus* (1589 ?).

Fay : Vide *Fairy, Elf.*

Feast : To dream that you are feasting without enjoying it is a forewarning of a great disappointment.

Feather : The presence of game feathers in a feather bed will prolong the agonies of death ; it is impossible to die on a pillow stuffed with feathers of doves or pigeons. (HAZLITT, p. 232).

Fêng-hwang : Chin. Myth. A pheasant-like bird of rich plumage and graceful form and movement, fabled to appear in the land on the accession of a sage to the throne, or when right principles are about to prevail. (MAYER, *Chin. Read. Man.,* p. 43). cf. *Phœnix.*

Fêng-shui : A system of spirit influence for good and evil, believed by the Chinese to attend the natural features of landscape.

Fenian : In Gaelic legend a band of heroes, forming a kind of free soldiery and chivalric order. Their leader was Finn.

Fenodyres : The Manx name for a brownie.

Fenrir : Norse Myth. A wolf, spawn of Loki, who fights with Tyr, and is afterwards cast into Niflheim by the Æsir. He killed Odin in a fight.

Fergus : Gaelic Legend. Son of Finn. He was a bard and an important member of the Fenians.

Feronia : An ancient Italian Goddess, a protectress of freedmen and markets.

Fetch : A double (q.v.). " In Ireland, ' a fetch ' is the supernatural facsimile of some individual, which comes to ensure to its original a happy longevity, or immediate dissolution ; if seen in the morning, the one event is predicted ; if in the evening, the other."—J. BANIM : *Tales of O'Hara Family, The Fetch.* (1825).

"The Earl of Cromwell met the fetch of his friend William Rufus."—TYLOR : *Primitive Culture.*

Fetish : A material object supposed by the savage tribes to possess magical powers, capable of bringing to issue the designs of the owner, or to preserve him from injury. Originally this name was applied to the rude wooden idols of the West Africans. but is now applied to similar objects all the world over. (cf. R. MARAN, *Batouala*, Lond., 1922, p 79).

Feu Follet : The French name for a Jack-o'-Lantern.

Fever : To cure fever, spill a can of water suddenly on the patient (SCHIFFER, *Urquell*, v. 223), or let him eat something he does not like. (*Jew. Enc.*, Vol. V., p. 223).

In Burma fever is caused by a demon seizing people trespassing in his domain. He shakes them with ague till he is exorcised. Apoplectic fits are similarly caused by other demons. (TYLOR, *P.C.* Vol. II, p. 124). Vide *Epilepsy, Bacon, Cockchafer, Spider, Nail, Willow, Eshshata, Agate, Magpie.*

Fianna Eirinn : Irish for Fenian.

Field : If a man dreams of green fields, he will marry a discreet, chaste and beautiful woman ; if a woman dreams the same, she will marry a loving and prudent husband, by whom she will have prudent and beautiful children.

Field-mouse : In parts of England it is believed that a field-mouse creeping over the back of a sheep gives it paralysis, and that this can be cured by shutting up a mouse in the hollow of a trunk of the witch-hazel or witch-elm tree, and leaving it to die of starvation. (BRAND, *Observations*, p. 739 ; cf. FRAZER, *Magic Art*, vol. i, p. 83).

Fiend : An infernal being, generally mixed up with the Devil.

Fiery Apparitions : Apparitions in the form of fiery dogs and other animals are usually the spirits of those who have committed some heinous crime in their lifetime. (ALPENBURG, p. 210, etc.).

G

Filth : Many spirits, generally of a malevolent nature, take up their abode in filth.

Finger : If the finger joints crack when pulled, it is a sign that someone loves you. (STRACKERJAN, Vol. I. 91).

Manx fishermen do not point at anything with a finger (RHYS, p. 396). Vide *Hare*.

Finn MacCoul : Gaelic Legend. Leader of the Fenians.

Finola : Irish Myth. The eldest of the four children of Ler, who were changed into swans by their jealous stepmother and doomed to retain this form, though without loss of human speech, for nine hundred years.

Fir (Tree) : If a fir tree be touched, withered or burned with lightning, it is a warning to the house that the master or mistress thereof will shortly die. (BRAND, *Observations*, Vol. III. p. 233).

Firbolg : Irish Legend. One of the tribes which settled in Ireland at a very early date, and who were nearly destroyed by the Tuatha De Danann. They were identified with the dark population of short stature, believed to be of Iberian affinities.

Fir Darrig : Irish lore. A little merry red man, not unlike in his disposition and movements to Puck.

Fire : If the fire springs out of the hearth, you will receive a visit (*Dutch*—THORPE, *N.M.*, Vol. III, p. 328).

The noise occasioned when the enclosed gas in a piece of burning coal catches fire is a sure indication of a quarrel between the inmates of the house (*Gt. Britain*).

If children play with fire at night, they are sure to wet the bed in their sleep. (STRACKERJAN, Vol. I., 45).

In Japan the following things foretell a fire : a cock crowing loudly in the evening, a dog climbing on the roof of a house or building, a weasel crying out once, and pulling up a peculiar kind of grass, called the "*hinode*" (sunrise), which grows on many houses. (GRIFFIS, *M.E.*, p. 471).

St. Christopher saves from fire, St. Agatha protects from it, but St. Florian should be invoked if a fire has already broken out.

If the fire burns brightly on Christmas morning, it betokens prosperity during the year ; if it smoulders, adversity. (RAGNER).

Making a cross with the bars of the grate and the poker drives the devil out of the chimney, and so enables the fire to burn. (*Gt. Britain.*—ELWORTHY, *E. E.*, p. 430).

In Ireland a fire is believed to be a great protection against fairies and witches. (ib. p. 436. cf. *Ethnologie du Bengale*, pp. 82, 92, 133 ; KÜHN UND SCHWARTZ, *Norddeutsche Sagen*, p. 92 ; WOLF, Beiträge, Vol. II, p. 303 ; PLOSS, *Das Weib*, Vol. I, pp. 615 *seq.* ; WUTTKE, p. 195 ; LADY WILDE, p. 118 ; TYLOR, *Primitive Culture*, Vol. II, p. 178 ; HYLTON-CAVALLIUS, *Wärend och Wirdarne*, Vol. I, p. 191 ; ATKINSON, *Glossary of Cleveland Dialect*, p. 597 ; HUBERT ET MAUSS, *Essai sur le Sacrifice*, *Année Sociol.*, Vol. II (1897-1898), p. 57, n. 7). Vide *Beehive*, *Agatha St.*, *Gipsy*, *Nail*.

Fire-Fly : Night blindness is cured by eating a fire-fly. (*Bengal*).

Fireplace : If the fire in the fireplace bursts with an explosive sound, it is a sign of a quarrel. (*Silesia, Hesse, Mark, Swabia*), but if you spit on it, you will not be the sufferer. (*Mark.*—WUTTKE, p. 37).

First : The first of April, August and December are unlucky days. (WUTTKE, p. 22 ; STRACKERJAN, Vol. II. p. 52).

First-born Children : They are believed to have the power of stopping rain ; according to the Muslims, they can do so by stripping naked and standing on their heads. In Calcutta, they need only make a candle of cloth and burn it (*Dic. Rel. Eth.* Vol. VIII, p. 291).

It is believed in India that a first-born son leaning against anything will attract a thunderbolt to it. (*Dic. Rel. Eth.* Vol. VIII, p. 290 ; *N.I.N.Q.*, I. (1891) 378).

First-buried : The spirit of the first-buried in a churchyard can never have rest, but must wander about eternally. (*Hessen, Westphalia*—WUTTKE, p. 215). cf. *Last Buried*.

Fish : If you count the number of fish you have caught, you will catch more that day. (*Gt. Britain*).

If you meet a priest while on your way to fishing, you will have a good haul that day. (*Gt. Britain ; Japan*—GRIFFIS, *M.E.*, p. 470).

Fish are sometimes transformed into birds (MAYER, *Chin. Read. Man.*, p. 301).

It is unlucky to dream of a single fish, but lucky to dream of a shoal.

Spirits and other malevolent demons are very fond of fish, especially fried (cf. *Ethnologie du Bengale*, p. 115 ; SKEAT, *Malay Magic*, p. 326). Vide *Net, Woman*.

Fisherman : Fishermen spit on their hansel for luck in fishing.

Fishermen everywhere avoid mentioning at sea the name of a pig, hare, salmon, trout, or dog, but go out of their way to find some other word when it is needful to indicate either of these. (ELWORTHY, *E.E.*, p. 313. BASSETT, p. 279). (For further superstitions, see BASSETT, *Legends and Superstitions of the Sea and Sailors*, Lond., 1885).

Fish, Great : The larger portion of the treasure of the North American Indians ; the smaller portion being called Little Fish. (RIDER HAGGARD, *Montezuma's Daughter*).

Fits : To cure fits, go into a church at midnight, and walk three times round the communion table. (LEAN, Vol. II., p. 996).

Five : In Japan new clothes or sandals should not be put on after 5 p.m. (GRIFFIS, *M.E.*, p. 472).

Flatfoot : It is a sign of low descent. Vide *Instep*.

Flea : A flea-bite on the hand is a precursor of good news (*Silesia, Hesse, Saxony.*—WUTTKE, p. 34), or it foretells that you will be kissed. (*Germany, Austria*).

Fleas will never come in a bed if the beds be aired on the Thursday before Easter. (STRACKERJAN, Vol. II, p. 111).

Fleas and bugs never infest a dying person. (LEAN, Vol. II, p. 579).

Flesh and Blood : Flesh and blood of the sacrificed were eaten and drunk by the Aztecs, because they thought that this would make them strong and powerful (WUTTKE, *Geschichte des Heidentums*, Vol. I, p. 268, etc.) ; or produce inspiration. (FRAZER, *G.B.*, Vol. I, p. 133).

Flint : Ghosts cannot bear the sight of sparks from a flint. (*Mark.*—WUTTKE, p. 224).

Flood : St. Christopher protects from floods. Vide *Frost*.

Flora : The goddess of flowers and gardens, the beloved of Zephyr, and mother of Spring.

Florian : Vide *Fire*.

Florimel's Girdle : It would loosen itself or tear asunder if any woman unfaithful or unchaste attempted to put it on. cf. *Bahman's Knife, Canace's Mirror, Sophia's Picture, Mantle, Grotto of Ephesus, Water of Jealousy*.

Flounder : According to a Sutherland tradition, the wry mouth of a flounder arose from making faces at the rock-cod. (CAMPBELL, *Sup. Scot. High.*, p. 223 ; cf. BASSETT p. 257).

The white side of a flounder is caused by the Virgin Mary's laying her hand on it. (*Finland.—Notes and Queries*, 15-11-1883).

Flour : It is a sin for a Bulgarian not to fumigate the flour when it is brought from the mill, especially if the mill is kept by a Turk ; this is done to prevent the Devil from entering into it. (St. CLAIR and BROPHY, *Bulgaria*, p. 46 ; TYLOR, *P.C.*, Vol. II, p. 146).

To meet a person carrying flour is a bad omen. (*India—* JACKSON, *F.L.N.*, Vol. I, p. 127).

Flower : If a flower be plucked from a grave and afterwards thrown away, the place where the flower falls will be haunted. (STRACKERJAN, Vol. I, p. 154).

Flowers or wreaths must not be laid on the bed of a sick person ; this is injurious to the invalid. (STRACKER-JAN, Vol. I, p. 49).

If you take a flower with you to dinner, wipe your lips with it after drinking some wine, and give it to your lover or sweetheart, he or she will fall madly in love with you. (PLOSS, *Das Weib*, Vol. I, 443).

Ghosts sometimes take up their abodes in flowers. (CROOKE, *P.R.I.*, Vol. I, p. 291).

Fly : Vide *Magpie, Vermin.*

Flying : The power of flying through the air may be acquired by eating the heart of an unborn babe. (STRACK, p. 21).

Witches are supposed to possess the power of flying through the air on brooms, goats, etc. (LEHMANN, *A.Z.*; GRIMM, *D.M.*)

If you dream you are flying, you are vainly ambitious and romantic.

Flying Dutchman : A legendary Dutch mariner condemned to sail against the wind till the Day of Judgment. His spectral ship, also called by this name, the seeing of which is considered a very bad omen by sailors, is said to sail about in the neighbourhood of the Cape of Good Hope with full sails in bad weather. (Capt. MARRYAT, *The Phantom Ship*; cf. WOLF, *Niederländische Sagen*, No. 130 ; THORPE, *N.M.*, Vol. III, p. 295). Vide *Ship Spectral.*

Foam : If the foam from a mule's mouth, mixed with warm water, be drunk by an asthmatic patient, he will at once recover, but the mule will die. (FRAZER, *G.B.*, Vol. III, p. 23.)

Fog :   " Fog on the hill
Brings water to the mill ;
Fog on the moor
Brings the sun to the door."
New York (BERGEN, *C.S.*, p. 112).

Folkvang :   Norse Myth. Frey's hall in Asgard to which went half of the battle-fallen heroes.

Fomor :   In Gaelic legend they were giants or sea-demons, powers of darkness and evil, believed to have been overcome by the Tuatha De Danann. Most of them were represented as huge and deformed, and some with animal heads.

Food : Food buried with the dead seems to have had the object of appeasing the spirit's hunger. (cf. *Ethnologie du Bengale*, p. 75 ; JOLLY, *Recht und Sitte*, p. 155 ; GREGOR, p. 21 ; LADY WILDE, p. 118 ; LE BRAZ, Vol. I, p. 267). Vide *Pindi*.

Fool's Paradise : Vide *Limbus Fatuorum*.

Foot :   While going along the street, if you scrape the ground with your right foot, you will meet a friend ; if with your left, you will meet with a disappointment. (*Gt. Britain*).
   Itching of the soles of the feet denotes a journey to some unknown place. (*Gt. Britain, India, Germany.*— WUTTKE, p. 41 ; among the Jews—*Jew. Enc.*, Vol. IX., p. 600).
   Bhûts enter a person's body by means of the feet (CROOKE, *P.R.I.*, Vol. I, p. 241). cf. *Hand*.

Footprint : The Devil is said to leave footprints pointing towards a backward direction. (See the story given by TYLOR in his *Primitive Culture*, Vol. I, p. 278).

Footwear : If they are lying on a table, they must be put on the floor before donning them, otherwise they bring bad luck. (STRACKERJAN, Vol. I, p. 46).

Fork :   A fork accidentally dropped signifies a visit from a woman. (*Gt. Britain*). Vide *Knife*.

Forseti : Teut. Myth.: A deity of Frisian origin whose chief seat was Heligoland. Norse Myth.: Son of Balder.

Fortuna : Class. Relig. An allegoric divinity of the Greeks and Romans. She was the goddess of Fortune; she is represented with a bandage round her eyes, and is standing either on a globe or on a circle.

Fossegrim : Another name for Grim

Fountain : Dirce, wife of Lycus, was changed into a fountain by Bacchus. cf. *Pirene.*

Four-leaved Clover : It is lucky to find a four-leaved clover (*Great Britain*), especially if it be sewn inside the clothes. (*Silesia.*—WUTTKE, p. 96.)

Fowl : "To bewitch till he die, take a black hen and pluck from it every feather, and this done keep them all carefully, so that not one be lost. With these you may do any harm to grown-up people or children." (LELAND, *Etruscan Roman Remains*, p. 354.)

Fox : The fox and certain other animals are said to possess a power of bewitching human beings by assuming phantom forms.

In Japan (GRIFFIS, CHAMBERLAIN, ASTON, BRINKLEY) and China (DE GROOT, GILES, MAYER) for example, the animal is said to have innumerable powers ; and, in fox-possession, the spirit of the animal intrudes itself into the body of a man or woman and exercises a more or less absolute control over the person in whose body it resides. (*Chin. Volksmärchen.*)

If the tongue of a fox be dried and worn near the heart, it will safeguard you against erysipelas in the face. (STRACKERJAN, Vol. I, p. 85.) Vide *Courage, Hare.*

Francus : Myth. Son of Hector. According to the poet Ronsard in his book *Franciade*, Francus is said to be the father of the French nation.

Frau Holle : Ger. Myth. A variation of the Wild Hunt. Vide *Holda.*

Freiherr von Güttingen : He collected the poor in a great barn and burnt them to death, mocking their cries of agony all the while. He, like Hatto, was invaded by mice and ran to his castle of Güttingen on Lake Constance, whither the vermin pursued him and ate him alive.

The Swiss legend says that the castle sank in the lake and may still be seen.

Freiherr von Güttingen had three castles, one of which was Moosberg.

cf. *Hatto, Graaf, Widerolf, Adolf.*

Frey : Teut. Myth. A Vanir deity of fruitfulness, love, prosperity and peace. He was united with Gerth, a giantess.

Freya : Norse Myth. The goddess of love and beauty, who also presided over the regions of the dead. She was one of the Vanir and daughter of Njörth, and sister of Frey. Her famous possession was the jewel or necklace Brisingamen, which was obtained from the dwarfs.

Friday : Nails should be cut on a Friday ; it brings luck and helps to keep toothache away (*Germany*), hair cut on this day grows well (*Silesia*) ; children born on this day have much to suffer (*Tyrol.*—WUTTKE, pp. 12, 17.).

"Never be born on a Friday, help it if you can."
—(*Great Britain*).

Sick persons should not be visited on a Friday. (LADY WILDE, p. 214).

Sailors will not sail on a Friday.

Friday derives its name from Freya or Frigg, to whom it is dedicated. Vide *Sunday, Wednesday, Thursday, Death Omens.*

Friendship : Vide *Needle, Knife, Dog, Garden, Pin.*

Frigg(a) : Norse Myth. Wife of Odin and goddess of the sky. She presides over marriage and domestic life. She rules not only in heaven, but also in the dark nether world, the abode of the dead.

Frog : When frogs croak more than usual, it is a sign of bad weather.

Frogs, lizards, owls and bats are used for various magical purposes, and as love charms. (PLOSS, *Das Weib*, Vol. I, pp. 440 *et seq.*)

To meet a frog is lucky (LEAN, Vol. II, p. 51) ; it indicates that the person is about to receive money.

Frogs or toads must not be killed on All Hallows Day, because " poor souls reside in them." (ZINGERLE, *Sitten*, p. 114.)

According to the Mongol Lamas, a frog supports the earth on its back. Vide *Jnūn.*

Frost : " Brouillard en Mars, bientôt il pleut ;
    Gelée en Mai plus qu'on en veut."
        Frost is foretold by the redness of the robin's breast. (*Gt. Britain*).

Fruit : Plucking fruits after nightfall is an extremely pernicious habit ; it disturbs the rest of the spirits living in the trees. (*India.*)

In Westphalia (WOLF, *Beiträge*, Vol. II, p. 301 ; WUTTKE, p. 88) and in Bohemia (GROHMANN), fruits and bread are thrown into the water as a peace-offering to the Nixies.

On Christmas Eve, South Slavonian and Bulgarian peasants swing an axe threateningly against a barren fruit tree. This is done thrice, and then another man intercedes. After that the frightened tree will certainly bear fruit next year. (KRAUSS, *V.R.B.S.*, p. 34.)

The Malays have a similar mode of horticulture. (SKEAT, *M.M.*, 198 seq.)   cf. *Jal Pari, Tree, Stone.*

Fukurukuju : Jap. Myth. A god of luck ; he is represented as possessing an extraordinarily long head and accompanied by a crane, a deer, and a tortoise.

Full Moon : Cabbages must not be planted at the time of the full moon ; if done, the seeds will come up on the top the next morning ; the moon draws them up ! (STRACKERJAN, Vol. I, p. 49.)   Vide *Moon.*

Furies : English name for the Erinyes.

Fye-token : It is the name given for a " waff " in Scotland.

Fylfot : Same as Swastika.

Fylgja : Norse Myth. Tutelary spirits which attended a person either as his soul or as guardian spirits.

G

Gæa : Gr. Myth. The earth as a goddess, the eldest born of Chaos.

Gal-alim : Babyl. Myth. A deity of a local character.

Galatea : Sicilian Myth. A sea-nymph beloved by Polypheme, a Cyclops. She herself had a heartache for Acis. The jealous giant crushed his rival under a huge rock and Galatea, inconsolable at the loss of her lover, was changed into a fountain. The word " Galatea " is used poetically for any rustic maiden. (DR. BREWER, *R.H.*, p. 401 ; *Petit Larousse*, p. 1335.)

Gale : A gale is caused by the spirit of the winds rushing through the air.

A gale is foretold by many crows getting together in the early morning. (*Tibet.*—WADDELL, p. 136.)

Gallu : In Babylonian superstition this was a demon ; the word signifies " the great one."

Gammadion : Another name for the Swastika (q.v.).

H

Gandini : Hindu Myth. Daughter of Kāsi Raja ; she had been twelve years in her mother's womb, when her father desired her to come forth. The child advised her father to present to the Brahmans a cow every day for three years and at the end of that time she would be born. This was done and the child on being born, received the name of Gandini, " cow daily." (DOWSON, *H.C.D.*, p. 106.)

Gandreid : " Spirit's ride " ; the Norse name for the " Wild Hunt " (q.v.).

Ganesha : Hind. Myth. The god of wisdom and prudence ; the remover of obstacles. He is the son of Siva and Parvati ; he is represented as a short, fat, yellow man with a large belly and with the head of an elephant. Generally, he is sitting cross-legged.

Ganymede : Gr. Myth. A beautiful shepherd boy of Phrygia, who was carried up to Olympus by Zeus, and made cup-bearer of the gods.

Garden : If you dream of a garden, and the trees are bare, your friends will become poor, or you will lose their friendship ; but if the trees are in blossom, you will have prosperity.

Gardsvor : " House-guardian " ; they are the household-spirits of the Scandinavians. cf. *Brownie, Nisse, Domovoy*.

Garlic : In Serbia rubbing the breast with garlic is a protection against a spirit that flies about at night.

The presence of Māmdos and other evil spirits is easily detected by the smell of garlic. (*India.*)

Danish mothers used garlic to keep evil away from children. (BRAND, *Observations*, p. 335.)

Garlic was an old English cure for a fiend-struck patient. (CHAMBERS, *Book of Days*, vol. i, p. 720.)

In India (CROOKE, *P.R.I.*, Vol. II, p. 35 ; *Ethnologie du Bengale*, pp. 118, 85 n. 3 ; cf. JOLLY, *Recht und Sitte*, pp. 157 seq. ; DURKHEIM, *La Prohibition de l'inceste, Année Sociologique*, Vol. I, 1896-1897, pp. 44 seq.), and in Macedonia (ABBOTT, p. 141), garlic is said to scare away demons.

Garm : Norse Myth. Hell's watch-dog, a monster who at Ragnarok breaks loose from his chains, bays terribly and slays and is slain by Tyr. cf. *Cerberus*.

Garnet : The garnet is an emblem of constancy and is, like the jacinth, dedicated to January.
This was the carbuncle of the ancients, which, they said, gave out light.

Garter : The exchange of a yellow garter means a proposal in six months. (*Washington, D.C.*—BERGEN, *C.S.*, p. 65.)
If a bride loses a garter, it is a sign that the marriage will be broken off. (STRACKERJAN, Vol. I, p. 35.) cf. *Veil*.

Garuḍa : (pron. Garur). The Garuḍa of Buddhist mythology is a mysterious being whose form is like that of a bird of prey, not unlike an eagle or vulture. Vide *Tengu*.

Gates of Gundoforus : No one carrying poison could pass through these gates. They were made of the horn of the horned snake by the Apostle Thomas. He built a palace of sethym wood for the Indian prince Gundoforus, and set up these gates. Vide *Horn, Nurjehan's Bracelet, Unicorn, Peacock, Rhinoceros, Venetian Glass*.

Gauri : Hindu Myth. Devi (q.v.) considered as a beneficent deity.

Gautami : Hind. Myth. An epithet of Durgā. (ii) Name of a fierce Rākshasi or female demon.

Gefjon : Norse Myth. A minor goddess resembling Freya. She shares Odin's knowledge of world's fates and to her come those who die as maids.

Geomancy : Divinations by means of points made in sand, or by means of pebbles or grains of sand placed on a piece of paper.

Germane, St. : The patron saint for children. Vide *Child*.

Gerstenalte : " Barley-gaffer " ; a Teutonic field-spirit of the human type.

Gerth : Teut. Myth. A giantess, wife of Frey.

Gertrude, St. : Vide *Mouse, Rat, Vermin*.

Geryon : Gr. Myth. A giant with three heads, who was killed by Hercules.

Getting out of Bed : You should not get out of bed with the left foot first ; if you do so, you will have ill luck the whole day. (*Silesia, Hesse, Saxony.*—WUTTKE, p. 131 ; *Oldenburg.*—STRACKERJAN, Vol. I, p. 35 ; *India, Great Britain, Bohemia, Persia, Turkey, etc.*)

Ghaddār : (Ar.). An evil spirit of Arabic superstition ; it is said to be an offspring of Iblis and is described as found in the borders of El-Yemen. It entices men and either tortures them or merely terrifies and then leaves them. (LANE, *A.S.M.A.*, p. 44.)

Gharrar : Another spelling for Ghaddār.

Ghost : The soul of a deceased person spoken of as appearing in a visible form or otherwise manifesting its presence to the living.

"*Ghost* : I am thy father's spirit ;
Doomed for a certain term to walk the night,
And for the day confined to fast in fires,
Till the foul crimes done in my days of nature
Are burnt and purg'd away. . . ."
SHAKESPEARE, *Hamlet*, i. v. 15.

To dream of a ghost tells you that persons you fancy to be your enemies are perhaps your best friends.

Ghoul : (Ar.). The Arabs regard it as a kind of Shaitān, that eat men and are capable of assuming various forms ; they haunt burial grounds and other sequestered spots and feed upon dead bodies. They are supposed to be the offsprings of Iblis. (LANE, *A.S.M.A.*, p. 43.)

In all Mohammedan countries they are supposed to rob graves and prey on human corpses ; they also kidnap children and devour them. (See the story given in *Grande Dictionnaire de la langue française*.)

"It sucks with the vampire, gorges with the ghoule."
—LOWELL, *Among my Books*.

Sergeant Bertrand who dug up dead bodies from the Cimetière du Père Lachaise and other cemeteries in and around Paris, and whose case created a great sensation in 1848, has been considered by Mr. Elliot O'Donnell (*Werewolves*) to have been possessed by a ghoul ; in the opinion of Dr. R. von Krafft-Ebing (*Psychopathia Sexualis.* Eng. tr. p. 70), it was a clear case of sadism. cf. TARDIEU, *Attentats aux mœurs*, 1878, p. 114; LEGRAND, *La folie devant les tribuns*, p. 514 ; PLOSS, *Das Weib*, Vol. II, p. 591.) Vide *Ankle-bone, Iron, Tooth*.

Ghritāchi : Hind. Myth. The name of an Apsaras or celestial nymph.

Giant : Gr. Myth. The offspring of Uranus and Gæa (Heaven and Earth), who rebelled against the gods.

A mythical manlike or monstrous being of a huge stature and of more than mortal but less than godlike power and strength. They appear very frequently in mediæval romances and nursery tales, as also in traditions and romantic fiction.

Giantess : The female counterpart of a giant.

Giavanel : Another name for the Dusou (q.v.)

Gift : Sharp instruments should not be given as gifts, they cut friendship ; neither pointed instruments. Vide *Scissors, Shoes.*

Gigantomachy : " The war of the giants."

Gigelorum : In Celtic superstition this is the smallest animal in the world. All that is known about it is, that it makes its nest in the mite's ear. (CAMPBELL, *Sup. Scot. Highl.,* p. 220.)

Gildas, St. : Guardian saint of idiots.

Gilgamesh : Babyl. Myth. A legendary king, hero of an epic bearing his name. With Eabani, his comrade, who dies, he is afflicted with foul diseases. Ut-napishtim (q.v.) cures him and directs him to the plant of immortality. Nergal grants him an interview with the ghost of Eabani who describes the sad lot of the dead in the underworld.

Gin-sai : A fabulous bird " capable of diffusing so venomous an influence that even its shadow poisons food." (GRIFFIS, *Corea,* p. 306.) cf. *Basilisk, Dragon, Bazaliček.*

Gipsy : Gipsies can cure various diseases and tell fortunes. (*Great Britain.*)
Gipsies can protect houses from burning. (WOLF, *Beiträge,* Vol. II, p. 376; SCHÖNEWERTH, Vol. II, p. 83; WUTTKE, p. 140.)

Girdle : If a girdle be accidentally loosed on a woman, it is construed into an omen of an easy delivery. (*Macedonia.*— ABBOTT, p. 99.) Vide *Stocking.*

Girru : Babyl. Myth. A deity symbolizing the element of fire.

Gjallhorn : Norse Myth. The horn belonging to Heimdall, warder of Asgard.

Gladsheim : Norse Myth. The abode of Odin in Asgard.

Glaisein : The Glaisein of the Isle of Man was a kind of brownie and was " very strong, he frequented farms, threshed corn and went to the sheep-folds." (CAMPBELL, *West Highland Tales,* Introd. liii.)

Glaisrig : Manx Folklore. A female fairy or goblin, half-human, half-beast.

Glaistig : Manx Folklore. A kind of she-goblin which takes the form of a goat.

The Glaistig of the Highlands of Scotland was " a tutelary being in the shape of a thin grey little woman, with long yellow hair reaching to her heels, dressed in green, haunting certain sites and farms, and watching in some cases over the house, in others over the cattle." (CAMPBELL, *Sup. Scot. Highl.*, p. 155.)

Glashan : In West Highland superstition it was a hirsute spirit that rebelled against clothing. cf. *Gruagach.*

Glass : You are sure to invite a quarrel if you look through a piece of broken glass. (*Great Britain.*)

A glass full of water which must not be drunk, protects the house from robbery and theft. (*Bohemia, Parts of Germany.*)

Glaucus : Gr. Myth. (i) A Boëtian fisherman who was later made a god of the waters.

(ii) Son of Sisyphus and father of Bellerophon. He was devoured (torn to pieces ?) by horses for having spoken derogatorily of Venus.

Gloso : " Glow sow "; a field spirit of Swedish folklore.

Glove : It is unlucky to lose a glove. (*Bathurst, N.B.*)

Glutton : If you cannot make your thumb and finger meet round your wrist, you are a glutton. (*Prov. of Quebec.*— BERGEN, *C.S.*, p. 35.) Vide *Mole.*

gNan : They are malignant Tibetan spirits who are believed to cause pestilential diseases ; they infest certain trees, rocks, and springs.

Gnat : When gnats fly low, it indicates rain at hand. When they fly high and are at all abundant, fine weather may be expected. (*Great Britain.*)

Gnome : A species of supernatural deformed dwarfs who, according to the Jewish cabbalists, inhabit the centre of the earth. They are supposed to be guardians of hidden treasures.

Goat : He-goats are the favourite mounts of witches. (GRIMM, *D.M.*, p. 1049 ; KÜHN UND SCHWARZ, 18, 232, 470 ; LEUBUSCHER, *Die Wahrwölfe* ; STRACKERJAN, Vol. II, p. 87.)

Witches and demons sometimes assume the form of he-goats. (ENNEMOSER, *Hist. Mag.*, Vol. II, p. 148.)

The Garos of Assam offer a black goat on the top of a mountain in times of drought. (DALTON, *Descriptive Ethnology*, p. 88).

Gobelinus : According to Ordericus Vitalis (12th century), it is the popular name of a spirit which haunted the neighbourhood of Evreaux.

Goblin : A kind of mischievous spirit of a grotesque shape. " Bhutas are evil spirits of the lowest order, corresponding to our ghosts and other goblins of the nursery." ELPHINSTONE, *Hist. of India* (1841).

God : The Jews and the Mohammedans do not call God by name, lest they commit the crime of blasphemy. " Thou shalt not take the name of the Lord, thy God in vain." *The Ten Commandments* (Exodus xx, 7). cf. *Qor'an, Shedim.*

God, Blind : A common epithet of Cupid, god of love.

God of Luck : Jap. Myth. There are in all seven gods of luck. They are : Fukurokuju, Daikoku, Hotei, Bishamon, Benten, Ebisu and Jurojin. (CHAMBERLAIN, p. 235 ; cf. ANDERSON'S *Catalogue of Japanese and Chinese Paintings in the British Museum*, pp. 27-46.)

God-father : A man must not be god-father to a baby girl, lest she die a spinster. (*Wetterau, Westphalia.*—WUTTKE, p. 199.)

God-mother : Pregnant women must not become god-mothers to other children ; if they do so, either their own or the god-children will die. (*Pomerania, Silesia.*—WUTTKE, p. 193.)

God-parents : God-parents whose god-children have died must not be god-parents again, lest the others die too. (*Wetterau, Westphalia.*—WUTTKE, p. 199.)

Gog : Gog and Magog were the popular names of two enormous wooden statues erected in 1708 in the Guildhall, London.

Goitre : Vide *Stones, Tattooing.*

Gold : To dream of gold denotes success and money.

Golden Age : A fabled primeval period of perfect human happiness and innocence, in which the earth yielded her fruits without toil and all creatures lived in peace.

Gold Fish : They were formerly supposed to live on gold. (CONWAY, *Demonology*, Vol. I, p. 228.)

Golden Fleece : The fleece of gold taken from the ram on which Phryxus was carried through the air to Colchis, and in quest of which the Argonauts sailed under Jason.

Golem : Everything that is in a state of incompletion, or everything not fully formed. Originally it meant " embryo."

Goll : Gaelic legend. The leader of a band which Finn out-witted.

Good Friday : Bathing on this day in the river is especially beneficent for the itch. (PANZER, *Beitr. zur deut. Myth.*, I, 258.)

One should not go into the garden on a Good Friday; caterpillars will be numerous if this be done. (WUTTKE, p. 18.)

Goose : A goose is the silliest animal on earth, hence the expression " a silly goose."

If the breast-bones of a roasted goose are white or bluish, it is a sign of a severe winter ; if brown, of a mild one. (STRACKERJAN, Vol. I, p. 25 ; HAZLITT, p. 284 ; Atkinson, *Cleveland Glossary.*)

Geese give warning of death by flying round a house. (OWEN, pp. 304, 205.) Vide *Barnacle, Holly, St. Matthew's Day.*

Gopis : Hind. Myth. The cowherd damsels and wives with whom Krishna (q.v.) sported in his youth. (DOWSON, *H.C.D.*, p. 113.)

Gorgon : Gr. Myth. They were monsters with snakes for hair ; their look was so terrible that it turned anyone into stone. They were three in number and were called : *Medusa, Euryale and Stheno* ; of these Medusa alone was mortal.

In modern Greek folklore a gorgon is represented as half woman, half fish. Their favourite resort, especially on Saturday nights, is reputed to be the Black Sea. (LAWSON, p. 185.)

Gorska makva : In Bulgarian superstition she is a hag who torments children by night. She is a frightful wood-spirit with the head like that of an ox, and is the exact counterpart of the Russian Kriksy.

Gout : Walking in the fields on a Friday morning before sunrise cures gout. (LEAN, Vol. II, p. 497.)

St. Wolfgang relieves people suffering from this disease.

Go-Vardhana : Hind. Myth. A mountain in Vrindāvana, which Krishna induced the cowherds and cowherdesses to worship instead of Indra. This enraged the god, who sent a deluge of rain to wash away the mountain and all the people of the country ; but Krishna held up the mountain with his little finger for seven days to shelter the people of Vrindāvana. Indra retired baffled and afterwards did homage to Krishna. (DOWSON, *H.C.D.*, p. 114.)

Graaf : A German count who, in order to enrich himself, bought up all the corn. One year a sad famine prevailed, and the count expected to reap a rich harvest by his speculation, but an army of rats pressed by hunger, invaded his barns, and swarming into his Rhine castle, fell on the old baron, worried him to death, and then devoured him. cf. *Freiherr von Güttingen, Hatto, Widerolf, Adolf.*

Graces : Class. Myth. Graceful and beautiful maidens, sister goddesses, represented as intimate with the Muses. They were three in number : *Aglaia* (Brilliance), *Euphrosyne* (Joy) and *Thalia* (Bloom) ; they were regarded as inspirers of the qualities which give charm to nature—love, wisdom, etc.

Grææ : Gr. Myth. Watchers for the Gorgons, daughters of a sea-deity. They were born with grey hair and had but one eye and one tooth between them. They were three in number and called ; *Deino, Enyo* and *Pephredo.*

Graha : The power that seizes and obscures the sun and moon, causing eclipses. Vide *Rāhu, Ketu, Maboya, Aracho.*

(ii) Evil spirits with which people, especially children, are possessed and which cause sickness and death. They are supposed to be amenable to medicine and exorcism. (DOWSON, *H.C.D.*, p. 114.)

Grāma-devatā : " Gods of the village " ; in North India they are generally non-human spirits.

Grand Veneur : At certain times of the year, a spectral huntsman, accompanied by his full ghostly pack of hounds, is said to hunt in the forest of Fontainebleu. He is the Wild Huntsman (q.v.) of France. cf. *Herne the Hunter, Wodan.*

Grape : It is a good omen to dream of eating grapes ; you will have profits.

Grass : If a dog eats grass, it is a sign of an approaching rain. (STRACKERJAN, Vol. I, p. 24). Cats chewing grass prognosticate the same.

On Christmas Eve, thrash the garden with a flail, with only your shirt on, and the grass will grow well next year (RAGNER).

Grass Demon : The name of a Teutonic field-spirit who lives in the meadows.

Grave : To dream of an open grave denotes sickness and disappointment.

Great Bear : Callisto (q.v.) after her death, became the constellation Great Bear.

Great Mother : The nature goddess of Anatolia whose chief name is Cybele.

Green : This is an unlucky colour and should therefore be avoided as much as possible. (*Great Britain.*)
"Brides in green
Keep sorrow unseen."
(*Great Britain.*)

Grey : This colour like black, is unlucky ; it denotes death and guilt.

Grigri : Another name for Juju.

Grim : Norwegian Superstition. A spirit of the waterfalls. In a story, a mysterious water-fairy, a musical genius, who plays to everyone and requires a white kid every Thursday. (THORPE, *N.M.*, Vol. II, p. 23.)

Gripes : St. Erasmus cures gripes.

Groats : In German folklore they are the hidden enchanted treasures of the dwarfs. (STRACKERJAN, Vol. II, p. 79.)

Grotto of Ephesus : Near Ephesus was a grotto containing a statue of Diana, attached to a reed, presented by Pan. If a young woman charged with dishonour, entered this grotto and the reeds gave forth musical sounds, she was declared to be a pure virgin ; if, on the other hand, it gave forth hideous noises, she was denounced and never seen more. (LORD LYTTON : *Tales of Miletus*, III.)
Vide *Florimel's Girdle, Mantle, Candle Glowing, etc.*

Gruagach : A spirit of Skipness who, like Glashan, rebelled against clothes.

Grumisel-rou : A kind of Swiss spirit, which appears in the form of a red ball of fire. (JALLA, *Lég. Vaud.*, p. 27.)

Guan Di : The Chinese god of war. His name is supposed to be a charm against a multitude of evils.

Guan Yin : Buddhist Folklore. A being who helps in time of need. She is the goddess of charity and pity ; she is represented as dressed in white and riding an elephant. (*Chin. Volksmärchen,* p. 202.)
Vide *Pu Hiän, Wen Ju.*

Gudrun : Volsunga Saga. A sister of Gunnar ; she wins Sigurd by the help of a magic draught and, after his death, marries Atli.

Gula : Babyl. Myth. The consort of Ninib.

Gun : Guns should neither be carried nor placed on the head ; this prevents a child from growing taller. (*Japan.*— GRIFFIS, *M.E.*, p. 470.)

Gundoforus : Vide *Gates of Gundoforus.*

Gunnar : Volsunga Saga.   Brother of Gudrun, husband of Brynhild.

Gunther : Nibelungenlied.   King of Burgundy, whose sister Kriemhild (q.v.) is married to Siegfried. After the murder of Siegfried, Gunther and his knights are treacherously slaughtered at the instigation of his widow, Kriemhild.

Gutrune : In the " Ring of the Nibelungen " she is Gunther's sister who became wife of Siegfried.

Gutta Percha : If you wear gutta percha soles to your boots or shoes you will have diseases of the eye and impaired sight. (LEAN, Vol. II, p. 165.)

Gwrach y Rhibyn : Welsh Folklore.   A spirit which gives warning of an approaching death. (RHYS, *C.F.*, p. 953.) cf. *Banshee, Smrtnice, Božaloshtsh, Death Warnings.*

Gwydion : Celt. Myth. A Cymric deity, husband of Arianrod, famous as a magician. He is a friend of mankind, a giver of arts and civilization, and is against the underworld powers.

Gwyn : Celt. Myth. A Cymric underworld deity, who conducts the souls of the dead to Annwn. In later Welsh legends, he is a king of the fairies.

Gwragedd Annwn : These are Welsh fairies of lakes and streams, and are neither mermaids nor sea-maidens. They are said to be descendants of villagers condemned to sink below the waters for reviling St. Patrick on one of his visits (SIKES, *Brit. Gob.*, p. 35).

They may be brought up by mortals by dropping bread and cheese in the water.   (ib., p. 41 ; BASSETT, p. 151.)

H

Habergeis : In Tyrol it is a malicious bird which is one of the Devil's tools. Its cry denotes death, and anyone imitating it would at once be torn to pieces. (ALPENBURG, *Mythen*, p. 385 ; ZINGERLE, *Sitten*, p. 42.)

Habsburg : The Habsburg family of Austria is said to have an ancestress who gives warning of an approaching death or deaths. By some authors she has been confused with the White Lady of the Hohenzollerns. cf. *Mélusine, White Lady.*

Hackelberg, Hackelberend : The Wild Huntsman of Germany is usually known by this name.

Hacketaler : This is the German equivalent of the Luck Penny. (On the method of obtaining one of these, see WUTTKE, *Der deutsche Volksaberglaube der Gegenwart,* p. 177.)

Haddock : The black spots on each side of a haddock near the gills, are the impression of St. Peter's finger and thumb, when he took the tribute money from the fish's mouth, or of Christ when he held the fish, at the time he fed the " multitude." (*Great Britain.* cf. *St. Matthew,* xiv, 16-21). A haddock's bones should not be burnt in Scotland. A haddock once said :

> " Roast me and boil me,
> But dinnah burn my behns.
> Or then I'll be a stranger
> Aboot yi'r hearth-stanes."
> (BRAND, *Observations,* Vol. III, p. 262 ;
> BASSETT, p. 260.)

Hades : Rom. Myth. The god of the lower worlds corresponding to Pluto of the Greeks.

Hæmorrhage : Topaz is favourable for hæmorrhages.

Hafaza : (Ar.) Moham. Myth. Certain angels who protect men from the jinni and the shaiṭāns. They are four in number, two of whom are on duty at daytime, and two at night. The hafaza write down the actions of man and keep an account of his good as well as of his bad deeds.

Haferbock : " Oat-goat " ; a field-spirit of German folklore.

Hagen : Nibelungenlied. A fierce knight in the court of King Gunther, who treacherously slays Siegfried (q.v.) and is himself slain by Kriemhild (q.v.), his widow.

Haimāvati : Hind. Myth. "Daughter of the Himalaya Mountains " ; one of the various epithets of Devi.

Hair : If a dog bites you, any evil consequences may be averted by applying three of the dog's hairs to the wound. (*Great Britain.*)

Hair should under no circumstances be thrown away, as other people finding it may perform many magical operations harmful to the owner. (*Great Britain, France, Germany, India, etc.*) In India, however, women may throw their hair away, provided they tie it to something. (DAY, *Folktales of Bengal*, p. 87.); or in Europe, spitting on cut hair before throwing it away will be sufficient to prevent it being used by witches. (ZINGERLE, *Sitten*, etc., Nos. 176, 580 ; *Mélusine*, 1878, c. 79 ; FRAZER, *G.B.*, Vol. I, p. 204 ; ELWORTHY, *E.E.*, p. 416.)

Men's hair turns grey upon a sudden and violent fright. " Thy father's beard is turned white with the news."
—SHAKESPEARE.

Hair is considered to be the seat of strength. (FRAZER, *The Magic Art*, Vol. I, pp. 102, 344 ; cf. the story of Samson.)

The Muslim exorcists of India tie a knot in the hair to prevent certain devils from escaping. (CROOKE, *Islam in India*, p. 237.)

The women of Leon believe that selling hair is equivalent to selling their souls. (LE BRAZ, Vol. I, p. 367.)

In Wales hair, after it has been cut, is carefully collected and hidden away, for to burn it would be injurious to the health. (RHYS, *C.F.*, p. 599.)

" A hairy man's a geary man, but a hairy wife's a witch." (LEAN, Vol. II, p. 39.)

If a Japanese should set his hair on fire, it is a sign that he will go mad. (GRIFFIS, *M.E.*, p. 468.)

A girl whose lover comes seldom to her, can remedy this by tearing out one of his hairs without his knowledge.

Hair should not be combed with a comb which has been used for a dead person ; if this be done, the person using it will die a speedy death. (*East Prussia.*—WUTTKE, p. 214.)

If a child's hair be cut before its seventh year, he will have no courage. (WOLF, *Beiträge*, Vol. I, p. 209.)

If you dream you are combing your hair, and it is long and fine, you will have many joys of short duration.

" Comb your hair after dark,
Comb sorrow to your heart."
—*Great Britain, India.*

Vide *Arm, Love, Pulling Hair, Nest, Age, Friday.*

Hair Cutting : A boy's hair must not be cut till he is seven years old ; this would prevent him getting strong. (*Wetterau, Westphalia.* WUTTKE, p. 202.)

If a child's hair be cut, an elf lock will grow. (*Jew. Enc.*, Vol. IV, p. 31 ; Vol. IX, p. 601.)

Hairpin : Hairpins dropping out of the head indicate that someone is thinking of you (*Great Britain*), or that you will lose a lover. (*Germany*.) cf. *Shoelace*.

Hairy Body : If a person's body is very hairy, it indicates that he will be lucky. (*Jew. Enc.*, Vol. VI, p. 158.)

If a man's chest be devoid of hair, it is a sure sign that he is, or will be, a thief. (*Bengal.*)

If a woman's body be hairy, she will either be unfaithful to her husband or be a widow. (*Northern India*.)

Haizum : Moham. Myth. The horse which Gabriel rode when he led a squadron of three thousand angels against the Koreishites in the famous battle of Bedr.

Hakenmann : Teut. Folklore. " Hook-man " ; a male nix who was armed with a hook, so that he might drag his victims down into the water.

Ham : Throwing ham, lard and other eatables in the fire is considered to be a protection against the house burning. (WUTTKE, p. 87.) This is done probably, to appease the spirits of the fire.

Hamadryad : Certain kinds of nymphs living in trees and mentioned in classical mythology.

Hand : On the night of Hosha'na Rabbah, anyone who tries to read his future from his shadow and does not see the shadow of the right hand, will lose a son during the year ; if he fails to see the left hand, he will lose a daughter ; if a finger, he will lose a friend. (*Jew. Enc.*, Vol. VI, p. 212, quoting BUXTORF.)

If a person has cold hands during your marriage, it is a sign that you will die soon. (*East Friesland.*—WUTTKE, p. 41.)

Cold hands at the beginning of a journey is an indication that the person will never return. (*Thuringia.*—ib.)

" Cold hands and a warm heart." (*Great Britain.* cf. *Kalte Hände, warmes Herz*).

Bhûts enter a person's body by means of the hands ; hence much is made of ablution. (*India.* CROOKE, Vol. I, p. 241.)

The dried up hand of an executed criminal is a powerful charm. (*India*, CROOKE, *P.R.I.*, Vol. II, p. 245.)

The hand of a dead man is used to stir the milk when butter will not form. (BRAND, *Observations*, p. 732 ; *N.I.N.Q.*, II, 215 ; LADY WILDE, *Legends*, 81 seq., 172.)

The Cornish miners sometimes see a dead hand holding a light. This is a sure indication of ill-luck. (LE BRAZ, Vol. I, p. 35, quoting *Revue des traditions populaires,* Vol. II, p. 474.)

On telling fortunes by the hand, see MRS. JOHN WHITE : *Shall I tell you your Fortune, my pretty Maid ?*

Hand of Gadkhāli : In popular Indian superstition this is the name by which a certain authentic(!) ghost of Gadkhāli, a village in Bengal, which was devastated by a cholera epidemic, is designated. The existence of this particular ghost is unquestionably recognized by the Bengal peasantry.

Han Siang Dsi : Chin. Myth. The seventh of the Immortals (q.v.).

Hantu : Among the Malays the demons or evil spirits are called by this name ; they are supposed to cause various diseases. (SKEAT, *Malay Magic* ; TYLOR, *P.C.*, Vol. II, p. 115. cf. the Ruaḥs of Jewish superstition.) Thus :

Hantu Kalumbahan : causes small-pox.

Hantu Kamong : brings on inflammation of the hands and feet.

Hantu Pari : sucks the blood of the wounded and thus causes blood to flow. Vide *Vampire.*
(For other kinds of Hantus, See SKEAT, *Malay Magic.*)

Hanumān : "Monkey God " ; in N. India he is installed at the foundation of every settlement.
In Hindu mythology he is the son of the wind and a monkey-nymph. He was the ally of Rāma (q.v.) in his war against Rāvana, the demon king of Lankā (*Ceylon*). He is represented as huge in stature, golden in colour with a ruby face, and is the hero of numerous exploits.

Hanging : The personal belongings or the dismembered parts of the body of a hanged person bring luck. (WUTTKE, p. 104 ; cf. GRIFFITH, *Chronicles of Newgate* ; LEAN Vol. II, p. 483.) Vide *Hand.*

Hapi : Egypt. Myth. The dog-headed genius of Amenti. He was associated with the South.

Hara-kiri : "Suicide by means of opening the belly " of the Japanese is probably a remnant of the belief that a dead man requires attendants in the spirit world to administer to his needs. Vide *Horse, Camel, Burial, Sati.*

Hare : In Great Britain, India, Germany (WUTTKE, p. 32) and in the Slavic countries it is a bad omen if a hare runs across one's path. (ELWORTHY, *E.E.*, p. 31 ; ABBOTT, p. 106. cf. F.L.J., 1883, p. 355 ; *Ethnologie du Bengale*, p. 108.)

Among the Kirghiz (SCHUYLER, Vol. II, p. 29), and in Alsace (LAMBS, p. 30), if a hare runs across a man's path while he is on a journey, it forbodes ill luck and he usually turns back.

It was believed at one time that hares changed their sex every year.

In Chinese superstition the hare conceives by gazing at the moon ; the female of the hare produces her young from the mouth. Like the fox, the hare attains the age of one thousand years, and becomes white when half that period is completed. (MAYER, *Chin. Read. Man.*, p. 233.)

Hare's fat cures bad fingers. (*Alsace.*—LAMBS, p. 30.)

In Cornwall, when a girl has loved not wisely but too well, she haunts her deceiver in the shape of a white hare. (HUNT, *Pop. Rom.*, p. 377.)

Hare is considered unlucky by sailors. (BASSETT, p. 279.)

The Albanians refuse to touch hare when it is killed. (ABBOTT, p. 106.)

The Roman augurs considered it an ill omen if a hare crossed their way ; they suspected they would be robbed or come to some mischance. Vide *Red Hare*, *Fisherman*.

Harmonia : Greek Legend. Wife of Cadmus. She was the proud possessor of a garment and a necklace which had the property of stirring up strife and causing bloodshed, and bringing evil to every possessor.

Harp : Vide *Teirtus's Harp*.

Harpocratos : Gr. Myth. A god of silence.

Harpy : " Snatcher " ; in Classical mythology they were fabulous monsters, rapacious and filthy, having the body and face of a woman and bird's wings and claws ; they were supposed to act as ministers of divine vengeance. They were malignant creatures ; they snatched up and carried off the souls of the dead, and executed vengeance by seizing or defiling the food of their victims. They were three in number and were called : *Aello, Ocypete* and *Celaeno* or *Podarge*.

Harut : In Mohammedan superstition it is an angel in Babel and is the Aramaic personification of mischief. (*Dic. Rel. Eth.*, Vol. VIII, p. 352.)

Hat : If a lady dons a gentleman's hat, it is a sign that she wants to be kissed. (*U.S.A.*—BERGEN, *C.S.*, p. 63.)

The Devil is said to wear a three-cornered hat. (STRACKERJAN, Vol. II, p. 138.)

If you dream you are wearing a torn and dirty hat, you will have damage and dishonour, but if you have one that pleases you, joy, profit, and success.

Hatchet : A hatchet is a protection against the machinations of witches. (STRACKERJAN, Vol. I, p. 354 ; Vol. II, p. 144.) This is probably because it is made of iron (q.v.)

Hate : You will be in need if you dream you hate any one.

Hathor : Egypt. Myth.: the goddess of mirth, love and social joy. The cow was sacred to her ; she is often represented with a cow's head and ears.

(ii) One of the seven genii or fairies who made their appearance at the birth of a child and foretold its fortune. cf. *Bidhātāpurusha, Fate, Parca, Norn, Sudičky*.

Hatif : (Ar.). In Arab superstition it is a spirit that is heard but not seen. It is generally the communicator of some intelligence in the way of advice, or direction, or warning. (LANE, *A.S.M.A.*, p. 46.)

Hatto : Archbishop of Metz. He was devoured by mice in the mouse-tower situated in a little green island in the midst of the Rhine, near the town of Bingen. cf *Freiherr von Güttingen, Graaf, Widerolf, Adolf*.

Haunting : Vide *Flower, Miser, Usurer*.

Havfrue : It is the Danish equivalent of a Nixie.

Havmand : It is the Danish name for a water-spirit and is the male counterpart of a Havfrue. (THIELE, *Danmarks Folkesagn*.)

Hay : It is lucky to see a load of hay coming towards you (*Great Britain, Germany, France, Spain, Bohemia, India*). Vide *Knife*.

Head : A great head is a sign of foolishness. (HAZLITT, p. 308.) The head is sacred among most peoples. (FRAZER, *G.B.*, Vol. I, p. 362 seq.)

Headache : The tooth of a corpse cures headaches. (*Hannover.* —WUTTKE, p. 102.)

A snake's skin worn round the head cures headaches. (*N. Lincolnshire.*)

Headaches may be cured by tying round the head a piece of cloth in which a corpse has been wrapped. (LADY WILDE, p. 82.)
Vide *Nest.*

Head-hunting : The Dyaks of Borneo thought that the spirit of the owner of every human head they could procure, would serve them in the next world.

Headless Spectres : In the folklore of various people phantoms apparently of murdered people, are met with, whose heads are wanting ; or at times they carry their heads in their hands or under their arms. Ghosts of animals are occasionally without a head.

These spectres are said to appear mostly in Tyrol. (See ALPENBURG, *Mythen und Sagen Tirols.*) cf. *Blemmyœ, A-Siras, Acephali.*

Health : Health can be obtained by drinking the blood of a stork.

It is unlucky to say you are very well. (RHYS, *C.F.,* p. 346.) Vide *Turquoise.*

Hearse : It is lucky to see an empty hearse coming towards you, but unlucky if you turn round to look at it. (*Great Britain.*)

Heart : The heart of an unborn child, if carried on the person, is sure to bring about a complete success in the thieving profession. (*Silesia.*—TETTAU UND TEMME, *Volkssagen Ostpreussens,* p. 266.)

If a person eats the heart of a bear, he will become a tyrant. (*Jews of Minsk.*)

Hearth : Ghosts frequently come to the family hearth, hence need of cleanliness there. (CROOKE, *P.R.I.,* Vol. I, p. 292.)

Heaven : In popular belief it is a place where there is no sorrow, and everything is happy and peaceful. The good and the upright go to heaven.

Hebe : Gr. Myth. The goddess of youth, daughter of Zeus and Hera ; she was cup-bearer of the gods before Ganymede. She was believed to have the power of restoring youth and beauty.

Hebigami : Jap. Myth. The serpent-god possession in Ino, Japan.

Hecate : Gr. Myth. Identified in later times with Persephone, the goddess of the infernal regions ; she was regarded as presiding over witchcraft and magical rites. She was a goddess combining the characters of moon-goddess, earth-goddess and underworld-goddess.

" Now witchcraft celebrates
Pale Hecate's warnings." SHAKESPEARE, *Macbeth*, ii, I.

Hecuba : Greek Legend. She was metamorphosed into a dog, and wandered howling through the country, stoned by its inhabitants.

Hedgehog : Hedgehogs foresee a coming storm.

They fasten themselves on the dugs of cows and drain off the milk. (*Great Britain, India.*) In Madagascar hedgehogs are not eaten for fear of becoming timid. (FRAZER, *Magic Art*, vol. i, p. 117).

Heimdal : Teut. Myth. The warder of Asgard, who dwells at the upper end of Bifrost. He can see a hundred leagues by day or by night, can hear the grass or the sheep's wool grow, and needs less sleep than a bird. He summons the gods by blowing on the Gjallarhorn.

Heinzelmännchen : In German superstition they are elves who work for people at night.

Heitlik : In Vancouver Island it is a snake-like scaly being who darts lightning with his red tongue. If seen, a bit of his tail should be cut off and preserved as an amulet.

Hejkal : " Wild man " ; it is the Bohemian name for a Lyesovic.

Hekkenfeldt : In popular belief this, like Blocksberg, was the favourite meeting place of the Danish witches. (LEHMANN, *A.Z.*, p. 112.) cf. *Brocken, Blakula, Blocksberg*.

Hekla : Mt. Hekla, in Iceland, was another favourite resort of the Danish witches. (LEHMANN, *A.Z.*, p. 112.) cf. *Brocken, Blakula, Blocksberg*.

Hel, Hela : Norse Myth. Daughter of Loki, goddess of the dead and queen of the lower world. Her dwelling was under one of the roots of the sacred ash-tree Yggdrasil (q.v.)

(ii) The underworld itself was also called Hel, Niflhel.

Helenus : Greek Legend. A son of Priam and Hecuba ; he was gifted with prophetic powers.

Helicon : The fountain which Pegasus produced by striking with his hoofs, and whence poets were fabled to draw their inspirations.

Helios : Gr. Myth. The sun-god, represented as driving a four-horse chariot through the heavens.

Heliotrope : Clytie was changed into a heliotrope.

Hell : In popular belief it is a place for the wicked. It is represented as a place of eternal torture. Satan is the king of hell.

Hell-shoon : Vide *Helskô*.

Helsko : Norse Myth. The shoes or sandals that were bound upon the dead man's feet for his toilsome journey along Helvegr to the other world.

Helvegr : Norse Folklore. "Hell way." The long, dark way along which a dead man had to go before he reached the other world.

Hem : If the hem of a garment turns up at the back, the wearer is destined to get a new one soon. (*Memoirs of the American Folklore Society*, IV, p. 142 ; ABBOTT, p. 100.)

Hemann : It is a kind of mischievous forest-spirit of Teutonic and Slavic folklore.

Hen : A crowing hen is unlucky. (*N. Germany, Tyrol.*— WUTTKE, p. 33 ; *China.*—DOOLITTLE, Vol. II, p. 328 ; *Macedonia.*—ABBOTT, p. 106 ; *Bengal.*—*Ethnologie du Bengale*, p. 110.)

In Bodethal a black hen is thrown into the water as a peace-offering to the Nixies. (WUTTKE, p. 88, quoting K.S., p. 426.)
"A whistling woman and a crowing hen
Is neither good for God nor men."
Great Britain.
If a woman dreams of a hen, she will be married to a widower with many children. Vide *Fruit, Fowl*.

Hena : In Vancouver Island it is a class of supernatural beings who can fly very rapidly ; they make a loud whistling noise and are identified with quartz crystals.

Henta : It is a magical picture by a village artist ; it is drawn by order of the Nicobarese magician as a cure for diseases and, after recovery, as a potent charm against further attacks. (C. B. KLOSS.)

Hephæstus : Gr. Myth. A god of fire, especially of volcanic and natural fire, and of the arts, such as pottery-making and metal-working, dependent upon fire. He was identified by the Romans with Vulcan.

Hera : Gr. Myth. An Olympian goddess, queen of Heaven, sister and wife of Zeus, whose power she shared. She was the Juno of the Romans.

Herb : Herbs plucked on Ascension Day are especially good for medicinal purposes. (WUTTKE, p. 21.)

Hercules : Class. Myth. A hero, son of Zeus and Alcmene ; he is celebrated for his strength. Juno infuriated against him at his birth, sent two huge serpents to devour him ; the baby who was already strong, squeezed the serpents to death.

Hercules is noted for his twelve heroic deeds, viz., (i) he squeezed to death the lion of Nemea ; (ii) he destroyed the Hydra of Lernæ ; (iii) he captured alive the wild boar of Erymanthea ; (iv) he subjugated the deer with the metal feet ; (v) he shot with arrows the birds of Lake Stymphale ; (vi) he conquered the bull sent by Neptune against Minos of Crete ; (vii) he slew Diomede, king of Thracia, who fed his horses with human flesh ; (viii) he was victorious over the Amazons (q.v.) ; (ix) he cleansed the stables of Augeas by forcing the river Alphea to flow over them ; (x) he fought with and killed Geryon, whose troops he took ; (xi) he got the golden apples from the garden of the Hesperides and (xii) he delivered Theseus from the infernal regions.

Besides these, he accomplished a host of other heroic deeds. For example, he pressed to death the giant Anteus, son of the Earth, under his arms ; killed the brigand Cacus, delivered Hesione from the monster which was going to devour her, separated the mountains Calpe and Abyla, freed Prometheus chained on Mt. Caucasus, and lastly killed the Centaur, Nessus, who was going to ravish his wife Deianera. This last victory indirectly caused him to lose his life. Vide *Nessus, Deianera, Cacus, Hesione.*

Hermes : Gr. Relig. An Olympian god, son of Zeus and Maia. His chief character was that of a herald and messenger of the gods. Further, he was a god of science and invention, of eloquence, cunning, trickery and theft, of treasure-trove and luck, of youth and gymnastic exercises and he was a conductor of the dead to Hades.

Hermes Trismegistus : "The thrice great." This was the name given by the Greeks to the Egyptian god Thoth. (q.v)

Hermione : Gr. Myth. Daughter of Menelaus and Helen. She became the wife of Neoptolemus, and later of Orestes.

Hermotimos : In a story by Pliny, the prophetic soul of Hermotimos went out from time to time to visit distant regions. During one of these absences, his wife thinking him to be dead, burnt his lifeless body on a funeral pyre. When the poor soul came back, there was no longer a dwelling for it to animate.

Herne the Hunter : English Legend. An ancient keeper of Windsor Park, who is believed to walk in the forest at midnight around an old oak, which still bears his name. He is said to be a malevolent spirit. (HAZLITT, p. 314.)

> " Herne the hunter,
> Sometime a keeper here in Windsor Forest,
> Doth all the winter-time, at still midnight,
> Walk round about an oak, with great ragg'd horns ;
> And makes milch kine yield blood, and shakes a chain
> In a most hideous and dreadful manner."
> SHAKESPEARE, *Merry Wives of Windsor*, iv. 4.

cf. *Wild Huntsman, Grand Veneur, Wodan, Frau Holle.*

Herregudsbuk : " The Lord's goat " ; a Norwegian field-spirit.

Hershef : Egypt. Relig. The tutelary deity of Heracleopolis ; a local form of Osiris. Hershef was known to the Greeks under the name of Arsaphes.

Hesione : Gr. Myth. Daughter of Laomedon, king of Troy. She was offered to a sea-monster, but was rescued by Hercules.

Hesperides : Gr. Myth. Daughters of Atlas. They were three in number and were the possessors of a garden, the trees of which bore golden apples. This garden was guarded by a dragon with a hundred heads. Hercules killed this dragon and thus accomplished the eleventh of his twelve famous deeds.

Hestia : Gr. Myth. A divinity of the family hearth corresponding to the Roman Vesta.

Hexe : The witches are so called in Germany.

Hiccough : If one has the hiccough it is a sign that someone is thinking of him. (*Great Britain, Bohemia, India.*)
Hiccough can be cured by a cross of paper, wetted and stuck on the forehead.
Hiccough, or in Macedonia choking over food or drink (ABBOTT, p. 111), is a sign that some backbiter is at work ; the method of curing it is to guess his name. (*Greece.—* LAWSON, p. 331.)

Hideous : Evil spirits usually take hideous human forms. (LANE, *A.S.M.A.*, p. 35.)

Himinbjorg : Norse Myth. Heimdal's house in Asgard.

Hinomisaki : A kind of possession, to be found in Bitchû and Bingo, Japan. It is a form of Kitsune-tsuki. (q.v.)

Hinzelmännchen : An occasional name of the Kobolds in Germany. Vide *Heinzelmännchen*.

Hippocrene : "Fountain of the horse." A fountain which flowed by the sides of Helicon. It was consecrated to the Muses and derived its name from Pegasus having made the fountain flow by striking his hoofs on a rock.

Hiranyaksha : Hind. Myth. "Golden Eye "; a daitya who dragged the earth to the depths of the ocean ; he was killed by Vishnu in the form of a boar. (DOWSON, *H.C.D.*, p. 121.)

Hlidhskjalf : Norse Myth. The cloud-throne above Asgard, whence Odin views the deeds of men, elves and giants in the lower worlds.

Hô : "The Crane." Next to the Fêng (q.v.), this bird is the most famous in Chinese legends. It reaches a fabulous age. When 600 years old, it drinks but no longer takes food. Human beings have repeatedly been changed into its shape, and it constantly manifests a peculiar interest in human affairs. (MAYER, *Chin. Read. Man.*, p. 56.)

Hoarseness : This can be cured by wrapping round the neck, before going to sleep, a discarded stocking belonging to the left foot. (STRACKERJAN, Vol. I, p. 82.)

Hobgoblin : Another name for Puck.

Hoder : Norse Myth. Hoder killed Balder with a dart of mistletoe, given to him by Loki ; mistletoe was the only thing on earth which had not taken an oath to do Balder harm. Cf. *Hotherus*.

Hog : In Celebes it is believed that earthquakes are caused by the world-supporting hog rubbing himself against a tree. Vide *Pig*.

Hohenzollern : The Hohenzollern family is said to have the apparition of the White Lady ; she is the ancestress of this family.

Hold : Folklore. The offspring of a witch by an evil spirit (cf. *Incubi, Succubi, Cuichi Supai, Tulûlu Supai*), often supposed to be an elf causing disease. They assume all forms, sometimes butterflies, sometimes worms, etc.

Holda : Teut. Folklore. A female spirit or sprite who leads the Host of the Dead in the mountains and in the wild ride through the air. She is also connected with the fruitfulness of both earth and women, and is often called Frau Holle. She could ride on the sea and waves, and was feared by sailors. (THORPE, *N.M.*, Vol. I, p. 204.) Vide *Wild Hunt.*

Holdiken : Same as Hold.

Holger : In Danish legend, a king who sits at a table, through which his beard is growing. cf. *Barbarossa; Arthur, King; Tell.* Vide *Charlemagne, Morgaine la Faye, Papillon.*

Holla's Troop : The German equivalent of the Wild Hunt.

Holle Frau : Vide *Holda.*

Holle kreish : The naming ceremony of a baby girl among the Jews of Germany is designated by this name. (For the origin see PERLES in *Grätz Jubelschrift,* 1887, p. 26.)

Holly : When hollies have many berries on them, it foretells a severe winter. (*Great Britain.*)
Holly must not be kept in the house after New Year's Day, it brings ill luck. cf *Goose.*

Holzweiber : Same as Buschweiber.

Honey : All kinds of precious stones cast into honey, become more brilliant thereby, each according to its colour.

Hoof : The Devil is supposed to be able to assume a variety of forms, but he cannot rid himself of his horns and hoofs. (STRACKERJAN, Vol. I, p. 249.) Vide *Cloven Hoof, Horn.*

Hoop : If a hoop comes off a cask on Christmas Eve, someone in the house will die that year. (RAGNER.)

Hoopoe : The country people of Sweden consider the appearance of a hoopoe as a presage of war. (BRAND, *Observations,* p. 701.)

Horæ : Gr. Myth. The three goddesses, daughters of Zeus and Themis, who followed the principal gods or some heroes, and were the guardians of the gates of Heaven. They were : *Thallo, Carpo and Auxo.*

Horn : It is unlucky to keep horns in a room. (*Great Britain, India.*)
The stag's horn is believed to give warning of an evil eye, and to be a safeguard against its malignant influences (*Spain*) ; the wound from a stag's horn never heals. (*Great Britain.*)

"The fear of the evil eye of a woman is very prevalent in Spain; but the panacea is to drink horn shavings." (MURRAY'S *Handbook to Spain*, by Richard Ford, 3rd Edition, 1855, p. 632.)

The tip of an ox's horn is used extensively in Africa, in the Philippine Islands and in America in order to extract blood and the devil along with it. (BASTIAN, *Der Mensch*, Vol. II, p. 117.)

The horn is a constant attribute of the Devil.

"No man means evil but the devil, and we shall know him by his horns."

> SHAKESPEARE, *Merry Wives of Windsor*, v, 2.

cf. *Hoof.*

Horse : If a person suffering from whooping cough, asks advice of a man riding on a piebald horse, the disease may be cured by doing what the rider tells him to do.

A piebald horse is a sign of luck. (*Great Britain.*)

Horses have the power of seeing ghosts and foretelling deaths. (STRACKERJAN, Vol. II, p. 83.)

In the Harz district of Germany, a horse is often buried alive in the belief that this would prevent other horses from being lost from the stable. (PRÖHLE in *Zeitschrift für deutsche Mythologie*, I, 202.)

It is lucky to dream of horses. (*Great Britain, India.*)

In Norway when a thunderstorm is brewing, the water-sprite comes in the shape of a horse. (BASSETT, p. 154, quoting FAYE, *Norsk Sagen*, 55.)

In Bohemia it is considered lucky to see a white horse.

A Pawnee warrior's horse is slain on the grave, to be ready for him to mount again in the spirit world. cf. *Camel, Sati, Boat.*

Horseshoe : It is extremely lucky to find a horseshoe. (*Great Britain.*—ELWORTHY, *E.E.*, p. 216 *et seq.* ; *France, Spain, Germany.*—WUTTKE, p. 36 ; HAZLITT, 330 ; See LAWRENCE, R. H., *The Magic of the Horseshoe*, Boston, 1898.)

A horseshoe fastened inside a door will preserve from the influence of witches and the evil eye (Great Britain) and bring luck. (*Swabia, Tyrol, East Prussia, etc.*—WUTTKE, p. 97 ; ELWORTHY, *E.E.*, p. 216 *et seq.*)

Horus : Egypt. Myth. The hawk-headed god of ancient Egypt. He is represented also as a hawk.

Hosha'na Rabba : Among the Jews it is the popular name for the seventh day of the Feast of Booths.

I

Ho Siän Gu : Chin. Myth. The seventh and the last of the Immortals (q.v.). She is the only woman among these divine eight. (*Chin. Volksmärchen*, p. 74.) She became immortal and disappeared from mortal view. She is said to have been seen in A.D. 750, floating upon a cloud, and again some years later in the city of Canton. (MAYERS, *Chin. Read. Man.*, p. 56.)

Host : Various superstitions are attached to the host or the sacred wafer of the Mass. (cf. *Jew. Enc.*, Vol. VI, p. 482.)

Hotei : A Japanese god of luck, who is represented as having an enormous belly ; he carries a sack on his back and a fan in his hand.

Hotherus : Legend. Son of a Swedish king ; he is said to have killed Balder with Miming's sword. cf. *Hoder*.

Houri : Moham. Myth. They are female beings who share, with other women, the society of the blessed. They are shining and pure and are, like all other inhabitants of Paradise, exempt from physical suffering.
" Femme du paradis de Mahomet."
Petit Larousse, p. 476.
cf. *Apsaras, Siren, Peri*.

House : Rats leave a house before a fall. (STRACKERJAN, Vol. I, p. 24.) Vide *Building*.

Howl : The howling of a dog denotes a speedy death in the house. (WUTTKE, p. 10.)
The plaintive howling of a dog in the night portends a death in some family in the vicinity of the animal. (*Great Britain, France, India, Japan.*—GRIFFIS, *M.E.*, p. 468.)

Hoymann : In Oberpfalz, Wodan (q.v.) appears as a frightful forest-spirit and is called either Hoymann or Wuzl. (STRACKERJAN, Vol. II, pp. 337, 342.)

Hu : It is the Chinese name for a fox (q.v.), a beast whose nature is highly tinged with supernatural qualities. (MAYERS, *Chin. Read. Man.*, p. 61.)

Hulderfolk : Same as Wild Hunt.

Huldrick, St. : He helps to destroy mice and other vermin.

Humming Bird : They are said to pick crocodiles' teeth.

Hunchback : It is lucky to meet a hunchback (*Great Britain, India*).

The camel got the " hunch " because he was never satisfied.

If you laugh at a hunchback, you will get a hump yourself. (*India, Persia.*)

Hunger : Vide *Bread, Sack, Pin, Clanking.*

Hunmamit : Egypt. Myth. They are either birds or beings with birds' heads.

Hurakan : In Central America he is the god of tempest, lightning and thunder. His name has been adopted into European languages as *hurricane* (Eng.), *huracan* (Sp.), *ouragan* (Fr.), *Orkan* (Ger.), *orkan* (Dan., Swed.), *urahan* (Russ.), etc.

Hurricane : Vide *Storm.*

Hütchen : A German household spirit.

Hutzelmännchen : Same as Heinzelmännchen.

Hwang Ch'u P'ing : Chin. Myth. One of the Sien or Immortals (q.v.). (MAYERS, *Chin. Read. Man.*, p. 74.)

Hyades : A cluster of stars in the head of Taurus, supposed by ancients to bring rain when they rose with the sun.

Hydra of Lerne : Greek Fable. A monstrous serpent with seven heads. As soon as one head was cut off, another grew in its place. To kill the monster it was necessary to cut off the seven heads in one blow. Hercules (q.v.) destroyed this monster and thus accomplished the second of his twelve famous deeds. cf. *Dragon.*

Hydrophobia : In Arabia it was believed that hydrophobia could be cured by drinking royal blood (HASTINGS, *Dic. Bib.*, Vol. IV, p. 603a) ; or, in England, by almost smothering the patient between two feather beds. (LEAN, Vol. II, p. 502.)

Hyldemoer : " Mother elder " ; in Danish superstition it is the spirit of the elder tree.

Hymen : Gr. Myth. God of marriage, son of Apollo.

Hyperion : Gr. Myth. A Titan, father of Helios the sun-god. In later mythology he is identified with Apollo, god of manly beauty.

Hypermnestra : Gr. Myth. One of the Danaides (q.v.). She was the only one who spared her husband, Lynceus.

Hypnos : Gr. Myth. A god of slumber; son of Erebus and Night.

I

Iapetus : Class. Myth. A Titan, father of Prometheus, Atlas and Epimetheus ; hence he was regarded as the ancestor of mankind.

Iarbas : Class. Myth. King of the Getules, son of Zeus. He wanted to marry Didon who, however, preferred death to union with him.

Iblis : Moham. Myth. The wicked angel who, assisted by his son, tempts mortals. He was cursed for refusing to prostrate himself before Adam. He has command of the jinni (q.v.), who are his agents with men. In Arabic demonology he is the Devil incarnate and is the chief of the Shaitāns. (LANE, *A.S.M.A.*, p. 30 ; MEAKIN, *The Moors*, p. 353.)

Icarus : Gr. Myth. A son of Dædalus, who, on account of his wax wings melting, fell and was drowned in the sea.

Ice : Witches make the water freeze. (LEHMANN, *A.Z.*, p. 111.) To dream of ice denotes that your desired is faithful and free from choleric passions.

Idæan Mother : An epithet of the Great Mother.

Idiocy : St. Gildas is the guardian angel of idiots. Vide *Drowning*.

Idolatry : It is not restricted to savage tribes. Thus, though the ancient Vedic religion did not recognize it, the Brahmans, recognized followers of the Vedic doctrines, are great idolaters. Even in modern Christianity it is largely practised. (See TYLOR, *Early History of Mankind* Chap. VI ; *Primitive Culture*, pp. 153 etc.)

Idomeneus : Gr. Myth. King of Crete, grandson of Minos. He was one of the heroes of the Trojan war.

Ifrit : In Arabic demonology it is a powerful evil jinn. (LANE, *A.S.M.A.*, p. 27.)

Igarat bat Maḥlat : Jewish Folklore. A queen of the demons who rides in her chariot and has a train of eighteen myriads of demons. (*Jew. Enc.*, Vol. IV, p. 517.) Vide *Lilith*.

Igigi : Babyl. Myth. A group of cruel heavenly spirits under the god Amu. In incantations they are associated with the Annunaki.

Ignis Fatuus : A phosphorescent light seen hovering over marshy ground. When approached, the *ignis fatuus* appears to recede, and finally to vanish, which led to the belief that it was the work of a mischievous sprite, intentionally leading benighted travellers astray. Also called *Jack-o'-Lantern, Will-o'-the-wisp.*

"An ignis fatuus that bewitches
And leads Men into Pools and Ditches."

BUTLER, *Hudibras* (1663).

cf. *Latawiec, Khu, Irrlicht, Feu Follet.*

Igumgehele : "Glutton"; this was the name of a Zulu club.

Ihanaga-hime: Jap. Myth. "The rock-long lady." Daughter of a mountain-god, sister of Konohana Sakuya-hime who married Ninigi (q.v.)

Iha-touchi-biko: Jap. Myth. "Rock-castle-prince." A god who was procreated by the gods Izanagi and Izanami (q.v.)

Ildico : A Teutonic princess by whose hand Attila was rumoured to have been slain on the night of their marriage.

Iliad : If the fourth book of Iliad be laid under the pillow of a patient suffering from ague, it will cure him at once.

Illness : All illnesses are caused by witches and other evil spirits. Vide *Baytree, Burial, Grave, Sickness.*

Imbubuzi : "Groan-maker"; this was the name either of a Zulu assegai (TYLOR, *P.C.*, p. 275), or of an axe that brought victory to the owner (HAGGARD, *Nada the Lily*, p. 114.)

Imilozi : "Whistlers." The ancestral manes (q.v.) of the Zulus, who talk in a low whistling tone.

Immortals : These are the eight divine beings of Chinese superstition. Vide *Sien, Ying, Chow, Peach.*

Imp : Folklore. A kind of malignant spirit closely allied to the goblins, elves, poltergeister, brownies and fairies.

Inada-hime: Jap. Myth. "Rice-land-lady." A goddess, probably the wife of a Rain-storm god.

Inari: Jap. Myth. A male Grain-deity. He is a comprehensive answerer of prayer for a good harvest and for the restoration of stolen property (ASTON, *Shinto*, p. 17.)

Shrines of Inari are to be seen in every village, and even in many houses, and may be recognised by two figures of forces which stand before them.

Inca : American-Indian Myth. The sun-god of the Peruvians.

Incas, Gold of the : Vide *Treasure Lost.*

Incest : The offspring of an incestuous union is a monster (See *Ethnologie du Bengale*, p. 75; cf. DURKHEIM, *La Prohibition de l'inceste, Année sociol.*, Vol. I ; GRIFFIS, *Mikado's Empire*, p. 472; FRAZER, *Psyche's Task*[2], p. 51; A. W. NIEWENHUIS, *Quer durch Borneo*, Vol. II, p. 99.)

Incubus : It was supposed to have been an evil spirit who descended upon persons in their sleep with the purpose of having carnal intercourse with women and producing supernatural births. In the Middle Ages their existence was recognized by the Ecclesiastical and Civil Law. (DALYELL, *Dark. Sup.*, p. 599.)

> " That fende that goth a nyght,
> Wymmen full oft to gyle,
> Incubus is named by right :
> And gyleth men other while,
> Succubus is that wyght."
> (CAXTON'S CHRONICLE, *Description of Walys*).

" The evil demons who trouble people in their sleep, the Incubi and the Succubi." TYLOR, *Early History of Mankind*, I, 7.

cf. *Succubus, Cuichi Supai, Tulûlu Supai, Khu, Jhoting, Latawiec.*

Indigestion : This can be cured by wearing red coral.

Indra : Hind. Myth. The Heaven-God, who, according to a Buddhist version, pursues Râhu with his thunderbolt and rips open his belly so that, although he can swallow the heavenly bodies, he lets them slip again. (BASTIAN, *Östlich. Asien*, etc., quoted in *Ethnologie du Bengale*, pp. 101 *seq.*)

In-é : " Fish-man." In Corea, a sort of siren that is supposed to inhabit the Sea of Japan. It is six or seven feet long and its upper part resembles that of a man ; it has a long slender tail like that of a horse. (GRIFFIS, *Corea*, p. 304.)

Infamy : St. Susan protects from infamy.

Infection : St. Roch protects from infections.

Inferno : Hell as conceived by the poet Dante.

Inflammation : Inflammations may be cured by external use of human excrement. (STRACKERJAN, Vol. I, p. 84.)

Initial : If your initials spell a word, it means that you will be rich. (*Massachusetts* and *Ohio*.—BERGEN, *C.S.*, p. 87.)

Inkosikaas : " Chieftainess " ; another name of the Imbubuzi.

Ino : Gr. Myth. A daughter of Cadmus, who, after her mad paramour Athamas had slain one of her two sons, threw herself and the other son Melicertes into the sea. She was changed into the sea-goddess Leucothea.

Insanity : Vide *Madness.*

Instep : If your instep is high enough to allow water to flow under it, you are of good descent. (*Brookline, Mass.*— BERGEN, *C.S.,* p. 34.)

Inugami : It is the name of the dog-god possession, said to be found in Bitchû, Awa, Tosa and parts of Kyûshû in Japan.

Invisibility : To become invisible go to the churchyard at a quarter of an hour before midnight, dig out a dead body, take the shirt off the corpse and put your own on it and dress yourself in that of the corpse ; but all this must be completed before it strikes midnight. (*Tyrol.*—ZIN- GERLE, *Sitten,* p. 38. See *Jew. Enc.,* Vol. XI, p. 600.)
A stone called Alectoria (q.v.) renders the wearer invisible; so does Agate.
The right eye of a bat carried in the waistcoat pocket, makes a man invisible. (*Bohemia.*—GROHMANN, p. 58.)
The blood from the genitals of an innocent boy makes a thief invisible. (STRACK, p. 22.) Vide *Dog's Blood.*

Io : Gr. Myth. The daughter of the river-god Inachus. She was changed into a heifer by Hera who also set a hundred-eyed Argus to watch over her.

Irial : In Blanche Bay it is a spirit and not a ghost.

Iris : Class. Myth. A messenger of the gods who was changed into a rainbow by Juno.

Iron : The Oriental jinni dread iron so much that even its very name is a charm against them ; in European folklore iron drives away fairies and elves and destroys their power ; similarly, witches are kept at bay by iron instruments. (LANE, Vol. I, p. 30; GRIMM, *D.M*[4]., pp. 435, 465, 1056 ; BASTIAN, *Mensch,* Vol. II, pp. 265, 287 ; Vol. III, p. 204 ; TYLOR, *P.C.,* Vol. I, p. 127 ; WUTTKE, pp. 15, 20, 122, 220 ; *Jewish*—BLAU, p. 159 ; *India, Ethnologie du Bengale,* pp. 92, 133 ; *Celtic.*—RHYS, Vol. I, p. 325 ; ELWORTHY, *E.E.,* p. 221 ; BASSETT, p. 19.)

Irrlicht : The German name for a Will-o'-the-wisp or an Ignis fatuus (q.v.).

Ishtar : Assyro-Babyl. Myth. The chief goddess of the pantheon, the Earth-Mother, goddess of the reproductive forces of nature ; with the Assyrians, goddess of war, pictured with bow and arrow and sometimes clothed in flame. She is probably the same as the other goddess worshipped under various names throughout Eastern Asia. (See SIR J. G. FRAZER, *Adonis, Attis and Osiris*[3].) cf. *Astarte, Great Mother.*

Ishunr : Babyl. Myth. A deity of a local character.

Isis : Egypt. Myth. Wife and sister of Osiris (q.v.), and mother of Horus. She was a goddess of medicine, marriage and agriculture, and the personification of the first Egyptian civilization. She and her husband were the chief deities of the Egyptian pantheon.

Ismene : Gr. Myth. Daughter of Œdipus and Jocosta, sister of Antigone.

Israfil : Moham. Myth. The angel who brings the orders of Allāh to their proper destination and who puts the souls into the bodies.

Itch : The itch can be cured by bathing in the river on a Good Friday. (PANZER, *Beiträge zur deut. Myth.*, Vol. I, p. 258).

Ithunn : Norse Myth. She was the wife of Bragi and had the golden apples of youth in her keeping.

Itongo : The Itongo of the Zulus is the shade of an ancestor which comes to him to warn him of some approaching danger. (?) (HAGGARD, *Nada the Lily*, pp. 28, 61, etc.)

Ixion : Gr. Myth. A king of the Lapithes, who was taken into Heaven by Zeus. He was deficient in respect to Juno and as a punishment, was thrown by Zeus into the infernal regions, where he was condemned to be bound to a flaming wheel and turned round and round eternally. He became the ancestor of the Centaurs.

Izanagi and Izanami : They were two deities of the Shinto religion, "symbols of Divine Will and Wisdom, or the Monad of Life and the Monad of Form, or Spirit and Matter." (GASKELL, *D.S.L.S.M.*, p. 403.) With these two deities Japanese myth begins (ASTON, *Shinto*, pp. 21 *seq.*) From Izanami's vomit, fæces and urine were born deities who personify the elements of metal, water and clay.

Izuna : The human-fox possession of Shinamo, in Japan, is called by this name. Vide *Ninko.*

J

Jacinth : This stone is dedicated to January.

Jack-o'-Lantern : Another name for the Will-o'-the-wisp or the Ignis Fatuus (q.v.). Vide *Knife, Swearing.*

Jackal : The jackal is the lion's provider ; it hunts with, and provides the lion with food by starting prey in the same manner as the dogs start the game.
   In India a jackal is endowed with all the attributes of the fox of European folklore. (CROOKE, *P.R.I.*, Vol. II, p. 243.)

Jack Frost : Frost personified.

Jagannâth, Car of : The Hindus believe that if they are run over and crushed by the wheels of this çar they will go to heaven. (*Ethnologie du Bengale*, p. 87).

Jahi : "Harlot." In the Avesta, she is a fiend of a particularly malicious type. She embodies the spirit of whoredom destructive to mankind.

Jalpari : In the Panjab it is the name of a water-fairy, which can be conciliated by offering a lamb and flowers on the banks of the watercourse. (*Ethnologie du Bengale*, p. 99.) Vide *Fruit.*

Jalyogini : In the Panjab it is a spirit which occupies wells and streams, and casts spells on women and children, causing sickness and even death. (ROSE.)

Jang Go : Chin. Myth. The second of the eight Immortals who was originally a white mouse. (*Chin. Volksmärchen*, p. 290.)

January : Vide *Amethyst, Garnet, Jacinth, Frost.*

Jason : Gr. Myth. Vide *Golden Fleece.*

Jaundice : Jaundice can be cured by drinking water in which something yellow has been cooked. (SCHIFFER, *Urquell*, Vol. V, p. 290 ; *Jew. Enc.*, Vol. V., p. 426.)
   A Bohemian remedy for jaundice is as follows : Take a living tench, tie it to your bare back and carry it about with you for a whole day. The tench will turn yellow and die. Then throw it into running water, and your jaundice will depart with it. (GROHMANN, p. 230 ; FRAZER, *G.B².*, Vol. III, p. 23.)

Jealousy : If your knee itches, you are jealous. (*Boston, Mass.*) Vide *Waters of Jealousy, Knee.*

K

Jehan-numa : A mirror belonging to Jamshīd, in which the whole world was reflected. (BECK, *Key to Neupersische Konversations—Grammatik*, p. 13.)

Jhoting : In the Deccan it is the spirit of a youth dying unmarried and leaving no relatives. It lives in trees, ruins or burial grounds ; it personifies absent husbands, and leads wayfarers into pools and drowns them. cf. *Incubus, Cuichi Supai, Tulúlu Supai, Ignis Fatuus, Khu, Latawiec.*

Jilâiyâ : In Bihar, it is a night-fiend which takes the shape of a night-bird, and is able to suck the blood of any person whose name it hears. (CROOKE, *P.R.I.*, Vol. I, p. 264.)

Jinn : (Pl. jinni) Muham. Myth. An order of spirits lower than angels, said to have the power of appearing in human and animal forms and to exercise supernatural influence over men. They are mostly servants of Iblis.

In eating they use the left hand. In whatever form they may appear, they will always have some animal characteristic, such as a paw in place of a hand. (*Jew. Enc.*, Vol. IV, p. 520.) Vide *Ankle-bone, Iron, Stumbling, Tooth.*

Jnūn : The Moors call the Jinni by this name. The Jnūn are usually supposed to assume the form of all animals— mostly however, frogs or toads. " Hence it is believed that anybody who kills or hurts one of these creatures will have fever or die in consequence ; and if a frog is found in a house or tent, it is politely asked to go away or is gently removed with a shoe." (WESTERMARCK, *The Belief in Spirits in Morocco*, p. 13.)

Jocasta : Gr. Myth. Mother and wife of Œdipus (q.v.). She, on learning that she was her husband's mother, committed suicide by hanging herself.

John Dory : Many superstitions are connected with this little fish. It is called Peter's fish from the legend that in its mouth was found the penny with which the temple tax was paid, and that the spots on either side of its mouth were caused by the apostle's thumb. (BASSETT, pp. 259 *et seq.*)

Jonah and the Whale : Jonah, a Hebrew prophet, was cast overboard during a storm. He was swallowed by a whale, and remained in its belly for three days and three nights before he was cast out. (*St. Matth.* xii. 40 ; cf. BASSETT, pp. 237-239.)

Jorth : Norse Myth. The earth as a goddess or giantess.

Juju : The native West African name for a fetish ; also called Grigri.

June : Vide *Agate*.

Jung Li Küan : Chin. Myth. The first of the eight Immortals. He has the power, beside others, of flying through the air. (*Chin. Volksmärchen*, p. 69.)

Juno : Class. Myth. Wife of Zeus, daughter of Saturn, and the goddess of marriage. The Greeks called her Hera. Poets consider her to have been a haughty, jealous and vindictive woman.

Jupiter : Rom. Myth. An ancient god of the Heavens, corresponding to the Greek Zeus (q.v.).

Jurôjin : Jap. Myth. A god of luck, a variation of Fukurokuju.

Juventas : Class. Myth. A nymph who was turned into a fountain by Zeus. This fountain is said to have the property of rejuvenating anyone bathing in it.

K

Ka-di : Babyl. Myth. A patron deity of Dur-ilu, a town situated near the Elamitic frontier.

Kagu-tsuchi: Jap. Myth. A god of fire. In giving birth to him Izanami was burnt so that she sickened, and lay down and died. Izanagi, in his grief and rage, slew him, thereby generating a number of other deities, two of whom Take-mika-tsuchi and Futsumushi were favourite objects of worship in later times. (ASTON, *Shinto*, p. 23).

Kâli : Hind. Myth. Devi in her malignant form is usually designated by the name of Kali, " the black " ; she is portrayed as dripping with blood, encircled with snakes and adorned with skulls. (For a description, see *Ethnologie du Bengale*, p. 57, quoting S. C. BOSE, *The Hindus as they are*, p. 137.)

Kâliya : Hind. Myth. A king of the serpents who was subjugated by Krishna (q.v.).

Kâma : Hind. Myth. A god of love corresponding to our Cupid. He is represented as a beautiful youth riding a parrot and attended by nymphs. He carries a bow of sugar-cane with a bowstring of bees, and each arrow is tipped with a flower. cf. *Cupid, Eros*.

Kâma-dhenu : Hind. Myth. The cow which grants all desires. (DOWSON, *H.C.D.*, p. 147.)

Kami: The ordinary Japanese word for god. It is applied to many other things besides deities, such as nobles, the authorities, etc. The Kami " are high, swift, good, rich, living, but not infinite, omnipotent and omniscient. . .
Not only human beings, but birds, beasts, plants, trees, seas and mountains and all other things whatsoever which deserve to be dreaded and revered for the extraordinary and pre-eminent powers which they possess, are called *Kami*." (ASTON, *Shinto*, pp. 5 *seq.*)
The Kamis possess two essential qualities without which it would be impossible to recognise them as deities, viz., sentiency and super-human power. They are of two classes : Nature-gods and Man-gods ; the first as a result of personification, the second of deification. Almost any Kami may send rain, bestow prosperity in trade, avert or cure sickness, or cure sterility, and so on.

Kamu-musubi: Jap. Myth. " Divine growth." A god of Growth.

Kappa : A Japanese water-demon who swallows boys who go down to swim without leave. (CONWAY, *Demonology*, Vol. I, p. 112.)

Karlagatch : A little bird whose tail is always twitching. If you keep this tail about you, it will ward off ill luck. (*Turkestan.*—SCHUYLER, Vol. II, p. 30.)

Kâsyapa : A Vedic sage to whom some hymns are attributed. All authorities agree in assigning to him a large part in the work of creation. (DOWSON, *H.C.D.*, p. 153.)
As this word means " tortoise," all creatures are said to be descendants of Kâsyapa.

Katie King : One of the best known examples of the modern materialization theory. With Florence Cook of Hackney as medium, Cook materialized (?) the spirit of Katie King, so that she appeared in human form. For a full description of this interesting experiment, vide *Materialization of Katie King*; PODMORE, *Modern Spiritualism*, Vol. II, p. 154, etc. ; and for an explanation, LEHMANN, *Aberglaube und Zauberei*, p. 327, etc.

Kaya-nu-hime: " Reed-lady." A Japanese goddess.

Kebhsnauf : Vide *Qebhsnauf.*

Kephu : It is the Karen wizard's stomach going forth in the shape of a head and entrails to devour the souls of men, so that they die. It corresponds to our own vampire (q.v.). (CROSS, *Karens*, p. 312.)

Ker : Gr. Myth. A ghost or disembodied soul, often represented as a winged mannikin. Frequently he was an avenging spirit, a spreader of disease and pollution. (Pl. Keres.)

Keraunia : "thunder-bitten"; an epithet of Semele.

Ketu : Hind. Myth. A monster who causes an eclipse by devouring the moon; he is represented as being red in colour (CROOKE, *P.R.I.*, Vol. I, p. 19; *Ethnologie du Bengale*, p. 102). cf. *Râhu, Maboya, Aracho.*

Key : The iron keys of a synagogue placed under the pillow of a dying child release him from death's grasp. (*Jew. Enc.*, Vol. IV, p. 486.)

A key kept under the pillow of a sleeping child protects him from the machinations of evil spirits and witches. (*India.*) Vide *Knife, Iron, Scissors.*

Keyhole : This is one of the favourite entrances of a mara. (SIMROCK, *Mythologie*, p. 545; WUTTKE, p. 161.)   cf. *Knothole.*

Kha : The Arabic letter Khâ, representing *khair* "good," is considered lucky by the Muhammedans. (MEAKIN, *The Moors*. p. 356.) cf. *Shin.*

Khabish : An Indian demon who resembles the Masān (q.v.) in his malignant nature and his fondness for burial grounds. (CROOKE, *P.R.I.*, Vol. I, p. 260.)

Khon pa : Siamese : " Men of the Wood "—apes. cf. *Monkey, Banmânush.*

Khu : (Pl. Khuu). Egypt. Myth. The demons. A khu is generally a wretched, wandering, unhappy, hungry being, a sort of outcast from the great crowd of the dead and other spirits. The Khuu of women dying in childbirth aim especially at causing infants to die. The Khuu of suicides, executed criminals and shipwrecked sailors are partly tormented and miserable. They appear suddenly to terrify the living, preferably in the neighbourhood of cemeteries, cause innumerable ills, violate women in lonely places, cause animals to die, in order to satisfy their craving for flesh.

" A Khu is a shining translucent part of the spiritual economy of a man which dwelt with his soul in the Sâhu or spiritual body."—BUDGE, *Book of the Dead*, Vol. I, p. lxii. cf. *Incubus, Succubus, Jhoting, Cuichi Supai, Tulûlu Supai, Ignis Fatuus.*

Khwăn : Chin. Myth. A fish of enormous length and breadth dwelling in that dark and vast ocean in the North, called the Pool of Heaven. The fish sometimes changes itself into a bird called Phang. (*Writings of Kwang-tze*, Bk. I, Pt. I, 3.)

Kincardines : This family has the apparition of the Bloody Hand.

King : To dream of a King denotes gain, honour, and joy. (For other superstitions, see ELWORTHY, *E.E.*, p. 426, *seq.*; SIR J. G. FRAZER, *The Magic Art*[1]).

Kingfisher : A kingfisher hanged by the bill shows what quarter the wind is by converting the breast to that point of the horizon whence the wind blows. (BRAND, *Observations*, Vol. III, p. 240.)

The cry of a kingfisher, heard on the right, indicates success in business ; if on the left, it is an evil omen (*Ethnologie du Bengale*, p. 113 ; cf. ELLIS, *Ewe-speaking Peoples*, p. 96.)

Kirin : Corean Folklore. It has the body of a deer and the tail of an ox. On its forehead is a single soft horn. It is said never to tread on or injure any living being ; it is the emblem of perfect rectitude. It is considered as the noblest form of animal creation, and its appearance on earth is regarded as a happy omen. (GRIFFIS, *Corea*, p. 303.)

Kirkegrim : In Danish superstition it is a Nisse attached to a church.

Kiss : If a lady dons a gentleman's hat, it is a sign that she wants to be kissed. (BERGEN, *C.S.*, p. 63.)

If you dream you are kissing a pretty maid, it shows you have some evil design. Vide *Dress, Lip, Prick.*

Kite : To cure rheumatic pains kill a kite on a Tuesday, cut up the bones and tie them to the affected part ; this brings about an immediate cure. (CROOKE, *P.R.I.*, Vol. II, p. 250 ; *Panjab Notes and Queries*, III, 81.)

The flesh of a kite gives keen eyesight.

Kite's foot is worn in South Africa to give swiftness to the feet. (TYLOR.)

Kitsune-tsuki : The fox-possession of Japan.

Kitten : To dream of kittens denotes the birth of children.

Kla : The vital soul among the Gold Coast negroes is called by this name. Vide *Sisa.*

Klabautermann : In German folklore this is the name of the guardian spirit of the ship. He dwells in the mast and warns the sailors of any imminent danger by certain noises. (BASSETT, p. 152 *et seq.*)

Klausenberg : A ruin of a castle in Germany, said to be haunted by a female spirit of a malicious type.

Klekaniček : In Bohemia this is a kind of spirit which gets hold of children remaining out of doors after the Ave Maria has been rung. (GROHMANN, p. 15.)

Klekanitsa : Moravian Folklore. A spirit who stalks around after the evening chimes and entraps children she still finds out of doors. cf. *Klekaniček, Bubák, Bogey.*

Klytemnestra : Gr. Myth. Wife of Agamemnon, symbolic of seductive sensation nature allied to the desire mind. (GASKELL, *D.S.L.S.M.*, p. 435.)

Knee : If your knee itches, you are jealous. (*Boston, Mass.*) Elephants have no knees.

Knife : Crossed knives denote a quarrel. (*Great Britain, India.*)
   If you let a knife accidentally drop on the floor, it is a sign that you will receive a visit from a gentleman. (*Great Britain.*)
   In Transylvania they will carefully see that no knife is left lying with the sharp edge upwards so long as a corpse remains in the house, or else the soul will be forced to ride on the blade. (ELWORTHY, *E.E.*, p. 223.)
   Jack-o'-Lanterns may be driven away by throwing a knife or a key at them. (*Silesia, Mecklenburg.*—WUTTKE, p. 220 ; THORPE, *Northern Mythology.*)
   When a gust of wind lifts the hay in the meadow, the Breton peasant throws a knife or a fork at it to prevent the devil from carrying off the hay. (SÉBILLOT, *Coutumes populaires de la Haute-Bretagne*, pp. 302 *seq.*) Vide *Razor, Sharpening, Drink.*

Knock : Three loud and distinct knocks at the bed's head of a sick person, or at the bed's head or door of any of his relations, is an omen of his death. (TYLOR, *P.C.*, Vol. I, p. 132.)
   If on three successive nights a knocking be heard at midnight at the door of a house, it is a sure sign of death. (DEANEY, *Peasant Lore from Gaelic Ireland*, pp. 55-60) ; or, in Scotland, three knocks at regular intervals of one or two minutes foretell the same (GREGOR, p. 203.).

To knock on the door and receive no answer is a sign of death. (*Virginia, Englewood.*—BERGEN, *C.S.*, p. 126.)

To hear a knock at the door and not to find the person knocking is an indication that the Devil has just entered. (*Great Britain.*)

Knocker : A spirit or goblin imagined to dwell in mines and to indicate the presence of ore by knocking. (HUNT, *Pop. Rom.*)

" In the Cardigan mines, the knockers are still heard, indicating where a rich load may be expected."— *Chambers' Journal*, II, 371-2 (1885.)

Knot : If two persons break a piece of cotton with a knot in it, it denotes the fulfilment of a wish for the person who gets the piece with the knot. (*Great Britain.*)

Witches were said to have had the power of making a marriage childless by tying a knot in a piece of string. (LEHMANN, *A.Z.*, p. 111 ; FRAZER, *G.B².*, Vol. I, p. 392 *seq.*).

If you are making a shroud, avoid knots. (WUTTKE, p. 210 ; *Jew. Enc.*, Vol. XI, p. 601.) Vide *Wart.*

Knothole : Knotholes in a piece of wood used for doors, etc., are the favourite entrances of fairies, maras and other nocturnal spirits. (cf. SIMROCK, *Mythologie*, p. 545 ; GRIMM, *D.M.* ; THORPE, *Northern Mythology* ; HARTLAND, *Science of Fairy Tales* ; WUTTKE, p. 161.)

Kobold : German Folklore. A familiar spirit haunting houses and rendering services to the inmates, but often of a tricky disposition.

Sometimes they are also underground spirits haunting mines and caves.

Kobud : The Wend name for a goblin.

Kokunochi: " Trees-father." A Japanese god of the tree.

Koma : It is the " shade " of the Wanika of East Africa, which cannot exist without food or drink. (KRAPF, p. 150 ; TYLOR, *P.C.*, vol. i (?) p. 27.)

Konshana-Sakuya-hime: " The lady who blossoms like the flowers of the trees." Daughter of a Japanese Mountain-god, wife of Ninigi.

Kornmutter : " Corn-mother " ; it is a Teutonic field-spirit in human form.

Kornwolf : " Corn-wolf " ; the name of a German field-spirit.

Kotavi, Kotari, Kottavi : Hind. Myth. A naked woman ; a mystical goddess ; the tutelary deity of the daityas, mother of Bâna the demon. (DOWSON, *H.C.D.*, p. 159.)

Kra : The vital soul among the Gold Coast negroes. Another spelling for Kla.

Kravyâd : Hind. Myth. " A flesh-eater." A Râkshasa or any carnivorous animal. In the Vedas, Agni is in one place called a Kravyâd of terrible power. Fire is also a Kravyâd in consuming bodies on the funeral pyre. (DOWSON, *H.C.D.*, p. 160.)

Kriemhild : Niebenlungenlied. The beautiful sister of Gunther, King of Burgundy, who becomes the wife of Siegfried. After Siegfried's death she marries Etzel, King of the Huns. Later, she brings about the slaughter of her kinsmen, the Burgundians, as a revenge for Hagen's murder of Siegfried.

Kriksy : Russian Folklore. A hag who torments children by night.

Krishna : Hind. Myth. The eighth Avatar of Vishnu, and one of the most widely worshipped deities of the Hindus. He is said to have been brought up by the cowherds as one of them. He is reputed to have dictated the Bhâgvat Gitâ, while Arjuna wrote it down ; he is the hero of innumerable exploits.

His body is supposed to have been turned blue from the poison of Kaliyâ, king of the serpents, whom he subjugated by standing on his head.

Kuda : The demon of disease of Jewish superstition, which attacks women in childbirth. (*Jew. Enc.*, Vol. IV, p. 517.)

Kukuchi: A Japanese god of trees, who represents a class (ASTON, *Shinto*, p. 11.)

Kuni no mihashiren: Jap. Myth. " August pillar of earth." A wind-god who is prayed to for good harvest.

Kuvera : Hind. Myth. God of wealth.

Kyffhâuser : German Legend. Barbarossa is said to sit at a marble table in Kyffhäuser.

Kyklopes : The correct spelling for Cyclops.

L

Labartu : In ancient Babylonian superstition this was the name given to a class of demons who were believed to be especially dangerous to children and their mothers.

Labasu : " One who throws down " ; in Babylonian superstition this was a demon who had the same powers as the Akhkhazu.

Lachesis : Gr. Myth. The goddess who determines the length of the Thread of Life.

Ladder : To walk under a ladder is not unlucky provided you cross your first two fingers. (*Great Britain.*)

Sailors say that you will be hanged if you pass under a ladder. (BASSETT, p. 433.)

To dream of going up a ladder denotes honour, but it is an evil omen to dream of going down it.

Ladybird : It is unlucky to kill ladybirds (*Great Britain*), because spirits of unfortunate beings animate them. (*India*).

Laertes : Class. Myth. A king of Ithaca, father of Ulysses.

Laius : Gr. Myth. King of Thebes, father of Œdipus by whom he was slain in an altercation.

Lakshman : Hind. Myth. Brother of Râma, with whom he went into exile when Râma was banished from the land.

Lakshmi : Hind. Myth. Goddess of fortune, wife of Vishnu. She is considered the type of Indian beauty and is represented sometimes with four arms, but oftener with two.

Lamb : If a sheep give birth to three black lambs, there will be a death in the family. (STRACKERJAN, Vol. I, p. 24.)

Witches cannot assume the form of lambs.

At Kilkenny, Ireland, it is believed that if the first lamb seen in the season be black, the person who sees it will die within the year. (LADY WILDE, p. 180 ; *Folklore*, X, p. 121.) cf. *Dove, Swallow.*

Lamia : Gr. Myth. She was a lascivious evil spirit in the form of a serpent with a woman's head and had the power of taking out her eyes. She was a kidnapper and murderess of children.

In modern Greek folklore the lamiæ are hideous monsters, shaped as gigantic and coarse-looking women for the most part, but with strange deformities of the lower limbs. They may have even more than two feet ; often one of them is of bronze, while others resemble those of animals. Their special characteristics, apart from their thirst for blood, are their uncleanliness, their gluttony and their stupidity. (LAWSON, p. 174.)

Lamp : To hold a lamp over a sleeping person causes death. (*Massachusetts.*)

A lamp should be kept burning night and day in a room where a baby is born till the mother is well again ; this is to keep the evil spirits away. (*Great Britain, India, Germany*.—KÜHN UND SCHWARZ, p. 92 ; WOLF, *Beiträge*, Vol. II, p. 303, etc. ; WUTTKE, p. 195.)

The spluttering of a lamp foretells misfortune. (*Greece* —LAWSON, p. 328.)

Langsuir : The Malays believe that a woman dying in child-birth becomes a *langsuir* and sucks the blood of the children. (*Enc. Brit.*, Vol. VIII, p. 6.) cf. *Choorail*.

Lan Tsai Ho : Chin. Myth. The fifth of the eight Immortals. (*Chin. Volksmärchen*, p. 71.)

Laocoon : Gr. Myth. A priest of Apollo at Troy, who incurred the wrath of Athena by throwing a spear at her wooden horse. As he was offering a sacrifice to Poseidon, he was destroyed with his two sons, by two huge serpents which the goddess had caused to come out of the sea.

Laodamia : Greek Legend. Wife of Protesilaus (q.v.), who, after the death of her husband, had him restored to life for three hours ; when it was time for him to return to the underworld, she accompanied him.

Lapithes : A mythical race inhabiting Thessaly. They were celebrated for their power of subjugating horses, and especially for their war against the Centaurs.

Lapwing : A handmaid of the Virgin Mary having purloined one of her mistress's dresses, was changed into a lapwing and condemned for ever to cry : Tyvit ! Tyvit ! (i.e., I stole it ! I stole it !)

Lapwings pick crocodiles' teeth, therefore they never harm them.

Lar : (Pl. Lares). A tutelary Roman divinity, usually a deified ancestor or hero.

Lard : Vide *Ham*.

Lark : If you drink three lark's eggs on a Sunday before the church bells ring, you will have a sweet voice.

Larva : (Pl. Larvæ). A disembodied spirit of the Romans and a malevolent one.

Last Buried : The person buried last in a churchyard does not have any repose, but must guard the others. (HADDON, " A Batch of Irish Folklore," in *Folklore*, Vol. IV, p. 363 ; LADY WILDE, pp. 82, 93, 213.) An analogous belief is current in Brittany. (LE BRAZ, Vol. I, p. 303.)

At Kilmurry the last buried has to carry water to moisten the lips of the souls in purgatory. (K. L. PAYNE, "A Burial Superstition in County Cork," in *Folklore*, Vol. VIII, p. 180.)

Last Piece : Do not take the last of anything remaining on a plate, you will be an old maid if you do so. (*Great Britain, Germany, Bohemia.*)

Whoever gets the last piece of cake from the plate at tea-time, will be the first to marry. (LEAN, Vol. II, p. 326.)

Lat : Hind. Myth. An ancient Hindu deity. (DUNCAN FORBES.)

Latawiec : Polish Folklore. A spirit which sometimes assumes the form of a man, sometimes of a fascinating maiden. He likes to beguile belated travellers from their right way. When he wishes to gratify his lust, he visits witches in the form of a flying fiery serpent. cf. *Ignis Fatuus, Incubus, Succubus, Jhoting, Cuichi Supai, Tulúlu Supai, Khu.*

Latona : The Romans called Leto by this name.

Lazarus, St. : He protects people from leprosy.

Leander : A Grecian youth, lover of Hero, priestess of Venus. He drowned himself in the Hellespont.

Leap Year : In Hesse and in Westphalia it is believed that the leap year is particularly suited for important undertakings. (WUTTKE, p. 24.) Vide *Twenty-ninth of February*.

Leather : Leather is said to scare demons away. (CROOKE, *P.R.I.*, Vol. II, p. 33.)

Leda : Gr. Myth. Wife of the Spartan king Tyndareus. According to the usual accounts, the father of Helen and Pollux was Zeus who took the form of a swan and had intercourse with Leda. Other accounts make both Pollux and Castor either sons of Zeus or of Tyndareus her husband. Her children were Castor and Pollux, Clytemnestra and Helen of Troy.

Left : Left to right is a good direction. (*Greece.*—LAWSON, p. 312.)

Leg : To see a man with a wooden leg coming towards you is an omen of good luck ; to see his back or to turn round to look at him portends ill luck. (*Great Britain.*)

Lemures : In Roman mythology they are the same as the Larvæ with whom the living find it hard to maintain a permanent peace. They were the malevolent spirits of the departed.

" Lest he behold one of these grim lemures."—
LYTTON, *Last Days of Pompeii.*

Leprosy : St. Lazarus the beggar protects from leprosy.
Bathing in human blood, especially the blood of a
maiden, cures leprosy. (STRACK, *Der Blutaberglaube*, p.
12 *seq.*, quoting PLINY, *Nat. Hist.*, XXVI, 1, 5.)
Richard, King of England, who was suffering from
leprosy, took counsel of a Jewish physician after all other
means had failed him. This Jew advised the King to
bathe in the blood of a new-born babe, and to eat its
warm heart raw as an infallible cure for this disease.
(SIMROCK, *Volksbücher*, XII, pp. 31, *et seq.* ; STRACK,
op. cit., p. 14.)

Ler : Celt. Myth. A Gaelic god of the sea.

Lethe : Class. Myth. The river of Hades, whose water, when
drunk, caused forgetfulness of the past.

Leto : Gr. Myth. The mother of Apollo and Artemis by Zeus
to whom she was married before he married Hera (Hesiod).
In a later story, she was only a mistress of Zeus and was
persecuted by Hera until her children were born at Delos.
She is called Latona by the Romans.

Letter : A moth flying towards a person, denotes a letter.
A bright spark from the burning wick of a candle
promises a letter.
If you dream of posting an unsealed letter to your
sweetheart, it means that your secrets will be exposed.
Vide *Cotton, Saliva.*

Leucothea : Gr. Myth. A goddess of the sea. Vide *Ino.*

Lichas : Gr. Myth. A servant of Hercules, who brought
him the poisoned shirt of Nessus. He was thrown from
a high mountain, and falling into the sea became a rock
which still bears his name and retains the human form.

Lichen : According to a legend this dry plant was not always
so ; it became dry as the result of the curse of a woman.
(JALLA, *Lég. Vaud*, p. 11.)
In the Hebrides fishermen refuse to wear clothes
dyed with the lichen found on the rocks, although it is
used in other cases. They say that it comes from the
rocks, and will go back there. (GOODRICH-FREER, *Outer
Isles*, 1902, p. 203 ; HAZLITT, p. 575.)

Lichoradka : Slavic Folklore. Demons of fever.

Lie : Vide *Tongue, Pimple, Speak.*

Light : In the superstition of nearly every nation, savage or civilized, it is generally admitted that light scares spirits away ; hence spirits appear only when it is either dark or in a state of semi-darkness. (cf. *Ethnologie du Bengale*, p. 95 ; SKEAT, *Malay Magic*, p. 15.)

Three lights burning in a room, is a sign of death. (ABBOTT, p. 99.)

If there are three lights in a straight line in front of an unmarried girl, she will soon be a bride. (STRACKERJAN, Vol. I, p. 23.)

Women, who can blow into flame the still glowing wick of a lamp or a candle, are virgins. (*S. Germany, Silesia, Tyrol.*—WUTTKE, p. 42.)

A light is seen on the grave of a very pious man. (PH. REDMOND, " Some Wexford Folklore," *Folklore*, X. 362.)

Before the death of a near relative, lights are seen moving before a person. No matter how hard the person tries to approach them, these lights always keep the same distance. (*Brittany.*—LE BRAZ, Vol. I, p. 260.)

A light going out of its own accord is an omen of death. (WUTTKE, p. 38.)

If the light is let go out on Christmas Eve, some one in the house will die. (RAGNER.)

Lightning : Witches generally cause lightning. (LEHMANN, *A.Z.*, p. 111.)

He who carries about him a piece of wood chipped off by lightning, will be extremely strong. (*Bohemia.*—GROHMANN, p. 40.)

To insure your house against lightning, burn the Yule Log on Christmas Eve. (RAGNER.)

If a person struck by lightning be immediately removed forty paces from the spot where the accident befell him, he will recover. (*Macedonia.*—ABBOTT, p. 229.)

Wreaths of red and white flowers hung up on Ascension Day over stable doors, safeguard the stables against lightning. (*Swabia.*—WUTTKE, p. 21.) Vide *Heitlik, Beetle.*

Lilis : Adam's wife before Eve was created. Lilis refused to submit to Adam, and was turned out of paradise ; she still haunts the air and is especially hostile to children and new-born babes. She is usually known as Lilith.

Lilith : Jewish Folklore. A female demon, worshipped by the Jews during the Babylonian captivity. She was the first wife of Adam who was compelled to repudiate her, Eve being created for him. In modern superstition she is the queen of demons, pictured with wings and long flowing hair. (*Jew. Enc.*, Vol. IV, p. 517.)

(ii) In the Middle Ages Lilith was a famous witch. (cf. GOETHE : *Faust.*) cf. *Igarat bat Mahlat.*

Lilitu : A female form of Lilu.

Lilu : "Night." In Babylonian superstition it was a kind of evil spirit who plied his trade at night under cover of darkness. cf. *Ardat lili.*

Limbo : (Lat. Limbus "an edge "). A sort of neutral land on the confines of paradise for those who are not good enough for heaven and not bad enough for hell, or rather, for those who cannot (according to the church system) be admitted into paradise, either because they have never heard the Gospel or have never been baptized. (DR. BREWER, *R.H.*, p. 614.)

Limbo of the Moon : In the moon are treasured up the time misspent in play, all vain efforts, all vows broken, all counsel thrown away, all desires that lead to nothing, the vanity of titles, flattery, great men's promises, court services and death-bed alms. (DR. BREWER, *R.H.*, quoting *Orlando Furioso*, XXXIV, 70.)

Limbus Fatuorum : Or the Fool's Paradise for idiots, madmen and others who are not responsible for their sins, but yet have done nothing worthy of salvation. (DR. BREWER, *R.H.*, p. 614.)

Limping : To limp with the left foot denotes good fortune ; with the right, the opposite. (*Bohemia.*)

Lin : Chin. Folklore. A supernatural creature with the body of a deer, the tail of an ox, and a single horn. It is said to attain the age of one thousand years and to be the noblest form of animal creation, the emblem of perfect good. (MAYERS, *Chin. Read. Man.*, p. 136.)

Lindwurm : "Dragon " ; in Tyrol it is believed that the Lindwurm watches treasures. (ALPENBURG, *Mythen*, p. 377 ; cf. KÚNOS, *Turkish Fairy Tales*, p. 135 ; LAWSON, p. 281.)

Lion : The lion will not injure a royal prince.

The ancient naturalists entertained the idea that the fiercest lion trembled at the crowing of a cock.

The lion hates the game-cock and is jealous of it ; some say because the cock wears a crown (its crest) ; others, because it comes into the royal presence " booted and spurred."

According to a legend the lion's whelp is born dead and remains so for three days, when the father breathes on it and it receives life.

Arab women in North Africa give their male children a piece of a lion's heart to eat to make them fearless (FRAZER, *G.B².*, Vol. II, p. 355.) Vide *Bear, Jackal.*

Lion-God, Double : Egypt. Myth. They were two lions seated back to back, supporting the horizon with the sun's disc, over which stands the sky ; the lion on the right is called Sef " yesterday," and that on the left Tuau " to-day." (BUDGE, *Book of the Dead*, p. 90.)

Lip : Itching of the lips is a sign that someone will kiss you. (*Great Britain, Boston.*—BERGEN, *C.S.*, p. 63.) A mole on the lip is a sign either of gluttony or of sensuousness.

Lir Majoran : In New Guinea, he is the god of husbandry, to whom first fruits are offered when the harvest is ripe. (FRAZER, *G.B².*, Vol. II, p. 463.)

Lisa's Ring : A ring which by its lustre told Lisa whether her lover was ill or dying. (ST. JOHN, *Leg. Chr. East*, p. 163.) cf. *Bahman's Knife*, etc.

Li Tia Guai : Chin. Myth. The sixth of the eight Immortals. (*Chin. Volksmärchen*, p. 71.)

Live Coal : It is a Scandinavian custom to cast live coals after the mother as she goes to be churched, in order to prevent the trolls from carrying her off bodily. (TYLOR, *P.C.*, Vol. II, p. 178, quoting HYLTEN-CAVALLIUS, *Wärend och Wirdarne*, Vol. I, p. 191, and ATKINSON, *Glossary of Cleveland Dial.*, p. 597.)

Lizard : The cut-off tail of a lizard lives some time after it has been separated from the body, and if by chance it touches the body it immediately joins itself to it and lives and grows along with it. (*Great Britain, India, Germany.*—STRACKERJAN, Vol. II, p. 110. cf. *F.L.J.*, 1883, p. 356.)

The lizard is man's special enemy, but warns him of the approach of a serpent. Food touched by a lizard becomes poisonous. (*Ethnologie du Bengale*, p. 116.)

Biscobra is the name of a kind of huge lizard. According to popular belief, its bite is fatal. (YULE & BURNELL, *Hobson Jobson²*, pp. 95, 367; ibid.[1], p. 765.)

When Queen Elizabeth sent a sculptured lizard to the wife of the Prince of Orange, the princess wrote back : " It is the fabled virtue of the lizard to awaken sleepers when a serpent is creeping up to them. Your Majesty is the lizard and the Netherlands the serpent. Pray God they may escape the serpent's tooth."

The Mohammedans say that the lizard is a treacherous reptile. It was a lizard which pointed out Mohammed to his pursuers while he was hiding in a cave.

If you let a lizard run over your hand, you will be a good needle-woman. (*Alsace.*—LAMBS, p. 30.)   Vide *Spider.*

Llen : Celt. Myth. A Cymric sun-god, son of Gwydion and Arianrod.

Llud : Celt. Myth. A Cymric god of the sky.

Llyr : Celt. Myth. A Cymric god of the sea.

Loadstone : Loadstone produces somnambulism. It is dedicated to Mercury, and in metallurgy means quicksilver.

Lock : In Cornwall death is believed to be retarded, and the dying person kept in a state of suffering by having any lock closed or any bolt shut in the dwelling. (HUNT, *Pop. Rom.*, p. 379 ; GREGOR, *F.L.N.E.S.*, p. 206 ; *Contemporary Review*, XLVIII, 108.)

The Arabs spit on a lock which cannot easily be opened. (DOUGHTY, *Arab Des.*, Vol. I, p. 227.)

Locust : In South Mirzapur, when locusts threaten to eat up the fruits of the earth, the people catch one, decorate its head with a spot of red lead, salaam to him, and let him go. After these civilities the locust immediately departs along with its fellows. (CROOKE, *Pop. Rel. Folkl. North India*, p. 380 ; FRAZER, *G.B*[2]., Vol. II, p. 424.)

Log : If logs crackle in the hearth, you will either have good news, or friends will arrive. (*Greece.*—LAWSON, p. 328.).

Loki : Norse Myth. A god, contriver of discord and mischief. He is adroit and cunning and is able to transform himself into innumerable shapes. He contrives the death of Balder, and is overcome by Thor. Skathi fastens a venom-dripping snake over him.

Longevity : Plenty of soup eaten slowly produces longevity. The Chinese worship the peepul-tree for long life. (WILLIAMS, *Mid. King.*, Vol. II, p. 259.)

Looking round : It is unlucky to look round at night. (STRACK-ERJAN, Vol. II, p. 20.)

Never look round when a ghost speaks to you ; if you do so, the ghost will immediately break your neck. (*Bengal.*) Vide *Beehive.*

Loom : If silver has been stolen from the house, the loom will be heard working in the dead of the night. (*Jutland*).

(For other superstitions connected with the loom, vide WIKMAN, *Die Magie des Webens.*)

Lorelei : In the Rhine district of Germany there is a belief that this is a Nixie or water-spirit, who entices mariners to destruction. She is represented as sitting on the Lorelei rocks, singing enchantingly and combing her hair with a golden comb.

" Ich glaube die Wellen verschlingen,
Am Ende Schiffer und Kahn ;
Und das hat mit ihrem Singen
Die Lorelei gethan."—HEINE, *Lorelei.*
cf. *Siren, Nixie, Alrinach, Jal Pari, Bugarik.*

Lost Goods : The saints Elain and Ethelbert lead to the recovery of lost goods.

Lot's Wife : She is said to have been turned into a pillar of salt. Vide *Wahela.*

Loup-garou : In France the werewolves (q.v.) are called by this name.

" Le peuple des campagnes appelait *loup-garou* ou *lycanthrope* un sorcier qui, travesti en loup, courait les champs pendant la nuit. Sa peau était à l'épreuve de la balle, á moins que celle-ci n'eût été bénite dans la chapelle de Saint-Hubert, patron des chasseurs, qui le tireur ne portât sur lui du trèfle à quatre feuilles, etc. Cette croyance ridicule disparait aujourd'hui de plus en plus."—*Petit Larousse illustré*, p. 569.

Lourdes : The water from the spring at Lourdes cures all diseases. (*Roman Catholic.*)

Louse : Lice on the bodies of children signify good luck. (STRACKERJAN, Vol. II, p. III.)

A louse taken from the body of a beggar and put into the hollow of an aching tooth instantly cures the pain. (STRACKERJAN, Vol. I, p. 85.)

In Lauenburg, a cross made of thorns is tied round a dog's neck to protect him from lice. (BASTIAN, *Der Mensch*, Vol. II, p. 116 note.)

Living lice on a corpse indicate the death of another member of the family. (*Alsace.*—LAMBS, p. 33.)

Love : According to the Greeks a cestus worn by women inspired love ; hence Aphrodite was irresistible on account of her cestus.

It is a West Highland superstition that a beauty spot cannot be resisted ; hence Diarmaid inspired masterless love by his beauty spot.

An Irish superstition is that, if a lover will run a hair of the object beloved through the fleshy part of a dead man's leg, the person from whom the hair was taken will go mad with love.

It is a Basque superstition that yellow hair in a man is irresistible with women ; hence every woman who set eyes on Ezkabi Fidel, the golden haired, fell in love with him. (For various love potions see *Ethnologie du Bengale*, p. 144 ; HOVORKA & KRONFELD, *Vergleichende Volks-medizin*, Vol. II, p. 179.) Vide *Salt, Cracking, Shoe, Urine, Perspiration, Menstruation, Blood, Flower, Frog, Chemise.*

Lucifer : The angel who rebelled against God ; the Devil.
" Know then that after Lucifer from heaven
. . . fell with his flaming legions through the deep
Into his place . . ."
MILTON, *Paradise Lost*, Bk. VII, 131.

Luck Penny : Such a coin kept on the person brings good luck. It can be obtained from the Devil himself.
(On the method of obtaining one, vide WUTTKE, p. 177.)

Lucina : Gr. Myth. The goddess who presided over child-birth, said by some to be the daughter of Jupiter and Juno ; by others, Juno herself.

Lucky Finds : It is extremely lucky to find the following things : horseshoes, bones, teeth, egg-shells and four-leaved clovers ; this last should be sewn inside the lining of one's clothes. (*Silesia.*—WUTTKE, p. 96.)

Lü Dung Bin : Chin. Myth. The third of the eight Immortals. (*Chin. Volksmärchen*, p. 69.)

Lug, Lugh : Celt. Myth. The Gaelic sun-god who aided the Tuatha De Danann to overthrow the Fomors. He was the son of Diancecht and Balor.

Lugal-banda : Babyl. Myth. An ancient sun-god of the violent type. The word signifies " mighty king." He and his consort Nin-Sun were worshipped in Erech.

Lumbago : To cure lumbago tie a skein of silk round the loins next the skin. (LEAN, Vol. II, p. 505) ; or a violin string round your waist.

Lusignan : An ancient illustrious feudal family whose ancestress, according to a legend, was the fairy Mélusine. (HARTLAND, *Sc. of Fairy Tales* ; *Petit Larousse*, p. 1436.)

Lutin : The Kobolds (q.v.) of French superstition.

Lycaon : Gr. Myth. An Arcadian king who, when Zeus came in disguise to him, set before the god a dish of human flesh in order to test his divinity. Zeus turned him into a wolf ; or in other versions, struck him dead by lightning.

Lycanthropy : (Gr. *lukos* " wolf " *anthropos* " man "). In ancient and mediæval times wizards were supposed to have the power of changing themselves at will into wolves, bears, tigers and the like. This metamorphosis could also be brought about by means of donning certain belts, or by rubbing the body with certain ointments, or merely by incantations. (Cf. O'DONNELL, *Werewolves*; S. BARING GOULD, *Book of Werewolves* ; GRIMM, *Deutsche Mythologie* ; LEUBUSCHER, *Währwölfe*, *Dic. Rel. Ethics*, s.v. " Lycanthropy.")

The werewolf not only existed in the imagination of our forefathers, but is firmly believed in in many countries to the present day. The Berserker of the Scandinavians, the Loup-garous of the French, the Fox of the Chinese and the Japanese, the Währwölfe of the Teutonic races, the Were-Tigers of the Indians and the Malays are all variations of our own werewolves. In reality it is a kind of insanity in which the patient imagines himself to be a wolf or some other wild animal. Vide *Werewolves*, *Loup-garou.*

" Persons accused of the crime of Lycanthropy."— SCOTT, *Demonology* (1830).

Lycus : Gr. Myth. A king of Thebes, husband of Dirce, who rescued Antiope from Epopeus.

Lyderhorn : A mountain near Bergen (Norway) ; this was supposed to have been a popular resort of the Norwegian witches. (LEHMANN, *A.Z.*, p. 112.) cf. *Blocksberg, Hecla, Brocken, etc.*

Lyesovic : " Wood king." In Russian folklore this is a forest-spirit. He looks very much like a man, but his hairy body betrays him. He has long hair and a green beard ; he has only one eye and lacks eyebrows ; he can change his size at will and often transforms himself into animals.

Lyesyj : Same as Lyesovic.

Lynceus : Gr. Myth. Husband of Hypermnestra, one of the Argonauts. He had such wonderfully sharp eyes, that he could see through a millstone, or look right down into the depth of the earth, and discover the treasures that were there.

M

Mabisalira : Among the Nyanjas of Nyassaland in Africa this is a professional witch-finder, generally a woman.

Maboya : Among the Caribs it is a demon, hater of all light, who seeks to devour the sun and the moon. cf. *Râhu, Metu, Aracho.*

Macbeth : Macbeth could not be killed by anyone who was born of a woman. (Shakespeare, *Macbeth*, viii.)

Machus : Gr. Myth. A god of the rivers, father of Io.

Madness : It is lucky to live in the same house with a madman. (*Gt. Britain, India, Germany, Greece* : LAWSON, p. 397).
  Among the Zulus madmen are supposed to be entered into by some departed spirit. (CALLAWAY, *Rel. of the Amazulu,* p. 147 ; TYLOR, *P.C.* Vol. II, p. 118 ; RIDER HAGGARD, *Nada the Lily*, p. 58); the same belief is prevalent in Polynesia (ELLIS, *Polynesian Researches*, Vol. I, pp. 363, 395 ; Vol. II, pp. 193, 274 ; TYLOR, *P.C.* Vol. II, p. 117), in East Africa and among the Barongos etc. (CASALIS, *Basutos,* p. 247 ; BURTON, *Cent. Africa*, Vol. II, pp. 320, 354).
  If you are bitten by a mad dog, take the dog's liver, burn it to charcoal, powder it and eat it with bread and butter. (STRACKERJAN, Vol. I, p. 81).
  If women step on egg-shells, they will go mad. (*Japan,* GRIFFIS, *M.E.* p. 469).
  Dogs will go mad if they eat of the afterbirth of mares. (STRACKERJAN, Vol. I, p. 49).
  If hair be set on fire, you will go mad. (*Japan,* GRIFFIS, *M.E.* p. 468).
  The saints Dymphna and Fillian cure madness.

Maenad : Class. Relig. A nymph attendant upon Dionysus.

Maelstrom : A whirlpool off the west coast of Norway. It was formerly believed that a spirit dwelt in it and sucked in all vessels which ventured near his dwelling.

Magnetic Islands : In several books there is mention of a magnetic island in some unknown sea where ships are wrecked. (cf. LANE, *Thousand and one Nights*, Vol. I, pp. 161, 217, Vol. III, p. 78; HEINRICH VON WALDECK, *Herzog Ernst's von Bayern Erhöhung etc.*, p. 65; LUDLOW, *Popular Epics of Middle Ages*, p. 221; SIR JOHN MAUNDEVILLE, *Voiage and Travaile*.)

Magog : Vide *Gog*.

Magpie : In Lancashire it is an omen of ill luck to see two magpies flying together.

When magpies chatter, it denotes that you will see strangers.

To see one magpie is unlucky, to see two denotes merriment, or a marriage, to see three, a successful journey, four, good news, five, company.

It is unlucky to see magpies (BASSETT, p. 275).

Magpies chattering on the house-top predict the coming of a friend and relatives from abroad (*Macedonia*, ABBOTT, p. 110).

Magpies shot during the Twelve Nights and burnt to powder, prevent fever. (KÜHN UND SCHWARTZ, p. 412).

If a magpie be shot in March and nailed on inside the cow-shed, it will stop the flies coming in. (STRACKERJAN, Vol. I, p. 67).

Among the Kirghiz, if a magpie be seen on the west it means a journey ; if on the east, guests ; if on the north, bad luck; if on the south, some remarkable event. (SCHUYLER, Vol, II, p. 30).

Among the Chinese, a magpie is a bird of good omen. (DOOLITTLE, Vol. II, p. 327). It is unlucky to kill a magpie (*Ethnologie du Bengale*, p. 112 ; ABBOTT, p. 110.)

" One for sorrow, two for mirth,
   Three for a wedding, four for a birth."
                                        Lincolnshire Proverb

To have a magpie perch on your house shows stability of the house. (LEAN, Vol. II, p. 16 ; *F.L.R.*, I, 8).

Alexander Ross tells us the battle between the Italians and the French, in which the former were overthrown, in the reign of Charles VIII, was foretold by a skirmish between magpies and jackdaws.
                        Arcana Microcosmi (Appendix, 219).
Vide *Pierides*.

Mahomet's Coffin : This is said to be suspended in mid-air between heaven and earth.

Mahu : The fiend prince that urges to theft.

Maia : Gr. Myth. Daughter of Atlas, mother of Mercury. The eldest and most beautiful of the Pleiades.
Rom. Relig. An ancient goddess, consort of Vulcan.

Maid : To dream of obtaining a maid denotes joy, but weeping and sorrow if you dream you are taking her away by force.

Maize : Plant maize when your stomach is full, and see to it that your dibble is thick ; this will swell the ear of the maize. (SKEAT, *M.M.*, p. 217 ; FRAZER, *G.B².*, Vol. I, p. 35).

Mala'ikat ar-rahma : Muham. Myth. The Angels of compassion. Vide *Azrâil.*

Mala'ikat al-adhab : Muham. Myth. The angels of punishments.

Malat : An ancient Hindu deity. (DUNCAN FORBES).

Malik : Muham. Myth. A terrible angel who guards over hell. He is assisted by Sbires (q.v.), of whom there are eighteen.

Mallt y nos : Welsh Folk-lore. A particular kind of night-fiend.

Mâmdo : In India it is the ghost of a Mohammedan ; it is of an extremely malevolent type. (*Ethnologie du Bengale*, p. 100.)

Mamony : "Wild women." The Divé ženy (q.v.) are called by this name in Poland.

Man : A person weighs more fasting than after a meal.
 The Jews maintained that man has three natures : body, soul and spirit. Diogenes Laertes calls the three natures : body, phren and thumos ; and the Romans called them : manes, anima and umbra. (Dr. BREWER, *R.H.*)

Mandrake : A kind of plant. It was believed to cry and groan like a child when pulled out by the roots. The fruit, when eaten by women, was supposed to promote conception. It is still the subject of many superstitions. In Persia it is said to cure barrenness. (PLOSS, *Das Weib*, Vol. I, p. 535)
 " I, last night, lay all alone
 On the ground to hear the mandrake groan."
 BEN JONSON, *Masque of Queens.*
 Whoever hears the mandrake cry must die. (HAZLITT, p. 385).

Manes : Rom. Myth. The deified souls of the departed ancestors as beneficent spirits; opposed to Larvæ and Lemures. They were gods of the lower world.

"Let eternal fame
Attend thy manes and preserve thy name."
POPE, *Thebais* (1703).

Mania : St. Vitus cures dancing mania.

Manito, Manitu : Among the Algonquin Indians it is one of the powers or spirits which dominate the forces of nature

Mantalini : A charlatan who professed to restore the dead to life.

Mantle : A boy brought to King Arthur's court a mantle which no one could wear who was unfaithful in love, false in domestic life, or treacherous to the king. If any such attempted to put it on, it puckered up, or hung slouchingly, or tumbled to pieces. (PERCY : *Reliques*). The same boy brought the Brawn's Head.

cf. *Florimel's Girdle, Water of Jealousy, Canace's Mirror, Grotto of Ephesus.*

Manucodiata : A bird resembling the swallow found in the Molucca Islands. It has no feet, and though its body is no bigger than that of a swallow, the span of its wings is equal to that of an eagle. These birds never approach the earth, but the female lays her eggs on the back of the male, and hatches them in her own breast. They live on the dew of heaven, and eat neither animal nor vegetable food.

"In these Ilands (Moluccas) onlie is found the bird, which the Portingales call *Passaros de Sol*, that is Foule of the Sunne, the Italians call it *Manu codiatas*, and the Latinists *Paradiseas*, by us called Paradice birdes, for ye beauty of their feathers which passe al other birds : these birds are never seene alive, but being dead they are found vpon the Iland ; they flie, as it is said, alwaies into the Sunne, and keepe themselves continually in the ayre . . . for they have neither feet nor wings, but onely head and bodie, and the most part tayle"—(LINSCHOTEN, *Discours of Voyages into ye Easte and Weste Indies*, 35 ; YULE & BURNELL, *Glossary*[1] (*Hobson Jobson*[1]), p 72.)

"Olha cá pelos mares do Oriente
As infinitas ilhas espalhadas

.   .   .   .   .   .

Aqui as aureas aves, que não decem
Nunca á terra, e só mortas aparecem."
CAMÕES, *Os Lusiadas*, x, 132

Englished by Burton :
> " Here see o'er oriental seas bespread
> Infinite island-groups and alwhere strewed
>
> .   .   .   .   .   .
>
> Here dwell the golden fowls, whose home is air,
> And never earthward save in death may fare."

cf. *Chakora*.

Mara : The nightmare-ghosts of Slavic and Teutonic mythology. They are the souls of living beings, mostly women, which leave their bodies by night, and visit sleepers for the purpose of tormenting them by sitting astride their chests. They usually make entrance either through a key-hole or through a knot-hole. The soles of their feet are flat and their eyebrows meet. They torment not only human beings, but also domestic animals, draining them of milk and sucking their blood.

> " The incubus which we call the mare."
>
> BACON, *Sylva* (1626).

> " The ten chief Sins came,
> Maras, mighty ones, Angels of evil."
>
> E. ARNOLD, *Light of Asia*, VI, xix,

Mardanu-'l-ghaib : Same as Rijâlu-'l-ghaib.

Marduk : Babyl. Myth. Originally the god of the city of Babylon, but later he became the official head of the pantheon. He is distinctly a solar god. His consort was Sarpanitum.

Margýr : "Sea-monster"; the name of a water-spirit in Iceland.

Marichi Deva : Buddhist Myth. " The personification of light, offspring of Brahmâ." (EITEL, *Handbook of Chinese Buddhism*).

Marid : They are the most powerful demons of Arabic demonology. (LANE, *A.S.M.A.*, p. 27).

Marriage : The English superstition is :

> " Change your name and not the letter ;
> You change for worse and not for better."

> " Marry in Lent,
> Live to repent."
>
> *New York.*

A marriage is foretold by the blossoming of an apple tree in autumn. (*Lower Saxony*, WUTTKE, p. 35). Vide *Bed, Bridal clothes, Chemise, Cradle, Magpie, Field, True, Wreath, Garter, Last piece, Myrtle, Needle, Pear tree, Plough, Purple, Wedding, Stones sepulchral*.

L

Mars : Gr. Myth. The god of War, in which character he is also regarded as a protector of the fields against hostile aliens, and as a leader of military colonists. The Romans considered him to be the father of Romulus.

Marsyas : Gr. Myth. A young Phrygian flute-player who defied Apollo in this art. The Muses declared the god to be the victor, and, as a punishment, Marsyas was tied to a tree and was flayed alive.

Martin : It is unlucky to kill a martin (*Gt. Britain*).
Martins forewarn miseries and unnatural wars by fighting against one another. (ALEXANDER ROSS, *Arcana Microcosmi*, p. 219.)

Martin, St. : Vide *Small-pox, Sudden Death*.

Martu : Babyl. Myth. Another name for Adad.

Marut : They were the storm winds of Vedic mythology, who tear asunder the forest kings, and make the rocks asunder, and assume the form of new-born babes.

Mârût : Like Harût, it was the Armaic personification of rebellion.

Masân : In the Himalayas this term is used to designate cemetery spectres. It is the ghost of a child, or a low-caste man, probably an oilman. (CROOKE, *P.R.*, Vol. I, p. 261 ; *Ethnologie du Bengale*, p. 100).

Masubi : Shinto Relig. The god of growth. (W. G. ASTON, *Shinto*, p. 172).

Match : To light three cigarettes (or in fact, three of any-thing) from the same match is considered unlucky ; one of the persons will die a sudden death. (*Gt. Britain*).

Materialization : In modern spiritualism it means the act of taking or assuming a material form.

Matmate : In the East Indies these are the spirits of ancestors, which are worshipped as guardian spirits or household gods. (FRAZER, G.B., Vol. II, p. 463).

Mathew, Father : He was well-known as the Apostle of Tem-perance.

Maug Moulach : The house of Tulloch Gorms in Scotland used to be haunted by Maug Moulach, or " the girl with the hairy hand." (STEWART, p. 144; DALYELL, *Dark Sup.*, p. 124).

May : Vide *Emerald*.

Mayflower : Mayflowers must not be brought inside a house, lest there be a death in the family. (*Gt. Britain*)

Maypole : Imparts fertilizing influence over both women and cattle as well as vegetation. (ELWORTHY, *E.E.*, p. 62 ; *Ethnologie du Bengale*, p. 84. See SIR J. G. FRAZER, *Golden Bough*, Vol. II, pp. 449-456).

May Queen : It is superstitiously believed that the girl chosen to be the May Queen will not live another year. (*Gt. Britain*).

" If you are waking call me early, call me early
   mother dear,
For I would see the sun rise upon the glad New
   Year,
It is the last New Year that I shall ever see,
Then you may lay me low i' the mould and think
   no more of me."

TENNYSON, *May Queen*

Maziqim : It is the Jewish equivalent of a *domovoy* or a brownie.

Meal : In some parts of Austria and Germany, when a storm is raging the people open a window and throw out a handful of meal, saying to the wind, " There, that's for you, stop ! " (FRAZER, *G.B.*, Vol. I, p. 127, note).

Measurement : If a corpse cannot immediately be disposed of, the best course is to measure it carefully, and then no malignant Bhût can occupy it. (CROOKE, *P.R.I.*, Vol. II, p. 76 ; *Ethnologie du Bengale*, p. 69.) Vide *Shadow*.

Meat : Warts can be cured by rubbing them with a piece of raw meat and then burying the meat.

Cholera may be detected by throwing up a piece of raw meat in the air.

Medea : Class. Myth. A female magician who brought back to life Acson, her father-in-law, by means of her magic arts. According to some legends she was in the habit of boiling old people in a large cauldron, under the pretence of making them young again. When her husband abandoned her, she revenged herself by killing her children.

Medicine Bottle : If empty medicine bottles be sold, you will want them filled again for yourself. (LEAN, Vol. II, p. 182 ; *F.L.R.*, i).

Medus : Gr. Myth. Son of Aegeus and step-brother of Theseus.

Medusa : Gr. Myth. The only one of the Gorgons who was mortal. She was a beautiful maiden noted for her splendid hair. The goddess Minerva being enraged with her, changed her hair into snakes, and endowed her with the terrible power of changing anyone into stone who looked at her. She was slain by Perseus who succeeded in cutting off her head while looking at its reflection in the shield. From her blood sprang Chrysaor and Pegasus.

Megaera : Gr. Myth. One of the three Furies.

Meleager : Gr. Myth. Son of Althea, Queen of Calydon. He was one of the Argonauts, and he slew the wild boar of Calydon. After the Calydonian hunt, he slew his uncles. Althea, enraged at this, thrust the brand into the fire, as it was foretold at his birth that his life would last no longer than this brand, and thus killed him. Meleager was in love with Atlanta. Vide *Amber.*

Meleagrides : Gr. Myth. The sisters of Meleager, who were turned into guinea-hens.

Melicertes : Gr. Myth. Son of Ino. After he was thrown into the sea by his mother, he became the sea-god Palaemon.

Melon : In Turkestan the " throat " of a melon must be cut before it is fit to eat. (Because the Qor'an says, it is unlawful to eat an animal before its throat is cut). (SCHUYLER, Vol. II, p. 29)

Melons planted on Ascension Day grow well (*North Germany*, WUTTKE, p. 21).

Melpomene : Gr. Myth. The Muse of Tragedy.

Mélusine : According to a French legend Mélusine, a fairy, was the ancestress of many noble families. She appears occassionally to give them warning of some approaching catastrophe. (HARTLAND, *Science of Fairy Tales*).

" . . . fée que les romans de chevalerie et les légendes du Poitou représentent comme l'aïeule et la protectrice de la maison de Lusignan."—*Petit Larousse illustré*, p. 1456. cf. *White Lady, Death Warnings*.

Meluzina : Bohemian Folk-lore. The spirit of the winds.

Memory : If you want to commit anything to memory, put the book containing the passage under the pillow before going to sleep. (*Silesia, Hesse, Tyrol*—WUTTKE, p. 186 ; *Denmark*, ANDERSEN, *Fairy Tales* (Little Tuk).

Menstruation : According to the Talmud, if a woman at the beginning of her period passes between two men, she thereby kills one of them ; if she passes between them towards the end of her period, she only causes them to quarrel violently. (J. BEIGEL, *Die Medizin der Talmudisten,* Leipzig and Berlin, 1885, p. 1593).

In Syria, a woman who has her courses may neither salt nor pickle, for the people think that whatever she salted or pickled would not keep. (FRAZER, *G.B.*, Vol III, p. 225, quoting EIJUB ABELA in *Zeitschrift des deutschen Palästina-Vereins*, VII (1885), p. 111).

The Guayquiris of Orinoco think that, when a woman has her period, everything upon which she steps will die, and that if a man treads on the place where she has passed, his legs will immediately swell up. (FRAZER, *ib.*)

In Brunswick people think that if a menstruous woman assists at the killing of a pig, the pork will putrefy. (R. ANDREE, *Braunschweiger Volkskunde*, p. 291)ᵢ

In the Greek island of Calymnos, it is believed that the presence of a menstruous woman in a boat will raise storms. (W. R. PATON in *Folklore*, I (1890), p. 524).

According to Pliny, the touch of a menstruous woman turned wine to vinegar, blighted crops, killed seedlings, blunted swords and razors, killed bees, brought down the fruit from trees, caused mares to miscarry, and so forth. (PLINY, *Nat. Hist.*, VII, 64*sq.*, XXVIII, 77*sq.*)

Menstrual blood is believed to be a powerful means of inspiring love. (PLOSS, *Das Weib*, Vol. I, p. 444) ; cf. *Ethnologie du Bengale*, p. 79 ; JOLLY, *Medicin*, (Grundr. d. Indo-Ar. Phil.), p. 50 ; VAN WATERS MIRIAM, *The Adolescent Girl among Primitive Peoples*, p. 23 ; L. K. A. K. IVER, *The Cochin Tribes and Castes*, Vol. I, p. 203. Vide *Barrenness*.

Mephistopheles : It is the name by which the Devil is called in Goethe's Faust and in Marlow's Life and Death of Dr. Faustus.

Mer : Babyl. Myth.   Another name for Adad.

Mercury : Rom. Myth.   Son of Zeus, messenger of the Gods, and himself a god of commerce, gain and eloquence. His worship was introduced into Rome from Southern Italy as early as 495 B.C.

Mermaid : An imaginary species of beings supposed to inhabit the sea ; they have the head and trunk of a woman, the lower limbs being replaced by the tail of a fish, and are often confused with the Sirens of Classical mythology. (LEHMANN, *A.Z.*, p. 15; BARING-GOULD, *Cur. Myths.*, p. 508; CONWAY, *Demonol.*, Vol. II, p. 218 ; THORPE, *N.M.*, Vol. II, pp. 27, 28, 173 ; BASSETT, p. 171 *et seq.*)

If a fisherman meets a mermaid, he will catch no fish that day. (THORPE, op. cit., p. 76).

Merman : The male counterpart of a mermaid.

Merrow : Irish Lore. A mermaid.

Meteor : Falling stars, eclipses, comets and other signs in the heavens portend the death or fall of princes. (LEHMANN).

Midas : Gr. Myth. A king of Phrygia, who obtained from Bacchus the power of changing everything he touched into gold. Even his food was changed into this metal the moment he touched it. To cure him of this marvellous and fearful power, the god made him bathe in the river Pactolus. For having preferred the flute of Pan to Apollo's lyre, Apollo made donkey's ears grow on him.

Midgard Serpent : Norse Myth. A sea monster, the offspring of Loki.

Midnight : Ghosts and other spirits wander about at this hour.
" In the dead vast and middle of the night,
. . . a figure like your father
. . appears before them. . . ."
SHAKESPEARE, *Hamlet*, I, 2.

Midzuha no me : In Japan the Water was made a female deity under this name.

Milford Haven : Fairies were supposed to attend the market of Milford Haven as late as the 19th Century.

Milk : Fairies are very fond of milk and often try to gratify their desires on " unsained " or unchurched women. (GREGOR, *Folk-lore of N.E. Scot.*, pp. 5, 60, 62).

All liquids spilled on the ground are supposed to go to the use of fairies. (STEWART, p. 124; DALYELL, *Dark Sup.*, p. 193).

It is considered a very good omen in India to see milk immediately on waking up in the morning.

Milk Tooth : Milk teeth should be swallowed, if nice, white teeth are desired. (*U.S.A.*, KNORTZ, p. 99). Vide *Tooth*.

Mill : In Slavic and Teutonic (STRACKERJAN, Vol. II, p. 142) folk-lore, mills are believed to be the haunts of all kinds of evil spirits.

Flour brought from a mill, especially one owned by a Turk, must be fumigated, in order to prevent the Devil from entering into it. (ST. CLAIR and BROPHY, *Bulgaria*, p. 46 ; TYLOR, *P.C.*, Vol. II, p. 146).

Mimas : Class. Myth. A giant who, warring against the gods, was killed by lightning.

Mimer : Norse Legend. A smith who reared Siegfried and incited him to slay Fafnir.

(ii) Another spelling for Mimir.

Mimi : In the " Ring of the Nibelungen " he is the smith who aids Siegfried to win the ring, and is slain by the hero for his treachery.

Miming : Teut. Myth. A forest spirit, the guardian of a power-ful sword.

Mimir : Norse Myth. A giant whose abode is a spring flowing from the root of the world-ash Yggdrasil. Drinking the waters of the spring, he knows all the past and the future. This was the water-spirit, into whose waters Odin had put his eye in pledge, in order to win wisdom.

Min : Egypt. Myth. A god of procreation, chief deity of Panopolis.

Minerva : Class. Myth. Daughter of Zeus, goddess of sagacity and arts. She presided over all artistic works and herself excelled in the arts of embroidery, etc. Vide *Arachne*.

Minjika, Minjikâ (f.) : Hindu Myth. Two beings who sprang from the seed of Rudra, which was spilt upon a mountain. They are to be worshipped by those who desire the welfare of children. (DOWSON, *H.C.D.*, p. 209).

Minos : Gr. Myth. Son of Zeus and Europa, king of Crete. After his death he was made a judge of the dead in Hades ; the other two judges were Eacus and Rhadamantos. Vide *Talos*.

Minotaur : Gr. Myth. A monster, half man and half bull, the offspring of Pasiphae (q.v.). It was confined in the laby-rinth in Crete, where it devoured the periodical tribute of seven youths and seven maidens till it was slain by Theseus, (q.v.) who volunteered to be one of the seven.

Miolnir : Norse Myth. The name of Thor's hammer.

Mirror : To break a mirror denotes seven years of poverty (*Pinsk, Jew. Enc.*, Vol. IX, p. 601 ; *U.S.A.*, KNORTZ, p. 37 ; HAZLITT, p. 225), or bad luck (*Gt. Britain*, BRAND, *Observations*, Vol. III, p. 169 ; GREGOR, p. 203).

If one looks at himself after eleven o'clock at night, he will see the reflection of the Devil's face beside his own. (*Mosel, Tyrol*—WUTTKE, p. 132 ; STRACKERJAN, Vol. I, p. 262 ; *Gt. Britain, India*).

A woman should not look at herself in the mirror for at least six weeks after she was brought to childbed, lest ghostly faces peer at her. (*Silesia*—WUTTKE, p. 207).

If a mirror be broken, it is a warning that someone in the house will lose a friend ere long ; or is prophetic that a person will never marry ; or if married, will lose the person wedded.

A mirror falling off the wall without any apparent cause is an omen of an impending disaster or of a death in the family. (*N. & C. Germany, Tyrol*——WUTTKE, p. 38 ; *Gt. Britain*).

If a mirror be held before a sleeping man during a hail or thunder-storm, the storm will cease. (LELAND, *Etruscan Roman Remains*, p. 93). Vide *Alasnam's Mirror, Ts'in King, Picture, Stuttering.*

Miser : The spirits of misers must return to earth.

The name of a miser should not be uttered the first thing in the morning ; if you do so, you will have nothing to eat that day. (*Bengal*—TAGORE, *Mashi and other Stories*, p. 92, Note I).

Mistletoe : It is no sin to kiss under the mistletoe at Christmas. Mistletoe was the only thing on earth which had not taken an oath to do Balder harm. (See FRAZER, *The Magic Art, passim.*)

Mithaoxta : Pers. Myth. A spirit which represented "false speech."

Mithras : Pers. Myth. A god of the light of the middle zone, a defender of truth, helper of Ahura-Mazda in his struggles with the powers of darkness.

Mitra : Vedic Myth. A celestial deity, probably the same as the Persian Mithras, who early sank to relative unimportance.

Mnemosyne : Gr. Myth. A Titaness, daughter of Uranus, goddess of memory. She was the mother of the Muses by Zeus.

Modu : Hind. Myth.   The prince of all devils that take possession of human beings.   (Dr. BREWER, *R.H.*).

Möen : Danish Folk-lore.   The king of the elves is supposed to reside at Möen.

cf. *Bornholm.*

Mole : Moles are blind ; hence the expression, " blind as a mole." (*Gt. Britain*).

If a mole digs up earth in a house there will be a death therein.   (STRACKERJAN, Vol. I, p. 24).

Mole-holes are the doors of ghosts.   (*Silesia*—WUTTKE, p. 224).

Mole-mark : A mole on the lip is a sign of gluttony and talkativeness ; on the neck it promises wealth ; on the nose it indicates that the person will be a great traveller ; on the thigh it forebodes poverty and sorrow ; on the throat, health and wealth, on the wrist, ingenuity.

A mole-mark on the arm-pits promises wealth and honour ; on the ankle bespeaks modesty in men, courage in women ; on the right breast it is a sign of honesty, on the left forebodes poverty ; on the chin promises wealth ; on the right ear, respect, on the left, dishonour ; on the centre of the forehead it bespeaks treachery, sullenness and untidiness; on the right temple it forebodes you will enjoy the friendship of the great, on the left it forebodes distress ; on the right foot, wisdom, on the left foot, rashness ; on the right side of the heart denotes virtue, on the left wickedness ; on the knee of a man it denotes he will have a rich wife, on the knee of a woman, she may expect a large family. (See *Ethnologie du Bengale*, pp. 128, 129; LEAN, *Collectanea*, Vol. II, p. 312 ; HAZLITT, *Faiths and Folklore*, pp. 413 *seq.* ; BRAND, *Observations*, Vol. III, p. 254).

" Moles on the neck,
Money by the peck."
Ohio (KNORTZ, p. 126)

Mole's Paw : Mole's paws are used in Gt. Britain to keep off cramp.

A mole's paw cures toothache (*F.L.R.*, I).

Monday : Monday is an unlucky day.

Servant girls appointed on a Monday break many things. (*Rhineland, Westphalia*—WUTTKE, p. 104). Vide *Sunday, Wednesday.*

M

Money : The Old Prussians furnished their dead with money to spend on his weary journey to the spirit world ; in Germany, France, China (false paper money) and Ireland this custom is kept up to the present day.

The Russian Jews (*Jew. Enc.*, Vol. IX, p. 598) and the Indians consider it unlucky to dream of money.

When taking money out of a purse leave at least a coin or two in it ; money attracts money. (*Grodno—Jew. Enc.*, Vol. IX, p. 601).

If they are compelled to give away the last piece of money they possess, the Bohemians say : " *Ty mùy milý posledečku, přivez mi jich na kolečku.*" (You my dear last one, bring me back a cartload like you). (GROHMANN, p. 227).

If you meet a frog, it denotes that you are about to receive some money.

To see blood is lucky ; it denotes money. (*Gt. Britain*).

It is unlucky to dream of money. (*Gt. Britain, India, U.S.A.*—KNORTZ, p. 43). Vide *Blood, Bubble, Cattle, Execution, Frog, Gold, Ant, Arm, Moon, Palm, Swallow, Blindness.*

Money Spider : To find small spiders of a golden colour, *Arenea scenica*, commonly called " money spider," on one's clothes is lucky—forebodes that you will be in receipt of some money soon. (*Gt. Britain.*)

Monkey : Monkeys are believed by various nations to be the forefathers of the human race. (cf. TYLOR, *P.C.*, Vol. I, p. 339 etc. ; DARWIN, *Origin of Species.*)

In Guinea monkeys found near a grave are believed to be animated by the spirits of the dead. (WILSON, pp. 210, 218 ; TYLOR, *P.C.*, Vol II, p. 7. cf. SKEAT, *Malay Magic*, pp. 184 *seq.*).

Monkeys' paws are used as vermifuge amulets in Formosa. cf. *Banmânush, Orang-utan.*

Monster : The offspring of incestuous unions are monsters. (cf. GRIFFIS, *M.E.*, p. 472).

Moon : Among the Mbocobis of South America the moon is the man and the sun his wife. (D'ORBIGNY). An Ottawa story describes the sun and the moon as brother and sister. (SCHOOLCRAFT). Among the Egyptians Osiris and Isis were the sun and the moon, brother and sister, husband and wife ; among the Peruvians it was the same as with the Egyptians. (PRESCOTT). In England and in France, the sun is the man (Eng. *the sun*, m., Fr. *le soleil*) and the moon is the woman (Eng. *moon*, f., Fr. *la lune*) ; in Germany, it is the reverse. (*der Mond.*, m., *die Sonne*, f).

When the " mone lies sain " on her back or when her " horns " are pointed towards the zenith, be warned in time, for foul weather is at hand.

Foul weather may be expected when the " new moon appears with the old one in her arms."

To see the new moon for the first time on the right hand side direct before you is lucky ; but to see it on the left hand, or to turn round and see it behind you is the contrary.

To sow under a waxing moon is beneficent for the crop.

Turn your money over when you see the new moon for the first time ; it brings luck. (*Gt. Britain.*)

If pregnant women look at the moon, the child will be " moon-struck." (*Silesia, Oberpfalz*—WUTTKE, p. 193).

The bacon of swine killed in a waning moon will waste much in cooking.

If you see the new moon over the right shoulder, take three steps backwards and repeat the following :

" New moon, true moon, true and bright,
If I have a lover let me dream of him to-night.
If I am to marry far, let me hear a bird cry ;
If I am to marry near, let me hear a cow low ;
If I am never to marry, let me hear a hammer
    knock."—*Tennessee.*

and one of these three sounds is always heard. (BERGEN, C.S., p. 117). Vide *Full-moon.*

Moonlight : He who sews by moonlight, sews his burial clothes. (STRACKERJAN, Vol. I, p. 47).

Moon, Spots on the : In Indian superstition the spots on the moon represent Krishna milking a cow under a spreading tree ; in England, " the man in the moon."

Moonstone : It has the virtue of making trees fruitful and of curing epilepsy.

Moonstone brings luck to the owner. (U.S.A.— WILKIE COLLINS, *Moonstone*).

It contains in it an image of the moon, representing the increase and decrease every month.

Moosburg : One of Freiherr von Güttingen's castles.

Moosweiber : Same as Buschweiber.

Morana : Bohemian Folk-lore. The goddess of death. She has been identified with the Greek Hecate. (GROHMANN, p. 6).

Moravaya panna : " Black woman " ; in Slavic countries this is a frequent disguise of the demon of pestilence.

Morgaine la Faye: " Morgaine the fairy." It is believed to the present day that she retains Holger the Dane entranced in Avalon in company with her brother, King Arthur, and other renowned knights.

Morpheus : Class. Myth. God of dreams, son of Night and Day.

Morta : Rom. Myth. One of the goddesses of fate. She is identical with the Greek Atropos.

Moss : To cure barrenness, boil some moss growing on the Temple walls and drink the water. (*Jews of Palestine* —SCHIFFER, *Urquell*, II, 235).

Moth : A moth flying round you presages the arrival of a letter. (*Gt. Britain*).

Mother Carey's Chicken : Vide *Petrel, Albatross*.

Mountain-climbing : The tongue of an eagle sewn in the collar of one's coat makes mountain climbing easier. (ALPENBURG, p. 384 ; WUTTKE, p. 164).

Mountain Mother : Same as Great Mother.

Mourning : Mourning clothes must not be exchanged for ordinary ones on a Sunday, or someone else will die ; they must neither be discarded without sufficient reason.

Mouse : Many mice signify war. (*Alsace*—LAMBS, p. 30).
    According to some legends mice are the souls of murdered people.
    If a mouse gnaws our clothes during the night, or nibbles a hole in a bag of flour (*Greece*—LAWSON, p. 328), it is indicative of some impending evil, perhaps even death.
    If food which a mouse has nibbled be eaten, it will give sore throat.
    A fried mouse is a specific for small-pox.
    St. Gertrude and St. Huldrick ward off mice.
    Suspending a live mouse by the tail before the fire and roasting it expels mice from the house. (LEAN, Vol. II, p. 418).
    In Bohemia the peasants, though they kill field mice and grey mice without scruple, always spare white mice. If a white mouse died, the luck of the house would be gone, and the grey mice would multiply in the house. (GROH-MANN, p. 60 ; FRAZER, *G.B.*, Vol. II, p. 426).
    Arab superstition regards a particular species of mouse as inhabited by the souls of an extinct Israelitish tribe. (BERTHOLET, p. 39). Vide *Field Mouse.*

Mouth : If anything falls in the corpse's mouth, the whole family will die. (*Franken*—WUTTKE, p. 212).

Mowing : If a sexton mows the churchyard, rain is sure to come. (STRACKERJAN, Vol. I, p. 47).

Mucus : The nasal mucus is considered by many primitive races to be a powerful amulet. (FRAZER, *Golden Bough*).

Mule : Vide *Foam.*

Mulkari : The Mulkari of the North-West Central Queensland is the "supernatural power who makes everything the blacks cannot otherwise account for ; he is a good, beneficent person, and never kills anyone." He is described as "a benevolent, omnipresent, supernatural being; anything incomprehensible." (LANG, *Magic and Rel.*, p. 40, quoting Mr. Roth).

Mumbo Jumbo : An African bogey, hideous and malignant, the terror of women and children. (DR. BREWER, *R.H.* p. 737).

Mummy : Mummies must not be carried in a ship or some misfortune would happen ; the same applies to corpses. (STRACKERJAN, Vol. I, p. 47). Vide *Corpse.*

Munda : Hindu. Myth. "Bald"; the name of a demon slain by Durgâ.

Munkir and Nekir : Moham. Myth. Two angels of the Arabs, who examine all the dead and torture the wicked in their graves. (LANE, *A.S.M.A.*, p. 26).

Mûra : The Mûras of Bohemian folk-lore are identical with the Polish *Upior* and our own Vampire (q.v.).

Murder : The spirits of murdered people must wander about on earth so long as they would have done had they been alive (*East Prussia*) ; likewise those of people dying an accidental death. (*Tyrol, Kärnthen*—WUTTKE, p. 217).
It is a bad omen to see a murder, or wild animals chased by dogs, or to pass a dead body lying on the ground. (*Tibet,* WADDELL, p. 135).

Muscatel : Muscatels kept in one's pocket is a cure for boils. (STRACKERJAN, Vol. I, p. 85).

Muses : Class. Myth. Daughters of Zeus and Mnemosyne. They were nine in number and presided over the arts; they dwelt with Apollo on Mt. Parnassus. They were as follows:
> Clio— the Muse of history.
> Euterpe—the Muse of music.
> Thalia—the Muse of comedy.
> Melpomene—the Muse of tragedy
> Terpsichore—the Muse of dancing.
> Erato—the Muse of elegiac poetry.
> Polymnia—the Muse of lyric poetry.
> Urania—the Muse of astronomy, and lastly
> Calliope—the Muse of eloquence and heroic poetry

Music : Persons bitten by the tarantula are supposed to be cured by music.

If you imagine you can hear music, it is a sure sign that you are in the presence of some well-disposed spirit (*India*).

Amphion is said to have built the walls of Thebes by the music of his lyre. Hirem and the capital of King Arthur's kingdom were also built to divine music. The city of Jericho was destroyed by music. (*Josh*. VI, 20).

If you dream of hearing music, you will receive acceptable news.

Mussel : A fountain near the waterless sea, which purges from transgression. So called because it is contained in a hollow stone like a mussel-shell. Those who test it enter the water, and, if they are true men, it rises till it covers their heads three times. (DR. BREWER, *R.H.*, p. 760).

Musubi : A Japanese god of growth, who represents an abstract quality. (ASTON, *Shinto*, p. 11), and is said to be a formidable rival of Amaterasu.

Mut : Egypt. Myth. Consort of Amon-Ra, the sun, mother of Chunsu, the moon. She is often represented as lion headed.

Mutilation : Among various tribes, as for example the Indians of Brazil, the Australians, the Chinese, the Japanese, etc., it is believed that the spirit or ghost of a man bears the same mutilation as the body of the man it originally inhabited. (TYLOR, *P.C.*, Vol. I, p. 407; *Enc. Rel. Eth.* Art. Demon—Japanese. Cf. FRAZER, *Golden Bough*, I, 204; *id.*, *On Certain Burial Customs as illustrative of the Soul*, in Journ. Anthrop. Inst., Vol. XV, p. 66; DURKHEIM, *Elementary Forms of Religious Life*, pp. 242 seq.; *Ethnologie du Bengale*, p. 90; TYLOR, *Early History*, Vol. I, p. 358, *id.*, *P.C.*, Vol. II, p. 230; CROOKE, *P.R.I.*, Vol. I, p. 280).

Myrrha: Class. Myth. Mother of Adonis. She was afterwards changed into a myrrh tree.

Myrtle : A girl engaged to be married must not plant myrtles or the wedding will be broken off. (*East Prussia*—WUTTKE, p. 204).

N

Nachzehrer : The Vampire (q.v.) is called by this name in some parts of Germany. (WUTTKE, p. 221).

Nâgas : " Snakes " ; the local spirits of the Hindus.

Nagual : The Nagual of Central America is a kind of guardian spirit in animal form.

Naiad : Class. Myth. Certain kinds of nymphs.

Nail : A white spot on the thumb nail promises a present ; on the index finger it denotes a friend ; on the middle finger, a foe; on the ring finger, a letter or a sweetheart; on the little finger, a journey to go. In England this is indicated by touching the fingers in turn and repeating the following doggerel verse :
> " A friend, a foe,
> Money to come, a journey to go."

The number of white spots on a person's nails determine the number of years he has to live. (*Alsace*—LAMBS, p. 39).

If the nails of a person suffering from fever be cut, and the parings stuck on with wax on a neighbour's door before sunrise, the fever will be transferred to the neighbour. (PLINY, *Nat. Hist.*, XXVIII, 86).

The Russian peasants place the parings of a dead person's nails along with the body in the grave, in the belief that the same has to climb a steep hill before reaching Paradise. (RALSTON, *Songs of the Russian People*, 109 ; cf. FRAZER, *Golden Bough*, Vol. I, p. 368*sq.*).

In America white spots on the nail are considered lucky.

In East Anglia spots on the thumb nail are more certain of fulfilment than the others. According to the local doggerel :
> " Spots on the fingers are sure to linger,
> Spots on the thumb are sure to come."

A girl who bites her finger-nails will bring forth children with great difficulty. (*Japan*—GRIFFIS, *M.E.*, p. 469).

Finger and toe nails should be carefully destroyed, otherwise other people finding them may perform magical operations. (*Gt. Britain, France, Germany, India*, etc.).

If while cutting nails, a piece springs into the fire, the owner will meet with a speedy death ; the consequences may however be averted by throwing some salt in the fire. Nails should be trimmed just before starting on a journey, and never at night. (*Japan*—GRIFFIS, *M.E.*, p. 467).

If babies' nails be cut before they are a year old, they will not grow.

If you cut your nails on a Monday, you will have luck all the week ; but if on a Friday, unluck (*Gt. Britain*), or it will bring luck and help to keep away toothaches. (*Germany*—WUTTKE, pp. 12, 17).

If you throw away nail-clippings in the fire either you yourself or your house will catch fire. (*Japan*—CHAMBERLAIN, *T.J*, Ger. tr. p. 18). Vide *European*.

Nail Iron : An iron coffin nail, if accidentally found, is used for various magical purposes, such as for curing diseases, punishing thieves, catching game, etc.

Name : If two children belonging to the same family bear the same name, one of them is sure to die. (*Pomerania*—WUTTKE, p. 197).

The real names of persons are often concealed, for fear that others ascertaining it, may perform various magical operations. (FRAZER, *G.B.*, Vol. I, p. 406 *sq.*) ; CROOKE, *P.R.I.*, Vol. II, p. 5).

The Finns and Esthonian peasants are very loth to mention wild beasts by their proper names, for they believe that either they will have poor sport, or that the creatures will do them much harm. (CASTREN, *Vorlesungen*, p. 201; BOECLER-KREUTZWALD, p. 120).

The Kamtchatkans abstain from mentioning the names of bears, whales and wolves, for they say that these can understand human language. (STELLER, p. 276).

Bengali women do not mention snakes and thieves by their proper names. (*N.I.N.Q.*, I, 15; *Ethnologie du Bengale* p. 83).

Various other animals and things are called by names different to their own, generally through fear of their vengeance. (FRAZER, *G.B.*, Vol. I, pp. 451-469).

In Brittany, the name of a deceased is not uttered. (LE BRAZ, Vol. I, p. 287). Vide *Child*.

Namtar : Babyl. Myth. They were plague-demons.

Nana : Egypt. Myth. Another name for Tashmit.

Nandini : Hindu Myth. The cow of plenty belonging to the sage Vasishtha, said to have been born of Surabhi. The cow of plenty that was produced at the churning of the ocean. (DOWSON, *H.C.D.*, p 218).

Nanna : Norse Myth. The daughter of King Gevarus of Norway. Balder is said to have been in love with her.

Narcissus : A flower. According to a Greek fable Narcissus fell in love with his own reflection in a fountain, and, having pined away because he could not kiss it, was changed into a flower which bears his name.

Navel : After the first human being was made, the Evil One spat in his stomach, but Allah hastened to tear out the contaminated flesh, and thus the navel originated. (*Turkish*, Kunos. *T.F.T.*, p. 2. For various superstitions see Ploss, *Das Weib*, Vol. II, pp. 277 *et seq.*).

Nebo : Assyro-Babyl. Myth. A god of Borsippa which is supposed to be older than Babylon itself. He is the representative of wisdom, and to him is the art of writing ascribed, even by the priests of Babylon.

Neck : If the neck of anyone grows stiff, or the muscles of the head are twisted awry, it is a portent that the person will die by the neck. (Hazlitt, p. 430).

Needle : You are inviting trouble if you utter the word "needle" soon after you wake up in the morning. (*Bengal*).
Death is presaged by the finding of a needle threaded with black cotton, on the way. (*Silesia*—Wuttke, p. 38).
If while sewing, the needle breaks in three pieces, it is a sign of a wedding in the near future. (*Gt. Britain, Germany, Bohemia.*)
Needles should not be lent to others, lest they " prick " your friendship. (*Tyrol*—Wuttke, p. 135).
It is unlucky to pick up a needle in the street. (*Gt. Britain*). Cf. *Pin*.
If a lizard runs over your hand you will be handy with the needle. (*Alsace*—Lambs, p. 30).

Negro : To dream of negroes portends illness or death. (U.S.A.—Knortz, p. 21).
To see a black man the first thing on waking up in the morning is an omen of luck (*Gt. Britain*).

Nek : Another name for the Nökke.

Nekhebit : Egypt. Myth. Nekhebit and Uatchit were taken by Horus in the form of two serpents, that they might consume the still-remaining rebels by fire. (Wiedemann, *Leg. of the Winged Sun-Disk*).

Nekir : Vide *Munkir*.

Nekkan : In Sweden it is the musical spirit of the water. He assumes various shapes and governs the sea. Sometimes he appears as a young man on the surface of the sea, and is especially severe to young maidens who have not treated their lovers well ; hence you should always carry a piece of iron (q.v.) or steel as a protection against him. (THORPE, *N.M.*, Vo.. II, p. 39; BASSETT, p. 96).

Nekogami : The cat-god possession of Japan.

Nemesis : Gr. Myth. An ancient goddess who was the personification of retributive justice.

Nemodilky : Bohemian Folklore. Beautiful maidens with coal-black hair falling loosely over their snow-white throats. They are dressed negligently in red, and go about at night enticing young men, whom they drown and are united to them. (GROHMANN, p. 11.)

Neoptolemus : Gr. Myth. The valiant son of Achilles and Deidamia, who, after the death of his father, joined his forces against Troy. After the fall of Troy, he married Andromache, wife of Hector. He was one of the heroes in the wooden horse, and the husband of Hermione. He was also called Pyrrhus.

Nephthys : Egypt. Myth. A goddess, daughter of Seb and Nut, sister and wife of Set, who, with Isis, was especially associated with the ritual of the dead.

Neptune : Rom. Myth. Son of Saturn, brother of Jupiter and Pluto, husband of Amphitrite. He was a god of the water, especially of the sea, whose worship was early introduced in Rome. He is usually represented as bearing a trident.

Nereid : Certain kinds of nymphs. Class. Myth. A sea-nymph. The Nereids, about fifty or hundred in number, were the daughters of Nereus and Doris, and attendants upon Poseidon. They are represented as riding sea-horses, and are either of entire human form or with the tail of a fish. cf. *Mermaid*.

Nereus : Class. Myth. A god of the sea, husband of Doris, father of the Nereids.

Nergal : Assyro-Babyl. Myth. One of the great gods. He is the god of the Midsummer sun, the sun in its burning aspect, also the god of war and pestilence. In Babylonian mythology, he is a sun-god who was worshipped in Cutah. In Assyria he was also a god of chase. Vide *Aralu*.

Nerthus : Teut. Myth. A goddess whose chief seat of worship was the island of Zeeland. According to Tacitus, her character was that of a deity of peace and fertility.

Nesnas : Arab. Folklore. It resembles half a human being ; it has half a head, half a body, one arm and one leg, and has the power of human speech. It is found in Ḥadramât and El-Yemen. (LANE, *A.S.M.A.*, p. 45.)

Nessus : Gr. Myth. A Centaur shot with a poisoned arrow by Hercules for trying to outrage the hero's wife, Deianira. She, by the advice of the dying Centaur, steeped her husband's shirt in his blood as a love charm ; when he put it on, this shirt poisoned Hercules' flesh and caused such agony that he killed himself.

Nest : If a bird finds a person's hair, and builds its nest with it, the person will suffer from headache. (*Germany.*— BIRLINGER, *Aus Schwaben*, p. 509 ; PANZER, *Beiträge*, Vol. I, p. 258 ; WOLF, *Beiträge*, Vol. I, p. 224 ; HAZLITT, p. 296.) Among the gipsies of Eastern Europe the same superstition prevails. (FRAZER, *G.B.*, Vol. I, p. 378, quoting WLISLOCKI, *Zigeuner*, p. 81.) Sometimes it is thought that the person whose hair is thus used will have an eruption on the head. (*Tyrol.*—ZINGERLE, p. 181.)

Net : Hurons and Athabascan Indians married their nets to young girls to obtain luck in fishing. (BASSETT, p. 411.)

News, Good : Good news is foretold by a flea-bite. (WUTTKE, p. 34.) Vide *Music, Nose.*

New Year : It is customary in China to cover the outside of doors and windows on this day with paper scrolls containing some mottoes, quotations from ancient literature, etc., as suggestive of material prosperity. (*Enc. Rel. Eth.*, Vol. VIII, p. 260.)

In Bengal people put on new clothes on this day, in the belief that they will not be in want for the rest of the year, and nothing is lent or sold on credit.

To meet a dark man immediately on getting up on New Year's morn is a prognostication of luck for the whole year. (*Great Britain.*)

In Tyrol and Silesia the peasantry believe to the present day that numerous phantoms such as wraiths, headless spirits, etc., can be seen on New Year's Eve.

If a person goes at midnight on New Year's Eve with a candle in each hand in front of a mirror and calls a dead man three times loudly by his name, the face of the deceased will be reflected on the glass. (General.— cf. WUTTKE, p. 224.)

"He who is born on New Year's morn,
Will have his own way as sure as you're born."

BERGEN, *Cur. Sup.*, p. 21.

Vide *Tear, Star.*

Neznama paní : In and around the district of Holitz, Death personified is designated by this name.

Nibelungs : Ger. Myth. The children of the mist; a race of dwarfs or demoniac beings, and the original possessors of the famous hoard and ring won by Siegfried (q.v.).

Nidaba : Babyl. Myth. A goddess of the agricultural type.

Nidhogg : Scand. Myth. A dragon or adder that gnaws the roots of the fabled ash-tree Yggdrasil.

Niflheim : Scand. Myth. A region of cold and darkness into which one of the roots of the ash-tree Yggdrasil descends.

Niflhel : Norse Myth. A name of the underworld.

Night : In Ireland, people born at night are said to have the power of seeing ghosts. (LADY WILDE, p. 204.)
St. Christopher protects people from night alarms.

Nightingale : Aëdon, after the death of her son, was changed into a nightingale by Zeus. cf. *Philomele.*

Nightmare : It is believed to be caused by a female demon called Mara (q.v.) sitting astride the sleeper's chest.
In Indian superstition nightmares are caused by the soul being tortured in its peregrinations during sleep.
Nightmares can be kept off by keeping a coal-rake in the bedroom. (*Yorkshire.*)

Nigi-haya-hi : Jap. Myth. "Gentle, swift sun." A sun-god who came down from heaven in a heavenly rock-boat, and became chieftain of one of the tribes subdued by Jimmu Tennō.

Nikasha : Hind. Myth. (i) A female demon, mother of Râvana. (ii) The mother of the carnivorous imps called Pisitâsanas.

Nin-agid-Khadu : Babyl. Myth. A goddess, probably of a local nature.

Nin-dara : Babyl. Myth. A deity of a local character.

Nin-gursu : Babyl. Myth. A solar deity, the patron deity of Sipurla.

Ninib : Assyro-Babyl. Myth. A solar deity, one of the chief gods of the pantheon. Primarily he was the god of the spring and the morning sun, and patron of agriculture. In Babylonian mythology he is essentially an agricultural deity who presides over the fields, and who is appealed to not merely to ensure fertility, but to protect the boundaries of the fields against unlawful invasion.

Ninigi : A grandson of the Japanese sun-goddess. Ninigi was despatched to earth, and descended on a mountain in Kiushiu. Here he married a mountain-god's daughter, named Konohana-sakuya-hime (*q.v.*), rejecting as too ugly her elder sister Ihanaga-hime. The latter uttered a curse, whereupon human beings became short-lived.

Ninko : The human-fox possession of Izumo, Japan. Vide *Izuna*.

Nin-mar : Babyl. Myth. An ancient goddess whose seat of worship lay in or near the Persian Gulf.

Nin-sun : Babyl. Myth. " The destructive lady " ; consort of Lugal-Banda.

Niobe : Gr. Myth. Daughter of Tantalus, wife of Amphion. Her pride in her fourteen children led her to compare herself to Leto who had only two, Apollo and Diana. To punish her Apollo and Artemis (Diana) slew all her children ; she herself was changed into a stone by Zeus, in which form she continued to mourn her loss. She is the personification of motherly love.

Niskai : Celt. Folklore. The water-nymphs are so called.

Nisse : Scand. Myth. A class of household spirits. In Danish superstition they are of the dwarf family. They are described as small as infants but have faces like old men ; they wear a grey dress and a pointed red cap. They are domestic spirits, and are often favourably disposed towards the members of the household. (THIELE, *Danmarks Folkesagn.*) cf. *Brownie, Domovoy, Gardsvor.*

Nithhögg : Same as Nidhögg.

Nixie : Teut. Myth. A class of water-spirits. The female nixies are noted for their beautiful singing by which they allured human beings into their toils. They sometimes intermarried with mankind. The male Nix was occasionally armed with a hook, with which he dragged people down under the water. cf. *Lorelei, Siren, Bugarik, Jalpari, Alrinach.*

Njord, Njorth : Teut. Myth. One of the Vanirs. He was the hostage given by the Vanir to the Æsir after their contest. He was protector of seafarers, having power over the winds.

Noatun : Norse Myth. Njord's dwelling in Asgard.

Nočnitz : Russian Folklore. " Night-hags " ; they torment children by tickling them or sucking their blood, or disturb their sleep by their mere touch.

Noise : Demons are said to be scared by noises. (CROOKE, *P.R.I.*, Vol. I, p. 167 ; cf. H. L. STRATFIELD, *'Ranchi, Journ. As. Soc. Bengal*, LXXII, pt. III (Cal. 1904), p. 36 ; FRAZER, *The Scapegoat*, p. 139 ; DOOLITTLE, *The Chinese*, Vol. II, p. 265 ; SKEAT, *Malay Magic*, p. 11 ; MARSDEN, *History of Sumatra*, p. 157 ; BASSETT, p. 33.)

Nökke : In Danish superstition he is a river-spirit who some- times appears in the form of a horse, sometimes as an old man ; oftener as a golden-haired boy who plays the harp most melodiously. (THIELE, *Danmarks Folkesagn*; THORPE, *N.M.*, Vol. II, p. 20 ; GRIMM, *Teut. Myth.*, Vol. II. p. 488.)
  They love to dance in the moonlight, and, like mermaids, foretell the future and are possessed of protean wisdom. (THORPE, *op. cit.*, Vol. III, p. 87.)

Nona : Rom. Myth. One of the goddesses of Fate. She is identical with the Greek Clotho.

Noorele : A being with three unbegotten sons, who lives up among the clouds. He is all-powerful and of a benevolent nature. He made the earth, trees, water, etc. He receives the souls (*ladko*=shades, umbræ) of the natives, who join him in the skies and will never die. (*Australian natives.*—LANG, *Magic and Religion*, p. 60.)

Norn : Norse and Teut. Myth. One of the demi-goddesses or giantesses who preside over and determine the fates of both men and gods. In Norse mythology they are usually spinners, weaving the fabric of Fate. They were three in number, and named : *Urth, Verthandi and Skuld.* cf. *Bidhâtâpurusha, Fates, Parca, Hathor, Sudičky.*

Nose : In India all ghosts are said to speak with a strong nasal accent. (DAY, *Folktales of Bengal*, p. 199 ; CROOKE, *P.R.I.*, Vol. I, p. 237 ; cf. SKEAT, *Malay Magic*, p. 31).

Itching of the nose prophesies corporal chastisement. (*Macedonia.*—ABBOTT, p. 113) ; or in Scotland, a letter. (CAMPBELL, *Sup. Scot. Highl.*, p. 258) ; or in America it denotes that the person is loved. (*Memoirs of the Amer. Folk Lore Soc.*, Vol. IV, p. 63.)

An irritation of the nose denotes, if inside, vexation ; if outside, pleasant news. (*Great Britain, India.*)

Three drops of blood dropping from a lover's nose, is an indication of the end of love. (*Rhineland, Westphalia.*— WUTTKE, p. 42) ; or the death of a parent. (GREGOR, p. 205.)

The bleeding of the nose can be stopped by tying a piece of wool round the little finger of the left hand (STRACKERJAN, Vol. I, p. 82) ; or by wearing a red ribbon or a skein of scarlet silk round the neck (LEAN, Vol. II, p. 486.) ; or by sniffing in cold water, or in grave cases, a big iron key is also placed on the back of the patient's neck (*India, Ethnologie du Bengale*, p. 140 ; cf. HOVORKÁ, *Vergleichende Volksmedizin*, Vol. II, p. 79).

If your nose itches, it is a sign that

> " You'll be mad,
> See a stranger,
> Kiss a fool,
> Or be in danger."

(*Prince Edward Island.*—BERGEN, *C.S.*, p. 140.)

Nosegay : It is unlucky to dream of making or gathering nosegays; our best hopes will come to naught. (KNORTZ, pp. 21, 138.)

November : Vide *Topaz.*

Nox : Rom. Myth. Goddess of night ; same as the Greek Nyx. Vide *Charon.*

Nu : Egypt. Myth. The double lion-god of Egypt. (BUDGE, *Book of the Dead*, p. 166.)

Nuada : Celt. Myth. A king of the Tuatha De Danann. He lost his hand in the battle in which the Firbolgs were overthrown, and replaced it by one of silver. Bress was chosen as king in his place, but was deposed and Nuada set on the throne again. He was killed by Balor. Probably he was an early war-god.

Nudd : Celt. Myth. A Cymric god of the sky. Same as Llud.

Num : A Samoyed water-god. (CONWAY, *Demonology*, Vol. l. p. 213.)

Nun : To dream of becoming a nun denotes confinement, disappointment in love or a rival.

Nurjehan's Bracelet : It gave warning of poison by a tremulous motion of the stones, which increased as the poison approached nearer and nearer.

Nusku : Assyr. Myth. A deity symbolizing the element of fire. Same as Girru.

Nut : Egypt. Myth. The heavens personified as a goddess, consort of Seb, and mother of Osiris, Isis, Nephthys, Set, Anubis, Shu and Tefnut. A winged picture of her is usually to be found painted on the outside of coffins. She is the feminine principle of Nû, that is, the watery mass out of which all the gods were evolved ; she is the goddess of the sky. (BUDGE, *Book of the Dead*, p. 4.)

Nymph : Myth. One of the numerous classes of semi-divine beings, imagined as beautiful maidens inhabiting the sea, rivers, fountains, hills, woods, or trees.
" By night they appear, and, like all the nymphs of ancient times, amuse themselves with graceful dances." (TOZER, *Highl. Turkey*.)
Vide *Obtaining*, *Nymph*.

Nyx : Gr. Myth. An ancient goddess, a personification of night. She is the daughter of Chaos, and mother of Day and Night ; she is identified with the Roman Nox.

O

Oak : Teut. Folklore. The oak is said to have sprung from the mouth of a king slain in battle ; it is the abode of departed souls (See FRAZER, *Spirits of the Corn and of the Wild*.)

Oak Speaking : Gr. Myth. A great oak tree at Dodona, which not only had human speech, but was oracular.

Oannes : Babyl. Myth. Under this form, Nebo (q.v.) is the god who instructs mankind in various arts, including writing. (CORY, *Ancient Fragments*, p. 57.)

Oar : In Icelandic belief if an oarsman leaves a little of the handle of the oar uncovered, the devil will use it (BASSETT, p. 89, quoting *F.L.R.*, 1879.)

Oats :

"Who in Janiver sows oats,
Gets gold and groats ;
Who sows in May,
Gets little that way."
(LEAN, Vol. I, p. 913.)

Oberon : Scand. Myth. King of the elves.

Oblā Bibi : The Hindus frequently invoke the help of Oblā Bibi in cases of cholera.

Obsession : The hostile action of the Devil or an evil spirit besetting anyone.

"These classes belong rather to obsession than to possession (q.v.), the spirits not actually inhabiting the bodies, but hanging or hovering about them."
TYLOR, *Primitive Culture*, II, 113.

Obtaining Nymphs : The Hindu Tāntra gives a detailed account of how a companion nymph may be acquired by a man, by means of worshipping her and repeating her name in a cemetery. (WARD, *Hindus*, Vol. II, p. 151 ; TYLOR, *P.C.*, Vol. II, p. 173 ; *Ethnologie du Bengale*, p. 101.)

Oceanid : Gr. Myth. Certain kinds of nymphs, daughters of Oceanus and Tethys.

Oceanus : Gr. Myth. The eldest of the Titans, son of Uranus and Gaea, the god of the stream bearing that name. He married his sister Tethys, their children being the rivers of the earth.

October : Vide *Opal.*

Ocypete : Gr. Myth. One of the Harpies (q.v.).

Odds and Evens : To discover whether the husband or the wife will die first, calculate the numerical value of the letters in the names of both. If the result be even, the man will die first ; if odd, the woman. (*Jew. Enc.*, Vol. IV, p. 486.)

Odin : Norse Myth. He is the supreme deity, and god of wisdom, poetry and war. He presided over Valhalla and was leader of the Furious Hunt. He is a man with only one eye, having left the other in pledge with Mimir (q.v.). His wife was Frigg ; he was the father of Balder and other gods.

Odysseus : Same as Ulysses (*q.v.*).

Œdipus : Gr. Myth. Son of Laius and Jocasta, king and queen of Thebes. At his birth an oracle said that he would kill his father ; he was therefore given away. Later, Œdipus not knowing his parentage, kills Laius in an altercation. About this time the Sphinx (q.v.) devastated the land ; Œdipus answered the Sphinx's riddle, ascended his father's throne and, as the oracle had foretold, married Jocasta, his mother. Eventually on discovering his parentage, Œdipus tore out his eyes, and Jocasta hanged herself. Œdipus was banished from his kingdom by his unnatural sons ; he went to Colones in Attica where, after cursing his sons, he expired. Vide *Sphinx, Jocasta.*

Œneus : Gr. Myth. King of Calydon, father of Deianira. Vide *Deianira, Hercules, Nessus.*

Oginius : A god of the Gauls, who has been identified with Hercules.

Ogre : A spirit who has the power of flying through the air.

Ogyges : Gr. Myth. An ancient king of Thebes, during whose reign there was a partial deluge.

Ogygia : An island where Odysseus was kept for seven years by the siren Calypso.

Ohonamochi : Jap. Myth. " Great-name-preserver." One of Susa-no-wo's children ; an Earth-god. Ohonamochi is frequently referred to as the " God who made the land." He had a numerous progeny by different mothers, among whom were the harvest and the food gods.

Oil : It is an evil omen to spill oil ; it portends poverty. (*Greece.*—LAWSON, p. 328.)

Oilman : In India it is unlucky to see the face of a *teli* or oilman immediately on getting up in the morning. The *Telis* belong to the lowest caste in India. (cf. *Ethnologie du Bengale,* pp. 122, 33.)

Ojhā : An exorcist who drives away ghosts from possessed persons.

Old Man of the Sea : A spirit or malicious demon appearing in *Alif laila wa laila,* "The Adventures of Sinbad the Sailor."

Old Nick
Old One
Old Serpent } : Different names for the Devil (q.v.).
Old Simmie

Omen : An occurrence supposed to portend or show the character of some future event.

A good omen is best at the beginning of a journey, less good, though not harmful at the middle and better near the end. (*Tibet.*—WADDEL, p. 136.)

Ondine : A nixie of French superstition.

Onion : To dream of onions portends good luck. (*U.S.A.*— KNORTZ, p. 43.) Strict Hindus do not eat onions, garlic, mushrooms and some other vegetables (JOLLY, *Recht und Sitte,* pp. 157 *sq.; Ethnologie du Bengale,* p. 85, n. 3).

Oni-tsuki : The name of the demon-possession of Japan.

Onufrius : The White Russians speak of their forest-spirit by this name. Vide *Lyesovik.*

Onyx : Onyx contains in it an imprisoned devil which wakes at sunset, and causes terror to the wearer, disturbing sleep with ugly dreams.

In the Zodiac onyx stands for Aquarius ; some say it is an emblem of August and conjugal love ; in Christian art it symbolizes sincerity.

Cupid with the sharp point of his arrows cut Venus's nails while she was asleep, and the parings falling into the Indus, sank to the bottom, and turned into onyxes.

Opal : This stone is believed to be fatal to love and sows discord between the giver and the receiver ; given, how-ever, as an engagement token, it is sure to bring luck.

Opal is an emblem of hope, and is dedicated to October Opal turns pale at the approach of poison.

Opals are unlucky (*Great Britain, Germany, France, Italy, U.S.A., India*), unless set with diamonds (*New York.*—BERGEN, *C.S.,* p. 84.)

Ops : An ancient Italian goddess of the harvest.

Orang-utan : " The man of the woods " ; Malay name for a monkey. cf. *Banmānush, Monkey.*

Oread : Certain kinds of nymphs.

Orestes : Gr. Myth. A son of Agamemnon and Clytemnestra. He revenges his father's murder by slaying his mother and Ægisthus. His friendship to Pyladus has remained proverbial.

Orion : Gr. Myth. A hunter who was changed into a con-stellation by Diana.

The Esquimaux say that the stars of Orion's Belt are the lost ones ; they are seal-hunters who lost their way home. (CRANZ, *Grönland*).

The natives of Australia say that the " stars are young men dancing a corroboree." (TYLOR, quoting STANBRIDGE.)

Orlando : Orlando was squeezed to death by Bernardo del Carpio.

Ormazd : Zoroastrianism. The supreme deity, the principal god, the creator of the world, and the guardian of mankind. He is attended by angels and archangels, and is represented as a bearded man enclosed in a winged circle. cf. *Ahur*.

Ormandine : The necromancer who threw St. David into an enchanted sleep for seven years, from. which he was reclaimed by St. George.

Oromazes : Pers. Myth. The principle of good.
Vide *Yezad*.

Orpheus : Class. Myth. Son of Œagres, king of Thracia, and the Muse Calliope. He was a poet and a musician, whose lyre could charm beasts and make trees and rocks move. He was one of the Argonauts. After his wife's death by snake-bite on the day of their marriage, he descended into Hades, and pleased Pluto so much, that he allowed Eurydice, his wife, to go back to the world again, but made a condition that Orpheus must not look back as long as he was not back on earth again. He neglected to keep this condition, and his wife had to retrace her steps to Hades.

Osiris : Egypt. Myth. The great god of the underworld, judge of the dead. He was the brother and husband of Isis, and father of Horus. He is said to have been a wise and beneficent king, who was treacherously slain by his brother Set. Osiris is considered to have been originally a corn-spirit. He is often identified with Râ as a source of life and fruitfulness.

Osprey : When fish see the osprey, they are so fascinated that they " swoon," and turning on their backs, yield themselves an easy prey to the bird. (cf. SHAKESPEARE, *Coriolanus*, Act IV Scene 7.)

Ostrich : An ostrich can digest iron (HAZLITT, p. 467) ; hence the popular expression, " A stomach like that of an ostrich."

Ottilie, St. : Bad eyes can be cured by invoking the aid of St. Ottilie.

Oudh : A province in India. According to a Hindu legend, this is considered to be the birthplace of the Aryan race. (*Petit Larousse illustré*, p. 1501.)

Ouranabad : A monster represented as a fierce flying hydra.

Oven : To dream of a hot oven denotes joy.

Never leave a stove or an oven empty ; if you have nothing to cook or bake in it, put a piece of wood in it ; if you leave it empty, you may not have anything to cook or bake when you want it. (*Minsk.—Jew. Enc.*, Vol. XI, p. 601.)

Ovinik : Russian Folklore. A kind of household-spirit, which lives in the drying kiln.

Owl : Owl's flesh is superstitiously believed to be a powerful charm, the eating of which causes a man to become a fool and lose his memory. (CROOKE, *Pop. Rel.*, Vol. I, p. 274 ; id., *Islam in India*, p. 243.)

It is unlucky to shoot an owl. (ELWORTHY, *E.E.*, p. 91.)

The cry of an owl in the immediate vicinity of a house forebodes calamity, sickness or death. (STRACKERJAN, Vol. I, p. 26 ; ABBOTT, p. 107 ; *Alsace*—LAMBS, p. 31 ; ELWORTHY, *E.E.*, p. 91 ; HAZLITT, p. 469 ; JACKSON, *F.L.N.*, Vol. II, p. 58 ; *Ethnologie du Bengale*, p. 112; DALYELL, *Dark. Sup. Scot.*, p. 503.)

One day an owl strayed into the Capitol, and the Romans, to avert the evil, underwent a formal lustration.

The death of Augustus was presaged by an owl screeching upon the top of the Curia.

The death of Commodus Aurelius, the emperor, was forboded by an owl sitting on the top of his chamber at Lanuvium.

The murder of Julius Cæsar was presaged by the screeching of owls.

The death of Valentinian was presaged by an owl, which perched on the top of the house where he used to bathe.

The great plague of Würzburg in Franconia in A.D. 1542, was foretold by the screeching of an owl.

Vide *Ascalophos*.

Oyster : Oysters in popular belief grow on trees. (GOODRICH, *Man upon the Sea*, p. 255.)

Whoever eats oysters on St. James' Day (August 5th), will never know want. (BASSETT, p. 265.)

Ozair : A prophet. One day riding on an ass by the ruins of Jerusalem, after its destruction by the Chaldeans, he doubted in his mind, whether God could raise the city up again. Whereupon God caused him to die ; he remained dead a hundred years, but was then restored to life. He found the basket of figs and wine as fresh as when he died, but his ass was a mass of bones. While he still looked on, the dry bones came together, received life, and the resuscitated ass began to bray ; whereupon the prophet no longer doubted the power of God to raise up Jerusalem from its ruins. (*Al Qŏr'an.* The legend is based on Neh. II, 12-20.)

P

Pactolus : A river of Lydia in Asia Minor, which was said to flow over golden sands. The modern name is Bagouly. Vide *Midas*.

Padalon : The Hindu hell under the earth. It has eight gates, each of which is guarded by a gigantic deity.

Paean : Gr. Myth. A doctor of the gods. He cured Ares who was wounded by Diomed.

Paian : A Greek name of Apollo.

Pain : All sudden pains are warnings of evil at hand.

Pairikas : (Late Persian : Peris). " Enchantresses " ; they were seductive beings like the Jahis.

Pakshirāj : " King of birds." The winged steed of Indian mythology. (DAY, *Folktales of Bengal* ; *Ethnologie du Bengale*, p. 102.)

Palæmon: Gr. Myth. The son of Ino, after being thrown into the sea by his mother, became the sea-god Palæmon.

Pales : Rom. Myth. A goddess who protected shepherds and their flocks.

Pallas : Gr. Myth. A name of Minerva (q.v.) considered as a goddess of war.

Palm : An outstretched palm of the hand is considered by the Moors to be a most effective charm against the " evil eye." (MEAKIN, *The Moors*, p. 354 ; *Hindus*.)

An irritation of the palm of the right hand promises money; of the left, it denotes that you will lose some money (*Great Britain, India, Ethnologie du Bengale,* p. 127 ; *Alsace.*—LAMBS, p. 39 ; *Greece.*—LAWSON, p. 390 ; *Macedonia.*—ABBOTT, p. 112) ; in America, it is the opposite. (*Memoirs of the Amer. Folk Lore Soc.,* IV, p. 135.)

Palsy : In cases of palsy, St. Cornelius should be invoked.

Pan : Class. Myth. Son of Hermes and the nymph Dryope. A god of flocks and pastures, patron of shepherds, hunters, fishermen, etc. Pan is represented as having the legs, and sometimes the horns and ears of a goat. cf. *Satyr.*

Panchajana: Hind. Myth. Name of the demon who lived in the sea in the form of a conch-shell. (DOWSON, *H.C.D.*, p. 225).

Pandion : A legendary king of Athens.

Pandora : Gr. Myth. The first woman created by Vulcan. Minerva, goddess of sagacity, endowed her with all the charms ; Zeus presented her with a big box and sent her down to man, decked with golden bands and garlands of spring flowers. Epimetheus, in spite of the warnings of his brother, Prometheus, took her. The wicked Pandora raised the lid of the great cask and shook out the evils that wander among mankind, and the diseases that by day and night bring ill. She set on the lid again, and shut Hope in, that evil might be ever hopeless to mankind.

P'an Ku : Chin. Myth. A being alleged to have been the first development out of chaos. He caused wind by breathing and created day by opening his eyes. (MAYERS, *Chin. Read. Man.*, p. 186.)

Panel : The cracking of wooden wall panels is a sign of approaching death. (BERTHOLET, p. 20 ; LADY WILDE, p. 138 ; OWEN, pp. 303, 304.)

Pantagruel : Pantagruel's tongue formed shelter for a whole army ; his throat and mouth contained whole cities.

Pantagruelion : A herb (hemp) symbolical of persecution. Rabelais says, Pantagruel was the inventor of a certain use for which this herb served ; it was, he said, extremely hateful to felons, who detested it as much as the "strangle weed."

Pāpa Purusha : Hind. Myth. "Man of sin." A personification of all wickedness in human form, of which all the members are great sins ; the head is brahmanicide, the arm cow-killing, the nose woman-murder. (DOWSON, *H.C.D.*, p. 229.)

Papillon : A great prince who was conquered by King Arthur, and condemned to spend three years in silence in the form of a horse. While in this form, he received Holgar the Dane in the castle of Avalon.

Paracelsus : Paracelsus is said to have kept a small devil prisoner in the pommel of his sword. For medicines he preferred metallic substances, while Galen preferred herbs. His full name was Philippus Aureolus Theophrastus Paracelsus, but his family name was Bombastus (1493-1541.)

Parcae : Rom. Myth. The Latin name for the goddesses of Fate. They were three in number : *Nona, Decima and Morta.* cf. *Fates, Norn, Bidhātāpurusha, Hathor, Sudička.*

Parizādi : Sister of Prince Bahman and owner of the famous knife.

Parthenope : Gr. Myth. One of the sirens, who threw herself into the sea, because she was unable to lure Odysseus to destruction. She was cast off by the sea near Naples, where there is an ancient town bearing her name.

Parting : If a woman's hair parts where it should not, it is a sign that she will be a widow.

Partridge : Vide *Talos.*

Pārvati : Hind. Myth. The goddess Devi is called Pārvati, " mountain-born," because she is the daughter of the Himalaya Mountains.

Pasiphae : Gr. Myth. Wife of Minos. On Minos refusing to sacrifice a bull sent to him by Poseidon, the god caused Pasiphae to become enamoured of it and thus give birth to the monster, Minotaur. Vide *Minotaur, Theseus, Minos.*

Pasitasanas : Hind. Myth. Carnivorous and cannibal imps descended from Nikashā. (DOWSON, *H.C.D.*, p. 235.)

Passover : In Galicia it is recommended not to leave a tank of water uncovered during this time ; even if water be poured in, it should be done through a cloth. (*Jew. Enc.,* Vol. IX, p. 519.)

Passport : There is a remarkable custom still surviving in Russia of placing in the hands of the dead a sort of passport to the nether world. (ELWORTHY, *E.E.*, p. 399.)

Path of Spirits : North American tribal name for the Galaxy, by which the souls travel to the land beyond the grave ; their camp fires may be seen blazing as brighter stars.

Patrocles : A hero, friend of Achilles, whom he followed to the siege of Troy.

Patronella, St. : The patron saint for ague.

Peach : A sprig of peach-blossom placed over the lintel is believed by the Chinese to act as a charm, and to drive away demons. (WILLIAMS, *Mid. Kingd.*, Vol. II, p. 255.)
   The fruit of the peach tree of the Genii, which grows by the borders of the Lake of Gems, confers the gift of immortality. (MAYERS, *Chin. Read. Man.*, p. 191.)

Peachwood : In China it is said to be a powerful asset in the art of exorcising. It is for this reason that 'peach twigs and peach blossoms are so often mentioned in Chinese fairy lore.

Peacock : The loud calling of a peacock presages death. (*Ethnologie du Bengale*, p. 111 ; *F.L.J.*, 1883, p. 227.)
   Peacocks give warning of poison by ruffling their feathers.
   It is a charm against snake-bite to smoke a peacock's feather in a pipe. (*India.*—CROOKE, *P.R.I.*, Vol. II, p. 250 ; JACKSON, *F.L.N.*, Vol. I, p. 141.)

Pearl : Pearls are concentrated tears, and bring tears to the owners. In the East a dissolved pearl is an essential ingredient of every love potion (MARR MURRAY in *New Magazine*, September, 1923, p. 578).
   A pearl wrapped up in leather was regarded by the Jews as a healing remedy for cattle. (HASTINGS, *Dic. of the Bible*, Vol. IV, p. 604.)
   The pearl acts as a charm against fire. (MAYERS, *Chin. Read. Man.*, p. 26.)
   Pearls are drops of rain swallowed by the oyster.
   " And precious the tear as that rain from the sky
   Which turns into pearls as it falls in the sea."
                                   MOORE.—*Lalla Rookh.*

Pear tree : A pear tree blossoming in autumn promises a marriage. (*Lower Saxony.*—WUTTKE, p. 35.) cf. *Apple tree.*

Peepul : It is a kind of tree ; it is worshipped by the Chinese for long life. (WILLIAMS, *Mid. Kingd.*, Vol. II, p. 259.)
   The peepul is sacred to the Hindus, and is not cut. It is considered to be reincarnation of a Brāhman. It is believed that the family of one who cuts it becomes extinct. If a corpse be burnt with its wood, the soul of the deceased attains salvation. (JACKSON, *F.L.N.*, Vol. I, p. 136.) Girls are often married to peepul trees. (ib., p. 138.)

Peewit : If your pockets are empty the first time you hear the call of a peewit in spring, you will be in want for the rest of that year. (STRACKERJAN, Vol. I, p. 25.) cf. *Plover*.

Pegasus : Gr. Myth. A winged steed that sprang from the blood of Medusa. With a blow of its hoof, it produced the fountain Hippocrene or Helicon. cf. *Pakshirāj*.

Pe-kar : It is one of the fiercest of the Tibetan spirits, and has been adopted as a special protector of the monasteries by the Yellow-Hat sect of Lamas.

Pelias : Gr. Myth. A king of Iolchos, son of Neptune. By the perfidious advice of Medusa, his children killed him in the hope of rejuvenating him.

Pelican : The pelican turns her beak against her breast, and pierces it till the blood comes, and then she nourishes her young with her own blood.

Pelops: Gr. Myth. Grandson of Zeus and son of Tantalus, king of Lydia. Pelops was killed by his father, and was served as a repast to the gods. Ceres alone, absorbed in his sorrows at the loss of his daughter, partook of this horrible food. Zeus brought back Pelops to life and replaced the shoulder eaten by Ceres with an ivory one. Later, Pelops married Hippodamia, daughter of Œnomaus. After his father-in-law's death, Pelops succeeded him and ruled over the Peloponnesians.

Penanggalan : She is the Vampire (q.v.) of Malay superstition. She is said to be a living witch and can be killed if caught ; she is especially feared in houses where a birth has taken place, and it is the custom to hang up a bunch of thistle to catch her. (*Enc. Brit.*, Vol. VIII, p. 6; SKEAT, *Malay Magic*.)

Penates : A general name for the domestic gods of the Romans. A continual fire was kept burning in their honour.

Penelope : Gr. Myth. The faithful wife of Odysseus. During her husband's absence, she was importuned by numerous suitors ; she postponed deciding among them till she had finished weaving a funeral pall for her father-in-law, Laertes. She secretly unravelled all she had woven by day, and thus put off her suitors.

P'eng Lai Shan : One of the three isles of the genii. (MAYERS, *Chin. Read. Man.*, p. 187.)

Penthesilea : Gr. Myth. Daughter of Ares, queen of the Amazons. She fought against the Greeks in the siege of Troy, and was killed by Achilles.

Pephredo : Gr. Myth. One of the Grææ.

Perchta : Teut. Folklore. An ancient goddess of the earth and its fruitfulness. She is connected with spinning and women's work generally.
An epithet of the White Lady.

Perchta's Host : A Teutonic name for the Wild Hunt.

Peri : Muham. Folklore. Fairies who live in paradise, free from care and sorrow.
" A being represented as a descendant of fallen angels, excluded from paradise till some penançe is accomplished."—CASSELL'S *English Dictionary.*
" The Peris are very beautiful, true believers and opponents of the evil demons, *div.* (REDHOUSE, *Turk. and Eng. Lex.*, Const., 1890, p. 446.)

Pernel, St. : Patron saint for ague.

Persephone : Gr. Myth. Daughter of Zeus and Demeter, wife of Hades (Pluto). She was allowed to spend two-thirds of the year with Demeter, her mother. Vide *Hecate.*

Perseus : Gr. Myth. Son of Zeus and Danae, who slew the Gorgon, Medusa. Perseus stole the eye and the tooth of the Grææ, and refused to give them up until they had instructed him how to proceed against Medusa.

Perspiration : The smell of perspiration is supposed to be a powerful asset in attracting persons of the opposite sex ; it also makes animals attached to you. (STRACKERJAN, Vol. II, p. 115 ; KRAFFT-EBING, *Psychopathia Sexualis,* Eng. tr., p. 27 ; PLOSS, *Das Weib*, Vol. I, p. 442.)
" Perspire red, you must work for your bread ;
Perspire brown, you must live out of town."
Popular Rhyme
Henry III is said to have fallen madly in love with Maria of Cleves by accidentally wiping his face with her handkerchief, wet with her perspiration ; and thus made her life, although she was the bride of the Prince of Condé, very unhappy.
The same is said of Henry IV with regard to his passion for the beautiful Gabriel.

Peter's Fish : The haddock (q.v.) is so called.

Petni : In Bengal she is a female malevolent spirit who usually lives on trees (*Ethnologie du Bengale*, p. 97.).

Petrel : A kind of sea-bird, so called in allusion to St. Peter's walking on the sea (Matt. xiv. 29). Sailors consider it unlucky to kill one of these birds. They are also called Stormy Petrel or Mother Carey's Chicken. cf. *Albatross.*

Petticoat :

"This Friday night while going to bed,
I put my petticoat under my head,
To dream of the living and not of the dead,
To dream of the man I am to wed,
The colour of his eyes, the colour of his hair,
The colour of the clothes he is to wear,
And the night the wedding is to be."

Rock Hall, Maryland (KNORTZ, p. 149).

Phaedra : Gr. Myth.. Wife of Theseus, daughter of Minos and Pasiphaë. She declared her incestuous love for Hippolyt, her step-son, who resented her advances ; she being incensed, falsely accused him of making approaches to her to her husband. Hippolyt was sacrificed to Neptune. Later Phaedra was troubled with remorse and committed suicide by strangling herself.

Phaethon : Class. Myth. The sun-god Helios, or his son.

Phallus : A figure of the male organ of generation, venerated as a symbol of the generating power in nature. cf. *Yoni.*

Phantom : Something that appears to the sight or other senses, but has no material substance ; a spirit ; a ghost.

"Hark the Phantom of the House
That ever shrieks before a death."

TENNYSON, *Elaine.*

Pheng Niao : Chin. Myth. A fabulous bird of a monstrous size, with wings like the clouds of heaven. It comes into being by metamorphosis from the Khwan fish, a monster of the deep. (*Writings of Kwang-tse*, Bk. I, Pt. I, 3 ; MAYERS, *Chin. Read. Man.*, p. 187.)

P'hepo : "Demon " ; the East African name for the sand-pillar (q.v.).

Philemon : Gr. Myth. Husband of Baucis. His and his wife's names have become symbolic of conjugal love. (cf. HAWTHORNE, *T.T.*).

Philomele : Gr. Myth. Daughter of Pandion, king of Athens. She and her sister were changed respectively into a nightingale and a swallow. cf *Aedon.*

Phœbe : Gr. Myth. A daughter of Gæa. According to a tradition, she bequeathed the Delphian Oracle to Apollo and Artemis, children of her daughter Leto.

Phœbus : Gr. Myth. Apollo as a sun-god.

Phœnix : Gr. Myth. Son of Agenor, king of Phœnicia, brother of Cadmus.

Folklore. A fabulous bird. There is said to have been but one phœnix in the world ; it lived for five hundred years or longer. In Arabia it was consumed by fire by its own act, and rose up again in youthful freshness from its own ashes. Before burning itself, it builds a funeral pyre, sings a melodious song, flaps its wings to fan the fire, is consumed to ashes, and rises again rejuvenated ; hence it is an emblem of immortality.

The phœnix has appeared five times in Egypt : (i) in the reign of Sesostris ; (ii) in the reign of Amasis ; (iii) in the reign of Ptolemy ; (iv) a little prior to the death of Tiberius and (v) during the reign of Constantine. Tacitus in his *Annals VI*, 28, mentions the first three. cf. *Fêng hwang*.

Phooka : Another spelling for a pooka (q.v.).

Phorcus : Gr. Myth. A sea-deity, father of the Grææ.

Phra-Harmakhis : Egypt. Myth. A solar divinity of ancient Egypt.

Picture : A picture falling off the wall without any apparent cause, is an omen of an impending disaster, or of a death in the family. (*N. and C. Germany, Tyrol.*—WUTTKE, p. 38 ; *Great Britain, India.*) cf. *Mirror.*

Pidzu Pennu : The rain-god of the Khonds who rests upon the sky above the hill country of Orissa, and pours down the showers through his sieve. (MACPHERSON.)

Pie : You will enjoy as many happy months during the next year as the number of mince pies you taste on Christmas day. (RAGNER.)

Pierides : Gr. Myth. The nine daughters of Pierus, king of Macedonia, who were changed into magpies for having disputed about the prize of singing with the Muses.

Sometimes the Muses themselves are designated by this name.

Pig : If going on a journey or business, a sow crosses the road, you will meet with disappointment, if not accident, before you return home.

Pigs denote good luck.

To meet a sow with a litter of pigs is extremely lucky ; it promises a successful journey.

If a woman be touched with pig's flesh without her knowledge she will be barren. (*Bakhtyurs.*—PLOSS, *Das Weib*, Vol. I, p. 508.)

When hogs run grunting home, a storm is impending.

The bacon of pigs killed in a waning moon will waste much in the cooking.

When pigs carry straw in their mouth rain is at hand.

When taking pigs from a sow, they should be drawn away backwards, otherwise the sow will be fallow.

In the forefeet of pigs is a very small hole, which may be seen when the pig is dead and the hair carefully removed. The legend is that the devils made their exit from the swine through the forefeet, and left these holes. There are also six very minute rings round each hole ; these are said to have been made by the Devil's claws. Vide *Menstruation, Fisherman.* (cf. FRAZER, *Taboo*, pp, 233, n. 4, 64.)

Pigeon : No person can die on a bed, or a pillow, containing pigeon's feathers. (ABBOTT, p. 232.)

If a white pigeon settles on a chimney, it bodes death to someone in the family.

A blue pigeon is held sacred in Mecca.

A black pigeon gave the responses in the temple of Ammon, another in Dodona.

In Kilcurry it is believed that pigeons enter a house and gently knock at the windows at the moment of death. (*Folklore*, X, p. 122.)

Pilgrim's Road : The Turkish name for the Galaxy

Pillalu : The Irish dirge.

Pillow : A Malay warrior's pillow and sleeping mat, while he is away at the wars, must be kept rolled up. If any one else were to use them, the absent warrior's courage would fail him and disaster would befall him. (FRAZER, *G.B².*, Vol. I, p. 31.) Vide *Pigeon.*

Pimple : A pimple on the tongue denotes that you have told a lie. (LEAN, Vol. II, p. 296.) Vide *Wren.*

Pin : If you pass a pin in the street, you turn your back on luck. (*Great Britain.*)
Pins given away as gifts "prick the friendship." (*Silesia.*—WUTTKE, p. 135.)

"See a pin and pick it up,
All the day you'll have good luck ;
See a pin and let it lie,
Come to sorrow by and by."

—New York.

"See a pin and let it lie,
You'll want that pin before you die."

—Peabody, Mass.

Pindi : The food offered by the Hindus to the spirits of their deceased relatives, in order to appease their hunger. This was formerly done at Gaya.

Pipe : Young people should never light their pipes at a lamp ; if they do so, they will not have good wives. The proper things to light pipes with are the glowing coals in the brazier. (*Japan.*—GRIFFIS, *M.E.*, p. 472.)

Pirene : Gr. Myth. Pirene disconsolate at the loss of her son, who was killed by the huntress Diana, wept so much that she was changed into a fountain which bears her name.
"This clear fountain was once a beautiful woman ; and when her son was killed by the arrows of the huntress Diana, she melted all away into tears. And so the water, which you find so cool and sweet, is the sorrow of that poor mother's heart."

HAWTHORNE, *Tanglewood Tales*, p. 139

Pirithous : Gr. Myth. A hero of Thessaly, son of Ixion, and king of the Lapithes. His marriage with Hippodamia was commemorated by the famous and bloody battle of the Lapithes with the Centaurs.

Pisācha : "Flesh-eater " ; in India these are the ghosts of madmen, habitual drunkards, the treacherous and the violent tempered. "It is an evil spirit produced by a man's vices, the ghost of a liar, adulterer, or criminal of any kind, or of one who has died unseen." (CROOKE, *P.R.I.*, Vol. I, p. 245 ; *Ethnologie du Bengale*, p. 102.)

Pisitasanas : Hind. Myth. A race of carnivorous imps. Vide *Nikashâ, Pasitâsanas.*

Pit : If you dream that you have fallen in a pit and cannot get out, some calamity will befall you, or your sweetheart will be false to you.

Pitheus : Gr. Myth. Father of Ægeus, grandfather of Theseus.

Pixie : Eng. Folklore. A certain class of fairies.

Pixie Ring : Eng. Folklore. A fairy-ring or circle.

Place : Do not change your place at the table ; it is very unlucky. (*New York.*—BERGEN, *C.S.*)

Plague : St. Roch cures plague.

Vinegar poured over a red-hot brick was believed as a plague preventive. (*Notes and Queries*, 29 October, 1925.)

If there is an epidemic write on the door of the house, " Here has typhus (or cholera, etc.) already been," and the house will remain untouched. Or hang on the door a locked " Schloss " and throw the key away. Or draw a black mark with coal (in India, red) on the outer wall. (*Galicia.*—*Jew. Enc.*, Vol. XI, p. 601, quoting SCHIFFER, *Urquell*, II, 80-82.)

Planchette : In modern spiritualism the planchette, a heart-shaped piece of wood with a pencil through it, is said to bring us in contact with the spirits in the other world.

Pleiades : Gr. Myth. The seven daughters of Atlas and Pleione, who killed themselves in despair. They were metamorphosed into constellations.

Folklore. People who cannot see the Pleiades, will die in a short time.

Plon : Among the Wends, a Plon is a dragon in the form of a fiery sphere. It can assume various forms ; the proper place to confer with it is a cross-road.

Plough : To dream of ploughing denotes success in life and good marriage.

Plover : If you have no money in your pocket when you hear the call of a plover for the first time in spring, you will be in want for the rest of the year. (STRACKERJAN, Vol. I, p. 25.) cf. *Peewit*.

In the wild Gieritz swamp in the Aar, in Switzerland, old maids become plovers. (BERTHOLET, p. 43.)

Plu : The Karens of South Asia say that *Plu* is the land of the dead. (TYLOR, *P.C.*, Vol. II, p. 25 ; CROSS, *Jour. Amer. Or. Soc.*, Vol. IV, p. 309 ; MASON, *Jour. As. Soc Bengal*, pt. II, p. 203.)

Plum : The Chinese attribute many magical qualities to this fruit.

Pluto : Class. Myth. Son of Saturn and Rhea, husband of Proserpina, brother of Zeus and Neptune, god of the lower worlds. The Greeks called him Hades and the Romans, Dis. cf. *Yama, Tha-ma, Yen Wang*.

Podarge : Another name of Celæno.

Poison : Vide *Opal, Peacock, Unicorn, Nurjehan's Bracelet, Gates of Gundoforus, Rhinoceros, Venetian Glass, Toad*.

Poker : Making a cross with the bars of the grate and the poker drives the devil out of the room, and helps to make the fire burn up brighter. (cf. ELWORTHY, *Evil Eye*, pp. 221, 426, 429). Vide *Iron*.

Polednice : Bohemian Folklore. Midday female spirits who fly about in the fields and woods, and steal little children who have been inadvertently left alone by their mothers in their dwellings. (GROHMANN.)

Poledniček : Bohemian Folklore. A little boy dressed in a white shirt who, at midday, passes from the forest into the field and punishes those whom he finds doing damage there. He sometimes leads people astray. cf. *Ignis Fatuus*.

Polevoy : The Russian name for the Polednice.

Pollux : Rom. Myth. One of the Dioscuri. Castor and Pollux were said to have been hatched out of an egg.

Poludnitsa : Polish Folklore. A spirit who walks abroad among cornfields, usually during the midday interval, and kills or infects anyone who cannot answer her questions or solve her riddles satisfactorily. cf. *Sphinx*.

Poludnitza : A Russian name for the Polednice.

Polymnia : Gr Myth. The Muse of lyric poetry. She is represented in an attitude of meditation.

Polynices : Gr. Myth. Son of Œdipus. He was slain in the war against his brother Eteocles and his uncle Creon for the possession of Thebes.

Polypheme : A Cyclop, a gigantic giant who fed on human flesh and whose only eye was blinded by Ulysses. (HOMER. *Odyssey* IX.)

Pomona : Rom. Myth. A goddess of fruits and gardens.

Poodle : A black poodle is seen on the graves of priests and clergymen who have not been true to the Faith. (*Franken.* —WUTTKE, p. 219.)

o

Pooka : Irish Folklore. A hobgoblin or a malicious sprite, generally believed to be the spirit of an animal.

" Irish superstition makes the Phooka palpable to the touch. To its agency the peasantry usually ascribe accidental falls."—T. CROFTON CROKER, *Fairy Legends* (1825).

Pool of Heaven : Chin. Myth. A dark and great ocean in the North, the dwelling of the fish called Khwan. (*Writings of Kwang-tse*, Bk. I, pt. I, 3.)

Poppy : Poppy seeds are used to determine the sex of a baby (q.v.)

Porcupine : When porcupines are hunted or annoyed, they shoot out their quills in anger.

Porcupine's feet are used by the Chawia women of North Africa as a protection during pregnancy, and by Arab women for sore breasts.

Porpoise : Porpoises sporting and chasing one another about ships foretell stormy weather. (BRAND, *Observations*, Vol. III, p. 240.) To dream of porpoises prognosticates a sea-voyage.

Portrait : If you have your portrait painted you will die. (FRAZER, *G.B²*., Vol. I, p. 297 ; cf. *Blackwood's Magazine*, Feb., 1886, p. 235 ; J. A. E. KÖHLER, *Volksbrauch etc. in Voigtlande*, p. 423 ; RALSTON, *Songs of the Russian People*, p. 117 ; F. H. GROOME, *In Gipsy Tents*, Edin., 1880, p. 337 *sq.* ; ABBOTT, p. 101 ; H. SPENCER, *Prin. of Sociology*, i. 305 § 157.)

Poseidon : Gr. Myth. God of the sea and watery element, son of Cronus and Rhea, husband of Amphitrite. He was also god of horses and chivalry. Vide *Amphitrite, Drebkuls*.

Possession : The fact of being possessed or occupied by a demon or spirit. The symptoms of demon possession are : "Some are struck dumb, others strike their heads, some go mad and walk about naked . . . lie down and become inactive." (CROOKE, *Islam in India*, p. 235.)

Pot : In Bulgaria, at the moment of death, all pots, kettles, etc. are turned upside down, in order to prevent the soul of the deceased taking refuge in one of them, and therefrom commencing a system of annoyance against the family. (ST. CLAIR AND BROPHY, p. 75.)

Poverty : Vide *Oil, Mirror*.

Prayer Book : The old Jews of Bohemia put a glass of water and a prayer book on the table as a protection against thunderbolts.

A prayer book keeps evil spirits away. Vide *Thunder, Glass, Bible, Qor'an.*

Precious Stones : All kinds of precious stones cast into honey become more brilliant thereby, each according to its colour.

A bouquet composed of diamonds, lodestones and sapphires combined renders a person almost invincible and wholly irresistible. (See under different names of precious stones.)

Pregnancy : Pregnant women must not be allowed to see a dead body, lest they give birth to still-born children (*Mecklenburg*) ; neither must they look at the moon, lest the child be " moon-struck." (*Silesia, Oberpfalz.*— WUTTKE, p. 193.)

If a pregnant woman takes anything belonging to another, the child will be a thief. (STRACKERJAN, Vol. I, p. 47.)

If pregnant women be left alone in the dark, evil spirits may do them some harm. (*India.* See PLOSS, *Das Weib,* Vol. I, p. 615 *et. seq.*) Vide *Double Fruits, Godmother, Lamp, Porcupine, Stones, Sepulchral, Sack, Moon, Porcupine, Suicide.* (For further superstitions see LEAN, Vol. II, p. 136 ; FRAZER, *The Magic Art,* Vol. II, p. 108.)

Pretni : Same as a Petni (q.v.).

Priapus : Gr. Myth. A god of gardens and vines.

Prick : If you prick your finger accidentally while making a dress, it presages that you will receive plenty of kisses. (*Berlin ; Germany* [?].)

Priest : If a priest pursues you on your journey, you will be cursed and bewitched by evil spirits, and despoiled by robbers. (*Tibet.*—WADDELL, p. 136.)

To dream of priests portends ill luck. (*U.S.A.,* KNORTZ, p. 43.)

Priests are especially liable to be struck by lightning. (*France.*—LEAN, Vol. II, p. 185.)

To meet a priest is unlucky. (*Greece.*—LAWSON, p. 306 ; ELWORTHY, *E.E.,* **p.** 23 ; ABBOTT, p. 105.)

Scotch fishermen do not allow you to say " minister " or " kirk " on their boats. (BASSETT, p. 109.)

Vide *Bonze, Poodle, Fish.*

Prince of Darkness : An epithet of the Devil.

Princess of Heaven : The Zulus have a "spirit which they call *Nomkubulwana*, or the *Inkosazana-ye-Zulu* (the Princess of Heaven). She is said to be robed in white, and to take the form of a young maiden, in fact an angel. She is said to appear to some chosen person to whom she imparts some revelation ; but, whatever the revelation may be, it is kept a profound secret from outsiders." (HAGGARD, *Nada the Lily*, p. xi, quoting F. B. FYNNEY, *Zululand and the Zulus* ; cf. *ib.* pp. 183, 190, 100.)

Procession, Funeral : When passing a funeral procession turn your money over ; this will ensure your always being in funds. (*Great Britain*.)

Procrustes : A legendary highwayman of Attica, who tied his victims upon an iron bed, and, as the case required, either stretched or cut off their legs to adapt them to its length. He was slain by Theseus who submitted him to the same torture.

Prometheus : Gr. Myth. A Titan, son of Iapetus and Clymene, regarded as the founder of civilization, and in later classical tradition, as the creator of the human race. Owing to his refusal to tell Zeus the source from which he would be overthrown, Prometheus was chained to a rock with a vulture eating his entrails and thus tortured till Chiron died for him.

Promise : If a promise be given to someone to appear to him after death, the spirit of the deceased will be compelled to keep his promise. (STRACKERJAN, Vol. I, p. 167.)

Proposal, Marriage : If a man dries himself on your worn chemise, he will surely propose marriage to you. (Vide *Perspiration*.)

The exchange of a yellow garter means a proposal of marriage in six months. (*Washington, D.C.*—BERGEN, *C.S.*, p. 65.)

Proserpina : Same as Persephone.

Protesilaus : Gr. Myth. Husband of Laodomia. He being slain at the siege of Troy, the dead body was sent home to his wife who prayed that she might talk to him again, if only for three hours. Her prayer was granted, but when Protesilaus returned to the region of the dead, she accompanied him.

Proteus : Gr. Myth. A god of the sea, who was gifted with the power of prophecy by his father Neptune.

Psaphon : Gr. Myth. A young Libyan who desiring to be honoured as a god, taught a great number of birds to say : Psaphon is a god. The people were imposed upon by this, and he was really worshipped as a god.

Ptah : Egypt. Myth. An ancient god who was identified with Osiris ; his seat of worship was Memphis. " Ptah was one of the most'active of the three great gods, who carried out the commands of Thoth. . . . He was self-created and was a form of the sun-god Ra as the ' Opener ' of the day. . . . His feminine counterpart was the goddess Sekhet." (BUDGE, *Egypt. Ideals, etc.*, p. 98.)

Puberty : For various customs connected with puberty see FRAZER, *G.B².*, Vol. III, pp. 205 *seq.*

Puck : An evil, malicious, or mischievous spirit or demon of popular superstition. In the Middle Ages, Puck was commonly identified with the Biblical Devil.

Pu Hiăn : In Chinese Buddhist folklore, he is a holy man who rides a lion ; he is a powerful helper in time of need. (*Chin. Volksmärchen*, p. 203.) cf. *Guan Yin, Wen Ju.*

Pukse : German Folklore. Another name for the Kobold.

Pulling Hair : If you pull a girl's hair, you will take her strength away. (*Bengal.*—cf. FRAZER, *The Magic Art*, Vol. I, pp. 102, 344.) Vide *Hair, Samson.*

Puluga : The Andaman Islanders have the idea of a being called Puluga—that is, " fire "—who is supposed to be invisible at present. He is held to know our thoughts and to punish murder, adultery and theft. (JOSEPH HUBY, *Christus, Manuel d'histoire des religions*, Paris, 1921, p. 94.)

Purple : Purple is a royal colour.
At a marriage ceremony no Japanese bride or bridegroom will wear anything of a purple colour, lest the marriage tie be soon loosed. (GRIFFIS, *M.E.*, p. 467.)

Pushpaka: Hind. Myth. The flower-adorned chariot of Kuvera, the god of wealth.

Put : Hind. Myth. A hell to which childless men are said to be condemned. A name invented to explain the word " *putra*," son. (DOWSON, *H.C.D.*, p. 250.)

Putana : Hind. Myth. A female demon, daughter of Bali. She attempted to kill the infant Krishna by suckling him, but was herself sucked to death by the child. (DOWSON, *H.C.D.*, p. 251.)

Pygmalion : Gr. Myth. A Greek sculptor who made a statue of Galatea. This statue was animated by Venus, and Pygmalion married his own statue.

Pygmy : A race of short-statured people. The ancients believed that they existed in various parts of the world, and especially in the region of the sources of the Nile. The word " pygmy " is used in modern language to denote a short person.

Pyladus : Gr. Myth. A friend of Orestes and husband of Electra.

Pyrrha : Gr. Myth. Wife of Prometheus, mother of Deucalion.

Pysk : Swedish Folklore. " Little goblin " ; a pixie.

Pythia : Gr. Myth. One of the priestesses of the Delphian Oracle.

Python : Gr. Myth. A monstrous serpent which arose from the mud left after the subsidence of the deluge which Deucalion survived. It dwelt in the caves of Mt. Parnassus, where Apollo (q.v.) slew it.

    Pythons are worshipped by the Ewe-speaking peoples of the Slave Coast (ELLIS, *The Ewe-speaking Peoples*, 54 *sqq.* ; FRAZER, *Adonis*, i. 83, n. 1.)

Q

Qâf : Moham. Myth. The mountains of Qâf are supposed to encompass the whole of the earth, and to be the chief abode of the Jinni. (LANE, *A.S.M.A.*, p. 37.) Vide *Sakhrat.*

Qahu : Egypt. Myth. This was the name by which the City of the Gods was designated. (BUDGE, *Book of the Dead*, Ch. CXLIX.)

Qebhsennuf : Egypt. Myth. One of the four children of Horus. He was hawk-headed, and represented the West ; he also protected the liver and the gall-bladder. (BUDGE, *Eastern Magic*, p. 89.)

Qebhsnauf : Another spelling for Qebhsennuf.

Quenching Fire : St. Florian will help to quench fires.

Qen-Qentel : Egypt. Myth. A pool of Sekhet-Hetepet.

Qetebh meriri : Jewish Folklore. A spirit of poisonous pestilence.

Qor'an : The Qor'an is the holy book of the Muhammedans, and is used by them in the same manner for telling fortunes as the Bible by the Christians ; it is opened at random, and the text thus found is said to give the key to the problem you have in mind.

The Qor'an is a powerful charm against evil spirits.

The uneducated Muslims of India do not mention the Qor'an by name, fearing to commit blasphemy thereby. (PHILLOTT, *Hindustani Stepping Stones*, Appendix.) cf. *Bible, Prayer Book, God, Shedim*.

Quaking-grass : There is a lingering superstition in the Midlands that the Briza brings ill-luck to its possessor. (LEAN, Vol. II, p. 639, quoting TOM BURGESS, *Old English Wild Flowers*, 1868.)

Quarrel : If you dream you are quarrelling, you will either receive some unexpected news, or your sweetheart will marry another. Vide *Apron, Fire, Fireplace, Glass, Knife, Shoe, Menstruation*.

Question : Spirits must never be questioned directly. (WUTTKE, p. 224.) Vide " *What is the matter with you ?* "

Quetzal : A Central American bird, worshipped either as a deity or as a symbol of a deity both by the Aztecs and the Mayas.

Quetzalocoatl : Aztec Myth. A king from whom has been derived the earliest Aztec culture. Quetzalocoatl driven away by his evil brother, Tezcatlipoca, set sail for the Golden Country of Tlapallan, promising to return at a later date. Quetzalocoatl represents the day-deity.

" By the sorceries of the Mexican god Tezcatlipoca (q.v.) he (Quetzalocoatl) was driven to the fabled country of Tlapallan, whence he had come. According to another account, he was supposed to have cast himself on a pyre, and after his death, his heart became the morning star. By some he is regarded as a sun-god, by others as a god of the air."—*Non-Classical Mythology*, p. 142.

Quinsy : St. Blaise cures quinsy.

Quirinus : Rom. Relig. An ancient god of war. As distinguished from Mars, he was a god of armed peace rather than that of aggressive warfare. In early times he, with Jupiter and Mars, formed the dominant triad of the Roman state.

Qutrub : Arab. Folklore. The male Ghoul is called by this name. (LANE, *A.S.M.A.*, p. 43.)

Qutrus : Moham. Folklore. They were demons who usually assumed the form of cats. (Mas'udi, *Muruj al-Dhabab*, III. 321.)

R

Ra : Egypt. Myth. The great god of the sun, the principal deity of historical Egypt. He was the son of Nut, the sky, and was believed to be engaged each night with the serpent Apepi. He is represented as a man with a sun-disc round his head.

Rabisu : Babyl. Folklore. A demon who springs upon his victim unawares.

Ragnarok : Norse Myth. The so-called "Twilight of the Gods," the final destruction of the world in the great conflict between the Æsir (gods) on the one hand, and on the other hand, the giants and the powers of Hel, under the leadership of Loki.

Rahab : Hebrew Myth. A great demon or dragon, who after a severe struggle, was overcome by Jähweh.

Rāhu : Hind. Myth. A demon of coal-black colour, who devours the sun, and thus causes a whole or a partial eclipse. (Crooke, *P.R.I.*, I, 19 ; *Ethnologie du Bengale*, pp. 101 *sq.*) Vide *Indra, Ketu, Mayoba, Aracho, Eclipse.*

Raiko and the Oni : This is one of the most famous of Japanese folktales. Raiko, the bravest man of his times, fights with monsters and ghouls, and kills all the wicked things in Japan, so that children may now sleep in peace, without being afraid of being carried away by ghouls, and the like. (Griffis, *M.E.*, pp. 491-493.)

Rain : Rain on a wedding day forebodes tears for the bride (Ploss, *Das Weib*, Vol. I, p. 451, quoting Karusio), or foretells the birth of many children (Strackerjan, Vol. I, p. 23.)

Rain is caused by witches. (Lehmann, *A.Z.*, p. 111.)

Gnats flying low foretell rain.

The croaking of a crow or a frog denotes rain.

Rain can be stopped by first-born children stripping naked and standing on their heads ; or, in Calcutta, by making a candle of cloth and burning it. (*Enc. Rel. Eth.*, Vol. VIII, p. 291.)

The Zulus cause rain by shooting at the sky with bows and arrows. Vide *Cat, Grass, Pig, Rake, Sexton, Whistle, Crow, Frog, Raven, Dog, Rice, Woman, First-born Children, Gnat, Mowing.*

Rainbow : The rainbow is considered by many nations to be a demon ; thus in New Zealand (TAYLOR), among the Karens of Burma, in Dahomey (BURTON), among the Indians of Ecuador (KARSTEN), the same superstition, with slight variations, is prevalent. (cf. TYLOR, *P.C.*, Vol. I, pp. 256, 266, 268 *sq.*)

Among the Indians, the rainbow is said to be the bow of Rāma; hence it is called Rāma-dhanuk, "Rāma's bow."

If the two extremities of a rainbow are within the limit of the same town, a death therein should be expected. (*Folklore*, X, p. 364.)

The appearance of a rainbow portends death. (DALYELL, *Dark Sup.*, p. 503.)

To dream of a rainbow on your right hand side is good, but if on the left. bad. Vide *Cuichi Supai*.

Rake : If a rake accidentally falls with the prongs pointing upwards, it is a sure sign of a heavy rainfall. (STRACKER-JAN, Vol. I, p. 35.)

Rākshasa : Hind. Myth. The giants, goblins or evil spirits of Indian mythology. They are of three sorts, and are not all bad. One is a set of beings like the Yakshas, the other a sort of Titans or enemies, and lastly, the demons who haunt cemeteries, disturb sacrifices, and devour human beings. (DOWSON, *H.C.D.*, p. 254 ; Vide DAY, *Folktales of Bengal* ; *Ethnologie du Bengale,* pp. 93 *sq.*)

Rākshasi : The female counterpart of the above. They have the power of assuming the forms of beautiful maidens in order to allure human beings. They are carnivorous, and are said to have devastated whole cities. Among other powers ascribed to them, they are believed to be capable of stretching their bodies to a distance of eighty miles. (cf. DAY, *Folktales of Bengal* ; CROOKE, *P.R.I.*, Vol. I, p. 250.)

Rakshe : A monster whose ordinary food was serpents and dragons.

Rāma : Hind. Myth. Hero of the great epic Rāmāyana, one of the incarnations of Vishnu. He was sent into exile for fourteen years at the desire of his step-mother. In his exile, he was accompanied by his wife Sitâ and his brother Lakshman. He exterminated the Rākshasas with the help of Hanumān, the monkey-king, and rescued Sitâ, whom their king Rāvana had kidnapped.

Ramman : Assyr. Myth. " Thunderer " ; an epithet of Adad.

Rán : Old Norse Myth. Wife of Ægir. She was a man-stealing demon of the sea, a hag who had no heart in her body. She lay in wait for sailors with her net, or tried to drag down ships with her arms to the depths. cf. *Nixie, Hakkenmann.*

Rarašek : Bohemian Folklore. It is either the spirit of a cyclone, or a kind of domestic spirit. (GROHMANN, p. 15, quoting JUNGMANN, *Slovnik.*)

Rat : Many rats coming suddenly in a house foretell death (*Folklore Journal*, V, p. 217) ; on board a ship, it is a sign of luck, but if they leave, the ship will be wrecked (STRACKERJAN, Vol. I, p. 24) ; similarly, they leave a house before a fall.

If a rat, during the night, gnaw the furniture of a room or our clothes, it is indicative of some impending evil, perhaps even death.

The Romans said that to see a white rat was a certain presage of good luck.

To destroy rats, St. Gertrude should be invoked.

In Macedonia if rats gnaw the clothes, it is taken as a hint that there is a dishonest servant in the house. (ABBOTT, p. 108.) Vide *Mouse.*

Ratatosk : Norse Myth. A squirrel who carries words of strife up and down. Vide *Yggdrasil.*

Rattlesnake : Rattlesnakes exercise so great a fascination over birds, that they fall an easy prey to them.

Some North American Indians will spare the rattlesnake, fearing the vengeance of the spirit, if slain.

Rāvana : Hind. Myth. The demon-king of Lankā or Ceylon. He was able to assume any form he pleased, and was malignant and terrible to the utmost degree. He had ten heads, twenty copper coloured arms and big shining teeth like swords ; his form was as thick as a mountain. He disguised himself like an old woman, and succeeded in carrying off Sitâ, which brought on the war with Rāma. Rāvana and his giants were conquered by the hero, and Sitâ was rescued.

Raven : Ravens are ill-omened birds (HAGGARD, *Nada the Lily*, p. 214 ; DALYELL, p. 503 ; ELWORTHY, *E.E.*, p. 94 ; BASSETT, p. 275) ; they forebode pestilence and death and call up rain ; hence the expression " to croak like a raven."

Ravens nailed up in stables protect from illnesses (*Alsace.*—LAMBS, p. 31.)

Ravens seen on the left hand side of a person bode impending evil. (*Great Britain, India.*)

If ravens gape against the sun, heat will follow ; but if they busy themselves in preening or washing themselves, there will be rain.

Ravens foster forsaken children.

A crowing raven in the vicinity of a house, or flying over one in which a person is lying ill, denotes his speedy death.   (*Germany.*—WUTTKE, p. 32 ; OWEN, p. 304 ; HAZLITT, p. 507.)

Ravens flying towards each other, presage a war. (*Swabia.*—WUTTKE, p. 33.)

The young of a raven, for nine days after it is hatched out of the egg, is snowy white ; after that time has passed, it changes its colour.   (STRACKERJAN, Vol. II, p. 103.)

The raven is said to be the most prophetic of "inspired birds." It bodes private and public calamities; hence the proverbial expression, "to have the foresight of a raven."

Among the North Pacific Coast tribes, the raven is important as a creator or transformer. In Vancouver Island, it is merely a greedy trickster.

According to the modern Indians, the raven is the " Messenger of Death."

In Cornwall, King Arthur is said to live in the form of a raven. (BERTHOLET, p. 34.)   Vide *Crow, Rook, Wolf*.

Pliny (*Nat. Hist.*, VII, 174) tells us that the soul of Aristeas of Proconnesus issued from his mouth in the shape of a raven.

Razor : It is unlucky to present a knife, razor, scissors or any sharp instrument, as they are apt to cut love and friendship. (BRAND, *Observations*, Vol. III, p. 250.)

To find a knife or a razor denotes ill luck and disappointment to the party. (*ib.*)

rDud : (Pron. *dut*). Tibetan Folklore. Evil genii or fiends of an actively malignant type.

Rebirth : According to most Orientals, people who have not fulfilled all their duties on earth, must be born again.

Red : Red is symbolic of love and pleasure. (STRACKERJAN, Vol. II, p. 69 : cf. HARTLAND, *Legend of Perseus*, Vol. II, p. 337.)

Evil spirits who wish to seduce people, are usually dressed in red.

Red Hare : Chin. Myth. A supernatural beast of auspicious omen, which appears when virtuous rulers govern the empire. (MAYERS, *Chin. Read. Man.*, p. 235.)   Vide *Hare*.

Red Riding Hood : In a German version of this well-known story, she and her grandmother are actually swallowed by the wolf ; they come out safe and sound, when the hunters cut open the sleeping beast.

Red Swan : The North American Indian Myth of the Red Swan is probably, as Longfellow suggests, only a vivid picture of the setting sun. (TYLOR, *P.C.*, Vol. I, p. 312.)

Reed : If reeds be planted in a house, a death will speedily follow. (GOODRICH-FREER in *Folklore*, XIII, p. 32.)

Regin : Volsunga Saga. A treacherous dwarf smith, brother of Fafnir, and foster-father of Sigurd whom he incites to slay Fafnir, plotting to kill the hero afterwards. His purpose was miraculously revealed to Sigurd who slays him.

Remarriage : At the remarriage of a widower, the ghost of his former wife appears at the wedding, and if she is satisfied with this arrangement, dances with the company. (*Usedom.*—WUTTKE, p. 216.)

Remora : A fish called the *remora* can arrest a ship in full sail. (BRAND, *Observations*, Vol. III, p. 259 ; BASSETT, p. 258 ; HAZLITT, p. 508.) cf. *Echinus.*

Return : To return after one has left the house, or to forget something on starting is unlucky (*Germany.*—WUTTKE, p. 36) ; but the misfortune can be averted by sitting down on your return and counting twelve. (*Great Britain, India* ; ABBOTT, p. 105.)

Rhadamantos : Gr. Myth. One of the three judges of the infernal regions, the other two being Eacus and Minos.

Rhea : Class. Myth. Daughter of Uranus and Gaea, wife of Cronus, mother of Zeus, Hades, Poseidon, Hera, Hestia and Demeter ; hence she was called "Mother of the Gods." She was regarded by the Greeks as a local form of the great nature goddess.

Rheumatism : The worn left stocking, or a skein of silk, wrapped round the part affected, cures rheumatism.
Horse chestnuts, or chestnuts (*Dutch*) carried in the pocket also cure rheumatism. Vide *Kite, Deer.*

Rhinoceros : If the horn of a rhinoceros be cut through the middle from one extremity to another, several little lines representing human figures will be seen.
If poison be put into a vessel made of rhinoceros's horn, the liquid contained therein will effervesce. cf. *Poison.*

Ribbon : A silk ribbon tied round a child's neck, cures various diseases. (STRACKERJAN, Vol. I, p. 80 ; Vol. II, p. 139.)

A piece of red ribbon protects children from bewitchment. (*Bohemia.*—GROHMANN, p. 112.)

A bow of some coloured ribbon on the child's head after dark, invites the evil eye. (*Bengal.*)

Rice : To throw rice denotes good luck ; hence rice is thrown after the newly-married pair (*Great Britain*) ; in India it is the reverse.

If young girls pour tea or hot water into a cup of red rice, their wedding nights will be rainy. (*Japan.*— GRIFFIS, *M.E.*, p. 472.)

Frequent and regular use of rice as an article of food is conducive to blindness. The vulgar name for rice on board ship is "strike-me-blind." (HAZLITT, p. 510.)

Riches : St. Anne and St. Vincent will help those who seek riches. Vide *Ant.*

Right : Vide *Left.*

Rijalu-l-ghaib : ("Hidden men") Muham. Folklore. Certain invisible spirits of the air who move in a circular orbit round the world. (CROOKE, *Islam in India*, p. 278.)

Ring : It is favourable to dream of a ring, but if it is on the wrong hand, your lover is deceitful. Vide *Wedding Ring.*

Ring, Bertha's Emerald : The duke Gondibert gave Bertha an emerald ring which, he said, would preserve its lustre as long as he remained faithful, but would become dull and pale if he proved false to her. cf. *Bahman's Knife, Sophia's Picture, Florimel's Girdle, Canace's Mirror.*

River : Spirits dwell in rivers.

As a rule, spirits are unable to cross rivers and other waterways. (GRIMM.) Vide *Water.*

Road of the Birds : In Lithuanian legend, it is the name of the Galaxy where souls of the good, fancied as fleeting away at death like birds, dwell free and happy. (HANUSCH.)

Road of Santiago : A Spanish name for the Galaxy.

Road of Souls : Same as the Path of Spirits (q.v.).

Road of the White Elephant : A Siamese name for the Galaxy.

Robber : The shin-bone of a sheep, placed above the door, keeps out robbers. (*The Kirghiz of Turkestan.*—SCHUYLER, Vol. II, p. 31.)

Robin : The red of a robin's breast is produced by the blood of Jesus. While he was on his way to Calvary, a robin plucked a thorn from his temples, and a drop of blood falling on the bird turned its bosom red. According to another version, the robin takes dew in its beak to cool the parched lips of the tortured in hell ; the flames of hell singed the feathers of the breast and turned it red.

It is unlucky either to keep or kill a robin ; if anyone attempts to detain a robin which has sought hospitality, some calamity will befall him.

If a robin finds a dead body unburied, it will cover up the face at least, if not the whole body.

The severity of a winter can be foretold by the redness of a robin's breast. If a deep red, it will be severely cold ; if pink mild.

> " Call for the robin-red-breast and the wren,
> Since o'er shady graves they hover,
> And with leaves and flowers do cover
> The friendless bodies of unburied men.
> Call unto his funeral dole
> The ant, the field-mouse, and the mole,
> To rear him hillocks that shall keep him warm,
> And (when gay tombs are robb'd) sustain no harm,
> But keep the wolf far thence, that's foe to men,
> For with his nails he'll dig them up again."
> —(quoted in *Word-Lore*, Vol. I, No. 5, p. 214.)

cf. *Goose, Stork, Swallow.*

Robin Goodfellow : Another name for Puck.

Roccia dla Fantina : In Switzerland, it is said to be the home of fairies. (JALLA, *Lég. Vaud.*, pp. 18, 23.)

Roch, St. : St. Roch cures plague.

Rockenmuhme : " Rye-aunt " ; a Teutonic spirit in human form.

Rockensau : " Rye-sow " ; a German field-spirit.

Roggenalte : Danish Folklore. A field-spirit in human form.

Roggenhund : " Rye-dog " ; a German field-spirit.

Rojenice : The Slovakian name for the Sudičky.

Rokhitu : Egypt. Myth. They were spirits full of wisdom, and were the personifications of the powers opposed to Egypt.

Romulus : Legendary founder of Rome. He is said to have vanished in the midst of a cloud.

Rook : Rooks forsaking a wood, foretell a famine. cf. *Crow, Raven.*

Rooke, St. : Vide *Boil, Disease, Scabs.*

Roque, St. : St. Roque protects from infection.

Rosary : A rosary protects from the machinations of evil spirits. (Roman Catholic.) cf. *Beads, Crucifix.*

Rose : According to a Teutonic superstition, rose trees spring up on the graves of lovers, and are the abodes of departed souls.

Rothmurchas : Vide *Bodachun Dun.*

Round Table : The table at which King Arthur (q.v.) sits. It belonged to him.

Rowan Tree : A twig of the rowan tree is effective against all evil things, including witches. (RHYS, *C.F.*, p. 325; cf. *Word-Lore*, Vol. I, p. 207, n. 33).

Royalty : Lions do not injure royalty.
Royal blood cures hydrophobia. (*Arabs.*—HASTINGS, *Dic. Bib.*, Vol. IV, p. 603.)

Ruaḥ palga : Same as Ruah zelahta.

Ruaḥ qezarit : Jewish Folklore. A particular spirit of nightmare. (*Jew. Enc.*, Vol. IV, p. 517.)

Ruaḥ tezarit : Jew. Folklore. A spirit of delirious fever and madness befalling man and beast. (*Jew. Enc.*, Vol. IV, p. 517.)

Ruaḥ zelaḥta : Jewish Folklore. The spirit of headaches, which dwells on palm trees.

Ruaḥ zenuim : Jewish Folklore. The spirit of sexual desire. (*Jew. Enc.*, Vol. IV, p. 517.)

Ruaḥ zeradah : Jewish Folklore. The demon of catalepsy.

Rubbing : If you see a person rubbing only one eye in the morning, you are sure to have a quarrel in the course of the day. (*Bengal.*)

Rübezahl : The most famous of the mountain spirits of Germany, who dwelt in Riesengebirge between Silesia and Bohemia. According to a legend, he once stole a princess and in order to please her, planted a big field with turnips (*Rüben*) ; she asked him to count (*zählen*) the turnips, and while he was doing so, escaped ; hence his ironic name : Rübezahl.

Ruby : Rubies are the blood of the sacrificed. (HAGGARD, *People of the Mist.*)

The Burmese believe that rubies ripen like fruit. They say, a ruby in its crude state is colourless, and as it matures, changes first to yellow, then to green, then to blue, and lastly to a brilliant red, its highest state of perfection and ripeness.

The ruby signifies Aries in the Zodiacal signs. It is given by some to December ; it is the emblem of brilliant success.

Rudha : Hind. Myth. " Howler." He is a howling god, the god of storms, and sometimes identified with the god of fire. Sometimes he is a destructive deity who brings about diseases upon men and cattle, and sometimes he is a beneficent deity for healing diseases. (DOWSON, *H.C.D.*, p. 269.)

Rudra : Hind. Myth. The god of thunder. He is usually represented as riding a bull.

Rusalka : Among the Slavs, these are more or less like the Vilas. They are delicate female beings who live in forests, fields and waters, and are mainly the souls of unbaptized children and women who have died by drowning. They seduce men by their voice and tickle them to death.

In Bohemian folklore they are kinds of water-spirits who entice young men and women to destruction. (GROHMANN, p. 8.)

In Russian folklore, they are female water-spirits who appear as beautiful maidens with long hair, bathing and sporting in the waters. They tickle bathers to death, cause storms and wind, and are thought to influence the luck of sailors and fishermen. (RALSTON. *Songs of the Russian People.* pp. 139-146.)

S

Saalah : Muham. Myth. An Arab evil spirit said to be found mainly in forests, and when " it captures a man . . . it plays with him as a cat plays with a mouse." It is described as a creature of a hideous form, and is supposed to be an offspring of human beings and men who eat men. (LANE, *A.S.M.A.*, p. 44.)

Sabazius : An ancient Greek deity who was worshipped with orgiastic rites and with nocturnal mysteries.

Sabbat : Mediæval Demonology. A nocturnal assembly in which demons and sorcerers were thought to celebrate their orgies.

Sabbath : Vide *Witch's Sabbath.*

Sabdag : Tibetan Folklore. "Earth owners"; numerous local spirits who inhabit the soils, springs and lakes. They correspond to our own "Elementals."

Sable : When Siberian sable-hunters have caught a sable, no one is allowed to see it and they think that if good or evil be spoken of the captured sable, no more sables will be caught. (FRAZER, *G.B².,* Vol. II, p. 403, quoting J. G. GMELIN, *Reise durch Sibirien,* II, 278.)

Sack : If a pregnant woman looks long in an empty open sack, the child will have to suffer hunger. (U.S.A.—KNORTZ, p. 8.)

Sacrifice : Gods of various nations can be appeased by offering sacrifices to them. There have been various theories to explain the meaning and importance of sacrifice. Thus Tylor saw in sacrifice an attempt to secure the favour of the gods. W. Robertson Smith explained sacrifice as a meal in which the worshipper was sharing the meal with his god, and Durkheim interpreted it in the same way. Frazer has thought that he can find in sacrifice an attempt to save the god of the worshipper from the inroads of old age. L. Marillier thinks that sacrifice is a magical rite to bend the will of the god to the will of the worshipper. And lastly, Westermarck regards the offering of a victim as an attempt to save the life of the worshipper, and Hubert and Mauss (*Essai sur la nature et la fonction du sacrifice,* Année Sociol., Vol. II, 1897-1898, p. 41) define sacrifice as follows : "Le sacrifice est un acte religieux, qui, par la consécration d'une victime, modifie l'état de la personne morale qui l'accomplit ou de certains objets auxquels elle s'intéresse."

The flesh and blood of the sacrificed were eaten and drunk by the Aztecs, as this was considered to make them strong and powerful. (WUTTKE, *Geschichte des Heidenthums,* Vol. I, p. 268, etc. ; FRAZER, *G.B².,* Vol. I, p. 133.)

Saga : An ancient Scandinavian legend, tale, or history ; hence any historical, mythical, or romantic tale of ancient times.

Sakhrat : Muham. Myth. The sacred stone on which Mt. Qāf rests. Mt. Qāf is a circular plain, the home of giants, and fairies. Anyone who possesses a single grain of the stone Sakhrat has the power of working miracles. Its colour is emerald, and its reflection gives a blue tint to the sky.

Sakti : Hind. Myth. The goddess Devi (q.v.) is called Sakti, because she is the female energy of Siva.

Salamander : The salamanders are the spirits of fires and live in them. They seek the hottest fire to breed in, but soon quench it by the extreme chill of their bodies.

Should a glass-house fire be kept up without extinction for more than seven years, there is no doubt but that a salamander will be generated in the cinders.

Food touched by a salamander (a kind of a lizard) is poisonous. (cf. HAZLITT, p. 531.)

Prester John in his letter to Manuel Comnenus, Emperor of Constantinople, describes the salamander as a worm, and says it makes cocoons like a silk-worm. These cocoons being unwound by the ladies of the palace are spun into dresses for the imperial women. The dresses are washed in flames and not in water.

"Diese Wesen können die Menschen ihre Umgebung beeinflüssen, indem sie deren Eigenschaften in Tätigkeit versetzen, und wir müssen immer daran denken, dass sie keine Unterscheidung von Recht und Unrecht haben; sie haben ihre eigene Gesetze von Moralität. Aber wie gesagt, wir kommen nicht viel mit ihnen in Berührung da sie der Menschlichkeit so fremd sind." DORA VON GELDER in *Theosophische Kultur*, January, 1925.

"Les salamandres, croyait-on, jouissaient de la propriété de traverser la flamme sans se brûler."— *Petit Larousse illustré*, p. 892.

Salemal · One of the four gods of Adite, the preserver of sickness

Saligen : Teut. Myth. A class of forest-spirits.

Saliva : The human saliva is a cure for blindness and a charm against fascination. (ELWORTHY, *EE.*, pp. 420, 663.)

A blacksmith who has to shoe a stubborn horse, spits in his hand to drive off the evil spirit.

To unbewitch the bewitched, you must spit into the shoe of your right foot.

If a pugilist spits on his hands, his blows will be more telling. (DALYELL, *Dark. Sup.*, p. 71.)

If you spit on a serpent, it will die.

Spitting for luck is a most common superstition. (cf.
HERRICK, *Hesperides, The Temple*; HAZLITT, p. 560;
SHIFFER, *Am Urquell*, Vol. II, p. 202; *Jew. Enc.*, Vol. XI,
p. 600; *Folklore*, Vol. IV, pp. 358, 361; FRAZER. *G.B²*.,
Vol. I, p. 204; ZINGERLE, *Sitten*, 176, 580; *Mélusine*,
1878, c. 79; ELWORTHY, pp. 416, 418; ABBOTT, p. 110;
DOUGHTY, *Arab. Des.*, Vol. I, p. 227; CROOKE, *Pop.
Rel.*, Vol. I, p. 167; *Ethnologie du Bengale*, p. 132;
F. W. NICOLSON, "The Saliva Superstition in Classical
Literature," *Harvard Studies in Classical Philology*, viii,
1897, 35 *sqq.*; J. E. CROMBIE, "The Saliva Superstition,"
International Folk-lore Congress, 1891, *Papers and Trans-
actions*, 249 *sq.*; C. DE MENSIGNAC, *Recherches ethro-
graphiques sur la salive et le crachat*, Bordeaux, 1892,
50 *sqq.*; FRAZER, *Taboo*, pp. 279, 287 *sqq.*)

Fishermen usually spit on their hansel for luck in fishing.
If you spit on a letter just before enclosing it in the
envelope, and then again before posting it, you will have
success. Vide *Spitting*.

Salmon : If, when a girl shows signs of womanhood, she eats
fresh salmon, she would lose her senses, or her mouth
would be changed into a long beak. (*Kolosh Indians of
Alaska.*—FRAZER, *G.B²*., Vol. III, p. 211, quoting FR.
BOAS, *Fifth Report*, p. 42.) Vide *Fisherman*.

Salt : Salt spilt towards a person indicates contention. (*General.*
—BRAND, *Observations*, Vol. III, p. 160), but the evil
may be averted by throwing a pinch of the spilt salt
over your left shoulder. (*Great Britain.*—DALYELL,
Dark. Sup., p. 127.)

Salt must not be bought at night, neither be sold
(*India*); it should be obtained at daytime, and a portion
of it be thrown in the fire to ward off all dangers, and
especially to prevent quarrels in the family. (*Japan.*—
GRIFFIS, *M.E.*, p. 470.)

In Bohemia a mother throws salt behind her daughter as
she is going out, as a preventive against her falling in love.
" As many grains of salt you spill,
So many days of sorrow you will fill."—U.S.A.

If on a Christmas Eve you make a little heap of salt
on the table, and it melts overnight, you will die the
next year; if, in the morning, it remains undiminished,
you will live. (RAGNER).

It is unlucky to help another person to salt. But to
whom the ill-luck is to happen does not seem to be settled.
(HAZLITT, p. 533.)

A sieve or salt must on no account be lent out of the house. The prosperity of the family will depart with them. (*Macedonia.*—ABBOTT, p. 101.)

Salt-cellar : If a girl omits to put the salt-cellar on the table, while laying it for dinner, it is a sure sign that she is no longer a virgin. (*Rhineland, Westphalia.*—WUTTKE, p. 43.) Vide *Virginity.*

If a salt-cellar be overturned, a ship will be wrecked. (*Holland.*—BASSETT, p. 438.)

Salzburg : Vide *Charlemagne.*

Samael : Semitic Lore. A known storm-demon, from whose name we have the samiel or simoom. (DR. BREWER, *R.H.*)

Samovílas : Slav. Folklore. These are the souls of deceased children and virgins, which dwell in woods, mountains and lakes, and fly in the clouds. They are noted for their dancing and exquisite singing ; they sometimes intermarry with men.

Samson : Samson's strength was said to have been in his hair (q.v.).

Sandal : New sandals must not be put on after five o'clock in the afternoon. (*Japan.*—GRIFFIS, *M.E.*, p. 472.)

Sandhyā-bala : " Strong in twilight." Rākshasas and other demons are supposed to be most powerful at twilight.

Sandmann : In German children's superstition it is a bogey which throws sand into the eyes of children who will not go to sleep. (cf. E. T. A. HOFFMANN, *Der Sandmann.*)
" Sandmännchen kommt geschlichen
Und guckt durchs Fensterlein,
Ob irgendwo ein Kindchen
Nicht mag zu Bette sein.
Und wo es nur ein Kindlein fand
Streut es ins Aug' ihm Sand."—
W. VON ZUCCAMAGLIO, *Sandmännchen* (1839).

Sand-Pillar : The whistling sand pillars of the desert are believed by the Muhammedans to be caused by the flight of an evil jinn. (LANE, BURTON.)

Sani : Hind. Myth. The god who brings ill luck and misfortune.

Sānkchinni : Indian Folklore. Female demons of a white complexion. They usually stand at the dead of the night at the foot of trees and look like sheets of white cloth. (DAY, *Folktales of Bengal*, p. 197 ; *Ethnologie du Bengale*, pp. 98 sq.)

Sänkini : In Bengal it is a kind of a female spirit, closely allied to Petni (q.v.), Dākini (q.v.), etc.

Sapphire : Sapphire produces somnambulism and impels the wearer to all good works.
Sapphire brings misfortune to the wearer. (*India*.)
In the Zodiac it signifies Leo ; in Christian art it is dedicated to St. Andrew, emblematic of his heavenly faith and good hope. This gem is dedicated to April.

Sarabha : Hind. Myth. A fabulous animal represented as having eight legs, and as dwelling in the Himalayas. (DOWSON, *H.C.D.*, p. 282.)

Saraswati : Hind. Myth. Wife of Brahma, the goddess of eloquence, learning and arts.

Sargon : "A fish supposed to be . . . our gilt-head. It was anciently supposed to have an extraordinary affection for goats, and to leap for joy when they approached the sea." (HAZLITT, p. 534.)

Sarpanit : Babyl. Myth. Consort of Marduk. She is sometimes identified with the mother-goddess Ishtar.

Sarugami : The monkey-god possession of Shikoku, Japan.

Satan : Theology. The chief of the demons. His name is mentioned several times in the New Testament, and especially in the Apocalypse.

Sati : The burning of widows in India on the funeral pyre of their deceased husbands, had probably its origin in the idea that dutiful wives should accompany the spirits of their dead husbands, and administer to their wants in the spirit world (cf. *Ethnologie du Bengale*, pp. 67 *sq.*) cf. *Horse, Camel, Dog*.

Saturday : In India this day is particularly unlucky, because it is dedicated to Sani, the god of misfortune.
Saturday derives its name from Saturn to whom it is dedicated. Vide *Wednesday, Sunday, Friday, Thursday*.

Saturn : Rom. Myth. The ancient god of the seed-sowing, whose temple in Rome was built in 497 B.C. In 217 B.C. the worship of Saturn was conformed to that of the Greek Cronus.

Satyr : Class. Myth. A sylvan deity or demi-god, represented as part human and part horse or goat, given to riotous merriment and lasciviousness. They were companions of Bacchus. cf. *Pan*.

Satyavāna : Hind. Myth. Husband of Sāvitri (q.v.).

Sāvitri : Hind. Myth. Wife of Satyavāna, who, after the death of her husband, compelled Yama, the god of death, by her devotedness, to restore her husband to life again. The story has been related by various authors. Sāvitri is considered by the Hindus to be a model of wifely devotion.

Sbires : Muham. Myth. The assistants of Malik, the demon of the underworld. They are eighteen in number.

Scabs : St. Rooke cures scabs.

Schachtmandl : German Folklore. The guardian-spirit of the mines.

Scinus : A legendary robber of Attica, who was thrown into the sea by Theseus. The sea, however, refused to take such a scoundrel, neither would the earth, after being rid of him once, take him back, so that he stuck fast in the air. (cf. HAWTHORNE, *T.T.*, p. 181.)

Scissors : If while using scissors they break in half, it is a sign of a great disappointment.

If you accidentally drop a pair of scissors and it fixes itself on the floor with the handle pointing towards you, you will receive a gift.

A pair of opened-out scissors keeps witches and other evil spirits at bay. (*India.*) cf. *Iron.*

Scorpion : Scorpions sometimes sting themselves to death. Scorpions have an oil which is a remedy for their stings. (HAZLITT, p. 536.)

Scrat : Slovenian Folklore. A demon which dwells in woods and mountains. This fact indicates that this demon was originally a forest-spirit.

Sea : There is a legend as to how the sea became salty. A sea-captain had robbed a young man of a magic mill which ground out anything that was asked for. After he had learnt the secret of setting the mill going from the owner, the wicked sailor pushed the young man overboard, but forgot to learn how to stop the mill. He wished for some salt, and the mill ground out salt in such quantity, that the ship sank in mid·ocean. The mill still grinds out salt from the bottom of the sea. (*Deutsche Märchen seit Grimm*, p. 266 ; cf. BASSETT, p. 21.)

The roaring of the sea predicts a storm. (BRAND, *Observations*, Vol. II, p. 240.)

A Berber superstition says that God made gnats to swallow the water of the rebellious ocean which was not salty then ; then when it promised obedience, caused them to vomit it up, but since then the sea is salty. (HAY in *Mélusine*, March, 1885.)

Scyros : Gr. Myth. An island in the Ægean Sea.

Sea-gull : It is unlucky to kill a sea-gull.
If you do not wish a sea-gull to fly away, put some salt on its tail.

Sea-Serpent : A great mythical sea-monster of ᵗ serpentine form and enormous length ; it is frequently reported to have been seen at sea. It is fabled to appear to announce some great calamity, such as the death of a king. (BASSETT, p. 221. See LEHMANN, *Aberglaube und Zauberei*.)

Seal : According to the Greenlanders, seals and wildfowls are scared by spectres " which no human eye but the sorcerer's can behold." (TYLOR, *P.C.*, Vol. II, p. 179 ; CRANZ, *Grönland*, p. 267.)
The Esquimaux believe that seals will be frightened away, if the heads of those taken are thrown into the water ; so they burn them or pile them up on the shore. (BASSETT, p. 246, quoting FARRER, *Primitive Customs*, p. 28.)

Seb : Egypt. Myth. The earth deified. The consort of Seb was Nut, the sky ; their children include Osiris, Isis, Nepthys and Set. Vide *Shu*.

Sebastian, St. : St. Sebastian cures diseases because he was martyred with arrows.

Second sight : The power of predicting or prophesying a future event. People having this power are said to foresee things.
Children born on a Sunday (q.v.) are gifted with the power of second sight.

Seewiesken : In some parts of Germany the water-nixies are called by this name. (STRACKERJAN, Vol. I, p. 419.)

Sef : Egypt. Myth. The lion-god (q.v.) on the right.

Sekhet : Egypt. Myth. The feminine counterpart of Ptah (q.v.).

Sekhet Hetep : Egypt. Myth. A field of peace.

Selene : Name of an idol or deity whom the Saracens are represented in mediæval romances as worshipping.

Semele : Gr. Myth. An earth goddess, daughter of Cadmus, mother of Dionysus. Zeus promised to grant any boon she asked for ; she begged to be allowed to see him in all his splendour, and was destroyed by his lightnings. Hence she was called " Keraunia "—" thunder-bitten."

Semiramis : A legendary queen of Assyria, to whom is ascribed the building of the famous hanging gardens.

Semnæ : Rom. Myth. One of the Erinyes.

Sennar : Name of a city. According to an Arab legend, it derived its name from a beautiful woman with teeth glittering like fire, who was found sitting on a river bank by the founders of the city. (SINNAR—tooth of fire.)

Serp : The Wend name for a Poledniček (q.v.).

Serpent : To dream of a serpent denotes danger, and perhaps prison.

Serpents' heads give strength to a man, and fidelity to a woman. (HAZLITT, p. 539.)

In Macedonia, it is a bad omen to meet a serpent on going out (ABBOTT, p. 106) ; in Lesbos, good. (G. GEORGE-AKIS ET LÉON PINEAU, *Le Folklore de Lesbos*, p. 339.) See *Snake*.

Set : Egypt. Myth. An evil destiny, brother and slayer of Osiris. He is represented with the head of a beast with high square ears and a pointed snout. His consort was Ta-urt.

Seven : The number seven is considered unlucky by the Moors. (MEAKIN, *The Moors*, p. 354.)

The seventh child of a woman becomes a mara (q.v.). (KÜHN UND SCHWARZ, p. 420 ; WOLF, *Beiträge*, Vol. II, p. 264 ; MÜLLENHOF, p. 242 ; cf. THIERS, *Traité des Sup.*, I, 436-7.)

Children should be introduced into their future profession before they are seven years old ; they will have luck in their professions. (*Hesse, Westphalia.*—WUTTKE, p. 202 ; WOLF, *Beiträge*, Vol. I, p. 206.)

The ages of seven and all multiples of seven are critical years for children. (*Great Britain.*) cf. *Thirteen, Three.*

Seven Sleepers of Ephesus : An early Christian legend in which seven noble youths of Ephesus fly to a cavern, are pursued by their enemies, and are walled in. They fall asleep and wake up after a lapse of two centuries. (cf. the Legend of Rip van Winkle ; see ELWORTHY, *The Evil Eye*, p. 407.) Vide *Al Raqim*.

Sexton : A sexton mowing the churchyard will bring about a rainfall. (STRACKERJAN, Vol. I, p. 35.)

Shabriri : Jewish Folklore. The demon of blindness. He rests on uncovered water at night, and inflicts blindness on those who drink it. (*Jew. Enc.*, Vol. IV., p. 517.)

Shadow : A shadow is a kind of a personal spirit, and is able under certain circumstances, to live apart from the owner. (cf. CHAMISSO, *Peter Schlemihl.*)

The Basutos say, if a man walks on the river bank, a crocodile may seize his shadow on the water and drag him in after it. (SIR J. LUBBOCK, *Origin of Civilization,* 1882, p. 219 ; cf. TYLOR, *P.C.*, i, 43 ; FRAZER, *Taboo,* p. 77 ; SPENCER, i. 180.)

The Jews believe that if the shadow of one's head be invisible against the wall in a house where a light is burning, on Hosha'na Rabbah Eve, it is an omen that the person is destined to die within a year. (*Jew. Enc.*, Vol. IV, p. 486.)

The Hindus say that the shadow is a ghost, and would not look at it after dark, for fear that they may be seized by it. (cf. H. SPENCER, *Principles of Sociology,* Lond., 1906, i, 116.)

He who does not throw a shadow on Christmas Eve, will surely die in the next year. (STRACKERJAN, Vol. I, p. 32), or is a ghost. (*India.*—CROOKE, Vol. I, p. 237 ; JACKSON, *F.L.N.*, Vol. I, p. 106.)

In modern Greece, a builder who cannot get a human victim, entices a man on to the site, secretly measures his body or his shadow and buries the measure under the foundation stone. It is believed that the man whose shadow is thus buried will die within the year. (SCHMIDT, *Das Volksleben der Neugriechen,* p. 196 *et seq.*; FRAZER, *G.B².*, Vol. I, p. 145 ; ELWORTHY, *E.E.*, p. 82.) The Roumanians have a similar belief. (ELWORTHY, p. 82.)

Shaitān: Muham. Folklore. ("The devil"). This word is commonly used to signify a Jinn. (LANE, *A.S.M.A.*, p. 27.)

Shaman : In its vulgar usage, it means a " medicine-man."

Shamash : Assyro-Babyl. Myth. The chief sun-god, a beneficent power, who drives away winter storms, as also demons and spirits that cause disease, and brightens the earth with verdure. He is a god of righteousness and order, and symbolizes the sun in general.

Shamrock : A four-leaved shamrock brings luck to the owner, especially if the owner be Irish. Vide *Lucky Finds.*

P

Shark : Sharks can tell a few days beforehand, if anyone on board a vessel is going to die (BASSETT, p. 240) ; they therefore follow a ship for days.

Sharpening : If you eat while someone is sharpening a knife, your throat will be cut that same evening or next morning at latest. (FRAZER, *G.B².*, Vol. I, p. 44.)

Shaving : One reason for the widespread custom of shaving on death of a near relative, is to change the appearance of the mourner, so that the pursuing ghost of the deceased person may be unable to recognize and to follow. (FRAZER; cf. *Ethnologie du Bengale*, p. 73.)

Shedim : "Demons." The Turkish Jews do not mention the Shedim by name. (GARNETT,, *Turkish Life*, p. 283 ; *Jew. Enc.*, Vol. IX, p. 599.) (cf. Good-folk of the Scotch for "fairies.")

In Chaldean mythology this was the name of the storm-demons of an ox-like form, as also the protective genii of royal palaces and the like. (DELITZSCH, *Assyrisches Handwörterbuch*, pp. 60, 253, 261, 646 ; JENSEN, *Assyr. Babyl. Mythen und Epen* (1900), p. 453.) cf. *Qor'an, God.*

Shedu : In Babylonian folklore they were strong and powerful demons. cf. *Utukku.*

Sheep : It is lucky to meet a drove of sheep on going out. (WUTTKE, p. 32.)

The shin-bone of a sheep placed above the door, keeps out robbers, or acts as a charm (*The Kirghiz of Turkestan.* SCHUYLER, Vol. II, p. 31), or the knuckle bone is a preventive against cramp. (ELWORTHY, *E.E.*, p. 437.)

"To have a black sheep was considered an omen of good luck to the flock where it was born, but if more than one sheep was the result of the lambing season, then it was the reverse of lucky." (HILLS in *Word-Lore*, Vol. I, p. 147.)

(Other superstitions connected with the sheep are given in SCHUYLER, *Turkestan*, Vol. II, pp. 31, etc.)

Shellfish : The Muhammedans abstain from shellfish, except shrimps. (LEAN, Vol. II, p. 208.)

Sheol : The Sheol of the ancient Hebrews corresponded to the Greek Hades, and was an under-world of awful depth.

Shibbeta : Jewish Folklore. A female demon who brings cramp to persons, especially children, who leave their hands unwashed in the morning. (*Jew. Enc.*, Vol. IV, p. 516.)

Shibta : Jewish Folklore. A spirit who clings to the finger tips, and afflicts people who eat with unwashed hands.

Shid : Babyl. Myth. An ancient goddess who belongs to the pantheon of Erech.

Shin : The Arabic letter Shîn, representing *sharr*, "evil," is considered unlucky by the Muhammedans. (MEAKIN, *The Moors*, p. 356.) cf. *Khâ.*

Shinatsu-Hiko : Shinto Religion. He was produced from Izanagi's breath when he puffed away the mists which surrounded the newly-formed country of Japan. (ASTON, *Shinto*, pp. 154, 155.) He is a symbol of spiritual mind on the higher mental plane of the soul. (GASKELL, *D.S.L.S.M.*, p. 686.)

Shinbone : Vide *Sheep.*

Shingles : Can be cured by laying the skin of a black cat on the part affected. (*New York, Massachusetts.*—KNORTZ, p. 128.)

Ship, Spectral : The appearance of a spectral ship foretells either a shipwreck (*Brittany.*—P. SÉBILLOT in *Revue des Traditions Populaires*, XII, p. 395 ; *Scotland.*—GREGOR, ibid, XI, p. 330 ; *Cornwall.*—BOTTRELL, *Traditions and Hearthside Stories*, p. 141 ; M. A. COURTNEY in *Folklore Journal*, V, p. 189), or a death (*Hebrides.*—GOODRICH-FREER, in *Folklore*, XIII, p. 52.)

The spectral ship is doomed to sail about for eternity, because the captain swore he would double the Cape, whether God willed it or not. (BASSETT, p. 363.) cf. *Flying Dutchman.*

Shipwreck : Rats forsake a ship before a wreck. (STRACKERJAN, Vol. I, p. 24.)

If the sound of a worm boring the planks of a ship be audible, it forebodes some catastrophe, probably shipwreck. (*Great Britain.*)

Children born with a caul will never be drowned in a shipwreck.

It is an evil omen to dream of a shipwreck. Vide *Cat.*

Shiqq : A demon of Arabic superstition, having the form of half a human being. (LANE, *A.S.M.A.*, p. 45.)

Shirt : If a shirt be spun, woven, and sewed by a pure, chaste maiden on Christmas day, it will be proof against lead or steel. (RAGNER.)

Shishchikul : In Vancouver Island, it is a large animal-like monster who lives inside a mountain, and whose red hair is a powerful amulet for success in war.

Shiver : If you suddenly shiver, it is a sign that someone is walking over your grave. (THORPE, *N.M.*, Vol. III, p. 331.)

Shoe : The Romans thought it a bad omen, to put a shoe on the wrong foot. (HAZLITT, p. 543.)

It is unlucky for lovers to give each other a present of shoes. (*Berlin.*)

Never walk in one shoe, or one slipper, lest your parents, or one of them, die. (*Jews of Minsk.—Jew. Enc.*, Vol. XI, p. 601 ; *India.*)

Old shoes are tied on to the bridal carriage for luck (*Great Britain*), or in Transylvania, to enhance the fertility of the union. (HARTLAND, *Legend of Perseus*, Vol. I, p. 171.)

If you leave shoes lying on their "uppers," you are sure to have a quarrel with someone during the course of the day. (*Bengal.*)

In Hessen, a woman in order to make her beloved love her, steals a pair of his shoes, wears them herself for eight days, and then returns them to him. (PLOSS, *Das Weib*, Vol. I, p. 443.)

In Poona, India, if a man feels that he has been struck by an incantation, he at once takes hold of an upturned shoe. (*N.I.N.Q.*, I, 86.)

If new shoes creak, it is a sign that you have not paid for them yet. (*Great Britain, India.*) cf. *Scissors, Knife, Slippers, Needle, Rice, Sandals, Footwear, Sleeplessness.*

Shoelace : If a shoelace comes undone, it denotes that someone is thinking of you. (*Great Britain.*)

If the shoelace comes unlaced
        " 'Tis a sure sign and true,
          At that very moment
          Your true love thinks of you."

                              New York (BERGEN, *C.S.*, p. 63.)
cf. *Hairpin.*

Shony : A spectral dog of Cornwall. It is said to predict a storm when appearing on the beach. (HUNT ; BASSETT, p. 279.)

Shooting : If you wish to have a successful day in shooting, allow a virgin to jump across your gun, before you set out. (STRACKERJAN, Vol. I, p. 98.)

Shooting Pains : All sudden pains are warnings of evil at hand.

Shot, First : If a hunter misses the first shot, it presages a very bad day. (STRACKERJAN, Vol. I, p. 35.)

Shroud : If you are making a shroud, avoid knots. (WUTTKE, p. 210 ; *Jew. Enc.*, Vol. XI, p. 601.)

Shu : Egypt. Myth. A solar deity typifying the sunlight. In some myths, Shu and his consort Tefnut are created by Tum, and became the parents of Seb (the earth), and Nut (the sky), whom Shu is represented as separating.

Shuck : A Norfolk ghost ; one of a numerous family of animal spirits (See *Word-Lore*, Vol. I, p. 167).

Shudder : If you shudder without any apparent cause, someone is walking over your grave. (*Great Britain, India.*)

Sickle : In Bulgaria, when a child is born, the witch brings a reaping-hook into the room and then proceeds to rub the infant all over with salt, and to fumigate the room in order to drive away evil spirits from mother and child. (ST. CLAIR AND BROPHY, p. 69.)

Sickness : In the Slave Coast of Africa the mother of a sick child believes that an evil spirit has taken possession of the child's body, and in order to drive him out, she makes small cuts in the body of the sufferer and inserts green pepper in the wounds. The poor child screams with pain, but the mother thinks that the demon is suffering. (ELLIS. *Yoruba-speaking Peoples*, p. 113 *sq.* ; cf. *Ethnologie du Bengale*, p. 130 ; FRAZER, *Taboo*, pp. 45 *sqq.* ; id., SCAPEGOAT, p. 139 ; TYLOR, *P.C.*, ii, 115, 134 ; DOOLITTLE, *The Chinese*, ii, 265 ; HOWITT, *Native Tribes*, pp. 356, 358 ; SKEAT, p. 11 ; MARSDEN, *Hist. of Sumatra*, p. 157 ; ROTH, in *North Queensland Ethnog. Bull.* No. 5, § 116 ; TAPLIN, *The Narrinyeri*, 62 *sq.* ; ST. JOHN, i, 217.)

Siddhas : Hind. Myth. A class of semi-divine beings of great purity and holiness, who dwell in the regions of the sky between the earth and the sun. They are said to be 88,000 in number. (DOWSON, *H.C.D.*, p. 292.)

Siegfried : The hero of the Nibelungenlied. He was brought up in the forest by the demoniac smith Mimir. In his youth he accomplished wonderful deeds, winning the hoards of the Nibelungs, the sword Balmung, Tarnkappe, and slaying the dragon, in whose blood he bathed himself to make himself invulnerable. The only part of his body which was vulnerable was a spot between his shoulders where a leaf fell, and thus prevented from coming in contact with the dragon's blood. He aids Gunther to win Brunhilde, and weds Kriemhild. Later, he is treacherously slain by the fierce Hagen, who gets the hoard of the Nibelungs and buries it in the Rhine. The widowed Kriemhild marries Etzel, a king of the Huns, and takes her revenge for the foul murder of Siegfried by slaying Gunther, Hagen and all their comrades. (KARL SIMROCK, *Das Nibelungenlied.*) Vide *Mimir, Nibelungs, Balmung, Tarnkappe, Gunther, Brunhilde, Kriemhild, Hagen, Etzel.*

Sien : Chin. Myth. Eight divine beings, living in Heaven and said to be immortal. They were : Jung Li Küän, Jang Go, Lü Güän (or Lu Dung Bin), Tsau Guo Giu, Lan Tsai Ho, Li Tia Guai, Han Siang Dsi and Ho Siän Gu. Vide *Immortal.*

Sieve : If children look at a sieve, they will suffer from a skin disease. (FRAZER, *G.B²*., Vol. I, p. 44.) Vide *Salt.*

Sight : Good eyesight may be obtained by eating the flesh of a kite.

Sigurd : The hero of the Volsunga Saga. He is reared by Regin, slays Fafnir, is engaged to be married to Brynhild, but after drinking of a magic potion, marries Gudrun. He was treacherously slain by Gunnar's brother. cf. *Siegfried.*

Silene : A Phrygian deity. According to Greek mythology, he was a jester in Olympia. He was foster-father of Bacchus.

Silk : To dream of being dressed in silk denotes honour ; to dream you are trading in silk is an indication of profit and joy. Vide *Lumbago, Nose, Ribbon.*

Silver : A Welsh witch shifts her form frequently into that of a hare, and while in this form no shot, except a silver coin can penetrate her body. (RHYS, *C.F.*, p. 294.)

Silver Fish : A kind of insect or book-worm. In China it is believed that if this insect gets inside a Taoist Classic and eats certain characters, its silvery body will become five coloured. If this five-coloured insect be subsequently caught and eaten, the one who eats it will overcome death and develop into a spiritual being. (*Enc. Rel. Eth.*, Vol. VIII, p. 261.)

Silver Fox : Chin. Folklore. These animals have the power of influencing human beings. They are yellow, red or white in colour ; some species of them can even learn to speak the human language in course of time, and are known as " Speaking Foxes." (*Chin. Volksmärchen*, p. 181.)

Sin : Babyl. Myth. A moon-god. The meaning and etymology of the word Sin is not quite clear.

Siren : Class. Myth. One of a group of sea-nymphs, generally represented as part woman, part bird. They were three in number, and were supposed to frequent an island near the coast of Italy. They lured mariners to destruction by their enchanting singing.
Theodore de Gaza saw several sirens on board ship in the Peloponnesian Sea, which were put back in the water. (LANDRIN, *Les Monstres Marins*, p. 265 *et seq.*, quoted by BASSETT, p. 169.)
cf. *Parthenope, Lorelei, Nixie, Bugarik, Alrinach, Jal Pari, Apsaras, Houris.*

Sisa : " Ghost ". The *kla* of the Gold Coast negroes of West Africa becomes a *sisa* after death, and can remain in the same house with the corpse, but is only visible to the spirit-doctor. (TYLOR, *P.C.*, Vol. I, p. 402, quoting STEINHAUSER.)

Sister : If two sisters are married within one year (*Altenburg*), or on the same day (*Silesia*), both, or at least one of them will be unhappy in her married life. (WUTTKE, p. 206.)

Sisyphus : Gr. Myth. Son of Eolus, king of Corynthia. He is famous for his brigandages and his cruelties. After his death he was condemned to roll a huge stone up a mountain in Hell. No sooner is this stone taken up to the summit, than it rolls down again.

Sitā : Hind. Myth. Wife of Rāma whom she accompanied on his exile. She was stolen by the giant-king, Rāvana, and, after a bloody war, was rescued by Rāma. Vide *Rāma, Rāvana.*

Siva : Hind. Myth. One of the gods of the Supreme Triad. He represents the reproductive and restoring power. He is a god of arts, especially dancing. He had a variety of names which, according to some authors, numbered more than one thousand.

Si Wang Mu : Chin. Myth. A fabulous being of the female sex dwelling upon Mt. Kwen-lun at the head of the troops of the genii, and holding from time to time intercourse with favoured imperial votaries. (MAYERS, *Chin. Read. Man.*, p. 191.)

Skadi, Skathi : Norse Myth. A goddess of Finnish origin, wife of Njorth. Vide *Loki*.

Skogsfruar: "Wood-nymphs"; forest-spirits of Swedish folklore.

Skrimsl : "Monster"; a water-spirit in Iceland.

Skrzatek : Polish Folklore. A winged creature which supplies corn, and flying about in the vicinity of houses, steals children.

Skuld : "Shall-be." One of the three Norns of Scandinavian mythology. She is the same as the Greek Atropos. According to the Edda, she was a water-nymph. (THORPE, *N.M.*, Vol. II, p. 13.)

Skull : A skull which is said to give forth piercing screams on being removed from its usual resting place, is believed to be preserved in a farm-house in Cornwall. (F. MARION CRAWFORD, *Uncanny Tales*; cf. P. SÉBILLOT, *Contes et légendes du Pays du Gouarec* in Revue de Bretagne, de Vendée et d'Anjou, XVIII, p. 60 *sq.*; LE BRAZ, Vol. I, p. 332.) There is such a skull at Chilton Cantelo in Somerset. (*Somerset Year Book*, 1925.)

The Jivaros and Tibolo Indians of Equador pound up and eat the skull and brains of human beings "so that the knowledge of the dead person may be added to their own." (MITCHELL-HEDGES, in *Cassell's Magazine*, No. 168, March, 1926, p. 34.)

Sky : The Muhammedans believe that the sky receives its blue tint from the reflection of the stone Sakhrat (q.v.).

Slamming : The German peasantry consider it a wrong thing to slam a door, because of the possibility of "pinching" a soul in it. (WUTTKE.) Vide *Door*.

Slaughter : If you pity the animals that are being slaughtered, it will prolong their death agony. (*Silesia, Wetterau.*—WUTTKE, p. 138.)

Sleep : If a girl falls asleep at work, she will marry a widower. (*Hanover.*—WUTTKE, p. 42.)

Sleeplessness : Insomnia can be cured by leaving the shoes with the toes pointing towards the bed. (*Mark. Silesia.*—WUTTKE, p. 136.)

Slippers : If you wish to forget something unpleasant, throw a slipper over your left shoulder. (STRACKERJAN, Vol. I, p. 96 ; Vol. II, p. 139.)

If you leave your slippers lying on their "uppers," you are sure to have a quarrel. (*Bengal.*)

In Cornwall, a slipper with the point turned up placed near the bed cures cramp. (HUNT, *Pop. Rem.*, p. 409.) cf. *Shoes.*

Small-pox : During a smallpox epidemic, the Japs put a notice outside their houses to the effect that the children are absent. This is supposed to keep out the disease. (GRIFFIS, *M.E.*, p. 468.)

Fried mouse cures smallpox.

St. Martin of Tours, or, in extreme cases, Oblā Bibi (*India*), may be tried by those objecting to vaccination.

The Chinese make their children hideous on the last night of the year with paper masks, so that the smallpox demon may pass them by. (DOOLITTLE, Vol. II, p. 316.)

Smell : If you imagine you can smell flowers, it is a sign of death (*Great Britain*), or the presence of snakes in the house (*India*).

Smile : A corpse with a smile on its lips, forebodes another death in the family. cf. *Eye.*

Smok : A flying dragon which appears in the folklore of all Slavic nations.

Smrtnice : Bohemian Folklore. A woman, haggard and dressed in white, who walks beneath the windows of a house in which someone is dying. If she sits down at the head of the bed, all hopes of recovery are lost ; but if at the foot, the invalid may recover. cf. *Banshee, Bodachun Dun, Corpse Candles, Åderyn y Corph, Edgewell Oak, Death Warnings, Habergeis, Božaloshtsh, Ahnfrau.*

Snake : In some parts of the world, snakes are not killed because they are the living homes of some "hapless souls."

Snakes are said to be the ancestors of some families (*India*). [A trace of totenism ?]

Q

Snakes smell of flowers. (HAGGARD, *When the World Shook*, Cassell's Pop. Ed., p. 91.)

If you spit on a snake it will die.

People bitten by a snake can be cured by drinking beer in which ash-leaves have been put (STRACKERJAN, Vol. I, p. 85.)

If you dream of snakes, it means you will receive some bad news. (*U.S.A.*—KNORTZ, p. 21.)

A snake seen in the house is a good omen ; it is the guardian spirit watching over its own. (*Greece.*—LAWSON, p. 328 ; *Russia*, RALSTON, *The Songs of the Russians*, 1872, pp. 175, 124.)

A snake's skin worn round the head cures headache (*N. Lincolnshire.*)

Snakes are said to fascinate frogs, birds, etc. (ELWORTHY, *E.E.*, p. 39 *et seq.*)

Hindu boatmen keep venomous serpents in their boats. If they are dull and irritable, they will not sail ; but if they are lively and good-natured, " it is thought a sign of an extremely lucky voyage." (DE FEYNES, *Voyage jusqu'à la Chine,* 1630, p. 207 ; *Mélusine*, Jan., 1885 ; BASSETT, p. 430.)

Snakes are most poisonous on Thursday and Saturday afternoons ; at these times some non-venomous snakes become venomous. (*Bengal.*)

The evil effects of a snake-bite may be counteracted by a mixture of pepper and clarified butter. (*India.*— JACKSON, *F.L.N.*, Vol. I, p. 141.)

" In ancient Mexican temples the serpent symbol is frequently seen. The approaches of the temple of El Castillo, at Chichen in Yucatan, is guarded by a pair of huge serpent heads, and a second pair protect the entrance to the sanctuary. Figures of serpents also appear in the mosaic relief designs of the façades, and within the sanctuary walls. So, too, in the temples of Palenque and other Mexican towns, serpents are everywhere plentiful in the decorations and sculptures. (Quoting *Amer. Antiq.*, Vol. XVIII, 1896, p. 141) . . . Visits from snakes are highly appreciated as auspicious events (cf. G.GEORGEAKIS et LEON PINEAU, *le Folklore de Lesbos*, p. 339), and reptiles are sure of a hospitable reception, because they are looked upon as tutelary divinities." (Dr. R. LAWRENCE, *The Magic of the Horseshoe*, Boston, 1898, pp. 62 *sq.*).

For Snake worship among the Romans see VIRGIL, *Æneid*, V, 84-93 ; among the Zulus and other African tribes, CALLAWAY, *Religious System of the Amazulu*, Pt. II, pp. 140-144, 196-200, 208-212 ; J. SHOOTER, *The Kaffirs of Natal*, p. 162 ; E. CASALIS, *The Basutos*, p. 246 ; *F.L.J.*, ii (1880), pp. 101-103 ; KRANT, *Natur und Kulturleben der Zulus*, p. 112 ; DUDLEY KIDD, *The Essential Kaffir*, pp. 85-87 ; W. A. ELMSLIE, *Among the Wild Ngoni*, pp. 71 *sq.* ; O. BAUMANN, *Usambara und seine Nachbargebiete*, pp. 141 *sq.* ; (SIR) H. JOHNSON, *The Uganda Protectorate*, Vol. II, p. 832 ; A. C. HOLLIS, *The Masai*, pp. 307 *sq.* ; S. L. HINDE and H. H. HINDE, *The Last of the Masai*, pp. 101 *sq.* ; G. SCHWEINFURTH, *The Heart of Africa*, 3 ed., Vol. I, p. 55 ; A. VAN GENNEP, *Tabou et Totémisme à Madagascar*, pp. 272 *sq.* ; H. W. LITTLE, *Madasgascar, its History and People*, pp. 86 *sq.* ; J. ROSCOE, in *Jour. Anthrop. Inst.*, Vol. XXXVII (1907) ; Maj. J. A. MELDON, *Jour. African Soc.*, No. XXII, p. 151 ; ELLIS, *Ewe-speaking Peoples*, pp. 54 *sq.* ; among the Hindus, *Ethnologie du Bengale*, pp. 58 *sq.* ; FRAZER, *Adonis*, Vol. I, p. 81 *sq.*

Vide *Emerald, Squirrel, Stag, Peacock, Serpent.*

Snakebane : It is a kind of flower, and is believed by the Coreans (GRIFFIS, *Corea*, p. 306), and by the Indians to keep away snakes.

Sneeze : Sneezing is due to demoniacal influence. (*India.*— CROOKE, *P.R.*, Vol. I, p. 240.)

To sneeze the first thing in the morning is lucky, but beware of sneezing the last thing at night !

If you, or another person, sneeze just as you are starting on a journey, or on a mission, you are sure to have a disappointment or to fail.

If a person sneezes on another's back, he immediately pinches the back in order to minimize the evil effects. (*India.*—CROOKE, *op. cit.*, I, 240.)

If you sneeze in the middle of a statement, it is a sign that you are telling the truth. (ABBOTT, p. 113 ; STRACKERJAN, Vol. I, p. 31.)

To sneeze three times is most unlucky. (TYLOR, *P.C.*, Vol. I, p. 97 ; BASSETT, p. 434.)

If you sneeze when I speak, it shows that I am right (*Turkestan.*—SCHUYLER, Vol. II, p. 29.)

At Raratonga sneezing is said to be caused by the soul returning to the body. (W. GILL, *Myths and Songs from the South Pacific*, p. 177.)

Sneezing is considered to be a call of death ; therefore the middle finger and the thumb are snapped as a charm. Sneezing with the face towards the West is considered auspicious, but sneezing while at work is inauspicious. (*India.*—JACKSON, *F.L.N.*, Vol. II, p. 54 *sq.*)

> " Once a wish,
> Twice a kiss,
> Thrice a disappointment,
> Four times a letter,
> Five times something better."

> Popular Rhyme (*Great Britain.*)

If you want to sneeze and cannot, it is a sign that someone loves you but does not dare to tell it. (*Boston.*—BERGEN, *C.S.*, p. 63.)

Sneezing indicates that absent enemies are speaking about you. (*Macedonia.*—ABBOTT, p. 113.)

> " Sneeze on Monday, sneeze for danger,
> Sneeze on Tuesday, kiss a stranger,
> Sneeze on Wednesday, receive a letter,
> Sneeze on Thursday, something better,
> Sneeze on Friday, sneeze for sorrow,
> Sneeze on Saturday, see your true love to-morrow,
> Sneeze on Sunday, your safety seek,
> Or the devil will have you for the rest of the week."

Crown Point. (BERGEN, *C.S.*, p. 145 ; cf. HAZLITT, p. 554.)

When sneezing, an evil spirit is expelled from the body. (TYLOR, *P.C.*, Vol. I, p. 97 ; LANG, *Custom and Myth*, p. 14.) A modern German says " *Wohl sein!* " or " *Gesundheit!* " if anyone sneezes in his presence.

The act of sneezing has found different interpretations in different countries at different times. The superstitions connected with sneezing in England at the time of Queen Elizabeth (" *Burghley Papers*," Lansdowne MSS., No. 121 in the British Museum, London ; *Twelfth Annual Report of the Thirteenth Club of New York*, January, 1894 ; LAWRENCE, *Magic of the Horseshoe*, pp. 212-214) were as follows :

I. Yf any man talk with another about any matter and snese twice or iiij times, let him by and by arise, yf he sett, or yf he be stand, let him move himself and go straightaway without any stays about his business, for he shall prosper.

II. Yf he snese more than iiij times, let him staye, for it is doubtful how he shall spede.

III.   Yf a man snese one or iij times, let him procede no further in any matter, but let all alone, for it shall come to nought.

IV.   Yf two men do snese both at one instant, yt is a good syne, and let them go about their purpose, yf that it be either by water or land, and they shall prosper.

V.   To snese twyse is a good syne, but to snese once or iij times is an yll syne.   Yf one come suddenly into the house and snese one tyme, yt is a good syne.

VI.   One snese in the nyght season made by any of the household betokeneth good luck to ye house, but yf he make two sneses, yt sygnifieth domage.

VII.   Trewe yt is that he who snesith takith pte (= part) of the signification in this condition, and that he pte some pte with other.

VIII.   Yf that any man snese twyse iij nyghtes together, yt is a tokyn that one of the house shall dye, or els some greatt goodness or badness shall happen in the house.

IX.   Yf a man go to dwell in a house and snese one time, lett him dwell there, but yf he snese twyse, lett him not tarry, neither lett him dwell therein.

X.   Yf a man lye awake in the bedde and snese one tyme, yt is a syne of greatt sickness or hyndraunce.

XI.   Yf a man sleape in his bedde and snese one tyme, yt betokeneth greatt trouble, the death of some person or extreme hyndraunce in the loss of substance.

XII.   Yf a man lye in his bedde and make a snese one tyme, yt is a good syne both of health and lucre, but yf he sleape yt is moche better.

XIII.   Yf a man snese twyse three nyghtes together, yt is a good syne whatsover he go about.

XIV.   Yf a man travell by ye ways and come to an Inne and snese twyse, lett him depart out of ye house and go on another, or els he shall not prosper.

XV.   Yf a man go forthe to seke worke and lay hands of yt and then snese one tyme, lett him depart, leaving his work behind him, and seke worke elsewhere, and so shall do well ; but yf he snese twyse lett him take his worke and go on further.

XVI.   Yf a man, after he haue made a bargayne with another for anything and then snese one tyme, yt sygnifieth that his bargayne will not continue.

XVII. Yf a man rise betymes on a Monday mornyng out of his bedde and snese one tyme, yt is a tokyn that he shall prosper and gayne all that week, or haue some other joye and comoditie.

XVIII. But yf he snese twyse, yt is cleane contrarie.

XIX. Yf a man lose a horse or anything els, and is stopping out of his dore to seek yt, he snese one time, yt is a tokyn he shall haue yt agayne.

XX. Yf a man rise betymes on Sonday and snese ii tymes, yt is a good tokyn, but yf he snese one tyme, yt is an yll tokyn.

XXI. Yf a man at ye very beginning of a dinner or supper be minded to eat, and do snese twyse, yt is a good tokyn, but yf he snese one tyme, yt is an yll syne.

XXII. Yf a man lye sicke in bedde and mistrusts himself, and snese one tyme, yt is a tokyn of deathe, but yf he snese twyse, he shall escape.

XXIII. A woman being very sicke, yf she snese one tyme, yt is a syne of health, but yf she snese twyse, she shall dye.

Snorting : The snorting of a horse while on a journey prognosticates good luck. (*The Kirghiz.*—SCHUYLER, Vol. II, p. 29.)

Snow : Snow is caused by witches. (LEHMANN, *A.Z.*, p. 111.)

Snuffing : In China, it is said that the snuffing by a cat or a dog will partly revive a corpse. (*Chin. Volksmärchen*, p. 202.)
cf. *Breath.*

Sodomy : In Persia and in China, sodomy is superstitiously believed to be a cure for venereal diseases. (KRAFFT-EBING, *Psychopathia Sexualis*, Eng. tr., p. 405.)

Soham : A monster with the head of a horse, four eyes and the body of a fiery dragon.

Sokkvabek : Norse Myth. The abode of Saga, the seeress in Asgard.

Sokotsu-wata-dzumi : Jap. Myth. " The bottom-sea-body." The chief sea-god of Shintoism. He, Nakatsu-wata-dzumi, " middle-sea-body " and Uhatsu-wata-dzumi, " upper-sea-body " were produced from Izanagi's ablutions in the sea. They are represented as forming one deity, and are much prayed to for safety from shipwrecks and for fair winds.

Soldier : Vide *War.*

Sole : According to a Russian story, the sole owes its shape to the fact that the queen of the Baltic ate one half of it, and threw the other back. (RALSTON, *Russian Folklore,* p. 330.)

Some say, it was restored to life, after half of it had been eaten, by the angel Gabriel. (BASSETT, p. 257.)

Somnambulism : Diamond produces somnambulism.

Song : Nixies and maras are said to have the power of singing enchantingly.

Singing in bed before getting up is unlucky. (*Great Britain*; cf. LAPHIN, in *L'Intrasigeant*, No. 17, 185, 24th August, 1927, p. 2.)

If a girl sings while at meals, she will have a drunkard for her husband (*Silesia.*—WUTTKE, p. 43), or it will bring ill luck (*Great Britain*), or poverty (*Paris*, LAPHIN, ib.)

If you sing at the table, you will have a disappointment (*U.S.A.*).

" Sing in the street,
Disappointment you'll meet." *U.S.A.*

In Wales it is said that persons on the point of dying can hear a melodious voice singing in the air. (OWEN, p. 305 *sq.*)

Soot : Flakes of soot hanging from the bars of a grate foretell the introduction of a stranger.

A volume of soot suddenly coming down the chimney promises a letter or money.

Sophia's Picture : Sophia's picture, given to Mathias, turned yellow if the giver was in danger or in temptation, and black if she could not escape from the danger, or if she yielded to the temptation. (MASSINGER, 1629.) cf. *Bahman's Knife, Canace's Mirror, Alasnam's Mirror, Florimel's Girdle, Ring, Bertha's Emerald.*

Soreness : Sore eyes can be cured by putting a spider in a nut-shell, and wearing it round the neck. (*Mark.*—WUTTKE, p. 165.)

St. Blaise when he was put to death, prayed that if any person suffering from a sore throat invoked his aid, he might be God's instrument in effecting a perfect cure. Vide *Spider, Amber.*

Soul : The Tyrolese peasants believe that a good man's soul issues from his mouth at death like a little white cloud (WUTTKE).

In India the soul of a saint is said to leave the body in the form of a miniature radiant being.

Among the ancient Romans, the nearest kinsmen knelt over to inhale the last breath of the departing.

At the death of Julius Caesar, a little animal, his soul, was seen to come out of his mouth.

Among the Seminoles of Florida, when a woman died in childbirth, the infant was held over her face to receive her parting spirit. (FRAZER, *G.B*²., Vol. I, pp. 247 *sq.*)

In Japan the soul is said to be a small, round, black body, and is capable of having adventures apart from the body. (GRIFFIS, *M.E.*, p. 472.)

The Ghost-Man of the natives of the Slave Coast of Africa continues its existence after death, and corresponds to our soul (ELLIS, *The Ewe-speaking Peoples*, pp. 105 *sq.*).

The Qŏr'an (*Sura XXXIX*) says : " God takes to Himself the souls of men at their death ; and He takes also to Himself the souls of those who do not die, while they sleep. He keeps with Himself the souls of those whose death He has ordained, but the others he sends back for a season. Truly herein lie signs for thoughtful men to ponder."

cf. *Ethnologie du Bengale*, pp. 88, 89, quoting GREGOR, p. 206 ; FRAZER, in *Folklore Journal*, Vol. III, p. 282 ; id., *Taboo and the Perils of the Soul* ; *On Certain Burial Customs*, Journ. Anthrop. Inst., Vol. XV, p. 66 ; id., *G.B*²., Vol. I, p. 204 ; RHYS, *Celtic Folklore*, p. 601 ; LE BRAZ, Vol. I, p. 214 ; LADY WILDE, p. 139 ; *Revue Celtique*, Vol. XII, p. 425 ; SPENCER AND GILLEN, *Native Tribes of Australia*, pp. 497, 508 ; BUDGE, *Book of the Dead*, Vol. I, p. lxii ; LORD in ROTH, Vol. I, p. 217 ; GRAAFLAND, *Die Insel Rote*, Mitteil. d. geogr. Gesells. zu Jena, VIII, p. 168 ; MEIJMERING, *Zeeden en gewoonten* . . . in Tijdsch. v. Nederl. Indië, VI, p. 363 ; HERTZ, *la Représentation collective de la mort*, Année Sociol., Vol. X, p. 59 ; JELLINGHANS, *Sagen, Sitten und Gebräuche der Munda Kolhs*, Zeitschr. f. Ethnologie, Vol. III (1871), p. 374 ; M. GRANET, *La religion des Chinois*, Paris, 1922, pp. 165 *sq.* ; TYLOR, *P.C.*, Vol. I, p. 407 ; id., *Early History of Mankind*, Vol. I, p. 358 ; CROOKE, *Pop. Rel.*, Vol. I, p. 280 ; DURKHEIM, *Elementary Forms of Religious Life*, p. 242 ; KRAFT, *Travels* . . . *in East Africa*, p. 150 ; *E.R.E*, § Demonology.

Soup : Plenty of soup eaten slowly promotes long life.

Sow : Vide *Pig*.

Sparks : If sparks from a burning log are thrown out into the room, troubles and anxieties must be expected. (*Greece.—* LAWSON, p. 328.) Vide *Death Omens*.

Sparrow : The chirping of sparrows portends much rain or snowfall (ABBOTT, p. III), or wet weather. (INWARDS, *Weather Lore*, p. 168.)

Speak : If a person appears just as you are speaking about him, it is a sign that he will live long. (*Great Britain, India.*)

    If you forget in the middle of your speech what you wished to say, you are telling a lie.

    If two persons say the same thing at the same time, they will have a fulfilment of their desire, provided that they wish before another word is spoken.

    In folktales all animals can speak.

Speaking Foxes : Vide *Silver Foxes.*

Spectre : An apparition, phantom, ghost, especially one of a terrifying nature or aspect.

Speed : Speed can be acquired by partaking of the flesh of a kite. cf. *Sight.*

Sphinx : An animal with the body of a lion and the head of a human being, which, according to the Egyptians repre-sented the sun. The ancient Greeks endowed the sphinx with mysterious powers and introduced it into their mytho-logy. It is said that in the time of Œdipus, a sphinx used to stop passers-by on their way to Thebes, and put certain enigmas to them ; if they could not answer these enigmas, they were devoured by the monster. It asked Œdipus the following : *Quel est l'animal qui marche à quatre pieds le matin, à deux pieds à midi et à trois le soir ?* Œdipus recognized the symbol of infancy, youth and senility in this riddle. The sphinx furious at this, threw itself into the sea, and was never seen any more. (*Petit Larousse Illustré*, p. 1602.)

Spider : The Mohammedans will never kill a spider, because they say that when Mohammed was flying from his enemies, he hid himself in a cave, and a spider spun its web over the entrance in order to give it an unsuspicious appearance. A lizard pointed Mohammed out to his followers.

    There are no spiders in Ireland, because St. Patrick cleared the island of all vermin.

    No spider will spin its web on an Irish oak.

    A spider enclosed in a quill and hung round the neck will cure the ague ; in cases of sore-eye or fever, it may be enclosed in a nut-shell and treated likewise.

The bite of a spider is venomous ; they envenom whatever they touch.

Spiders will never set their webs on a cedar roof.

Spiders spin only on dark days, and have a natural antipathy for toads ; they indicate where gold is to be found.

> " Une araignée au matin, c'est du chagrin,
> Une araignée au midi, c'est du plaisir,
> Une araignée au soir, c'est de l'espoir."

Vide *Money, Spider, Soreness, Arachne.*

Spindle : In Italy, women were forbidden by law to walk on the high roads twirling a spindle, because this was supposed to injure the crops. (FRAZER, *G.B*²., Vol. II, p. 461 note ; PLINY, *Nat. Hist.*, XXVIII, 28.)

Spinning : Women in childbed should not spin, lest they spin a halter for the baby. (*Franken.*—WUTTKE, p. 196.) Vide *St. Matthew's Day.*

Spinster : Vide *Last Piece, Tea, Godfather.*

Spirit : A supernatural, incorporeal, rational being or personality, usually regarded as imperceptible at ordinary times to the human senses, but capable of becoming visible at will, and frequently conceived as troublesome, terrible or horrible to mankind.

> " It faded on the crowing of the cock."
>
>   SHAKESPEARE, *Hamlet,* I, 1.1

Vide *Midnight.*

Spitting : If you spit on the first money received during the day, you will have more. (*Great Britain, India, Germany.* —WUTTKE, pp. 80, 186 ; cf. HAZLITT, p. 560 *sq.*)

Cattle will thrive if you spit on their food. (*Mark, Silesia.*—ib.)

Great virtue is and was always believed to belong to fasting spittle, both as curative and protective. (ELWORTHY, *E.E.,* p. 418, quoting HERRICK, *Hesperides,* " The Temple."

In Macedonia, spitting is considered a great precaution against disease. (ABBOTT, p. 110.)

The Arabs believe that human saliva can cure a multitude of diseases ; further they will spit upon a lock which cannot easily be opened. (DOUGHTY, *Arab. Des.,* Vol. I, p. 226.) Vide *Saliva, Hair.*

Splashing : If a girl splashes herself while washing clothes, it forebodes that her husband will be a drunkard. (STRACKERJAN, Vol. I, p. 45 ; *Great Britain, U.S.A.*)

Spøgelse : A common name in Denmark for the Bulderbasse or the Poltergeist.

Spot : If you accidentally make some ink-spots while writing, it is an omen of good luck.

In West Highland superstition, a beauty-spot cannot be resisted, hence Diarmaid inspired masterless love by his beauty-spot. Vide *Nail*.

Spriggan : In Cornwall these were certain demons said to guard treasures. (HUNT, *Pop. Rem.*, p. 81.)

Sprite : Same as spirit ; in ordinary language it denotes an elf.

Squint : It is very unlucky to meet a man who squints. (ELWORTHY, *E.E.*, p. 32, 417.)

Squirrel : Squirrels are so charmed by snakes that they fall an easy prey to them. Vide *Ratatosk*.

Saints : (See also under the first names of the saints.)

St. Alfonso di Liguori : He is believed to have had the power of preaching in church and confessing penitents at home at the same time. (J. GARDNER, *Faiths of the World*.) Vide *Bilocation*.

St. Ambrose : When St. Ambrose died on Easter Eve, several newly-baptized children claimed to have seen the holy bishop, and pointed him out to their parents, but these with their less pure eyes could not see him (CALMET).

St. Ammonius : St. Anthony saw the soul of St. Ammonius carried to heaven by a company of angels, the same day the holy man died at a distance of five days' journey in the desert of Nitria.

St. Dunstan : St. Dunstan's harp discoursed most enchanting music without being struck by any player. cf. *Teirtus' Harp*.

St. John : The first words of the Gospel of St. John have always been held of great virtue when carried on a person. These should be written upon virgin parchment, enclosed in a goose-quill an hour before sunrise on the first Sunday in the year. (THIERS, *Traité des Sup.*, Vol. I, p. 414 ; ELWORTHY, *E.E.*, p. 400.)

On May 16, St. John Nepomuc is honoured in Magyar lands, by throwing his image in the Danube, while people follow in boats, playing musical instruments, etc. (*Magyar Folklore* in " Notes and Queries," 27 Dec., 1883 ; BASSETT, p. 415.) .

St. John's Eve : Folklore. It is believed that fasting watchers may, on this day, see the apparitions of those doomed to die during the year come with the ministers to the church-door and knock. These apparitions are the souls which come forth from their bodies. (TYLOR, *P.C.*, Vol. I, p. 440 ; RHYS, Vol. I, p. 329.)

St. Matthew's Day (24th February) : If you spin on this day, it will go ill with the geese. (*East Prussia.*—WUTTKE, p. 21.)

Stag : Stags draw serpents from their holes by their breath, and then trample them to death.

A wound from a stag's horn never heals.

A stag's horn gives warning of the evil eye and is a safeguard against its malignant influences (*Spain*).

Stair : To pass another on the stairs is unlucky.

If while coming down the stairs you fall down, it fore-bodes some misfortune ; but if you stumble while going up, it promises a wedding.

Star : The Esthonians believe that if anyone sees a falling star on New Year's night, he will die or be visited by some serious illness that year. (BOECLER-KREUTZWALD, p. 73 ; FRAZER, *G.B².*, Vol. II, p. 22.)

If you point to a star, your finger will get fixed in that position. (STRACKERJAN, Vol. I, p. 44.)

If a shooting star takes a direction towards some particular house, it is a sign that someone will die therein (STRACKERJAN, Vol. I, p. 23 ; ELWORTHY, *E.E.*, p. 424.)

A shooting star denotes the birth of a child (*Great Britain, India*; cf. W. ELLIS, *Polynesian Researches²*; iii, 171.)

The Moors say that shooting stars are missiles hurled by God at evil spirits to make them desist from trying to reach heaven. (MEAKIN, *The Moors*, p. 353 ; LANE, *Mod. Egypt.*, Ch. X ; C. VELTEN, *Sitten u. Gebräuche der Suaheli*, p. 339 *sq.*)

When you see the first star, wish for something and say
" Star light, star bright,
First star I see to-night,
I wish I may, I wish I might
Have the wish I wish to-night "
and your wish will come to pass provided of course, that you do not divulge it to anyone. (*Eastern Massachusetts.*— BERGEN, *C.S.*, p. 69.)

When you see a shooting star, the wish you form before its disappearance will be fulfilled. (LEAN, Vol. II, p. 280.)

In Ruthenia a shooting star is looked upon as the track of an angel flying to receive a departed spirit, or of a righteous soul going up to heaven. In the latter case, if a wish be uttered at the moment the star shoots by, it will go straight up with the rejoicing spirit to the throne of God. So when a star falls the Servians say : " Someone's light has gone out," meaning someone is dead. (RALSTON, *Songs of the Russian People*, p. 116.)

" It is then (6th century B.C.) that we find stars worshipped in particular cities and that the twelve signs of the Zodiac were believed to control the destinies of states. Particular stars or groups of stars were worshipped in the supposed causes of fires and such-like calamities. . . . In 540 B.C. there is a more detailed account of the same worship in the *Tso chwen*, and at the same time, in *Kwo Yü*, we find abundant proof that the Chinese then believed that the various baronies of China were all controlled by particular stars " (*China Review*, XIII, 416-418, quoted by BENOY KUMAR SARCAR, *Chinese Religion through Hindu Eyes*, Shanghai, 1918, p. 62).

For other superstitions about shooting stars and meteors, see FRAZER, *The Dying God*, London, 1920, pp. 60-68.

Stepping over a Child : If you step over a child it will stop growing (*Jews of Kiev* ; *Virginia.*—BERGEN, *C.S.*, p. 23) ; to make it resume growing, repeat the action (*Jews of Galicia, India*, some parts of *England*. cf. SCHIFFER, *Urquell*, VI, 111.)

Stheno : Gr. Myth. One of the Gorgons.

Stihija : A Bulgarian household-spirit in the form of a snake ; also called Tolosom.

Stija : Bulgarian Folklore. A class of water-spirits. They are remarkable for their long hair, which they sometimes employ to choke those who fall into their power.

Stocking : To put the left stocking on first denotes ill luck, but putting the right one on first protects the wearer from rheumatism. (STRACKERJAN, Vol. II, p. 18.)

To put on a pair of stockings with the wrong side out is lucky, provided you do not change (CHAMBERS, *Book of Days*, Vol. II, p. 321 ; ABBOTT, p. 144 ; *Ethnologie du Bengale*, p. 124).

The wife is recommended to carry a piece of her husband's stockings or girdle as a safeguard against premature birth. (WUTTKE, p. 195.)

" Wear at the toe,
Spend as you go ;
Wear at the heel,
Spend a good deal ;
Wear at the side,
You'll be a rich bride ;
Wear at the ball,
You'll live to spend all."

—*U.S.A.*

Vide *Hoarseness, Throatache.*

Stomach : If you stir drinks with a knife, you will have a stomach ache. (STRACKERJAN, Vol. I, p. 49.)

Stones : Stones grow on the earth as long as they are not touched by hand ; they receive nourishment through a " vein " by which they are joined to the earth. (STRACKER-JAN, Vol. II, p. 71.)

To find a perforated stone is a presage of good luck. (See SPENCER, *Pr. of Sociology*, i, 310 *sq.*)

In India (CROOKE, *Islam in India*, p. 241), and in East Africa (C. W. HOBLEY, *J.R.A.I.*, XLI, 432f), it is believed that throwing stones is a common habit of some mischievous devils.

Engraved stones with short sentences on them are worn by the Chinese women and children, and are supposed to have great efficacy in preventing evil. (WILLIAMS, *M.K.*, Vol. II, p. 256.)

" Meeting anyone carrying stones, bringing a bride, or an animal under yoke, or anyone suffering from goitre, means mischief and loss ; the king of devils will injure your familiar good spirit ; so *spit at him* ! " (*Tibet.*— WADDELL, p. 136.)

On Christmas Eve, put a stone on every tree and they will bear more fruit. (RAGNER.)

Stones, Sepulchral : Pregnant women either sit on, or slide down them to ensure an easy delivery ; unmarried girls do the same to procure a husband. (BERENGER-FÉRAUD, Vol. I, p. 529 ff ; T. A. TROLLOPE, *A Summer in Brittany*, (Lond. 1840), II, 229 ; W. C. BORLASE, *The Dolmens of Ireland* (Lond. 1897), II, 841.)

Stork : It is unlucky to kill a stork.

A stork flying over a house promises an addition to the family (*Silesia.*—WUTTKE, p. 32.)

Perfect health can be obtained by drinking the blood of a stork.

According to a Swedish legend a stork fluttered round the cross of Jesus crying : *Styrkê* ! *Styrkê* ! (Strengthen ye ! Strengthen ye !), and was hence called the *styrk* or stork, but ever after lost its voice.

Storm : Storms are caused by demons.   (*Slavic countries* ; cf. LEHMANN, *A.Z.*, p. III.)

A storm may be caused by whistling.

When pigs run grunting home a storm is impending.

St. Barbara may be invoked to abate storms.

According to the Edda, Giants and Giantesses caused storms. (GRIMM, *Teut. Myth.*, Vol. II, p. 637.)

If a storm breaks out while a grave is still open, it is a sign that the deceased has led a wicked life, and has sold his soul to the devil. (GREGOR, p. 214.)

In North Wales, thunder and storm presage the death of an important personage in the parish. (*Archaeologia Cambrensis*, 1872, p. 333.)

In the Gulf of Carnero, storms and hurricanes were caused by sorcerers, who, when offended, kindled great fires in caverns, causing the enraged earth to send forth their storms. (JONES, *Credulities*, p. 72 ; BASSETT, p. 104.) Vide *Meal, Cat, Deo, Whistling, Menstruation, Sea, Porpoise, Cuttlefish, Shony, Hedgehog, Mirror.*

Stranger : Unless a dead man is watched by someone from another town, his soul will not rest in peace. (F. MARION CRAWFORD, *A Roman Singer*, Ch. XIII.)   Vide *Nose, Magpie, Soot.*

Straw : If a person succeeds in getting hold of a mara (q v.), he will find only a piece of straw in his hand. If this piece of straw be nailed to the wall, or otherwise made fast, the mara will be compelled to show herself next night (WUTTKE, p. 123), or the next morning in her true form. (cf. GRIMM, *D.M.* ; THORPE, *North. Myth* ; TYLOR, *P.C.* ; STRACKERJAN, etc.)

If while sweeping the room, you find a piece of straw, it is a sign that someone will shortly pay you a visit (*Germany*).

It is unlucky to see a load of straw.

It is a bad omen to find two pieces of straw crossed in one's path.   (*Westphalia, Rhineland.*—WUTTKE, p. 35.)

Straw was once a powerful means of bewitching one's neighbour. Getting possession of the straw was said to carry with it possession of everything belonging to the other man. (RHYS, *C.F.*, p. 345.)

Straw Road : This is the Persian and Syrian name for the Galaxy, who compare it with their lanes littered with morsels of straw that fall from the nets they carry it in.

Stream : " The modern Albanian still sees the stain of slaughter in streams running red with earth, as to the ancient Greeks the river that flowed by Byblos bore down its summer floods the red blood of Adonis." (TYLOR, *P.C.*, Vol. I, p. 367.)

Strength : Hair is the seat of a person's strength. (FRAZER, *The Magic Art*, Vol. I, pp. 102, 344.)
   If you carry about with you a piece of wood chipped off by lightning, you will be strong. (*Bohemia.*—GROH-MANN, p. 40.) Vide *Sacrifice, Hair, Topaz, Elephant, Thunder, Haircutting, Lion, Lightning, Ash Wednesday.*

Striges : In Modern Greece they are usually confused with the Lamiæ (q.v.) because of their taste for blood, which they share with those demons. In reality, striges are women who possess the power to transform themselves into birds of prey and other animals. (LAWSON, 179.)

String : It is unlucky to burn string (*Great Britain, India.*)

Stringed Instrument : The Elle-women are said to be capable of playing most enchantingly on stringed instruments. (THIELE, *Danmarks Folkesagn.*)

Stromkarl : " River-man." In Norway it is the name of the spirit of the water-fall ; in Sweden it is any water-spirit.

Stumbling : The Moors believe that if a person stumbles in the dark, the reason for it may be that he has trod on a Jinn (q.v.). (WESTERMARCK, *The Belief in Spirits in Morocco*, p. 15.)
   Among the Kirghiz, the stumbling or the snorting of a horse while on a journey is a prognostication of good luck. (SCHUYLER, Vol. II, p. 29.)

Sturgeon : The sturgeons of the Yellow River, in China, make an ascent of the stream in the third moon of each year, when those which succeed in passing above the rapids of the Lung Mên (" Dragon Gate ") become transformed into dragons. (MAYERS, *Chin. Read. Man.*, p. 320.)

Stuttering : Children who are allowed to look at themselves in the mirror before they are a year old become stutterers. cf. *Tickling.*

Sty : A sty on the eye can be effectually cured by rubbing it with a wedding ring. (STRACKERJAN, Vol. I, p. 83.)

Styx : Gr. Myth. The river which surrounded the infernal region seven times, and separated the world of the living from the world of the dead. cf. *Vaitarini.*

Sübeh : The Sübeh of Syrian superstition is a demon " in the shape of a fabulous animal or as a woman with coarse hair on her head, immense eyes, and long pendent breasts." (WESTERMARCK, *The Belief in Spirits in Morocco*, p. 149, quoting VON KREMER, *Studien* iii-iv, 34 *sq.*, SNOUCK HURGRONJE, ii, 123 *sq.*)

Succubus : In the Middle Ages this was a demon in female form ; she was supposed to have carnal intercourse with men in their sleep.
"For forty years, he (Benedict of Berne) had kept up an amatory commerce with a succubus, called Hermeline."
C. K. SHARPE, *Law's Memorialls*, Pref., p. xx (1818)
cf. *Incubus, Cuichi Supai, Tulûlu Supai.*

Suckle : German Folklore. The dead mother comes back again during the night to suckle her infant she has left behind on earth.

Suddenness : St. Martin saves from sudden deaths.

Sudička : Bohemian Folklore. The three white women who come to a room where a child is born and decide its future. They are the three goddesses (?) of fate. (GROHMANN, p. 7.)
cf. *Fates, Norn, Parcae, Bidhâtâpurusha, Hathor.*

Sugar : If a pregnant woman puts sugar on the window-sill, she will give birth to a baby girl. (*Bohemia.*)
Sugar is put in the mouth of an infant the first time it enters the house of a stranger. (DALYELL, *Dark. Sup.*, p. 96 ; cf. E. CHAVANNES, *Documents sur les Tou-Kiue* (*Turcs*) *Occidentaux*, p. 134 ; FRAZER, *Magic Art*, i, 157.)

Suhijini : Sand has been deified under this name in Japan.

Suicide : The spirits of those who have committed suicide cannot rest ; they must haunt the place where the crime was committed (*East Prussia, Silesia.*—WUTTKE, p. 217 ; *Great Britain, France, Bohemia, India, Japan.*)
It is a recognized practice in Modern China for widows to commit suicide, in order to accompany their husbands to the spirit world ; this is sometimes even performed in public. (See DE GROOT, *Religious System of China*, Vol. II, Bk. I, pp. 720 *sqq.*)
The body of a suicide does not sink. (GREGOR, p. 208.)
If a pregnant woman walks over a suicide's grave, she will have a miscarriage. (ibid., p. 215.)

Epilepsy can be cured by drinking out of the skull of a suicide. (G. HENDERSON, *Survivals in Belief among the Celts*, p. 302.)

If the body of a suicide be buried in view of the sea, herrings will not be caught. (CAMPBELL, *Sup. Scot. Highl.*, p. 243.)
cf. *Sati, Horse, Camel.*

Suitengu : Jap. Myth. An obscure deity who is worshipped in Tokio at the present day as a protector against the perils of the sea, burglary, and the pains of parturition.

Sumeru : Hind. Myth. A mountain ; the abode of Indra and his consort.

Sun : There is a " bird with three legs," or a spirit, in the sun. (MAYERS, *Chin. Read. Man.*, p. 81.)

In India, it is believed that girls may be impregnated by the sun. (FRAZER, *The Golden Bough*[2], Vol. II, p. 234 ; HARTLAND, *Legend of Perseus*, Vol. I, pp. 99, 138, 170 ; CROOKE, *P.R.I.*, Vol. I, p. 11 ; *Ethnologie du Bengale*, p. 66.) Vide *Moon, Virgin.*

Sunday : Of all the days in the week, Sunday is the luckiest. It is unlucky to cut nails, or hair, on a Sunday.

Children born on a Sunday have the gift of foresight, and if they be christened on a Sunday too, spirits, though invisible to others, will be visible to them at all times. (WUTTKE, p. 10.)

> " Sunday's child is fair of face,
> Monday's child is full of grace ;
> Tuesday's child is full of woe,
> Wednesday's child has far to go ;
> Thursday's child has much to borrow,
> Friday's child is full of sorrow ;
> Saturday's child must beg for its living
> And never have rest night and morning."
>
> Popular Rhyme (*Great Britain.*)

Surā : Hind. Myth. Wine or spirituous liquor personified as Sûra-devî, a goddess or nymph who was produced at the churning of the ocean.

Surabhi : Hind. Myth. " The cow of plenty " was produced at the churning of the ocean. It granted every desire, and is reverenced as the fountain of milk and curds. (DOWSON, *H.C.D.*, p. 209.)

Susa no wo : Jap. Myth. A god of Rain-storm, who provides mankind with useful trees. He and his wife are regarded as gods of wedlock. He was at first appointed to rule the sea, but after his mother Izanami's death, preferred to join her in Yomi (Hades). (ASTON, *Shinto*, pp. 17, 24.)

Susan, St. : Vide *Chastity, Defilement, Infamy.*

Sut : Moham. Myth. Son of Iblis, a jinn who suggests lies. (*Jew. Enc.*, Vol. IV, p. 521.)

Swallow : It is unlucky to kill a swallow.

Swallows forecast bad weather by flying low, and fine weather by flying high.

If a swallow builds its nest on a house, it is sure to bring good luck.

Swallows spend the winter underground.

The swallow is said to bring home from the sea-shore a stone which gives sight to her fledglings.

If you turn the money in your pocket the first time you see a swallow in spring, you will never be short of funds. (*Thuringia, Silesia.*—WUTTKE, p. 177.)

Witches are said to be incapable of assuming the form of swallows. (STRACKERJAN, Vol. I, p. 327.)

According to a Scandinavian legend, the swallow hovered over the cross of Christ crying *Svalê! Svalê!* (Cheer up ! Cheer up !), and hence it received the name of *Svalê* or Swallow, "the bird of consolation."

Swallows forewarn miseries and unnatural wars by fighting against one another. (ALEXANDER ROSS, *Arcana Microcosmi*, p. 219.)

If a woman accidentally treads on swallows' eggs lying on the ground, she will be barren. (PLOSS, *Das Weib*, Vol. I, p. 508.)

cf. *Robin, Stork, Dove, Peewit, Plover, Lamb, Philomele.*

Swan : Swans cannot hatch without a crack of thunder.

Swans retire from observation when about to die, and sing most melodiously ; hence the expression " Swan-song." Vide *Cygnus, Red Swan.*

Swan Maiden : In mythology these are elves or fairies capable of becoming maidens or swans at will by donning or doffing a magic garment, the Swan-shift, or covering of swan's feathers.

The Norse and German literature constantly make mention of swan-maidens " who fly through the air, come swimming along to bring tidings, or through putting aside their swan-shifts have come into the power of him who has taken it away." (DE LA SAUSSAYE.) (See GRIMM, *D.M.* ; HARTLAND, *Science of Fairy Tales.*)

Swarth : The Cumberland name for a " waff."

Swastika : A mystical religious mark placed upon persons or things, and thought to be a charm or a talisman. It is a sign of good luck and benediction. It is in the form of a Greek cross with the ends bent round (卐). (ELWORTHY, E.E., p. 289.)

Swearing : Jack-o'-Lanterns can be driven away by swearing at them ; praying has no effect on them. (cf. WUTTKE for Germany, JONES for Wales, THORPE for Northern Countries.)

Sweeping : If you throw sweepings out of the room at night, you run the risk of dying. (*Jews of Galicia.—Jew. Enc.*, Vol. XI, p. 601.)

The Japs never sweep a house immediately after one of the inmates has set out on a journey ; this would sweep out all the luck with him. (GRIFFIS, *M.E.*, p. 467.)

If sweepings be left accumulated in a corner of the room, a female spirit, called *Kune,* is sure to take up its abode there. cf. *Ethnologie du Bengale,* pp. 100 *sq.*)

It is lucky to see a sweeper the first thing on getting up in the morning. (*Great Britain* and *India.*)

Sweet Flag : Leaves of the sweet flag (Acorns) and Artemisia tied in a bundle, and placed near beds drive away demons. (*China.*—WILLIAMS, *M.K.*, Vol. II, p. 255.)

Sweetheart : If a man dreams of his sweetheart and she is fairer than usual, she is chaste and constant, but if pale, black and sickly, she has broken her faith.

Swiftness : Vide *Kite.*

Swine : To meet a herd of swine at the beginning of a journey is an omen of ill luck. (WUTTKE, p. 32.) Vide *Pig.*

Swinging : " The custom of swinging has been practised as a religion or rather magical rite in various parts of the world. . . . People appear to have resorted to the practice from different motives and with different ideas of the benefit to be derived from it." (FRAZER, *G.B*[2]., Vol. II, pp. 449-456.)

Sycamore : Sycamore was sacred to Horus. (WIEDEMANN, *Legend of the Winged Sun-Disk.*) cf. *Acacia.*

Sylph : Celt. and Teut. Myth. The sylphs are the elves of the air, and are the most developed among them. They are of a human form, and are usually of a beautiful colour, which reminds one of opal. They have more intelligence than other elves.

T

Table : You will never have a husband if you sit at the corner of the table.

Lie down on the table and you will die within a year. (*Mattawamkeag, Me.*)

In modern spiritualism three-legged tables are used extensively for table-rapping.

Table of Emerald :
"Deep . . . under yonder pyramid, has for ages lain concealed the Table of Emerald, on which the thrice-great Hermes engraved, before the flood, the secret of alchemy that gives gold at will."—MOORE, *Epicurean.*

Tail : It is believed that various tribes scattered all over the world have tails. For example the gigantic Patagonians, the Ghilanes, a race of men " beyond the Sennar," the Niam Niam tribe of Africa, the Narea tribes, certain other tribes south of Harrar in Abyssinia, the natives of Formosa are all supposed to be men adorned with tails.

Taka-mika-dzuchi : Jap. Myth. Formerly a god of thunder, at present he is universally recognized as a war-god and as a god who predicts the weather.

Takar-bune : " Treasure-ship " ; a Japanese emblem of luck. (CHAMBERLAIN, *Ger. Tr.*, p. 235.)

Talisman : A stone with a hole through it is sometimes hung on the handle of a stable door to ward off evil spirits.

In order to free the house of vermin, the figure of the obnoxious animals should be made in wax in " the planetary hour."

Talos : Gr. Myth. Son of Perdrix, sister of Daedalos, inventor of the saw, compasses and other mechanical instruments. His uncle jealous of him, threw him down the citadel of Athens, and he was changed into a partridge.

Talos : A man of brass made by Hephaestus (Vulcan). This wonderful automaton was given to Minos to patrol the island of Crete. It traversed the island thrice a day, and if a stranger came near, made itself red-hot, and squeezed him to death ; it is also said to have challenged every vessel coming to the island.

Tamarind : The Oraons of Bengal revere the tamarind and bury their dead under its shade. (DALTON, *Descriptive Ethnology*, p. 189 ; see *Ethnologie du Bengale*, pp. 62, 92.)

Tammuz : Babyl. Myth. A god of agriculture, and spirit of vegetation. He marries Ishtar by whom he is slain, and later, is brought back again from the lower world.

Tan : Chin. Folklore. The Elixir of Gold, the mystical compound by means of which the Taoist alchemists professed themselves able to produce gold and to confer the gift of immortality. It constituted the " potent drug which, if one-half of its bulk be swallowed, confers perpetual longevity on earth, whilst the entire quantity gives at once the power of ascending on high among the genii." (MAYERS, *Chin. Read. Man.,* p. 217.)

Tangaloo : The principal god of the Australian natives, who is represented as the common god of the heaven and sea, as well as the creator of the world.

Tanit : Egypt. Myth. Ancient Phoenician deity, one of the forms of Astarte who was worshipped at Carthage.

Tank : A tank of water should not be left uncovered during Passover ; even if water be poured in, it should be done through a cloth. (*Galicia.—Jew. Enc.,* Vol. IX, p. 519.)

Tantalus : Class. Myth. He was made to stand in water breast deep ; but every time he, tortured by thirst, bent down to drink, the water receded. Hence the expression " tantalising."

Tanuki-gami : The badger-god possession of Japan.

Taromaiti : Persian Myth. A spirit of arrogance.

Tarantula : A kind of spider supposed to be extremely poisonous.

Music will cure the venomous bite of a tarantula.

A person bitten by a tarantula laughs and dances in a kind of frenzy till he dies.

Tarnkappe : Siegfried's (q.v.) cap (or cloak) which had the power of making the wearer invisible.

Tashmit : Egypt. Myth. Nebo's consort is usually designated by this name. She was also called Nana.

Task : In Ross this is a kind of a warning light, and is the same as the " waff."

Tasnim : Moham. Myth. A fountain in Mahomet's paradise ; so called from being conveyed to the very highest apartments of the celestial mansions.

Tasting Death : The Rabbis say, there are three drops of gall on the sword of Death ; one drop in the mouth and the man dies ; from the second the pallor of death is suffused ; from the third his carcase turns to dust.

Ta tsiao : Chinese Folklore. It is the name of a mass celebrated to appease the wandering and hungry ghosts of the wicked men. (WILLIAMS, *M.K.*, Vol. II, p. 257.)

Tattooing : In Bengal tattooing is used as a cure for goitre. (CROOKE, *P.R.I.*, Vol. II, p. 33.)

In Bengal, high caste Brahmans will not drink from the hands of a girl who does not wear the Ulkhi or star-shaped tattoo-mark between the eyebrows. (ib. p. 32 ; *Ethnologie du Bengale*, p. 133.)

Ta-urt : Egypt. Myth. A goddess having the body and head of a hippopotamus, the hind quarters of a lion, and the tail of a crocodile. She presided over the birth of kings and gods, and was an important personage in the underworld. She was the wife of Set.

Tea : If young girls pour milk into the tea before putting in the sugar, they will die as spinsters. (STRACKERJAN, Vol. I, p. 49.)

Fortune can be told by tea-leaves.

Tear : Tears should not be allowed to drop on a corpse, or the mourner will die himself. (*Mecklenburg.*—WUTTKE, p. 210.)

Witches are incapable of shedding tears. (WUTTKE, p. 115.)

Tears of mourners are collected in a bottle by the Persians in the belief that a single drop will restore a dying man. (MORIER, *Second Journey through Persia*, 1818, p. 179.)

Pearls bring tears. (*Great Britain.*)

If the eyes suddenly fill with tears, it is a sign that the person will soon mourn the death of a dear one. (*Brittany.* —LE BRAZ, Vol. I, p. 12.)

(ii) Torn clothes must not be worn on a New Year's Day. (*India.*)

Tefnut : Egypt. Myth. A lion-headed goddess, sister and wife of Shu.

Teirtus' Harp : A harp which played of itself merely by being asked to do so, and when desired, ceased playing. cf. *St. Dunstan.*

Telegraph Wire : In Japan some people will not go under telegraph-wires, or at least cover their heads with a fan, for fear of some diabolic possession. (CHAMBERLAIN, *Ger. tr.*, p. 534.)

Telephassa : Gr. Myth. Wife of Agenor, mother of Cadmus, Europa, Phocius, Clix.

Telephus : Gr. Myth. A king of Mysia, who was wounded by the lance of Achilles. His wound was immediately cured by a plaster made from the rust of this same lance.

Tell : According to a legend the three Tells, founders of the Helvetic Confederacy, sleep peacefully in a cavern near Lake Lucerne, till that time when their country shall have need of them. cf. *Barbarossa, King Arthur, Charlemagne.*

Temmangu : A Japanese god of learning and calligraphy. He is, or was until recently, one of the most widely worshipped of Shinto deities, especially by pedagogues and schoolboys.

Temperance : Father Mathew is called the " Apostle of Temperance."

Tempest : St. Barbara who flourished in A.D. 235, abates tempests. Vide *Storm*.

Tench : Vide *Jaundice*.

Tengu : Jap. Myth. Mysterious beings who appear as priests, riding on foxes, carrying sometimes swords like the *samurai* ; but their commonest form is like that of a bird of prey, not unlike an eagle or a vulture. The favourite haunts of these beings are famous temples. They are the prototype of the *Garuda* of Buddhist mythology.

The popular explanation of this term is " heavenly dog " ; it also means " heavenly fox."

Terme, Terminus : Rom. Myth. A Roman god, protector of boundaries and limits.

Terpsichore : Gr. Myth. The Muse of singing and dancing She is usually represented with a lyre.

Tersus : A legendary king of Thracia, husband of Procne.

Tethys : Gr. Myth. A Titaness, daughter of Uranus, sister of Cronus, wife of Oceanus, and mother of the Oceanides.

Teutates : A certain god whom the inhabitants of Gaul regarded as their father.

Tezcatlipoca : The evil brother of Quetzalocoatl (q.v.) who represents the conquering night.

In Mexican mythology he was the personification of the breath of life. He was a life-giver, and had also the power to end existence. He is represented as holding a dart in his right hand, and his mirror-shield and four other darts in his left hand. He was a god of fate and fortune. (*Non-Classical Mythology*, p. 167.)

Thalia : Gr. Myth. The Muse of comedy and idylls. She is represented with a mask and a garland of ivy.

(ii) One of the three Graces (Horae, q.v.).

Tha-ma : The Burmese name for Yama, the god of death.

Tha-tha-pali : A deity. He is regarded by the Wathi Wathis of Central Australia as a powerful spirit, or perhaps a supreme supernatural being. They say that he comes from the far North, and now lives in the sky. He told each tribe what language they were to speak. He made men and women, and dogs ; and the latter used to talk, but he took the power of speech from them. (LANG, *Magic and Religion*, p. 71, quoting from Mr. CAMERON.)

Theft : If you steal anything at Christmas without being caught, you can steal safely for a year. (RAGNER.) Vide *Glass, Heart.*

Thei : Gr. Myth. A Titaness, wife of Hyperion.

Themis : Gr. Myth. A form of the Earth goddess. She is a Titaness, daughter of Uranus, wife of Zeus, mother of Prometheus. She was a goddess of justice, and is represented with a pair of scales.

Theseus : Gr. Myth. The chief Attic hero, son of Ægeus, grandson of Pittheus. He rid Attica of Procrustes and other evil doers, slew the Minotaur, conquered the Amazons, and took part in the Calydonian Hunt.

Thetis : Gr. Myth. One of the Nereids, mother of Achilles. She plunged her son into the waters of the Styx in order to make him invulnerable.

Thief : If one can obtain some articles of clothing belonging to a thief, and if these be beaten, the thief himself will fall ill. (*Prussia.*—TETTAU UND TEMME, *Volkssagen*, p. 283.)

If an article touched by a thief be put into a coffin, all those who participated in the theft will die. (*Lauenberg.*—WUTTKE, p. 83.)

If a pregnant woman takes anything belonging to another, the child will be a thief. (STRACKERJAN, Vol. I, p. 47).

R

Thirst : Agate quenches thirst.

Thirteen : Thirteen is an unlucky number.
  If thirteen people sit down to dinner at the same table, one of the company will die within a year (*Christian*).

Thistle : The vampire of Malay folklore may be caught by hanging up a bunch of thistle. (*Enc. Brit.*, Vol. VIII, p. 6.) cf. *Brushwood, Thorn.*

Thomas à Becket : This saint cures blindness.

Thor : Norse Myth. Son of Odin. The god of thunder, the same as the Teutonic Donar. In Norway and Iceland he was the most widely worshipped god. He was killed by the Midgard Serpent (q.v.) whom he also slew at Ragnarok. He sent thunder and dashed waves against the coast. (THORPE, *N.M.*, Vol. I, p. 24, 195 ; see *Mundra Edda*, 20.)

Thorn : If thorns remain sticking on to the clothing of an unmarried girl, she will be married to a widower. (*Hanover.*—WUTTKE, p. 42.)
  The Khonds attempt to keep away diseases, such as smallpox, etc., by " placing thorns and brushwood in the paths leading to places decimated by that disease, in the hope of making the disease-demon retrace his steps." (*Enc. Brit.*, Vol. VIII, p. 6 ; *Ethnologie du Bengale*, p. 132. cf. TYLOR, *P.C.*, Vol. II, pp. 115, 134 ; ST. JOHN, *Far East*, Vol. I, p. 217 ; *Jew. Enc.*, Vol. IV, p. 517 ; ROTH, *Superstitions, Magic and Religion*, in *North Queensland Ethnogr. Bull.*, No. 5, § 116 ; TAPLIN, *The Narrinyeri*, pp. 62 *sq.* ; HOWITT, *Native Tribes*, pp. 356, 358 ; ELLIS, *Yoruba-speaking Peoples*, pp. 113 *sq.*)

Thoth : Egypt. Myth. A scribe of the gods, measurer of time, and inventor of numbers. In the Judgment Hall of Osiris he records the result of the weighing of the heart. He is represented with the head of an ibis. He was identified with Hermes by the Greeks.

Thread : A scarlet thread suspended from the horse's head will protect him from the evil eye. (HASTINGS, *Dic. Bib.*, Vol. IV, p. 605.)
  If a thread gets tangled in sewing, that suggests that the garment on which it is employed will bring health and prosperity to the person who is destined to wear it. (*Macedonia.*—ABBOTT, p. 100.)

Three : Three is a mystical number. (Note how this number occurs in mythology.)

The number three is unlucky.   (*Greece.*—LAWSON,
p. 313 ; *Celtic*—RHYS, Vol. I, p. 343.)

Throat : Throat ache can be cured by wrapping an old stocking
round the neck before going to sleep. (*Silesia, Hesse*—
WUTTKE, p. 165 ; *Great Britain*—LEAN, Vol. II, p. 512.)
Vide *Amber, Mouse.*

Thruthvang : Norse Myth. Thor's abode in Asgard.

Thrymheim : Norse Myth. The dwelling of Skadi in Asgard.

Thumb : Press your thumbs to bring about a fulfilment of
your desires : "*Daumen drücken*" (*Germany* ; LEAN,
Vol. II, p. 341.)
In some parts of India the thumbs and great toes of a
corpse are tied together in order to prevent the spirit
from walking ; among the Bhutiyas, they are tied up in
a cotton bag. Vide *Glutton.*

Thunder : Thunder on Sunday portends the death of some
learned man, judge or author ; on Monday, the death of
women ; on Tuesday, plenty of grain ; on Wednesday,
the death of harlots or bloodshed ; on Thursday, plenty
of sheep, cattle and corn ; on Friday, the death of some
great man or a battle; on Saturday it forebodes pestilence
or sickness.
Thunder is caused by witches. (LEHMANN, *A.Z.*, p. 111.)
When you hear the first thunder, shake something
heavy ; then you will be strong. (*Bohemia.*)
If you keep a glass full of water on the table, thunder
will do your house no harm.
A prayer-book kept on the table serves the same purpose as a glass of water. (*Jews of Bohemia.*)
Swans cannot hatch without a clap of thunder.
If you kill a beetle, it will bring rain, thunder and
lightning. (LEAN, Vol. II, p. 136.)
> " Thunder in the morning,
> All the day storming ;
> Thunder at night
> Is the sailor's delight."—Popular Rhyme.

Thunder Bird : Among the North American Indians, the
Dacotas, Brazilians, Caribs, Karens, Bechuanas, Basutos,
etc., thunder is believed to be caused by the thundering
of an old bird. It is the young birds that do the mischief.
(TYLOR.)

Thunderbolt : The Indians believe that the thunderbolt is the missile thrown by Indra when he is angry.

Thunderbolt may be attracted to anything by a first-born child leaning against it. (*Enc. Rel. Eth.*, Vol. VIII, p. 290, quoting *N.I.N.Q.*, i, (1891) §378).

A thunderbolt can be " caught " by quickly covering it with some cow-dung. (*India.*)

Thursday : Of all days of the week this is the unluckiest in Germany. No marriages should be celebrated, or important businesses undertaken, or children sent to school for the first time on a Thursday. (WUTTKE, p. 11 ; *India.*)

Thursday derives its name from Thor or Donar to whom it is dedicated. Vide *Sunday, Wednesday.*

Tickling : Tickling a baby causes stuttering. (*Georgia.—* BERGEN, *C.S.*, p. 28.)

Tide : Children cannot be born till the tide comes in ; neither can anyone die until the tide goes out (*Portugal.—* SÉBILLOT, *Légendes, Croyances et Superst. de la Mer,* Vol. I, p. 132 ; DICKENS, *David Copperfield*, Ch. XXX), or is beginning to recede. (*Spain.—*SÉBILLOT, *loc. cit.,* SAUVÉ in *Mélusine*, Sept., 1884; BASSETT, p. 29 ; FRAZER, *The Magic Art*, Vol. i, p. 167.)

Tiger : The peasantry of India and the Malay Archipelago believe that a man under certain circumstances can change himself into a tiger. (Vide *Lycanthropy, Werewolf.*)

In Corean superstition a tiger is supposed to have the power of flying, or emitting fire, or hurling lightning. (GRIFFIS, *Corea.*)

The tiger lives to the age of one thousand years. When five hundred years old, his colour changes to white. His claws are a powerful talisman, and ashes prepared from his skin worn about the person, act as a charm against sickness. (MAYERS, *Chin. Read. Man.*, p. 65 ; WILLIAMS, *M.K.*, Vol. II, p. 256 ; ELLIS, *Ewe-speaking Peoples,* p. 93 ; *Ethnologie du Bengale*, p. 106.)

The Indians do not mention a tiger by name. (CROOKE, *P.R.I.*, Vol. II, p. 212.)

Tigers are amenable to courtesy, and will not harm anyone who is polite to them (CROOKE, *P.R.I.*, Vol. I, p. 249 ; cf. J. MACLAREN COBHAM, *The Red Sultan* (The Nelson Library), pp. 90 *sq.* ; *Ethnologie du Bengale,* pp. 106, 91, n. 8.)

Tii : The *Tii* are the Polynesian vampires, and are represented as the ghosts of the dead, which leave their graves and peep into houses by night, and devour the heart and entrails of the sleepers, so that they die. (J. R. FOSTER, *Observations During a Voyage Round the World*, p. 543.)

Time : The ancients had personified time in the form of an old man with two wings.

Tindalo : The *Tindalo* of the Melanesians is a ghost as distinct from the *vui* (q.v.).

Tiphys : Gr. Myth. One of the Argonauts ; he was appointed helmsman during the expedition.

Tir : Moham. Myth. Son of Iblis, a jinn who brings about calamities and injuries. (*Jew. Enc.* Vol. IV, p. 521.)

Tisiphone : Gr. Myth. One of the three Furies. She was entrusted with punishing the guilty the moment they entered the infernal regions.

Titanus : Gr. Myth. One of the primeval deities, children of Uranus and Gæa. The great event in Titan history was the Titanomachy, or war of the Olympian gods in Thessaly. The Titans were the earliest children of the Earth, older than even the Greek gods, and were sons of the Earth, their mother. (G. E. WOODBERRY.) They attempted to reach the heaven by piling one mountain upon another, and were destroyed by lightning by Zeus.

Tizona : " The Firebrand " ; the name of the mighty sword of the Cid. cf. *Excalibur, Balmung*.

Tlapalan : Aztec Folklore. The Red Land of the South East, whence Quetzalocoatl originally came and later went back to.

Toad : Toads spit poison, but they carry in their head an antidote.

Toads are not found in Ireland, because St. Patrick cleared the island of all vermin.

Bodies of toads killed slowly are a specific remedy for warts ; hung inside the stable doors, they protect the cattle from diseases. (ZINGERLE in *Wolfs Zeitschrift*, I, 16 ; WUTTKE, pp. 95, 96.)

People who have hidden treasures, guard them after death in the form of a toad till someone finds them. (ALPENBURG, *Mythen*, p. 215, etc.)

In some Teutonic countries it is considered unlucky to kill toads, because they are the homes of some unfortunate souls.

The Jnūn of the Moors are usually supposed to assume the form of toads. Hence anybody who kills or hurts one of these creatures will have fever or die in consequence. (WESTERMARCK, *The Belief in Spirits in Morocco*, p. 13.)

Toads are used for various magical purposes (see PLOSS, *Das Weib*, Vol. I, p. 440.)

cf. *Scorpion, Snake, Frog.*

Tobyo : (meaning unknown.) It is a kind of possession to be found in Bitchu and Bingo in Japan, and is a form of the Kitsune-tsuke.

Toe : Toe-nails should be carefully destroyed, lest other people finding them may perform magical operations. (*India.*) Vide *Thumb.*

Toelu : The Welsh name for a phantom funeral.

Tolā : In the Himalayas, the *tolâs* are the spirits of children and bachelors, sometimes appearing in the form of a will-o'-the-wisp, sometimes prowling about in the form of bears and other wild animals. They are as a rule harmless, and their present state only temporary. (CROOKE, *P.R.*, Vol. I, p. 261, quoting TRAILL, *Asiatic Researches*, XVI, 137 *sq.* ; *N.I.N.Q.*, ii, 27 ; *Ethnologie du Bengale*, p. 99.).

Tolosom : A Bulgarian household spirit in the form of a snake.

Tomb : To dream of erecting a tomb denotes marriages, weddings and births of children ; but if falling to ruin, sickness and destruction to yourself and family.

Tom Cat : A tom cat of a black colour brings good luck. Vide *Cat.*

Tomte : "House-spirit." Another form of Gardsvor (q.v.).

Tongue : If you bite your tongue, it promises a gift of sweets, or some pleasant news, or it indicates that you are telling a lie. (*India.*)

If the tongue of a fox be dried and worn near the heart, it will safeguard the wearer against erysipelas in the face. (STRACKERJAN, Vol. I, p. 85.)

Tooth : A child's first tooth must not be thrown away, but hidden in a mouse-hole. (*Great Britain, India.*)

Teeth set wide apart warn a person to seek his fortune away from his native place.

The teeth of a cat or of a fox are believed by Arabs to be a powerful weapon against Jinns, Ghouls, and even Satan himself. (HASTINGS, *Dic. Bib.*, Vol. IV, p. 603.)

If a child gets the upper teeth first, it is a sign that he will not outlive his milk-teeth ; but if the bottom row first, he will live long. (*Bavaria.*—ZINGERLE, *Deutsche Mythologie*, p. 101.)

In Dahomey if a child was born with a complete set of teeth, the chief magician upheld the event being a reincarnation of the King who had returned to devour his son, and the child was drowned (BERTHOLET, p. 27) ; in European countries such a child is considered to be a monster.

At Penvénan if a person loses a tooth in a cemetery at the moment he sees a priest, it is a sure sign of his speedy death. (LE CALVEZ in *Revue des Traditions Populaires*, VII, p. 90.)

To dream of teeth (U.S.A.—KNORTZ, p. 43) falling out is very unlucky ; it denotes the death of some near relative. (STRACKERJAN, Vol. II, p. 117 ; ST. CLAIR TISDALL, *Modern Persian Conversation Grammar* (1920), p. 41.) Vide *Lucky Finds, Bread, Church bell, Comb, Headache, Milktooth, Nail, Mole's paw, Toothache.*

Toothache : A paw cut from off a live mole cures toothache. (*W. Sussex.*—*F.L.R.*, 4.)

The tooth of a person fallen in war, or dying a violent death cures toothache if the suffering tooth and that side of the face be rubbed with it. (*Mecklenburg, Silesia.*— WUTTKE, pp. 101, 102.)

A louse taken from the body of a beggar and put into the hollow of an aching tooth, instantly relieves the pain. (STRACKERJAN, Vol. I, p. 85.)

St. Appolina cures toothache, because all her teeth were pulled out before she was burnt alive.

A splinter of wood from a gibbet cures toothache. (LEAN, Vol. II, p. 515.)

To cure toothache, rub the gum with the finger of a corpse. (STRACKERJAN, vol. i, p. 19.)

As a remedy for toothache, carry an amulet with the word ὤφελε on it. (*Jew. Enc.*, Vol. V, p. 426.)

Silesian mothers swallow their children's cast teeth in order to save their offspring from toothache (GROHMANN, p. 111, § 823 ; WUTTKE, p. 330, § 527).

Topaz : Topaz is favourable for hæmorrhages ; it imparts strength and promotes digestion.

The topaz is an emblem of fidelity ; it is dedicated to November and in the Zodiac it signifies Taurus.

Torngak : An Esquimaux familiar demon which may be the soul of a deceased parent. (CRANZ, *Grönland*, p. 268.)

Torngarsuk : The great spirit of the Greenlanders, as opposed to the Manitous, to whose happy land only those come, who have been valiant workers. (CRANZ, *Grönland*, p. 259 ; BASTIAN, Vol. II, p. 109.)

Tortoise : The Hindus believe that a tortoise supports the world-bearing elephant. (BASSETT, p. 263.)

The North American Indians say that earthquakes are caused by the movement of the world-bearing tortoise.

In Macedonia the tortoise is regarded as lucky, and the killing of one is a great sin. (ABBOTT, p. 109.)

In Corea the tortoise is a symbol of immortality and strength. (GRIFFIS, *Corea*, p. 303.)

In a Chinese legend a tortoise emerged from the Yellow River, on the shell of which a sage found a system of numerals, and thus obtained the rudiments of mathematics and philosophy.

In China divers marvellous tales are narrated with regard to the fabulous longevity and the faculty of transformation of the tortoise. It is said to conceive by thought alone ; hence the Chinese use the term " son of a tortoise " to denote a bastard. (MAYERS, *Chin. Read. Man.*, p. 101.)

Totem : A family symbol.

Totemism : The term " totemism " is used to signify the belief that " man is related to a particular species of animal, or is even descended from it. The believer then takes the name of his totem animal, as we take our family names." (BERTHOLET, p. 4.)

" A large number of peoples believe that after death, the soul does not remain disincarnate for ever, but presently animates another living body, and the primitive mind, drawing no definite line of demarcation between the souls of men and of beasts, admits without difficulty the transmigration of human souls into the bodies of the lower animals (TYLOR, *Primitive Culture*, II, p. 6). The animal thus serving as a receptacle for a venerated being becomes a holy thing, the object of a cult, that is, a *totem*, for all the descendants of the ancestor, who form the clan descended from him." (DURKHEIM, *Elementary Forms of Religious Life*, p. 168, quoted in *Ethnologie du Bengale*, p. 17.)

Towel : If lovers wipe themselves on the same towel, their love will come to an end.

Tower of London : It is believed to be haunted.

Toyo-tama-hiko : Jap. Myth. "Rich-jewel-prince." A sea-god.

Toyo-tame-hime : " Rich-jewel-maidens.". Daughter of the Japanese sea-god ; wife of Hohodemi, a son of Ninigi. On discovering her changing her form into that of a *wani* (sea-dragon), her husband abandoned her after barring the passage between the realms of land and sea.

Traitor : Vide *Brawn's Head, Drinking Horn.*

Trance : In popular belief a trance is caused by the soul leaving for a certain time the body it inhabits. If the soul does not return, death ensues.

Treasure : Treasures are watched over by dragons. (*Tyrol.*— ALPENBURG, *Mythen*, p. 377 ; *Greece*—LAWSON, p. 281 ; *Turkish*, KÚNOS, *T.F.T.*, p. 135, etc.)

Yaks (q.v.) keep watch over treasures (*Bengal*); Bhûts also do the same (CROOKE, Vol. I, p. 286.)

To dream of treasures, big or small, is an evil omen.

If there be any buried treasure in an old occupied house, the owner of the treasure remains there in the form of a ghost. (JACKSON, *F.L.N.*, Vol. II, p. 59.)

Vide *Groat, Toad.*

Treasure, Lost : The wealth of the Incas is said to have been hidden in two separate parts, known respectively as the Great and the Little Fish. This happened after the fall of Montezuma, and the secret of it is now lost to the world

Tree : The Izhuvans of India believe that trees are inhabited by spirits, therefore proper notice of ejection is given to them before a tree is cut down. (cf. JACKSON, *F.L.N.*, Vol. I, p. 136.)

In Franconia, on St. Thomas's Day, the girls go to a tree, knock upon it three times with due solemnity, and listen for answering knocks within telling them what sort of husband they will get. (BERTHOLET, p. 19.)

In Sicily, they tie stones to fruit trees in order to ensure a crop of fruit. (G. PITRÉ, *Usi e costumi, credenze e pregiudizi del popolo siciliano*, Palermo, 1889, ii, 113 *sq.*)

The Khâsiyâs of East Bengal lay the bodies of their dead dead in the hollow of a tree. (CROOKE, *P.R.I.*, Vol. II, p. 85.)

The Indians do not like plucking fruits at night, for fear of disturbing the spirits living in the trees.

In Japan trees are the abodes of ghosts and evil spirits ; good spirits rarely dwell in them. (GRIFFIS, *M.E.*, p. 473.)

Beat the trees on Christmas night and they will bear more fruit. (RAGNER.)

To dream of trees in blossom signifies a happy marriage and many children.

s

Triangle : A piece of iron of a triangular shape is used for various magical rites. (AUBREY, *Remains*, p. 57 ; CROOKE, *P.R.I.*, Vol. II, p. 39.) cf. *Circle*.

Trimurti : Hind. Myth. Trinity ; composed of Brahmā, the Creator, Vishnu, the Preserver, and Siva, the destroyer, representing the three powers of nature.

Trinavartta : Hind. Myth. A demon who assumed the form of a whirlwind and carried off the infant Krishna, but was overpowered and killed by the child. (DOWSON, *H.C.D.*, p. 321.)

Tri-pada : Hind. Myth. " Three-footed." Fever personified as having three feet, symbolizing the three stages of fever —heat, cold and sweat. (DOWSON, *H.C.D.*, p. 321.)

Triton : Gr. Myth. A demi-god of the sea, son of Poseidon (Neptune) and Amphitrite, represented as having the lower part of his body fish-like and blowing a spiral shell. Later mythology imagined a number of Tritons, attendants on the sea-gods.

Trold : Danish Folklore. These are dwarfs, and are represented as misshapen, stumpy and humpbacked. They are generally ill-natured, of a thieving disposition, they live underground and are rich in gold and silver. (THIELE, *Danmarks Folkesagn*.)
(ii) *Trold* is the Scandinavian name for a witch.

Troll : Teut. Folklore. A supernatural being, conceived sometimes as a dwarf, sometimes as a giant, fabled to inhabit caves, hills, and like places. Later, this word came to mean a familiar but impish dwarf.

Trout : Vide *Fisherman*.

Trude, Trute : In the Tyrol district of Germany the *mara* is usually designated by this name.

Tsao Guo Giu : Chin. Folklore. The fourth of the eight Immortals. (*Chin. Volksmärchen*, p. 71.)

Tsin King : A magic mirror which had the property of reflecting " the inward parts of those who looked upon it and revealing the seats of disease." (MAYERS, *Chin. Read. Man.*, p. 251.)

Tsuki-yomi : A Japanese moon-deity. He has shrines at Ise and other places and occupies a far less prominent part in Japanese mythology and cult than his elder sister, Amaterasu.

Tuamatef : Egypt. Myth. The ape-headed genius of Amenti. He was associated with the East.

Tuatha De Danann : Irish Legend. The divine race, children of Danu, who invaded Ireland, overthrew the Firbolgs and Fomors, and were finally overthrown by the Milesians, by whom they were worshipped as gods.

Tuau : Egypt. Myth. The lion-god (q.v.) on the left is known by the name of Tuau.

Tuckbolde : In the provinces of Mark and Lower Saxony this is another appellation of the Jack-o'-Lantern. Vide *Ignis Fatuus.*

Tuesday : Tuesday is a propitious day for marriages and other important undertakings. (WUTTKE, p. 10.)

In Modern Greece, Tuesday is an unlucky day, because it is called Τρίτη " third day." (LAWSON, p. 313.)

Vide *Sunday, Wednesday, Three.*

Tulong : The Ta-ta-thi of Central Australia regard him as a deity. He is a powerful spirit or perhaps a supreme supernatural being. They say that he comes from the far North and now lives in the sky. He told each tribe what language they were to speak, and created men, women and dogs ; the latter could once speak like human beings. The Ta-ta-thi do not like to speak much of *Tulong*, and say that he does not come much to earth. (LANG, *Mag. Rel.*, p. 71, quoting MR. CAMERON.)

Tulsi Plant : The Hindus regard the *tulsi* or the sweet-basil plant or its leaves as a powerful charm against all kinds of evil spirits (*Ethnologie du Bengale*, p. 62 ; MONIER WILLIAMS, *Hinduism*, p. 170 ; *F.L.J.*, 1883, p. 377 ; WARD, *Hindus*, Vol. II, p. 203 ; DAY, *Govinda Sāmanata*, Vol. I, p. 18 ; J. T. BENT, *The Cyclades*, p. 328).

" Veneram a planta chamada Tulosse, por dizerem é do pateo dos Deoses, e por esso é commun no pateo de suas casas, e todas as manhãs lhe vão tributar veneração " (Annaes Martimos, III, 453, quoted by YULE and BURNELL, *Hobson Jobson*[2], p. 931 ; idem[1], p. 710).

It is a great sin to uproot this tree, though no sin attaches to the plucking of its leaves during daytime. (JACKSON, *F.L.N.*, Vol. I, p. 136.) cf. *Bay, Assides, Chikuli, Rowan tree.*

Tululu supai : The Canelos believe this to be a demon who, when he wants to visit a woman, may take the form of a black nocturnal bird which they call *tulúlu*. It enters a house and has intercourse with the woman while she is sleeping. (KARSTEN, *Indian Tribes of Equador*, p. 71.) cf. *Incubus, Succubus, Cuichi supai.*

Tum : Egypt. Myth. A sun-god regarded as the "Closer" of the day, and often as the creator of the world. He is represented as carrying ankh and sceptre. Vide *Shu.*

Turk : Turks are more liable to become vampires than Christians. (*Greece.*—LAWSON, p. 369 note.)

Turmeric : In Indian superstition turmeric is an infallible test in discovering whether a person is really human, or a ghost in human form, or a possessed ; no ghost is able to endure the smell of burnt turmeric. (DAY, *Folktales of Bengal*, p. 199 ; CROOKE, *P.R.*, Vol. I, p. 237.)

Turning : If a person turns round on the way to his wedding, it is a sign that one of the party will die. (*Thuringia.*—WUTTKE, p. 43.)

Turpentine : If you think you can smell turpentine when there is none in the vicinity, it is an omen of death. (STRACKERJAN, Vol. I, p. 31.)

Turquoise : It is a precious stone found in Persia. Several virtues are ascribed to it :

It indicates by its hue the state of the wearer's health.

It indicates by its change of lustre if any peril awaits the wearer.

It removes animosity between the giver and the receiver.

It rouses the sexual passion.

Turquoise given by loving hands carries with it happiness and good fortune.

The turquoise is an emblem of prosperity, and is dedicated to December. It is a Saturnian stone, and stands for lead in metallurgy.

Twanyrika : The Aruntas of Central Australia believe that the roaring noise of a wooden slat tied to a string and swung about is the "voice of the great spirit Twanyrika." This spirit lives in wild and inaccessible regions and is mostly believed in by women and children. (LANG, *Mag. Rel.*, p. 65, quoting SPENCER and GILLEN.)

Twelve Nights : Teut. Folklore. The twelve nights beginning from Christmas and extending to Epiphany. At this time the gods, especially Wodan and his wife Frigg hold their processions with the good spirits. It is also the time of the Wild Hunt (q.v.), and of the activity of Holda, Perchta, etc.

In Northern Germany, it is said that as the weather is during each of these twelve days, so it will be during each month of the year. (KÜHN UND SCHWARTZ, *N.D.S.*, p. 411 ; BASSETT, 131.)

Twenty-ninth of February : People born on this day have an especial aptitude for seeing ghosts, while others cannot even feel their presence. (*Rhineland, Westphalia.*— WUTTKE, p. 24.)

Twilight : Râkshasas and other spirits are strongest at twilight. Vide *Râkshasas, Sandhyā-bala.*

Twins : The Indians at Canelos never eat two bananas which have grown together, believing that if they eat them, their wives will give birth to twins. (KARSTEN, *Indian Tribes of Equador,* p. 74 ; cf. BAARDA, pp. 466, 468.)

If pregnant women eat fruits which have grown double, they will be delivered of twins. (*Mecklenburg.*—WUTTKE, p. 193 ; *Great Britain, India ; Ethnologie du Bengale,* p. 81.)

Tychon : Gr. Myth. The spirit of good luck.

Tyndareus : Gr. Myth. Legendary king of Sparta, husband of Leda, father of Castor, Pollux, Helen and Clytemnestra.

Typheus : Gr. Myth. The chief of the giants who scaled the heavens. He was struck by lightning by Zeus.

Typhon : Egypt. Myth. An ancient god of wickedness, darkness and sterility.

Typhus : The Polish peasants believe that the hand of a dead Jew is effective against typhus. (SCHIFFER, *Urquell,* Vol. III, pp. 123, etc.)

Tyr : Teut. Myth. An ancient war or sky god. His name has been connected with Zeus, Jupiter and Dyaus.

Tyrant : If a person eats the heart of a bear, he will become a tyrant. (*Jews of Minsk.*)

U

Uatchit : Egypt. Myth. The goddess of the North who, along with Nekhebit, was taken by Horus, in the form of two serpents, that they might consume with fire any rebels who still remained. (WIEDEMANN, *Leg. of the Winged Sun-Disk.*)

Uazit : A variation of Uatchit.

Ugly Females : These are to be found in Yomi (q.v.).

Uhatsu-wata-dzume : See Sokotsu-wata-dzume.

Uhijini : Mud has been deified under this name in Japan.

Ukemochi : A Japanese Food-goddess who, with the Sun-goddess, is worshipped at Ise. She is said to be the child of Ohonomochi, the great Earth-god.

Ukhat : Babyl. Myth. The word literally means a " wailing woman." Ukhat lured Eabani into the service of Gilgamesh. Vide *Eabani, Gilgamesh.*

Ulcer : The tongue of a dog cures ulcers. (LEAN, Vol. II, p. 516.)

Ulysses : Gr. Myth. A legendary king of Ithaca, son of Laertes, father of Telemachus, and husband of Penelope. He was one of the principal heroes in the Siege of Troy, and is noted for his sagacity and prudence. The principal episodes of his life in chronological order are : (i) the ruse he employed in order to single out Achilles disguised as a maiden and living with the daughters of the king of Lycomeda, to take him to the siege of Troy ; (ii) his dispute with Ajax for the possession of Achilles' arms ; (iii) his entry into the cave of the giant Polyphemus whose only eye he blinded ; (iv) the metamorphosis of his companions into pigs brought about by the wicked enchantress Circe ; (v) the manner in which he escaped the allurements of the sirens by binding himself to the mast of the ship and stopping his own and his companions' ears ; (vi) his reception in the court of Alcinoüs, king of the Pheacians ; (vii) the flight of the image of Ithaca before him ; (viii) the touching manner of his recognition by his dog and his faithful nurse Euryclea, after an absence of twenty years. Vide *Circe, Penelope, Euryclea.*

Umā : Hind. Myth. Devi, the consort of Siva, is also called Umā, " light."

Umbrella : In Eastern countries the umbrella is a symbol of supremacy. If a king is present, no one is allowed to carry an umbrella. (Monier Williams, *Buddhism*, p. 523.)

It is unlucky to open an umbrella inside the house ; it denotes a speedy death (*general*), or that you will remain unmarried all your life. (*U.S.A.*—Knortz, p. 39.)

Umkulunkulu : The supreme spirit of the Zulus (Callaway). His character seems to vary from the idea of an ancestral spirit, or the spirit of an ancestor, to that of a god. (Haggard, *Nada the Lily*, pp. xii, 206.)

Underclothing : A woman must not change her underclothing for a period of six weeks after she has given birth to a child ; if she ignores this precaution, she will give birth to a baby every year. (*Mark.*—Wuttke, p. 207.)

Unfaithful : Elephant hunters of East Africa attribute their want of success in hunting to the unfaithfulness of their wives ; in such case they think they will be killed or severely wounded. (P. Raichard, *Deutsch-Ostafrika*, Leipsic, 1892, p. 427.)

Unicorn : Unicorns can be caught only by placing a virgin in their haunts.

The horn of a unicorn dipped into a liquor will show if it contains poison. (cf. Hazlitt, p. 605 *sq.*)

Unicorns do not eat anything but virgins. Vide *Chichi Vache, Poison, Virgin, Venetian Glass, Drinking Horn, Rhinoceros, Dragon.*

Unlucky Days : There are forty-two unlucky days in the year of which three are the most unlucky, viz., 1 April, the day of the birth of Judas Iscariot ; 1 August, the day of the destruction of Sodom and Gomorrah ; and 1 December, the day on which Satan was driven out of Heaven.

The forty-two unlucky days are : January 1, 2, 6, 11, 17, 18 ; February 8, 16, 17 ; March 3, 12, 13, 15 ; April 1, 3, 15, 17, 18 ; May 8, 10, 17, 30 ; June 1, 17 ; July 1, 5, 6 ; August 1, 3, 17, 20 ; September 1, 2, 15, 30 ; October 15, 17 ; November 11, 17 ; December 1, 7, 11. (Strackerjan, Vol. II, p. 52 ; cf. Hazlitt, pp. 374-379.)

Upasruti : Hind. Myth. A supernatural voice which is heard at night, revealing the secrets of the future. (Dowson, *H.C.D.*, p. 326.)

Upior : The vampire of Polish superstition.

Upir : The vampire of Russian superstition.

Urania : Gr. Myth. The Muse of astronomy. She is represented with a compass and a globe.

Uranus : Class. Myth. The most ancient of the Greek gods, father of Saturn, the Ocean, the Titans, the Cyclops, etc.

Urdhr : Scand. Myth. "Was." One of the Norns or goddesses of Fate. She corresponds to the Greek Lachesis. According to the Eddas she was a water-nymph. (THORPE, *N.M.*, Vol. II, p. 13.)

Urganda : A fairy of the Middle Ages, who was beneficent to the knights. Sometimes she appeared as an old woman and sometimes as a charming maiden.

Uriel : An angel whose name is often mentioned in Eastern liturgies.

Urine : Urine is an excellent means for keeping away all evil-intentioned spirits and ghosts. (LEAN, Vol. II, p. 460 ; RINK, *Tales and Trad.*, p. 56.)
If a girl urinates in a man's shoe, he will fall madly in love with her. (PLOSS, *Das Weib*, Vol. I, p. 443.)

Urisk : Celt. Folklore. " The Urisk was a large, lubberly supernatural being of solitary habits and harmless character that haunted lonely and mountainous places. . . . There were male and female Urisks, and the race was said to be the offspring of unions between mortals and fairies." (CAMPBELL, *Sup. of Scot. Highl.*, p. 145.)

Urshu : Egypt. Myth. Spirits who played the part of the watchers.

Urth : Same as Urdhr.

U-simbela-banta-bami : " He digs-up-for-my-children." This was the peaceful name of a Zulu assegai. (CALLAWAY, *Relig. of the Amazulu*, p. 186.)

Usurer : The spirits of usurers must return to earth.
If you mention the name of a usurer the first thing in the morning, you will have nothing to eat that day (*Bengal*). cf. *Miser*.

Ut-napishtim : Babyl. Myth. A hero who by special favour of the gods has secured immortal life, and to whom Gilgamesh (q.v.) applies for the secret of immortality. He is the hero of the Babylonian deluge myth, of which he and his household are the only survivors.

Uttama-pada : Outstretched, supine. In the Vedas, a peculiar creative source from which the earth sprang. Supposed to refer to the posture of a woman in parturition. (DOWSON, *H.C.D.*, p. 329.)

Utukku : Babyl. Folklore. They were like the Shedu, strong and powerful demons.

V

Vadava, Vadavānala : Hind. Myth. The submarine fire which " devours the waters of the ocean " causing it to throw off the vapours which are condensed into rain and snow (DOWSON, *H.C.D.*, p. 330.)

Vaitarani : Hind. Myth. The river which separates the land of the living from the land of the dead. cf. *Styx*.

Valentine, St. : He should be invoked as a last resource in cases of epilepsy.

Valhalla : Norse Myth. The hall of Odin, in which he receives the souls of heroes slain in battle; it is the palace of immortality. From its 540 gates the warriors go each morning to fight, and at night they return to feast with the gods, Valkyries being their servitors.

Vali : Norse Myth. One of the Æsir, son of Odin, and avenger of Balder. He survives Ragnarok.

Valkyrie : Norse Myth. One of the twelve maidens of Odin, awful and beautiful, who hover over the field of battle choosing those to be slain, and conducting the worthy heroes to Valhalla (q.v.).

Vampire : A spirit of a dead person or his corpse reanimated by his own spirit or by another, returning to sap the life of the living by sucking their blood. The vampire is often one who has died an untimely death, or one who in his turn has been killed by a vampire. The superstition is very widespread, and may be found among the Slavs, the Greeks, the Malays, the Chinese, etc.
When a grave is opened, a vampire may easily be recognized owing to the body remaining in perfect preservation and the lips being stained with blood.

When the body of a vampire is found, the most effectual way of ridding the world of this horrible monster is to cut off the corpse's head, and thrust an ash stake through the breast ; whereupon a profuse flow of fresh blood gushes forth, and the corpse utters a fearful scream. Next the head and the body should be burnt to ashes, and the ashes scattered to the winds ; or the body may be re-buried beyond a stream (M. RANFT, *Tractat von dem Kauen und Schmatzen der Todten in Gräbern*, Leipzig, 1734). Other methods of destroying the power of the monster have also been advocated, such as sprinkling the corpse with holy water, but the above is said to be the most effectual. (KRAUSS, *Vampirglaube in Serbien und Lithauen* in " Mittheil d. Anthrop. Gesellschaft in Wien," Vol. XVIII, 183 ; ABBOTT, p. 217 ; RALSTON, *Songs of the Russian People*, p. 412.)

There is an authentic (?) case of vampirism of one Arnold Paolo, a Heyduck, in the Balkans. Several military and medical gentlemen of the time were commissioned to investigate the facts of this case, and they signed a protocol setting out all the details. It is said that this Heyduck who had been once sucked by a vampire prior to his death, had been killed by a fall from his carriage. After his decease, he revisited his native place as a spirit, and sucked the blood of various people. These died, and in their turn became vampires. Not only this, but as cattle were also drained of their blood by these monsters, people drinking the milk of these cows or eating the flesh of the cattle, became vampires themselves after death. Thus there was a regular epidemic of vampirism. Later all the bodies were exhumed, and were found to be fresh and ruddy. Their heads were cut off, a stake thrust through their hearts and the remains afterwards burnt to ashes ; thus was the vampire epidemic put an end to. Further, the said Arnold Paolo is said to have had intercourse with his wife during sleep, so that she gave birth to a solid piece of flesh which crumpled up in the course of a few days. (RANFT, *Tractat, etc.* ; CALMET, *Dissertation sur les esprits etc.* ; O'DONNELL, *Werewolves* ; ENNEMOSER, *Hist. Mag.*, Vol. II, pp. 185, 480.)

(Vampirism has been made the subject of many tales, and has been masterfully dealt with by MR. BRAM STOKER in his *Dracula*, T. GAUTIER in his *La Morte Amoureuse* and E. T. A. HOFFMANN in his *Serapion Brothers*.)

cf. *Tii, Vyestitsa, Water-colt, Upior, Upir, Mûra, Nočnitz, Alukah, Langsuir, Hantu Pari, Penanggalan Kephu, Incubus, Succubus, Cuichi Supai, Túlulu Supai, Khu, Jhoting, Jiláya.* Vide *River, Water, Cat, Eyebrow.*

Vanir : Norse Myth. The three deities Njorth, Frey and Freya who forced the Æsir to allow them to share their sacrifices. They were wealthy gods of trade and commerce, and came from the South.

Varāha : Hind. Myth. " The boar." The demon Hiranyaksha dragged the earth to the bottom of the sea. To recover it, Vishnu assumed the form of a boar ; and, after a contest of a thousand years, succeeded in slaying the demon and raising the earth.

Vargamor : Slavic Folklore. A certain class of witches who preside over werewolves, and whose especial duty is to supply the beasts with food ; the werewolves in their turn are bound to obey all her commands. She is a kind of queen over these animals. (O'DONNELL, *Werewolves.*)

Varulpe : The Danish equivalent of a werewolf.

Varun : Hind. Myth. In the Vedic period he was the god of the heavens, creator and ruler of the world, and bestower of rewards and punishments for good or evil. In later mythology his sovereignty is restricted to the waters and the regions of the West. 'He is represented as riding a sea-monster, and holds a snaky cord in his hand, with which to bind the offenders.

Vasishṭha : Hind. Myth. Most wealthy. A celebrated Vedic sage to whom many hymns are ascribed. Vasishṭha was the possessor of the cow of plenty called Vandini which had the power of granting him all things (vasu) he desired ; hence his name. (DOWSON, *H.C.D.*, p. 339.)

Vatnskratti : " Water-wraith." In Iceland it is the name of a water-spirit.

Vauderie : The French name for witchcraft.

Veil : It is unlucky for a bride to lose a veil. (STRACKERJAN, Vol. I, p. 35.) cf. *Garter.*

Vein : A blue vein on the child's forehead extending down upon the nose is a sure sign of an early death. (*Maine and Massachusetts.*—BERGEN, *C.S.*, p. 34) ; across the nose, it has the same meaning. (U.S.A.—ib., p. 36 ; LEAN, Vol. II, p. 142.)

Veipsey : A spring in Yorkshire. It is called " prophetic," because it gives due warning of dearth by rising to an unusual height.

Venereal Disease : Vide *Sodomy, Virgin.*

Venetian Glass : If poison be put into a liquor contained in a vessel made of Venetian glass, the vessel will crack and fall to pieces. cf. *Unicorn, Drinking Horn, Rhinoceros, Gates of Gundoforus.*

Venison : Young men and warriors may not eat venison, because it would make them timid. (FRAZER, *G.B².,* Vol. II, p. 353 ; *Ethnologie du Bengale,* p. 107.)

Venus : Rom. Myth. An ancient Italian goddess of bloom and and beauty, and protectress of gardens. She was born of sea-foam.

Verdhandi : Scand. Myth. " Is." One of the three goddesses of Fate. According to the Edda, she was a water-nymph. (THORPE, *N.M.,* Vol. II, p. 13.) Vide *Norn.*

Vermilion Mark : If a Hindu married woman takes off the red mark on her forehead, she will be a widow. cf. *Wedding Ring.*

Vermin : In Ireland there are no vermin because St. Patrick cleared the island of them.

To get rid of vermin, put a few of them in a gun and shoot up the chimney. (WUTTKE, p. 171.)

Vermin are caused by witches.

To dream of any kind of vermin denotes enemies.

The saints Gertrude and Huldrick help to destroy vermin.

If you wear something sewed with thread spun on Christmas Eve, no vermin will stick to you. (RAGNER.)

Verthandi : Another spelling for Verdhandi.

Vertumnus : A Roman divinity of Etruscan origin, who presided over the seasons.

Vesta : Rom. Myth. A divinity of the family hearth. cf. *Hestia.*

Vestice : They are the " Wild Women " of Bohemian folklore. They can assume the form of every animal. They steal new-born babies and leave " changelings " in their places (GROHMANN, p. 14.)

Vetāla : In the Deccan he is a guardian spirit who appears as a demon tenanting dead bodies. He is represented in human form, but his hands and feet are turned backwards. His eyes are tawny green, and his hair stands on end. He is to be usually met with in cemeteries. (*Vetāla Pañchaviṁsati.*) cf. *Devil.*

Vetrnice : Bohemian Folklore. The spirit of the winds.

Vilas : Bulgarian Folklore. They are the souls of deceased children and virgins. They are beautiful, white-robed, light-footed damsels who dwell in woods, mountains and lakes, and fly in the clouds. They are noted for their dancing and exquisite singing. They sometimes even intermarry with men. The state of the weather depends to a certain extent on them.

Vincent, St. : He helps those who seek riches.

Vinegar : Vide *Plague.*

Violet : Violets sprang from the blood of Attis (q.v.).
Violets do not smell any more after the first thunder. (*Bohemia.*—GROHMANN, p. 40.)

Violin : Violin strings worn round the waist cure lumbago. (*Great Britain.*)

Viper : Young vipers destroy their mothers when they come to birth.
Vipers are usually connected with witches.
". . . And beat
The ground with vipers, till it sweat."
BEN JONSON, *Masque of Queens.*

Virgin : Sexual intercourse with a virgin, or children, is, in some countries, supposed to be a cure for venereal diseases. (KRAFFT-EBING, *Psychopathia Sexualis,* Eng. tr., p. 405.) Vide *Chichi Vache, Unicorn, Shooting, Bastard, Water, Shirt, Cage, Light.*

Virgin Goddess : Diana (q.v.) was called by this name.

Virginity : In Posen virginity can be proved by going through a swarm of bees without being stung.
If a girl can blow into a flame a still-glowing candle or a light, it is a sure sign that she is a virgin. (*South Germany, Silesia, Tyrol.*—WUTTKE, p. 42.)
To be able to look at the sun is a sign of one's having the maidenhead. (LEAN, Vol. II, p. 359, quoting PEGGE, *Anonymiana,* X, 46.)

In Caucasus it is held to be a sure sign of a girl having lost her virginity, if her breasts have developed to any extent. (PLOSS, *Das Weib*, Vol. I, p. 360.)

Vide *Salt-cellar, Chastity, Grotto of Ephesus, Water.*

Virgo : Astræa after her death became the constellation Virgo.

Vishnu : Hind. Myth. The second god of the Hindu Trimurti, called the preserver in contrast to Brahmā, the creator, and Siva, the destroyer. He is the object of a widely extended and very popular worship. The holy river Ganges is said to spring from the feet of Vishnu. As a preserver and restorer Vishnu is a very popular deity, and the worship paid to him is of a joyous character. In early times he was a sun-god. (See MACDONELL, *Vedic Mythology*, pp. 37 *sq.* ; KEITH, *Hindu Mythology*, pp. 29 *sq.* ; *Rig Veda*, I, 155-v, VII, 99-ii.)

Vision of Charles XI : Charles XI of Sweden, accompanied by other members of the royal household, saw an apparition (vision) of the murder of a Swedish king, and the subsequent trial and execution of the murderer, which really took place a number of years after the death of Charles XI. He was so impressed by this vision, that he kept a record of the events he witnessed, attested by all those present, who actually saw the (future) murder being committed. (See PROSPER MERIMÉE, *Mosaïque.*)

Visit : If you are visiting a house where there are children, you should sit down for a few minutes ; otherwise you will take the children's " peace of mind " away with you. (*Wetterau, Westphalia.*—WUTTKE, p. 201.)

If the fire springs out of the hearth, you are sure to receive a visit. (*Dutch.*—THORPE, *N.M.*, Vol. III, p. 328.)

Vide *Knife, Fork, Straw, Weaving, Cat, Bee.*

Vitar : Norse Myth. A hero who kills Fenrir.

Vitus, St. : He cures dancing mania.

Vizaresa : Persian Myth. A fiend that drags the soul of the wicked to hell.

Vlkodlak : The Bohemian name for a werewolf.

Vlukolak : The Bulgarian name for a werewolf.

Vodyannies : In Russian folklore these were male water-spirits who influenced the weather and luck of fishermen. Their wives were drowned women. They are the male counterparts of the *Rusalka* (q.v.). In the Ukraine, when the sea is rough, these water-spirits are often seen on the surface where they sport themselves and sing enchantingly ; therefore it is not safe for bathers to go in the water after sunset, nor without a cross about their necks. (RALSTON, *Songs of the Russian People*, 106, 129, 146). Sometimes they are also called Pharaohs, and are believed to be the ghosts of the host drowned in the Red Sea. (ib. p. 171.)

Voe : In Central America the *voe* is a bird, and is the messenger of Hurakan (q.v.). (TYLOR, *P.C.*, Vol. I, p. 328.)

Voice : A sweet voice may be obtained by drinking three larks' eggs on a Sunday before the church bells ring. (*Germany, Bohemia, Austria.*)

Völves : Among the ancient Norsemen the *Völves* were sorceresses who used their magical powers as a means of intercourse with the dead. The Eddas often tell of men and gods who visited the grave of a Völva for the purpose of obtaining knowledge of the future.

Voodoo : A system of magic, snake worship, and probably, in extreme forms, of human sacrifice and cannibalism practised by Creoles and negroes in Hayti and other parts of the West Indies and in the Southern States. (See PUCKETT, Ch. III, pp. 167-310.)

Vougha : Celt. Myth. A kind of water-spirit.

Vovkulak : The Russian name for a werewolf.

Vrykolakas : (Gr. Βρύκολακας). In Modern Greece the were-wolves are so called. (LAWSON, p. 362 *sq.*)

Vui : The *vui* or spirits of the Melanesians have been described by Codrington as follows : It lives, thinks, has more intelligence than a man ; knows things which are secret without seeing ; is supernaturally powerful with mana ; has no form to be seen ; has no soul, because itself is like a soul.

Vukodlak : The Serbo-Croatian name for a werewolf.

Vulcan : Class. Myth. Son of Zeus and Juno, husband of Venus, god of the fiery element, especially in its fearful aspect. Later he was represented as a god of metal working.

Vulture : These birds live in the underworld, and are the messengers of Death (*India*).

Vyestitsa : Serbian Folklore. The *vyestitsa*, or sorceress, harbours a demoniac spirit which leaves her during sleep, and flying among the houses in the shape of a bird or butterfly, feeds upon people—especially children—whom she finds asleep, tearing out their hearts and devouring them.

W

Wade : Teut. Myth. A giant, regarded as a storm- or sea-demon.

Waff : In Northumberland a " warning light " is called a *waff*.

Wag-at-the-Wa' : A spectre supposed to haunt and to take its station on the chimney. It is seen to wag backwards and forwards before the death of anyone of the family (*Roxburghshire*).

Wahela : Lot's wife who was confederate with the men of Sodom, and gave them notice when any stranger came to lodge in the house. Her sign was smoke by day and fire by night. Lot's wife was turned into a pillar of salt.

Waist : Measuring one's waist, as· for a dress, will bring ill luck. (BERGEN, *C.S.*, p. 85 ; ABBOTT, p. 99.)

Waka-hirame : " Young-sun-female." A Japanese sun-deity who is no doubt a personification of the morning sun.

Wake : In Ireland a " wake " is the watching of a dead body, prior to burial, by friends and neighbours of the deceased, with lamentations often followed by merry-making. (HAZLITT, p. 341.)
   People holding a wake must not sleep with their feet pointing towards those of the corpse, because during sleep life flows to the feet, and it .is therefore possible that the corpse may receive some life and be partly revived. (*China. Chin. Volksmärchen*, p. 202.)

Waking : In the East it is considered unlucky to behold certain people, such as misers, usurers, etc., immediately on waking up in the morning. (*Ethnologie du Bengale*, p. 122.)
   Many people believe that it is dangerous to wake a sleeping man ; his soul might have left his body and might be unable to return immediately, in which case his body would be left soulless. (LE BRAZ, Vol. I, p. 212 ; RHYS, *C.F.*, pp. 602, 603, 606 ; G. HENDERSON, *Survivals in Beliefs among the Celts*, pp. 83-85 ; BERTHOLET, p. 8.)

Walking : If you walk into the winter corn on Christmas Eve, you will hear all that will happen in the village the following year. (RAGNER.)

Walpurgis Night : (First of May). If it rains at daytime on the 1st May there will be a bad crop ; if at night, a good one. (WUTTKE, p. 19.)

Dew on the morning of this day signifies plenty of butter (ib).

1st May is particularly suited for all kinds of magic. (ib).

The evening before the May Day is believed by Teutonic races to be the occasion for the witches' sabbath on the Brocken. The Devil attends these meetings in person. (cf. GOETHE, *Faust.*) Vide *May Queen.*

Walriderske : German Folklore. It is the spirit of nightmare corresponding to the *maras.* These spirits usually appear in the form of rough-haired animals, and are of a black, brown or even white colour. Mostly they are female spirits. (STRACKERJAN, Vol. I, p. 375.)

Wandering Jew : Vide *Eternal Jew.*

War : If children play at soldiers in the street, it is a sign of an approaching war. (LEAN, Vol. II, p. 323.)

Ravens flying towards each other foretell a war. (*Swabia.*—WUTTKE, p. 33.)

The Aurora Borealis gives warning of an impending war. (STRACKERJAN, Vol. II, p. 63.)

In Sweden the appearance of a hoopoe presages a war. (BRAND, *Observations*, p. 701.) Vide *Shishchikuli, Mouse, Comet.*

Warning Stone : Bakers in Wiltshire and in some other counties used to put a certain kind of pebble in their ovens to give them notice when the oven was hot enough for baking. When the stone turned white, the oven was fit for use.

Wart : If you count others' warts, you will have them yourself. (STRACKERJAN, Vol. I, p. 49.)

Stolen bacon is a specific remedy for warts. (STRACKERJAN, Vol. I, p. 83 ; Vol. II, p. 85.)

Toads killed slowly also cure warts. (ZINGERLE in *Wolfs Zeitschrift*, I, 16.)

Warts can be cured by rubbing them with a piece of fresh meat, and afterwards burying it. (cf. *Notes and Queries*, 24 October, 1925.)

To cure warts, make as many knots in a string as the number of warts you have, and then bury the string in the gutter. (*Tyrol.*—WUTTKE, p. 157), or tie the string round your hand. (RHYS, Vol. I, p. 297.)

Lard or green elder will charm away warts. (LORD BACON, *Nat. Hist.*, X, 997.)

To cure warts " steal a piece of fresh butter, chop leaves of viper's bugloss, mix, and apply with a wish away." (*Notes and Queries*, 24 October, 1925). Or take a dew-snail and rub it on the wart, then stick the snail upon a thorn, and as the snail dries up, and " goes away," so will the wart. (ELWORTHY, *E.E.*, p. 59). Or rub them with the blood from another man's warts, but not your own. (STRACKERJAN, Vol. I, p. 83.)

Washerman : In India it is considered terribly unlucky to see the face of a washerman (Dhobi) immediately on getting up in the morning ; even his name should not be mentioned.

Washing : If a milkmaid neglects to wash her hands after milking, the cows will go dry (*Great Britain*).

" Wash and wipe together,
Live in peace together."
Vide *Towel*.   —*Northern Ohio*.

Water : To dream of water or fish denotes misfortune in India, and in some parts of Germany. (STRACKERJAN, Vol. I, p. 32.)

To dream of smooth water means good luck, of rough water means ill luck. (*St. John, N.B.*—BERGEN, *C.S.*, p. 75.)

If you step over water that has been spilt, you will die a speedy death. (*Silesia.*—WUTTKE, p. 132.)

Virgins have the power of rolling water into balls. (GRIMM, *Deutsche Rechtsalterthümer*, 1828, p. 932.)

Vampires and other spirits are, as a rule, unable to cross salt water. (*Greece.*—LAWSON, p. 368.)

The spilling of water is a presage of good success, especially in a journey. (*India, Greece.*—LAWSON, p. 328.)

In certain provinces of France, it is believed that between eleven and twelve o'clock on Christmas Eve, water turns to wine. (RAGNER.)

On the death of a sailor, his wife can hear the sound of falling drops of water at the head of the bed. (SAUVÉ in *Mélusine*, Vol. II, col. 245.)

To dream of running water foretells sorrow (*India*), or death. (GOODRICH-FREER, *More Folklore from the Hebrides*, in " Folklore." XIII, p. 37.)

It is not advisable to give water out of the house after sunset. (*Macedonia.*—ABBOTT, p. 101.)

Vide *River*.

Water of Jealousy : This was a beverage which, the Jews used to assert, no adulteress could drink without bursting. (*Five Philosophical Questions Answered*, 1653.)

Water of Life: This is the water of a certain spring in the underworld, which has the property of making anyone immortal who bathes in it. (GREY.)

Water-bull : Celt. Folklore. The water-bull haunts pools and swamps, and is the parent of strangely formed beasts and monsters.

Water-colt : Celt. Folklore. It is the nearest approach to a vampire. It is thoroughly vicious and sucks the blood of maidens. (RHYS, *Celtic Folklore*, Vol. II, p. 673.)

Water-dog : Celt. Folklore. The Water-dog or *Dobhar-Chu* is a formidable animal of popular superstition. (CAMPBELL, *Sup. of Scot. Highl.*, p. 216.)

Water-horse : Celt. Folklore. A kind of supernatural animal that haunts lochs. (CAMPBELL, *Sup. of Scot. Highl.*, p. 202 ; SIKES, *Brit. Gob.*, p. 36 ; BASSETT, p. 155.)

Water-kelpie : Celt. Folklore. It has the form of a grey colt ; it wanders over the banks of the streams at night, and haunts streams and torrents. (CAMPBELL, *Sup. of Scot. Highl.*, p. 215 ; BASSETT, p. 154 ; STEWART, p. 147.) It is described as an aquatic creature emerging from its native element only to pursue human prey. (HAZLITT, p. 352.)

Waterman : A recent account, as late as 1864, says that Bohemian fishermen do not venture to save a drowning man from the waters, for fear that the waterman would bring them ill-luck in fishing and drown them at the first opportunity (GROHMANN).

Waterspout : The Chinese believe that waterspouts are occasioned by the ascent or descent of the dragon. (DOOLITTLE, Vol. II, p. 265.)

The Arabs account for them as caused by gigantic jinns. (LANE.)

The Japanese believe the same as the Chinese, and beat drums and gongs to dissipate the dragons. (BASSETT, p. 33.)

Water-wagtail : Immediately you see the first water-wagtail in spring, you should roll yourself on the ground, no matter where you may be ; this will ensure good luck. (STRACKERJAN, Vol. I, p. 66.)

Wave : The ninth is thought to be the greatest wave by boat-men of many lands. (BASSETT, p. 24 *et seq.*)

Way : If you lose your way in your own house, it is a sign someone will die. (STRACKERJAN, Vol. I, p. 35.)

Way of the Gods : The Basuto name for the Galaxy.

Way of the Spirits : The Ojis call the Galaxy by this name ; they say that souls go up to heaven by this way.

Wealth : St. Vincent helps those seeking wealth, and St. Anne bestows wealth to those who pray for it. Vide *Riches, Arm, Moles.*

Weapon : The weapons of a deceased warrior were, among the Hindus, the Norsemen, the Teutons, and other civilized as well as savage races, burnt or buried or otherwise disposed of along with the corpse. (cf. BERTHOLET, p. 22 ; MACDONELL, *Vedic Mythology*, p. 165 ; *Ethnologie du Bengale*, p. 68 ; *Handbook to the Ethnographical Collections of the British Museum*, 1910, p. 33, fig. 30.)

Weasel : If you see a weasel, you will die before the year is out. (LE BRAZ, Vol. I, p. 5 ; ELWORTHY, *E.E.*, p. 31.)
    You can never catch a weasel asleep.
    It is unlucky to meet a weasel either in the house or in the road (JACKSON, *F.L.N.*, Vol. I, p. 127 ; *Greece—* LAWSON, p. 327) ; or it is a good omen (*Macedonia—* ABBOTT, p. 108). Vide *Fire.*

Weather : Bad weather is caused by witches. (LEHMANN, *A.Z.*, p. 111.)
    Crows gaping at the sun foretell hot weather.
    If ravens gape against the sun, heat will follow ; but if they busy themselves in preening or washing themselves, there will be rain.
    When frogs croak more than usual, it is a sign of bad weather.
    When dogs wallow in the dust, expect foul weather.
    When cats are very assiduous in cleaning their heads and ears, it prognosticates bad weather.
    Bad weather may be driven away by striking the door-sill with an axe. (*Prussia.—*TETTAU UND TEMME, *Volkssagen*, p. 284.)
            " Red at night,
             Shepherd's delight ;
             Red in the morning,
             Shepherd's warning."

If it rains during cohabitation, a daughter will be born ; if it be fine weather, a boy. (*Germany.*—PLOSS, *Das Weib*, Vol. I, p. 551.)

> " Evening red and morning grey
> Will speed the traveller on his way.
> Evening grey and morning red
> Will bring the rain upon his head."

Vide *Ant, Crow, Swallow, Dolphin, Twelve Nights.*

Weaving : If many threads of cotton break while weaving, guests are sure to come. (*Sweden.*—WIKMAN, *Die Magie des Webens*, p. 3.)

Wedding : To dream of a wedding forebodes a quarrel. (STRACKERJAN, Vol. II, p. 124.)

A wedding is foretold by the blossoming of an apple tree in autumn. (*Lower Saxony.*—WUTTKE, p. 35.)

If you stumble while going up the stairs, it is a sign of a wedding. Vide *Pear tree, Crow, Turning, Marriage, Rain.*

Wedding Cake : If a piece of a wedding cake be put under the pillow before retiring at night, a maiden will dream of her future husband. (*Great Britain.*)

Wedding Day : The bride and bridegroom should not see each other on this day till they meet at the altar. (*Great Britain.*)

If the bride looks round on the way to the church on her wedding day, she will be unfaithful to her husband.

Wedding Ring : If the wedding ring be taken off the finger of a married woman, she will become a widow.

If an unmarried woman puts on a wedding ring, she will remain a spinster.

To lose or break the wedding ring during the marriage ceremony is an omen of extreme ill luck ; it presages the death of one or both of the parties. (*Hesse, Tyrol.*— WUTTKE, p. 40.) Vide *Wreath, Vermilion Mark, Sty.*

Wednesday : This is generally considered to be an unlucky day ; even stables are not cleaned out on Wednesdays and Saturdays. (*Germany.*—WUTTKE, p. 10.)

The Jews thought it dangerous to drink water on Wednesday or Friday nights. (HASTINGS, *Dic. Bib.*, Vol. IV, p. 603.)

Wednesday derives its name from Wodan to whom it is dedicated.

" Monday for health,
Tuesday for wealth,
Wednesday the best of all,
Thursday for losses,
Friday for crosses,
And Saturday no luck at all."

New England (KNORTZ, p. 23.)

Weeping : To dream that you are weeping is indicative of mirth.

Weeping Chamber : A chamber in the house of a certain merchant in Beyrout. "Invariably before one of its (the house) members sickened unto death, a shower of heavy drops, as from a thunder cloud, pattered upon the pavement of the Weeping Chamber, and was heard distinctly at night through the whole house." (ST. JOHN, *Leg. Christian East*, p. 29.) cf. *Edgewell Oak, Death Warnings.*

Weight : A person weighs more fasting than after a good meal. (LEAN, Vol. II, p. 625.) Vide *Egg.*

Weird Sisters : The Norns of Scandinavian mythology were designated by this name.

Wen : The hair from the tail of a horse is commonly regarded as a cure for wens. (BLACK, *Folk Medicine*, p. 152.)

Wen Ju : Chin. Myth. In Buddhist superstition he is the third divine being who helps in time of need. He is represented as riding a werewolf. (*Chin. Volksmärchen*, p. 202.) Vide *Pu Hiang, Guan Jin.*

Were-tiger : In the East there is a belief prevalent that a man, by magic or otherwise, can transform himself into a tiger. Vide *Lycanthropy.*

Werewolf : In Slavic and Teutonic countries wizards were said to have the power of transforming themselves into wolves and other animals. The metamorphosis is brought about by means of magic incantations, or by rubbing the body with certain ointments, or by wearing certain belts. Not only do these people howl like wolves, but the metamorphosis is so complete that even their appearance is changed into that of a wolf. (Vide O'DONNELL, *Werewolves*; BARING-GOULD, *Book of Werewolves*; LEUBUSCHER, *Wahrwölfe*; ELWORTHY, *E.E.*, p. 29 *et seq.* ; DALYELL, *Dark. Sup.*, p. 559; ENNEMOSER, *Hist. Mag.*, Vol. II, p. 145; ABBOTT, p. 215.) cf. *Loup-garou, Varulpe, Vroykolakas, Vovkulak, Vlkodlak, Vlukolak, Vukodlak.* Vide *Lycanthropy, Loup-garou.*

Western Royal Mother : Chin. Folklore. A fabulous being of the female sex, " dwelling upon Mount Kw'ên-Lun at the head of the troops of genii and holding from time to time intercourse with favoured imperial votaries." (MAYERS, *Chin. Read. Man.*, p. 191.)

Whale : According to the Japanese, and the Hovas of Madagascar (BASSETT, p. 237), whales creep under the earth and cause earthquakes.

To ensure a good catch of whales, the wife must lie fasting till the husband returns from the whale-fishing. (FRAZER, *G.B²*., Vol. I, p. 28.)

In the Georgian islands, whales were scared and not killed. (TYLOR, *P.C.*, Vol. II, p. 270.)

The appearance of whales forebodes trouble. A whale coming up the Thames during Cromwell's protectorate greatly alarmed that iron man. (BASSETT, p. 236, quoting AUBREY, *Miscellanies*.)

" What is the matter with you ? " : Such direct questions must not be put to a spirit. Say instead : " What is the matter with me ? " and the ghost will answer : " Nothing with you, but there is something the matter with me," and forthwith relate everything. (*Tyrol*, WUTTKE, p. 224.)

Wheat : To prevent wheat from burning, pick up some seeds silently above your head, and repeat the formula :
"Weizen, ich setze dich auf den Band !
Gott behüte dich vor Trespe und Brand."
Harz.—PRÖHLE in *Zeitschrift für deutsche Mythologie*, I, 200.

Whirlpool : Over every *vodyanny's* (water-spirit) house there is a whirlpool. (RALSTON, *Songs of the Russian People* ; BASSETT, p. 22.)

Whirlwind : Whirlwinds are caused by demons.
The demon of whirlwind may be seen by looking through the sleeve of one's coat (*Serbia*.)
A Whirlwind can be stopped by throwing a knife into the midst of it. (*Tyrol*, *Overpfalz*.—SCHÖNEWERTH, Vol. II, p. 113.)

Whistle: Whistling at night is extremely unlucky. (STRACKER-JAN, Vol. II, p. 20.)
Whistling is considered bad in Turkestan. If a husband whistles, something will befall his wife; if the children whistle, their father or mother will die. (SCHUYLER, Vol. II, p. 30.)

The Kirghis frequently whistle to bring about rain (ib.), or it increases wind. (BRAND, *Observations*, Vol. III, p. 240.)

> " A whistling woman and a crowing hen
> Are neither good for God nor men."
> Popular Rhyme (*Great Britain*).

Whistling at sea brings about a storm.   (*Germany.*— BASSETT, p. 145.)

White : White is the colour of innocence ; hence spirits with hopes of redemption are dressed in white. (STRACKERJAN, Vol. II, p. 68.)

White Lady : According to a tradition, a spirit dressed in white appears to some one of the household or guard of the Hohenzollern family, to announce the death of a prince of Hohenzollern, or any important event in the history of Germany. This spirit is said to be that of an ancestress and is known by the name of Bertha. She was duly seen on the eve of Prince Waldemar's death in 1876. cf. *Mélusine.*

Whooping Cough : This disease can be cured by following the advice of a man riding a piebald horse. Vide *Horse, Ass.*

Wichtelmännchen : Same as Hinzelmännchen.

Widerolf : Widerolf, Bishop of Strassburg, was devoured by mice in the seventeenth year of his episcopate, because he suppressed the convent of Selten on the Rhine.   cf. *Hatto, Freiherr von Güttingen, Graaf, Adolf.*

Wick : A glowing ball on the burning wick of a candle promises a letter for the person towards whom it is pointing. (STRACKERJAN, Vol. I, p. 33.)

Widow(er) : If you are the third—or fourth, etc.—husband (or wife) of a widow(er), you will die soon after the marriage. (*Jews of Vilna.*—*Jew. Enc.*, Vol. IX, p. 601.)

If a woman's hair parts where it should not, it is a sign that she will be a widow.

The point formed by the hair growing on the forehead is called a *widow's peak.* In a woman it indicates that she will be a widow. Vide *Hen, Thorn, Hairy Body, Wedding Ring, Vermilion Mark, Work.*

Wights : Old Norse Folklore. Wights were tutelary spirits who had their abode in groves, hills and waterfalls, and were able to dispense fortune or misfortune to human beings. In German superstition, they were vivacious spirit-like creatures who assisted men in their work for some remuneration.

Wild Dove : If a wild dove flies in a circle round a house, it is a sign of some misfortune, probably death. (STRACKER-JAN, Vol. II, p. 26.)

Wild Fowl : Wild fowls are said to be scared by spectres which no human eye can behold. (CRANZ, *Grönland*, p. 267.)

Wild Hunt(sman) : In European folklore this was supposed to be a night-time chase of spectral hunters through the wilderness or athwart the sky. The leader of this hunt was the Wild Huntsman who was Odin or Wodan, god of the wind and of the dead ; his attendants were the souls of the dead. In certain places, above all in cross-roads, the spirit host is believed to come and hunt for the souls. The principal time for the manifestation was the season of Epiphany. In reality, it was the sound of the wind in long winter nights, which gave rise to this superstition.

The curse of a deathless life has been passed on the Wild Huntsman, because he desired to chase the red deer for evermore. (BARING-GOULD, *Cur. Myths.*, p. 29 ; BASSETT, p. 363.) Vide *Holda, Herne the Hunter, Grand Veneur, Wodan.*

Will : If you make your will, you will die. (LEAN, Vol. II, p. 563.)

Willis : According to a Bohemian tradition it is the name given to certain young women who after their death, are condemned to leave their graves every night and dance till dawn. (*Petit Larousse*, p. 1652.)

Will-o'-the-wisp : Northern Folklore. A spirit which comes in the form of a light, and takes belated wayfarers out of their way. They are the souls of unbaptized children. Vide *Ignis Fatuus, Swearing, Knife.* cf. *Blud, Feu Follet, Jack-o'-Lantern, Irrlicht, Jhoting, Khu, Latawiec.*

Willow : According to a legend, Niobe at the loss of her children was so disconsolate that she was changed into a willow-tree.

Willow is used for various magical purposes. (LEAN, Vol. II, p. 379.)

T

If you run three times round a willow-tree at sunrise crying, " The fever shall take thee and the sun shall warm me," the fever will depart. (*Bulgaria.*—STRAUSS, *Die Bulgaren*, p. 400 ; FRAZER, *G.B²*., Vol. III., p. 27.)

Wind : Wind, rain, snow, ice, thunder, lightning and bad weather are superstitiously believed to be caused by witches (LEHMANN, *A.Z.*, p. III ; FRAZER, *G.B²*., Vol. I, p. 123 *sq.*)

In Melanesia the wizard makes wind by waving the branch of a tree and chanting the appropriate charm. (COD-RINGTON, pp. 200, 201.)

> " Comes the rain before the wind,
> Then your topsails you must wind ;
> Comes the wind before the rain,
> Haul your topsails up again."

Cape Cod, Mass.

Vide *Whistling, Dolphin. Kingfisher.*

Winding Sheet : A film of tallow, called a " winding sheet," shot from the top of a lighted candle, gives warning to the house of an approaching death.

Window : In many parts of the world, the window of a house where a person is dying is thrown open in order to give the departing soul a free passage. (RHYS, *C.F.*, p. 601 ; BERTHOLET, p. 4 ; LE BRAZ, Vol. I, p. 214.)

If a person watches a burial from a window, he himself will follow the defunct to his grave. (GREGOR, p. 214.) cf. *Soul, Door.*

Wine :

> " Drink up your cup,
> But not spill wine.
> For if you do
> 'Tis an ill sign."

HERRICK, *Hesp.*, ccxii.

The spilling of wine is a good omen ; it portends plenty. (*Greece.*—LAWSON, p. 328.) Vide *Water.*

Winter : The severity or mildness of a winter can be foretold from the breast-bones of a roast goose, or by the redness of a robin's breast, or by the number of berries on a holly branch.

Wish : If two persons say the same thing at the same time, their wish will come to pass provided they wish for something before another word is said.

If two people break together the "wish-bone" of a chicken, the one in whose hand the part with the bit sticking out is left will have the fulfilment of his wish.

If the palm of your hand itches, wish for something and then if you

"Rub it on brass,
It's sure to come to pass."

If you sneeze once, you will have your wish.

When you see the first star wish for something and say:

"Star light, star bright,
First star I see to-night,
I wish I may, I wish I might
Have the wish I wish to-night,"

and your wish will come to pass provided that you do not mention it to anyone. (*Eastern Massachusetts.—* BERGEN, *C.S.*, p. 69.) Vide *Star, Speak, Thumb.*

Witch : These are women who deny God, and renounce Him and His grace ; who have made a compact with the devil, and have given themselves up to him body and soul ; who attend his assemblies and sabbaths, and receive from him poison-powder to injure and destroy men, animals and property, and who by their devilish arts stir up storms, call down lightning, damage the corn, fields, etc., and confound the powers of nature. Many superhuman powers are ascribed to them, such as flying through the air on broomsticks, goats, etc., instantly assuming various forms at will, causing and spreading diseases at will by mere glance. They are supposed to come back to earth as ghosts after death. (HAZLITT, pp. 641-662.)

"To make ewes cast their lambs, swine eat their farrow,
And housewives' tun not work, nor the milk churn !
Writhe children's wrists, and suck their breath in sleep,
Get vials of their blood ! and where the sea
Casts up his slimy ooze, search for a weed
To open locks with, and to rivet charms,
Planted about her in the wicked feat
Of all her mischiefs ; which are manifold."

BEN JONSON, *The Sad Shepherd* (1637)

Vide *Dancing, Goat, Broomstick, Sabbath, Blood, Iron, Scissors, Catseye, Coral, Broom, Blocksberg, Brocken, Hekla, Calf, Cat, Dove, Flying, Horseshoe, Tulsi, Key, Knot, Ice, Rain, Lightning, Storm, Rowan-tree, Urine Vermin, Weather, Thunder, Illness, Saliva.*

Witchcraft : Bringing cattle in and out of stables backwards protects them against witchcraft. (STRACKERJAN, Vol. II, p. 17.)

Spitting in the right shoe is a talisman against witchcraft. Vide *Circasea Lutetiana, Witch.*

Witch-doctor : Among the Africans, especially the Kaffirs, a magician whose business is to "smell out" or detect witches, and to counteract magic spells by sorceries.

Witch Hazel : A forked twig of witch hazel made into a divining rod was supposed in the 15th, 16th and 17th centuries, to give warning of witches, and to be efficacious in discovering them.

Witch's Sabbath : Folklore. A midnight orgy in which witches and devils are supposed to participate, often with travesties of Christian ceremonies.

Wodan, Wode : The leader of the Wild Hunt or spirit-host was given the name of Wodan. In process of time Wodan was deified, and in some Teutonic countries came to be recognized as a supreme god.

Wodejäger : The German prototype of the version of the Wild Huntsman.

Wolf : If a wolf sees a man before the man sees the wolf, the man will be struck dumb.

Men are sometimes changed into wolves. (Vide *Lycanthropy*.)

A wolf's tooth used at one time to be hung on the neck of a child to charm away fear.

If you mention the word "wolf" in the month of December, you run the risk of being torn to pieces by werewolves. (TETTAU UND TEMME, p. 281 ; FRAZER, *G.B².*, Vol. I, p. 454.)

In Vancouver Island the wolf is important in ritual, legend and crest representation, and is believed to grant power and medicine. The wolves are supposed to form a supernatural community of their own with the raven as news-teller.

In popular superstition of many lands, wolves are the ghosts of the dead. (cf. RIDER HAGGARD, *Nada the Lily*.) Vide *Lycanthropy, Werewolves, Bereserker, Raven, Lycaon.*

Wolfgang, St. : This saint relieves people suffering from gout.

Wolta : According to a superstition of the Gold Coast negroes, ghosts build themselves houses and dwell on the banks of the river Wolta. (TYLOR, *P.C.*, Vol. II, p. 7.)

Woman : In Sweden if a woman steps over a fishing-rod, no fish will bite. (JONES, *Credulities*, p. 134 ; BASSETT, p. 427.)

If seven women stand together at the cross-roads, there will be rain. (STRACKERJAN, Vol. I, p. 29.) (For numerous superstitions connected with women see PLOSS, *Das Weib*.) Vide *Amethyst, Canace's Mirror, Alasnam's Mirror, Florimel's Girdle, Sophia's Picture, Boar's Head, Ring, Bertha's Emerald, Drinking Horn, Water of Jealousy, Grotto of Ephesus, Candle, Glowing, Salt-cellar, Bee, Virgin, Blood.*

Woo-rie : The *woo-rie* of the Watchandis of Australia is the spirit of the warrior's victim, which enters the warrior's body and becomes his warning spirit. It takes its abode near the liver, and informs him of the approach of danger by a scratching or tickling sensation. (OLDFIELD, *Aborigines of Australia* in *Tr. Eth. Soc.*, Vol. III, p. 240.)

Wong : Wong is the Gold Coast negro's generic name for a fetish-spirit.

Woodcutter and the Wen : It is a popular Japanese story and describes how a woodcutter's happy disposition and dancing were the means of curing himself of a wen by the help of the elves. An envious neighbour came the next day to cure himself too, but the elves were enraged at his bad dancing and gave him the other wen too. (GRIFFIS, *M.E.*, p. 494.)

Work : If a girl falls asleep at work, she will marry a widower. (*Hanover.*—WUTTKE, p. 42.)

Worm : If, on your way to a sick person, you pick up a stone and find no living thing under it, it tells you that the sick person will die ; but if you find there a worm or an ant, it presages the patient's recovery.

If the sound of a worm boring the planks of a ship be audible, it forebodes some catastrophe, probably shipwreck.

Wound : Vide *Desert, Goat, Stag.*

Woutan : Ger. Legend. The equivalent of Wodan.

Wraith : An apparition of a living person in the exact likeness, thought to be seen just before his death. The Celtic people are firm believers in " wraiths."

King James tells us that the wraith of a person newly-dead, or about to die, appears to his friends.

Wreath : The wreath or the ring of a bride accidentally falling off during the marriage ceremony presages that the marriage will be unhappy. (*North and Central Germany*.— WUTTKE, p. 40.)

Wreaths must not be laid on the bed of a sick person. (STRACKERJAN, Vol. I, p. 49.)

Wreck : Vide *Shipwreck.*

Wren : If anyone kills a wren, he will break a bone before the year is out (BRAND, *Observations*, Vol. III, p. 195), or the cows will give bloody milk (CHAMBERS, *Pop. Rhymes of Scot.*, p. 188), or in France, his house will be struck by lightning (SEBILLOT, Vol. II, p. 214.)

In Brittany, people think that if children touch the young wrens in the nest, they will suffer from pimples on the face, legs and so on. (SEBILLOT, *Trad. et Sup. de la Haute-Bretagne*, Vol. II, p. 214 ; FRAZER, *G.B*²., Vol. II, p. 443.)

Sailors say it is unlucky to kill a wren. (BASSETT, p. 275). cf. *Word-Lore*, Vol. I, p. 161. Vide *Robin.*

Wudu-mære : " Wood-spirit." The Anglo Saxon name for an echo (q.v.)

Wu Lao : Chin. Myth. The five old men who were the spirits of the five planets. (MAYERS, *Chin. Read. Man.* p. 279.)

Wuzl : In Oberpfalz Wodan appears as a frightful forest-spirit, and is called either Wuzl or Hoymann. (STRACKER-JAN, Vol. II, pp. 337, 342.)

X

Xaragua : According to an American Indian superstition, there is a lake in the province of Xaragua, on the banks of which the spirits of the good men live united to those of their beloved and ancestors in " shady and blooming bowers, with lovely females, and banquet(ed) on delicious fruits." (W. IRVING.)

Xisthorus : A Greek corruption of Atra-khasis, " very clever " ; an epithet of Ut-napishtim (q.v.) who was probably the hero of the deluge in the second Babylonian version of the myth

Xisusthrus : In the Babylonian creation myth, after man was created, they became evil and it was decided to destroy them. One man, Xisusthrus, alone, with his family and servants was saved. " He took riches, seeds of all kinds, his family and his servants in the ark and closed the door. For six days and nights the storm continued and began to subside on the seventh. He then sent forth a dove which returned. After that a swallow which did the same, and lastly a raven which did not return. Xisusthrus, after that, came forth with his family and servants and offered sacrifices " (S. BURROWS, *The Open Door*, Lond., 1926, p. 158). He was later made a demi-god and his family became a race of giants. He corresponds to Noah of the Biblical deluge myth. (For other parallels of the deluge myth see FRAZER, *Folklore in the Old Testament*, Vol. I.)

Xmas : Vide *Christmas, Beans, Coal, Birth, Carrying, Bread, Crumb, Cross-roads, Water, Pie, Tree, Dog, Light, Shirt, Grass, Theft, Stone, Hoop, Vermin, Elder, Egg, Salt, Lightning, Fire, Walking, Yule Log, Fruit, Call.*

Xuthus : Gr. Myth. Husband of Io.

Y

Yaai : In Vancouver Island these are fairy-like beings who dwell on the summit of mountains. They are illusive and disolve at will like foam.

Yak : (pron. jak). In Bengal it is a ghostly custodian of a treasure with which it was buried alive. Formerly misers and others buried little boys alive with ceremonial rites along with their treasures, under the impression that they themselves would re-acquire their wealth in one of their future births. (TAGORE, *Mashi and other Stories*, p. 104 ; KAṄKĀVATI ; *Ethnologie du Bengale*, pp. 97, 98.)

Yakshas : Hind. Myth. A class of supernatural beings. They have no very special attributes, but they were generally inoffensive and classed as good people, but they occasionally appear as imps of evil. (DOWSON, *H.C.D.*, p. 373.)

Yama : Hind. Myth. The deification of the first mortal to die, who became king and judge of the dead and chastiser of the souls. In the Vedic period his abode was supposed to be in the sky ; later, like Pluto, he was the lord of the infernal regions. He is green in colour, with red garments, has inflamed eyes, rides a buffalo, and carries a club and noose.

Yarrow : To dream of this weed denotes, to the married, deaths in the family' ; to the unmarried that they will be deprived of the object of their affection.

Yatus : " Sorcerers." These are the male partners of the Pairikas (q.v.).

Yawn : In Turkestan yawning is a most sinful and dangerous habit ; it rises from an evil place in the heart (SCHUYLER, Vol. II, p. 29), or in India, a Bhût may go down your throat, or part of your soul may escape. (CROOKE, *P.R.*, Vol. I, p. 240.)

Yawning is caused by Death calling you. Snap your middle finger and the thumb as an antidote. (*India.—* JACKSON, *F.L.N.*, Vol. II, p. 54.)

Ydalir : Norse Myth. Uli's dwelling in Asgard.

Yeast : If you dream of yeast, it tells you what you next undertake will prosper and your wife will be in the family-way.

Yebisu : A modern Japanese deity. He is represented with a shining countenance and wearing an old Japanese costume ; he is pictured as an angler with a fish dangling at the end of his line. Merchants pray to him for success in trade.

Yedogonya : Serbian Folklore. They are demons who influence the state of the weather, and are said to fight with each other among the mountains, their missiles being huge boulders and uprooted trees.

Yedza : The Polish equivalent of the Baba-Yaga (q.v.).

Yellow : Evil spirits are afraid of yellow. (*India.—*CROOKE, Vol. II, p. 28.)

A yellow leaf in peas or beans foretells a death. (STRACK-ERJAN, Vol. II, p. 69.)

Jaundice can be cured by drinking water in which something yellow has been cooked. (*Jew. Enc.*, Vol. V, p. 426 ; SCHIFFER, *Urquell*, Vol. V, p. 290.)

In China charms are written on yellow paper. (Doo-LITTLE, Vol. II, p. 308.)

Yen Wang : The Chinese equivalent of Pluto or Yama.

Yew : To dream of a yew tree denotes the death of an aged person, through which you will receive some benefit.

Yezad, Yezdam : Persian Myth. The principle of good as opposed to Ahriman, the principle of evil. Yezad created twenty-four good spirits and, to keep them from the power of the evil one, enclosed them in an egg ; but Ahriman pierced the shell ; hence there is no good without some mixture of evil. The Greeks called him Or(o)mazes.

Yezibaba : The Slovakian equivalent of the Baba-Yaga (q.v.).

Yezidi : One of a sect of reputed devil-worshippers of Armenia and the Caucasus.

Yggdrasil : Norse Myth. The great tree which supports the universe. A wise eagle sits at the top ; the roots are gnawed by *Nithhogg* and other serpents. The squirrel *Ratatosk* carries words of strife up and down. The tree binds Heaven, Earth and Hell together. Its branches extend over the whole earth, its top reaches heaven, and its roots descend to hell. The three Norns (q.v.) sit under the tree, spinning the events of man's life.

Ying Chow : Chin. Folklore. One of the three isles of the genii. In the island there is a spring whose water resembles wine ; " whoso quaffs a few measures of this beverage becomes suddenly inebriated, and eternal life is given by the draught." (MAYERS, *Chin. Read. Man.*, p. 289.)

Ymir : Norse Myth. The primeval giant from whose body the gods created the world.

Yogini : In the Panjab it is a kind of fairy who haunts waterfalls.

Yomi : Shinto Relig. It is supposed to be a land of darkness where deities, ugly females, armies and road-wardens are also to be found. (ASTON, *Shinto*, p. 54.)

Yoni : The Hindu symbol of the fertility of nature under which the consort of a male deity is worshipped ; it is represented by an oval figure (the female organ). cf. *Phallus*.

Yugas : Hind. Cosmogony. One of the four ages of the world.

Yule Log : This log was supposed to be a protection against evil spirits and to assure safety against lightning and thunder. (RAGNER.)

U

Yun Hwa Fu-jen : Chin. Myth. A daughter of Si Wang Mu. She is reputed to haunt the peaks of Wu Shan. (MAYERS, *Chin. Read. Man.*, p. 291.)

Z

Zagreus : Gr. Relig. Dionysus as a bull-god. " He is essentially a ritual figure. the centre of a cult so primitive, so savage, that a civilized literature instinctively passed him by, or at most figured him as a shadowy Hades." (WEBSTER quoting J. E. HARRISON.)

Zaḥḥak : A Persian monarch who had two boils on his shoulders. To ease the pain of these boils he killed two men every day and applied their brains to the wounds. (BECK, *Key to Neupers. Kon. Gr.*, p. 14.)

Zahuiti : Egypt. Myth. Another name of Thoth (q.v.).

Zainmyangwa : (Tortoise). It " is an evil creature that destroys from midnight to dawn thousands of creatures of the good spirit." (VENIDAD, XIII.)

Zalambur : Moham. Myth. A son of Iblis, a jinn, who presides over places of traffic. (*Jew. Enc.*, Vol. IV, p. 521.)

Zamalmal : Babyl. Myth. An ancient sun-god worshipped in the city of Kish.

Zemaka : Persian Myth. The spirit of winter personified.

Zemi : Among the North American Indians he is an inferior deity, a kind of tutelary god.
" They believed in a supreme being. . . . They never addressed their worship directly to him, but to inferior deities, called Zemes, kind of messengers or mediators. . . . Each family had a particular *zemi* as a tutelary or protecting genius, whose image, generally of a hideous form was placed about their houses. . . . They believed their *zemes* to be transferable. . . . Some had sway over the elements . . . some governed the seas and forests, the springs and fountains. . . . They gave success in hunting and fishing . . . and if incensed caused them (streams) to burst forth into floods and torrents, inundating and laying waste the valleys." W. IRVING, *Life of Columbus* (1828.)

Zemzem : According to Arab superstition, the souls of believers remain in the well of Zemzem, and those of infidels in a certain well in the province of Ḥadramôt, called Barahoot. (LANE, *A.S.M.A.*, p. 264.)

Zephyr : Gr. Myth. The West Wind personified. It has been introduced into modern language to mean a "light breeze."

Zerana-Akerana : In the Zoroastrian religion it is a symbol of the Absolute. the Eternal unmanifest Being, the Emanator of the Universe. (GASKELL, *D.S.L.S.M.*, p. 839.)

Zethus : Gr. Myth. A son of Zeus and Antiope, twin brother of Ampion.

Zeus : Gr. Myth. Son of Saturn and Rhea, brother of Pluto and Neptune. He conquered the Titans, deposed his father, gave the sea to his brother Neptune, and the underworld to Pluto, and kept for himself the heavenly kingdom. Zeus was regarded by the Greeks as a god of the Hellenic race, the original seat of whose worship was Thessaly. He is known as the "father of the gods." He was identified by the Romans with Jupiter.

Zitna matka : Slavic Folklore. A midday spirit who walks among the corn-fields, and kills anyone who cannot satisfactorily answer her riddles. She has been identified with the Poludnitsa of the Poles.

BIBLIOGRAPHY

ABBOTT, G. F.: *Macedonian Folklore.* (Cambridge, 1903.)
ACHELIS, TH.: *Über Mythologie und Kultus von Hawaii.* (Berlin, 1895.)
ADAMS, W. H. D.: *Curiosities of Superstition and Sketches of some Unrevealed Religions.* (Lond., 1882.)
ALPENBURG, J. N. VON: *Mythen und Sagen Tirols.* (Zürich, 1857.)
AM UR-QUELL: *Monatschrift für Volkkunde.* (Hamburg.)
ANDERSEN, HANS CHRISTIAN: *Danish Fairy Tales and Legends.* (Paisley, 1910.)
ANDERSON: *Catalogue of Japanese and Chinese Paintings in the British Museum.*
ASTON, W. G.: *Shinto.* (Lond., 1921.)
ATKINSON, J. C.: *Glossary of the Cleveland District.* (Lond., 1868.)
AUBREY, J.: *Miscellanies.* (Lond., 1696.)

BAARDA, M. J. VAN: "*Fabelen, verhalen en overleveringen der Galslareezen,*" in *Bijdragen tot de Taal- Land- en Volkenkunde van Nederlandsch-Indië.* Vol. xlv. (1895.)
BACHOFEN, J. J.: *Das Mutterrecht.* (Stuttgart, 1861.)
BALSALOBRE, GONÇALO DE: *Relacion autentica de las supersticiones de los Indios.* (Mexico, 1892.)
BANIM, J.: *Tales of the O'Hara Family.* (Lond., 1825.)
BARING-GOULD, REV. S.: *The Book of Were-Wolves.* (Lond., 1865.)
— *Curious Myths of the Middle Ages.* (Lond., 1877.)
BARTSCH, K.: *Sagen, Märchen und Gebräuche aus Mecklenburg.* 2 vols. (Vienna, 1879-1880.)
BASSETT, FLETCHER: *Legends and Superstitions of the Sea and Sailors.* (Lond., 1885.)
BASTIAN, ADOLF: *Der Mensch in der Geschichte.* 3 vols. (Leipzig, 1860.)
— *Ethnologische Forschungen,* 2 Vols. (Jena, 1871-1873.)
BAUDET, POL.: *Superstition populaire.* (Le Mans, 1907.)
BECK, SEBASTIAN: *Schlüssel zur Neupersischen Konversations-Grammatik.* (Heidelberg, 1915.)
BENJAMIN, S. G. W.: *Persia and the Persians.* (Lond., 1887.)
BERENGER-FÉRAUD: *Superstitions et survivances etudiées au point de vue de leur origine et de leurs transformations.* 5 vols. (1895-1896.)

BERGEN, FANNY D.: *Current Superstitions.* (Boston, 1896.)
— *Animal and Plant Folklore.* (Boston, 1899.)
BERTHOLET, DR. ALBERT: *The Transmigration of the Soul.* Tr. by Rev. H. J. Chaytor. (Lond., 1909.)
BIART, L.: *The Aztecs, their History, Manners and Customs.* (Eng. tr. by Garner. Chicago, 1887.)
BIBESCO, PRINCESS: *Le Pays de Saules.* (Paris, 1923.)
BIBLE, THE HOLY.
BIRLINGER, A.: *Aus Schwaben, Sagen, Legenden, Aberglauben, Sitten, Rechtsbräuche, etc.* 2 vols. (Wiesbaden, 1872-1874.)
BLACK, W. G.: *Folk Medicine.* (Lond., 1883.)
BOECLER-KREUTZWALD: *Der Ehsten abergläubische Gebräuche, Weisen und Gewohnheiten.* (St. Petersburg, 1854.)
BOISMOREAU, DR.: *Coutumes médicales et superstitions populaires du Bocage vendéen.* (Paris, 1911.)
BONNERJEA, BIREN: *L'Ethnologie du Bengale.* (Paris, 1927.)
BORLASE, W. G.: *The Dolmens of Ireland.* (Lond., 1897.)
BOTTRELL, W.: *Traditions and Hearthside Stories of West Cornwall.* (Penzance, 1873.)
BOWRING, SIR JOHN: *Servian Popular Poetry.* (Lond., 1827.)
BRAND, JOHN: *Observations on the Popular Antiquities of Great Britain.* 3 vols. (Lond., 1848-1849.)
BRAY: *The Borders of Tamar and the Tavy, etc.* (Lond., 1879.)
BRAZ, ANATOLE LE: *La Légende de la Mort.* 2 vols. (Paris, 1923.)
BREWER, DR.: *Reader's Handbook.* (Lond., 1911.)
BRINKLEY, CAPT.: *Japan, its History, Arts and Literature.* (Lond., 1904.)
BRINTON, D. G.: *Myths of the New World.* (New York, 1899.)
— *National Legends of the Chahta-Musoka Tribes.* (New York, 1870.)
BROCKHAUS: *Konversations-Lexicon.*
BRÜHL: *Jahrbuch.*
BUDGE, E. A. WALLIS: *Egyptian Magic.* (Lond., 1899.)
— *The Book of the Kings of Egypt,* 2 vols. (Lond., 1908.)
— *Egyptian Literature,* 2 vols. (Lond., 1912.)
BURNOUF, EUGÉNE: *Venidad Sadé.* (Paris, 1829-1842.)
BURTON, R.: *A Personal Narrative of a Pilgrimage to Al Medinah and Mecca.* 2 vols. (Lond., 1898.)
— *Alif laila wa laila.* 12 vols. (Lond., 1894.)
— *Zanzibar, City, Island and Coast.* 2 vols. (Lond., 1872.)
BUTLER: *Hudibras.* (1663.)

CALLAWAY, BISHOP : *The Religious System of the Amazulu.* (Lond., 1868-1872.)
— *Nursery Tales, Traditions and Histories of the Zulu.* (Lond., 1868.)
CALMET, DOM AUGUSTIN : *Dissertation sur les apparitions des Esprits et sur les Vampires, etc.* 2 vols. (Paris, 1749.)
CAMPBELL, J. F. : *Popular Tales of the West Highlands.* 4 vols. (Glasgow, 1890.)
— *Superstitions of the Highlands and Islands of Scotland.* (Glasgow, 1900.)
CASALIS : *Les Bassoutos, ou Vingt-trois années d'études et d'observations au Sud de l'Afrique.* (Paris, 1859.)
CASSELL'S ENGLISH DICTIONARY.
CASTREN, M. : *Vorlesungen über die finnische Mythologie.* Vol. 3. (St. Petersburg, 1853-1862.)
CATLIN, G. : *Manners, Customs and Conditions of the North American Indians.* (Lond., 1891.)
CHADEYRAS, F. : *Superstitions et légendes d'Auvergne.* (1900.)
CHAMBERS' JOURNAL. (1885.)
CHAMBERS, R. : *Book of Days.* 2 vols. (Lond., n.d.)
CHAMBERLAIN, BASIL HALL : *Uojiki, in " Trans. As. Soc. of Japan."* 1883.
— *Things Japanese.* (Ger. tr. by Bernhardt Kellermann, Berlin, 1912.)
CHANTEPIE DE LA SAUSSAYE, P. D. : *Lehrbuch der deutschen Religionsgeschichte.* (Tübingen, 1905.)
CHINESISCHE VOLKSMÄRCHEN. (Eugen Diderichs Verlag. Jena, 1921.)
CODRINGTON, R. H. : *The Melanesians.* (Oxford, 1891.)
CONWAY, M. D. : *Demonology and Demon Lore.* 2 vols. (Lond., 1879.)
CRANZ : *Historie von Grönland, enthaltend die Beschreibung des Landes und der Einwohner.* 2 vols. (Barby, 1770.)
CRAWFORD, F. MARION : *Uncanny Tales.*
— *A Roman Singer.*
CRAWFORD, J. : *On the Classification of the Races of Man,* in *Trans. Ethnol. Soc.*, N.S. (Lond., 1861.)
CROKER, T. CROFTON : *Fairy Legends and Traditions of the South of Ireland.* (Lond., 1825.)
— *Popular Songs of Ireland.* (Lond., 1886.)
CROOKE, W. : *Herklot's Islam in India.* (Lond., 1921,)
— *The Popular Religion and Folklore of Northern India.* 2 vols. (Westminster, 1896.)
CROOKES, W. : *Researches in the Phenomena of Spiritualism.* (Lond., 1874.)

CURTIN, J. : *Tales of the Fairies and of the Ghost-World*. (London, 1895.)
— *Myths of the Modocs*. (Lond., 1912.)
— *A Journey in Southern Siberia*. (Lond., 1909.)

DALYELL, J. G. : *The Darker Superstitions of Scotland*. (Edin., 1834.)
DANON, ABRAHAM : *Les Superstitions des juifs ottomans* (w.p.d.).
DAVIS, F. H. : *Myths and Legends of Japan*. (Lond., 1912.)
DAVIS, SIR JOHN : *The Chinese*. 2 vols. (Lond., 1836.)
DAY, REV. LAL BEHARI : *Folk Tales of Bengal*. (Lond., 1883.)
DEENEY, DANIEL : *Peasant Lore from Gaelic Ireland*. (Lond., 1900.)
DE GROOT, J. J. M. : *The Religious System of China*. 6 vols. (Leyden, 1896-1910.)
— *Les fêtes annuelement célébrés à Emoui (Amoy)*, etc. tr. par G. Chavannes. (Paris, 1886.)
DELITZSCH, F. : *Assyrisches Handwörterbuch*. (Leipzig, 1896.)
DENNISTON, J. : *Legends of Galloway*. (Edin., 1825.)
DENNYS, N. B. : *Folklore of China*. (Lond., 1876.)
DEUTSCHE MÄRCHEN SEIT GRIMM. (Eugen Diederichs Verlag, Jena, 1919.)
DODS : *Spirit Manifestations examined and explained*. (New. York, 1854.)
DOOLITTLE, JUSTUS : *Social Life of the Chinese*. 2 vols. (New York, 1867.)
DORÉ, HENRI : *Recherches sur les superstitions en Chine* (Shanghai, 1911.)
DORMAN, R. M. : *The Origin of Primitive Superstitions*. (Phil., 1881.)
DOUGHTY, C. M. : *Travels in Arabia Deserta*. (Cambridge, 1888.)
DOUTTÉ, E. : *Magie et Religion dans l'Afrique du Nord*. (Alger., 1909.)
DOWSON, JOHN : *Hindu Classical Dictionary*. (Lond., 1914.)
DRAKE, S. A. : *The Myths and Fables of To-day*. (Boston. 1900).
DU CHAILLU, P. B. : *Afrique Equatoriale*. (Paris, 1863.)
DURKHEIM, E. : *Elementary Forms of Religious Life*, Eng. tr. by Swain.
— *La prohibition de l'inceste*, in *Année Sociologique*, Vol. I. (Paris, 1896-1897.)
DUTT, TORU : *Ancient Ballads and Legends*. (Lond., 1885.)
DYER, T. F. T. : *Popular Customs*. (Lond., 1876.)

EITEL, REV. E. H. : *Handbook of Chinese Buddhism.* (Hong Kong, 1870.)
ELLIS, E. B. : *The Tschi-speaking Peoples of the Gold Coast of West Africa.* (Lond., 1888.)
— *The Ewe-speaking Peoples.* (Lond., 1890.)
— *The Yoruba-speaking Peoples.* (Lond., 1899.)
ELWORTHY, F. T. : *The Evil Eye.* (Lond., 1895.)
ENCYCLOPÆDIA BRIȚANNICA. 25 vols. (Lond., 1875-1889.)
ENCYCLOPÆDIA OF RELIGION AND ETHICS. 12 vols. (Edin.)
ENNEMOSER, J. : *Geschichte der Magie.* (Leipzig, 1844.)
— *History of Magic.* 2 vols. (Lond., 1854.)
EYRE : *Journals of Expeditions of Discovery into Central Australia.* Vols. 1-2. (Lond., 1848.)

FOLKLORE, a quarterly journal of myth, tradition, institution and custom. (Lond., 1890, *et seq.*)
FOLKLORE JOURNAL. 7 vols. (Lond., 1883-1889.)
FOLKLORE RECORD. The Folklore Society. 5 vols. (Lond., 1878-1882.)
FORTIER, A. : *Louisiana Folk Lore.* (Boston, 1895.)
FRAZER, SIR JAMES G. : *The Golden Bough.* 3 vols. Second Ed. (Lond., 1900.)
— *Psyche's Task.* Second Ed. (Lond., 1913.)
— *Totemism and Exogamy,* 4 vols. (Lond., 1910.)
— *Folklore in the Old Testament.* (Lond., 1914.)
— *The Golden Bough,* 12 vols. Third Edition.

GALE, J.S. : *Korean Folk Tales, Imps, Ghosts, etc.* (Lond., 1913.)
GARNETT, LUCY : *Turkish Life.* (Lond., 1904.)
GASKELL, G. A. : *A Dictionary of the Sacred Languages of all Scriptures and Myths.* (Lond., 1923.)
GIBSON, A. C. : *The Folk Speech of Cumberland and some Districts Adjacent.* (1869.)
GIBSON, FRANK : *Superstitions about Animals.* (Lond., 1904.)
GILES, HERBERT ALLEN : *Strange Stories from a Chinese Studio.* 2 vols. (Lond., 1880.)
GILL, REV. WILLIAM WYATT : *Myths and Songs of the South Pacific.* (Lond., 1876.)
GOETHE, W. VON : *Sämtliche Werke.*
GOMME, SIR G. L. : *Folk-lore.* (The Antiquary's Books.)
GREGOR, REV. W. : *Notes on the Folk-lore of the North-east of Scotland.* (Lond., 1881.)
GREY, E. : *Polynesian Mythology and Ancient Traditional History of the New Zealand Race.* (Lond., 1855.)
GRIFFIS, W. E. : *The Mikado's Empire.* (New York, 1876.)
— *Corea, the Hermit Nation.* (New York, 1911.)

GRIFFITHS, MAJ. ARTHUR: *Chronicles of Newgate.* 2 vols. (Lond., 1884.)
GRILLPARZER: *Sämtliche Werke.*
GRIMM, J.: *Deutsche Mythologie.* (Göttingen, 1844.)
— *Deutsche Sagen.* 2 vols. 3 Aufl. (Berlin, 1891.)
— *Deutsche Rechtsalterthümer.* (Göttingen, 1835.)
GROHMANN, J. V.: *Aberglauben aus Böhmen.* (Prague, 1864.)
GROOME, F. H.: *Gipsy Folk Tales.* (Lond., 1899.)
GROSE, F.: *Provincial Glossary.* (Lond., 1790.)
GUBERNATIS, A. DE: *Zoological Mythology, or Legends of Animals.* 2 vols. (Lond., 1872.)
GUÉBHARD, DR. ADRIEN: *Sur l'Antiquité des Superstitions attachées aux coquilles fossiles.* (Le Mans, 1907.)

HAAS, A.: *Rügensche Sagen und Märchen.* 3 Aufl. (Stettin, 1903.)
HAGGARD, H. RIDER: *Nada the Lily.* (Tauchnitz Ed.)
HALE, H.: *Iroquois Book of Rites.* (Phil., 1883.)
HALLE, J. S.: *Magie oder die Zauberkräfte der Natur.* Vol. 1-4. (Berlin, 1874-1886.)
HALLIDAY, W. R.: *Folk-lore Studies: Ancient and Modern.* (Lond., 1924.)
HANNUSCH: *Wissenschaft der slawishchen Mythus.*
HARDWICK, C.: *Traditions, Superstitions and Folk-lore.* (Lond., 1872.)
HARDY, R. SPENCE: *Manual of Buddhism.* (Lond., 1853.)
HARLAND AND WILKINSON: *Lancashire Folk-lore, etc.* (Manchester, 1867.)
— *Lancashire Legends.* (Manchester, 1873.)
HARLEZ, C. DE: *La Religion des Tartares Orientaux.* (Paris, 1887.)
HARTLAND, E.: *Science of Fairy Tales.* (Lond., 1891.)
— *Ritual and Belief.* (Lond., 1914.)
— *The Legend of Perseus.* 3 vols. (Lond., 1894-1896.)
HASTINGS, DR. J.: *Dictionary of the Bible.* 5 vols. (Edin.)
HAUNTED HOMES OF ENGLAND.
HAWTHORNE, NATHANIEL: *A Wonder Book* and *Tanglewood Tales.* (New York, 1910.)
HAZLITT, W. C.: *Faiths and Folk-lore.* 2 vols. (Lond., 1905.)
HEARNE, L: *Some Chinese Ghosts.* (Boston, 1910.)
HEINEMANN, FRANZ: *Aberglaube.* (Berne, 1907.)
HELWIG, KARL: *Zur Psychologie.* (Elberfeld, 1911.)
HOMER: *Odyssey.* Eng. tr.
HOVORKÁ, O. VON, and KRONFELD, A.: *Vergleichende Volksmedizin. Darstellung volksmedizinischer Sitten und Gebräuche, Anschauungen, Heilfaktoren, etc.* 2 vols. (Stuttgart, 1908-1909.)

HOWELLS, WILLIAM : *Cambrian Superstitions, comprising Ghosts, Omens, Witchcraft, Traditions. etc.* (Tipton, 1831.)

HOWITT, W. : *Literature and Romance of Northern Europe.* (Lond., 1852.)

HUART, CLÉMENT : *Superstitions et rites populaires des Arabes anté islamiques.* (Alençon, 1913.)

HUBERT H. ET MAUSS M. : *Essai sur la nature et la fonction du Sacrifice,* in *Année Sociol.,* Vol. II. (Paris, 1897-1898.)
— *Esquisse d'une theorie générale, de la Magie,* in *Année Sociol.,* Vol. VII. (Paris, 1902-1903.)

HUNT, ROBERT : *Popular Romances of the West of England, or the Drolls, Traditions and Superstitions of Old Cornwall.* (Lond., 1865.)

HYSLOP, JAMES HARVEY : *Science and Future Life.* (Boston, 1905.)

INWARDS, R. : *Weather Lore.* (Lond., 1893.)
IRVING, WASHINGTON : *Life of Columbus.* (1828.)

JACKSON, A. M. T. : *Folk-lore Notes.* 2 vols. (Bombay, 1915.)

JACOBS, J. : *Celtic Fairy Tales.* (Lond., 1892.)
— *Indian Fairy Tales.* (Lond., 1891.)

JAHN : " *Über den Aberglauben des bösen Blickes,*" in *Berichte der Gesellschaft der Wissenschaften.* (Leipzig, 1855.)

JALLA, PROF. JEAN : *Légendes des Vallées Vaudoises.* (Torre Pellice, 1911.)

JAMES, KING (of England) : *Dæmonologie.* (Edin., 1537.)

JELLINGHANS, TH. : *Sagen, Sitten und Gebräuche der Munda-Kohls in Chota Nagpore,* in *Zeitschrift für Ethnologie.* 1871.

JENSEN : *Assyrisch-Babylonische Mythen und Epen.* (Leipzig, 1910.)

JEWISH ENCYCLOPÆDIA. (Lond. and New York.)

JOHNSON, C. : *What they say in New England.* (Boston, 1896.)

JOHNSON, R. F. : *Lion and Dragon in Northern China.* (Lond., 1910.)

JOLLY, JULIUS : *Recht und Sitte* (*Grundr. der Indo. Ar. Phil.* Strassburg, 1896.)

JONES, W. : *Finger-Ring Lore.* (Lond., 1877).

JONSON, BEN : *Masque of Queens.*

JOURNAL OF THE AMERICAN ORIENTAL SOCIETY.

JOURNAL OF THE ANTHROPOLOGICAL INSTITUTE. (*J.R.A.I.*).

JOURNAL OF THE ASIATIC SOCIETY OF BENGAL.

KALEWALA : Das National Epos der Finnen. Ger. tr. by
Anton Schefner. (Helsingfors, 1852.)
KARSTEN, RAFAEL : Indian Tribes of Ecuador. (Åbo, 1920.)
KEITH , A. BERRIDALE : Indian Mythology. (Boston, 1917.)
KENNEDY, PATRICK : Legendary Fiction of the Irish Celts.
(Lond., 1891.)
KIESEWETTER, C. : Faust in der Geschichte und Tradition.
(Leipzig, 1893.)
KINGSLEY, MARY : West African Studies. (Lond., 1899.)
KNOOP, O. : Ostmärkische Sagen, Märchen und Erzählungen.
(Lissa, 1909.)
KNORTZ, KARL : Amerikanischer Aberglaube der Gegenwart.
(Leipzig, 1913.)
KNOWLES, J. H. : Folktales of Kashmir. (Lond., 1888.)
KOEHLER, J. A. E. : Volksbrauch, etc., in Vogtlande. (Leipzig,
1867.)
KOHUT, A. : Jüdische Angelologie und Demonologie. (Leipzig,
1866.)
KRAFFT-EBING, DR. : Psychopathia Sexualis. Eng. tr. by
Chaddock. (Phil., 1894.)
KRAPF, DR. J. L. : Travels, Researches and Missionary Labours
. , . in Eastern Africa. (Lond., 1860.)
KRAUSS, F. S. : Volksglaube und religiöser Brauch der Südslawen.
(Wien, 1885.)
— Sagen und Märchen der Südslawen. (Leipzig, w.d.)
— Das Geschlechtsleben der Japaner. (Leipzig, 1907.)
KÜHN, F. F. A., UND SCHWARTZ, W. : Norddeutsche Sagen,
Märchen und Gebräuche aus Mecklenburg. (Leipzig, 1848.)
KUNOS, DR. IGNACZ : Forty-four Turkish Fairy Tales. (New
York, w.d.)

LAMBS, A. : Über den Aberglauben in Elsass. (Strassburg,
1880.)
LAMMERT, G. : Volksmedizin und medizinischer Aberglaube in
Bayern. (Würzburg, 1869.)
LANE, E. W. : Account of the Manners and Customs of the
Modern Egyptians. (Lond., 1896.)
— Arabian Society in the Middle Ages. (Lond., 1883.)
LANG, A. : Magic and Religion. (Lond., 1901.)
— The Book of Dreams and Ghosts. (Lond., 1899.)
— Myth, Ritual and Religion. (Lond., 1899.)
— Making of Religion. (Lond., 1902.)
— Modern Mythology. (Lond., 1897.)
LAROUSSE : Grand Dictionnaire de la langue française.
LAWRENCE, ROB. H. : The Magic of the Horseshoe. (Boston
1898.)

LAWSON, JOHN CUTHBERT : *Modern Greek Folk-lore and Ancient Greek Religion.* (Cambridge, 1910.)

LEAN, V. S. : *Lean's Collectanea.* Vol. 1-2. (Bristol, 1902-1903.)

LEHMANN, DR. ADOLF : *Aberglaube und Zauberei.* Ger. tr. by Peterson, 2 Aufl. (Stuttgart, 1908.)

LEGGE, REV. JAMES : *Chinese Classics.* (Hong Kong, 1861-1871.)

LELAND, C. G. : *Etruscan Roman Remains in Popular Traditions.* (Lond., 1892.)

LESKIEN, A., and BRUGMANN, K. : *Litauische Volkslieder und Märchen.* (Leipzig, 1882.)

LETOURNEAU, CH. : *La Condition de la femme dans les diverses races et civilisations.* (Paris, 1902.)

LEVI, ELIPHAS : *Histoire de la Magie.* (Paris, 1880.)

LIEBICH, RICHARD : *Der Zigeuner.* (Leipzig, 1863.)

LIVINGSTONE, D. : *Travels and Researches in South Africa.* (Lond., 1840-1856.)

LONGFELLOW : *Poetical Works.*

LUBBOCK, SIR JOHN (Lord Avebury) : *Origin of Civilization.* (Lond., 1892.)

LUZEL, F. M. : *Contes populaires de Basse-Bretagne.* 3 vols. (Paris, 1887.)

LYTTON, LORD : *Tales of Miletus.*

MAAS, ALBERT : *Allerlei provenzalischer Volksglaube.* (Berlin, 1896.)

MACANNALLY, D. R. : *Irish Wonders, the Ghosts, Giants, Pookas, etc.* (Lond., 1888.)

MACCULLOCH, J. A. : *The Misty Isle of Skye.* (Edin., 1905.)
— *The Religion of the Ancient Celts.* (Edin., 1911.)

MACDONALD, J. : *Religion and Myth.* (Lond., 1893.)

MACDONELL, A. : *Vedic Mythology.* (Grundr. der Indo-Ar. Phil. Strassburg, 1897.)

MACKENZIE, ALEXANDER : *The Prophecies of the Brahan Seer.* (Inverness, 1878.)

MAGNUS, HUGO : *Der Aberglaube in der Medizin.* (Breslau, 1903.)

MARLOW, CHRISTOPHER : *History of Dr. Faustus.* (1589.)

MARRETT, R. R. : *The Threshold of Religion.* (Lond., 1909.)

MARRYAT, CAPT. : *The Phantom Ship.*

MATERIALIZATION OF KATIE KING.

MATHERS, MCGREGOR : *The Kabbalah Unveiled, containing the chief Books of the Zohar.* (Lond., 1887.)

MAYERS, W. F. : *Chinese Reader's Manual.* (Reprinted from Shanghai, 1874.)

MEAKIN, BUDGETT : *The Moors*. (Lond., 1902.)
MÉLUSINE. *recueil de mythologie, littérature populaire, traditions et usages, dirigé par H. Gaidoz*. (Paris, 1878, et seq.)
MEMOIRS OF THE AMERICAN FOLKLORE SOCIETY.
MEMOIRS OF THE ASIATIC SOCIETY OF BENGAL.
MENZ, W. M. : *Demoniac Possession in the New Testament*. (Edin., 1902.)
MEYER, K. : *Der Aberglaube des Mittelalters und der nächstfolgenden Jahrhunderte*. (Basel, 1884.)
MICHELET, J. : *La Sorcière*. (Paris, 1862.)
MIR, HASSAN ALI, MRS. : *Observations on the Mussalmans of India*. 2 vols. (Lond., 1832.)
MOGK, E. : *Germanische Mythologie*. 2 Aufl. (Strassburg, 1898.)
MOLINA, JUAN IGNACIO : *Geographical, Natural and Civil History of Chili*. (Lond., 1809.)
— *Historia de Chile*. (Santiago de Chile, 1901.)
MONE : *Geschichte des Heidenthums im nördlichen Europa*. (Leipzig, 1822.)
MONNIER, D. : *Traditions populaires comparées*. (Paris, 1854.)
MOORE, A. W. : *The Folk-Lore of the Isle of Man*. (Lond., 1891.)
MOORE, T. : *Lalla Rookh.*
MORIER : *Second Journey through Persia*. (Lond., 1818.)
MULLENHOF, K. : *Sagen, Märchen und Lieder d. Herzogthum, Schleswig-Holstein und Lauenburg*. (Kiel, 1899.)
MULLER, MAX : *Chips from a German Workshop*. (Lond., 1893.)
MÜLLHAUSE, E. : *Die Urreligion des deutschen Volkes, u.s.w.* (Cassel, 1860.)
MURRAY, DR. : *The Oxford Dictionary*. A new English Dictionary on Historical Principles ; founded mainly on the Materials collected by the Philological Society and edited by Sir James A. H. Murray, Dr. Bradley, Dr. Craigie and Mr. Onions. 10 vols. (Oxford.)
MYTHOLOGY OF ALL RACES. (Boston, w.d.)

NAPIER, J. : *Folk-lore.* (Paisley, 1879.)
NASSAU, R. H. : *Fetichism in West Africa*. (Lond., 1904.)
NIEBELUNGENLIED, DAS. : Ger. tr. by Karl Simrock.
NICOLAY, FERNAND : *Curiosités des lois et coutumes*. (Paris, 1901.)
NON-CLASSICAL MYTHOLOGY.
NORTH INDIAN NOTES AND QUERIES (N.I.N.Q.)
NOTES AND QUERIES (N. & Q.)

O'DONNELL, ELLIOT : *Werewolves.* (Lond.)
OTTO, RUDOLF : *Das Heilige.* (Breslau, 1921.)
OWEN, REV. ELIAS : *Welsh Folk-lore, a Collection of Folk-tales and Legends of North Wales.* (Oswestry and Wrexham, 1896.)

PANZER : *Beiträge zur deutschen Mythologie.* 2 vols. (München, 1848, 1855.)
PESCHEL, O. : *Völkerkunde.* (Leipzig, 1874-1897.)
PLINY : *Naturgeschichte.* (Ger. tr. by Wittstein, Leipzig 1881-1882.)
PLOSS, DR. H. : *Das Weib in der Natur und Völkerkunde.* 2 vols. 4 Aufl. (Leipzig, 1895.)
PODMORE, F. : *Modern Spiritualism.* (Lond., 1902.)
POESTION, J. C. : *Lappländische Märchen, Volkssagen, Räthsel und Sprichwörter.* (Wien, 1896.)
POLAK, DR. J. E. : *Persien, das Land und seine Bewohner.* 2 vols. (Leipzig, 1865.)
PONCHON, A. : *Les Contre-Sorts.* (Cayeux sur Mer, 1904.)
POPULAR SUPERSTITIONS. (Phil., 1832.)
POWELL, F. YORK : *Origines Islandicæ.* 2 vols. (Oxford, 1909.)
PRAGER TAGBLATT. 21st April, 1925.
PRESCOTT : *History of the Conquest of Peru.* 2 vols. (Lond., 1864.)
PUCKETT, N. N.: *Folk Beliefs of the Southern Negro.* (Chapel Hill, 1926.)

QOR'AN, THE. English translation by Sale.

RABAUD, CAMILLE : *Phénomènes psychiques et superstition populaire.* (Castres, 1908.)
RADLOFF, WILHELM : *Aus Sibirien.* 2 vols. (Leipzig, 1884.)
RAGNER, BERNHARD : *Legends and Customs of Christmas,* in *The Chicago Tribune,* Eur. Ed., Christmas number, 1925.
RALSTON, W. : *Folk-tales of the Russians.* (Lond., 1873.)
— *Songs of the Russian People.* (Lond., 1872.)
— *Tibetan Tales.* (Lond.)
RANFT, M. : *Tractat von dem Schmatzen und Kauen der Todten in Gräbern.* (Leipzig, 1734.)
REDHOUSE : *Turkish-English Lexicon.* (Constantinople, 1890.)
REINACH, S. : *Cultes, Mythes et Religion.* (Paris, 1905.)
REVUE DES TRADITIONS POPULAIRES, *dirigée par P. Sébillot.* (Paris, 1885, *et seq.*)
RHYS, JOHN : *Celtic Folklore, Welsh and Manx.* 2 vols. (Oxford, 1901.)

RICHARDSON, J. : *Travels in the Great Desert of Sahara.* (Lond., 1848.)
RIEDEL, J. G. F. : *De shiek- en Kroesharige rassen tusschen Selebes en Papua.* The Hague, 1886.)
RINK, DR. H. : *Tales and Traditions of the Esquimaux.* (Lond., 1875.)
RIVIERE, EMILE : *Folk-lore.* (Le Mans, 1911.)
ROBERTSON-SMITH, W. R. : *The Religion of the Semites.* (Lond., 1894.)
RODD, RENNEL : *The Customs and Lore of Modern Greece.* (Lond., 1892.)
ROTH, H. LING : *The Natives of Sarawak and British North Borneo.*

SAYCE, A. H. : *Babylonians and Assyrians, Life and Customs.* (Lond., 1900.)
SCHINDLER : *Der Aberglaube des Mittelalters.* (Dresden, 1856.)
SCHOOLCRAFT : *Informations regarding the History, Conditions and Prospects of the Indian Tribes of the United States.* 6 vols. (Phil., 1851-1857.)
— *Algic Researches.* (Phil., 1839.)
SCHUYLER, EUGENE : *Turkestan.* 2 vols. (Lond., 1856.)
SCOTT, SIR W. : *Minstrelsy of the Scottish Border.* (Kelso, 1802-1803.)
— *Letters on Demonology and Witchcraft.* (Lond., 1830.)
SÉBILLOT, PAUL : *Le Folk-lore de France.* 4 vols. (Paris, 1904-1907.)
— *Légendes, Croyances et Superstitions de la mer.* 2 vols. (Vannes, 1892.)
— *Traditions et Superstitions de la Haute-Bretagne.* (Paris, 1882.)
SEIFART, K. : *Sagen, Märchen, Schwänke und Gebräuche aus Stadt und Stift Hildesheim.* 2 Aufl. (Hildesheim, 1889.)
SEYFARTH, C. : *Aberglaube.* (Leipzig, 1913.)
SHAKESPEARE : Collected Works.
SHARPE, C. K. : *Law's Memorialls.* (Lond., 1818.)
SHORTLAND : *Traditions and Superstitions of the New Zealanders.* (Lond., 1856.)
SIKES, WIRT : *British Goblins, Welsh Folk-lore, Fairy Mythology, Legends and Traditions* (Lond., 1880.)
SIMROCK, KARL : *Rheinsagen.* 10 Aufl. (Bonn a/R., 1891.)
SKEAT, W. W. : *Malay Magic.* (Lond., 1900.)
SMITH, DR. W. : *A Dictionary of Greek and Roman Mythology.*
SÖDERBLOM, N. : *Das Werden des Gottesglaubens.* (Leipzig, 1915.)
SOLDAN, W. G. : *Geschichte der Hexenprozesse.* 2 vols. (Neubearbeitet von H. Heppe, Stuttgart, 1880.)

SPENCER, B. AND GILLEN, F. : *The Native Tribes of Central Australia.* (London, 1898.)

ST. CLAIR, S. G. B., and BROPHY, C. L. A. : *A Residence in Bulgaria.* (Lond., 1869.)

ST. JOHN, BAYLE: *Legends of the Christian East.* (Lond., 1856.)

STEERE : *Swahili Tales.* (Lond., 1889.)

STELLER, G. W. : *Beschreibung von Kamtschatka.* (1774.)

STERNBERG, T. : ·*Dialect and Folk-lore of Northamptonshire.* (Lond., 1851.)

STEWART, W. G. : *Popular Superstitions of the Highlands of Scotland.* (Edin., 1823.)

STOKES, MARGARET : *Three Months in the Forests of France.* (Lond., 1895.)

STRACK, H. : *Der Blutaberglaube bei Christen und Juden.* (München, 1891.)

STRACKERJAN, L. : *Aberglaube und Sagen aus dem Herzogtum Oldenburg.* 2 vols. (Oldenburg, 1867.)

STRAUSS, A. : *Die Bulgaren.* (Leipzig, 1898.)

SUE, EUGENE : *Le Juif errant.* 10 vols. (Paris, 1844-1845.)

TAGORE, SIR RABINDRANĀTH : *Mashi and other Stories.* (Lond., 1918.)

TALMUD. English translation.

TAWNEY, C. H. : *Kathâ—sarit—sâgara.* 2 vols. (Calcutta, 1880.)

TAYLOR, HENRY OSBORN : *The Mediæval Mind.* 2 vols. (Lond., 1911.)

TEMPLE, R. C. : *Legends of the Panjâb.* (Bombay, w.d.)

TENNENT, SIR J. E. : *Ceylon.* 2 vols. Second Ed. (1859.)

TENNYSON, ALFRED LORD : *Poetical Works.*

TETTAU UND TEMME : *Die Volkssagen Lithauens und Ostpreussens.* (Berlin, 1837.)

TETZNER, FRANZ : *Die Slawen in Deutschland.* (Braunschweig, 1902.)

THEOPHRASTUS : *The Characters.* Eng. tr. by R. C. Jebb. (Lond., 1870.)

THIELE : *Danmarks Folkesagn.* (Kopenhagen.)

THIERS, J. B. : *Traité des superstitions qui regardent les sacramens.* (Paris, 1679).

THOMS, W. J. : *Anecdotes and Traditions.* (Lond., 1839.)

THORPE, BENJAMIN : *Northern Mythology.* 3 vols. (Lond., 1851.)

TISDALL, REV. W. ST. CLAIR : *Modern Persian Conversation Grammar.* (Heidelberg, 1920.)

TOEPEN, M. : *Aberglauben aus Masuren, mit einem Anhange enthaltend masurische Sagen und Märchen.* (Danzig, 1867.)

TRANSACTIONS OF THE ETHNOGRAPHICAL SOCIETY.
TREMEARNE, A. J. N. : *Hausa Superstitions and Customs.*
(Lond., 1913.)
TROLLOPE, T. A. : *A Summer in Brittany.* (Lond., 1840.)
TURNER : *Nineteen Years in Polynesia.* (Lond., 1868.)
TURNER, WM. : *A Tour in the Levant.* 3 vols. (Lond., 1820.)
TYLOR, E. B. : *Primitive Culture.* 2 vols. (1871.)
— *Early History of Mankind.* (Lond., 1888.)
— *Anthropology.* (Lond., 1881.)

USENER, H. : *Götternamen, Versuch einer Lehre von der religiösen Begriffsbildung.* (Bonn a /R., 1896.)

VAMBÉRY, A. : *Die primitive Kultur des turko-tatarischen Volkes auf Grund sprachlicher Forschungen.* (1879.)
— *Das Türkenvolk in seinen ethnologischen und ethnographischen Beziehungen geschildert.* (Leipzig, 1885.)
VAUX, J. E. : *Church Folk-Lore.* (Lond., 1894.)
VERNALEKEN, TH. : *Alpensagen.* (Wien, 1858.)
— *Mythen und Bräuche des Volkes in Oesterreich.* (Wien, 1859.)
VETĀLA PAÑCHAVIMSATI.

WADDELL, L. AUSTINE : *Lhasa and its Mysteries.* (Lond., 1905.)
WAITZ : *Anthropologie der Naturvölker.* (Leipzig, 1859-1871.)
— *Quellenkunde der deutschen Geschichte.* (Leipzig, 1907, 1912.)
WAKE, G. STANILAND : *Serpent Worship and Other Essays.* (Lond. 1888.)
WARD, WILLIAM : *Account of the Writings, Religion and Manners of the Hindus.* (Serampore, 1811.)
WARDROP, MARJORIE : *Georgian Folk Tales.* (Lond., 1894.)
WELLHAUSEN : *Reste arabischen Heidentums : Skizzen und Vorarbeiten.* (Berlin, 1897.)
WESTERMARCK, EDWARD : *The Belief in Spirits in Morocco.* (Åbo, 1920.)
— *History of Human Marriage.* (Lond., 1901.)
WIEDEMANN: *Magie und Zauberei in alten Aegypten.* (Leipzig, 1905.)
WIEGER, L. : *Folklore chinois moderne.* (Paris, 1909.)
WIENER, LEO : *The History of the Yiddish Literature in the Nineteenth Century.* (New York, 1899.)
WIKMAN, R. : *Die Magie des Webens.* (Åbo, 1920.)
WILDE, LADY : *Ancient Legends, Mystic Charms and Superstitions of Ireland.* (Lond., 1888.)

WILKINSON, J. GARDNER : *The Egyptians in the Time of the Pharaohs*. (Lond., 1857.)

WILLIAMS, S. WELLS : *The Middle Kingdom*. 2 vols. (New York, 1883.)

WOLF : *Beiträge zur deutschen Mythologie*.

WORD-LORE, The " Folk " Magazine, Vol. I. (Lond., 1926.)

WRIGHT : *Historical Caricatures*. (Lond., 1865.)

WUTTKE, DR. A. : *Der deutsche Volksaberglaube der Gegenwart*. (Hamburg, 1860.)

YATE, WILLIAM : *An Account of New Zealand*. 2 vols. (Lond., 1835.)

YULE AND BURNELL, *Hobson Jobson*. *A Dictionary of Anglo-Indian terms*. (Lond., 1903, and 1st ed. Lond., 1886.)

ZEITSCHRIFT FÜR ETHNOLOGIE.

ZENKER, DR. TH. : *Dictionnaire turc-arabe-persan*. (Leipzig, 1876.)

ZINGERLE, J. V. VON : *Sitten, Bräuche und Meinungen der Tiroler Volkes*. 2 Aufl. (Innsbruck, 1871.)

ZÖLLNER : *Wissenschaftliche Abhandlungen*. Vol. 1-3. (Leipzig, 1878-1879.)

ZUCCAMAGLIO, W. VON : *Gedichte*.